The Archaeology of Citizenship

The American Experience in Archaeological Perspective

UNIVERSITY PRESS OF FLORIDA

Florida A&M University, Tallahassee
Florida Atlantic University, Boca Raton
Florida Gulf Coast University, Ft. Myers
Florida International University, Miami
Florida State University, Tallahassee
New College of Florida, Sarasota
University of Central Florida, Orlando
University of Florida, Gainesville
University of North Florida, Jacksonville
University of South Florida, Tampa
University of West Florida, Pensacola

The Archaeology of
CITIZENSHIP

STACEY LYNN CAMP

Foreword by Michael S. Nassaney

University Press of Florida
Gainesville · Tallahassee · Tampa · Boca Raton
Pensacola · Orlando · Miami · Jacksonville · Ft. Myers · Sarasota

All illustrations are by the author unless otherwise noted.

This book may be available in an electronic edition.

First cloth printing, 2013
First paperback printing, 2019

24 23 22 21 20 19   6 5 4 3 2 1

Library of Congress Cataloging-in-Publication Data
Camp, Stacey Lynn.
The archaeology of citizenship / Stacey Lynn Camp ; foreword by Michael S. Nassaney.
pages cm.—(The American experience in archaeological perspective)
Includes bibliographical references and index.
Summary: An examination from an archaeological perspective of how those in power have tried to mold the citizenship and composition of the United States and the various and often conflicting strategies that have been employed to "Americanize" both immigrant and native non-white populations.
ISBN 978-0-8130-4459-0 (cloth : alk. paper)
ISBN 978-0-8130-6419-2 (pbk.)
    1. Citizenship—United States. 2. Americanization. 3. Immigrants—United States. 4. Nationalism—United States. 5. Assimilation (Sociology)—United States. 6. United States—Social conditions. I. Nassaney, Michael S. II. Title.
JK1759.C326 2013
323.60973—dc23   2013007064

The University Press of Florida is the scholarly publishing agency for the State University System of Florida, comprising Florida A&M University, Florida Atlantic University, Florida Gulf Coast University, Florida International University, Florida State University, New College of Florida, University of Central Florida, University of Florida, University of North Florida, University of South Florida, and University of West Florida.

University Press of Florida
2046 NE Waldo Road
Suite 2100
Gainesville, FL 32609
http://upress.ufl.edu

To Lana and Ty

Contents

List of Illustrations   ix

Foreword   xi

Preface and Acknowledgments   xv

List of Abbreviations   xxiii

Introduction   1

1. Who Is an American?   19

2. Historical Archaeologies of Citizenship   40

3. Tourism and Citizenship   72

4. The Archaeology of Citizenship   94

5. The Future of Citizenship   130

References   145

Index   161

Illustrations

Maps

3.1. Location of Mount Lowe Resort and Railway 78

4.1. Reconstruction of 1924 PERC map 116

4.2. Excavated features and units in 2005 and 2006 117

Table

4.1. Employees at Echo Mountain 104

Figures

2.1. Clay pipes recovered from German immigrant households 60

3.1. Lowe Observatory and Echo Mountain House 79

3.2. Echo Mountain House, date unknown 79

3.3. Children "riding" fish at Santa Catalina Island 83

3.4. Photograph at the top of Mount Lowe's Incline 85

3.5. Mount Lowe Resort and Railway brochure 89

3.6. White Chariot railway car 92

4.1. PERC article depicting Mexican immigrant children and section camps 101

4.2. PERC article illustrating camp nurses and inspectors 101

4.3. Ye Alpine Tavern 103

4.4. Only known photograph of the section house 103

4.5. Lid to a child's miniature porcelain tea set 107

4.6. Frozen Charlotte doll 107

4.7. Gladding, McBean & Company pipe 111

4.8. Cement-lined cesspool 111

4.9. Aerial photograph of excavated section house 115

4.10. Partial aerial view of excavation areas in 2006 115

5.1. Artwork found at Kooskia Internment Camp 137

5.2. Gaming pieces found at Kooskia Internment Camp 139

Foreword

Contemporary archaeologists are acutely aware of the relevance of their work for the present, particularly those who study the recent past. Moreover, their practice and findings often challenge ideologies that naturalize relations of power and homogenize categories of belonging. A critical examination of citizenship is especially poignant for this book series, which aims to elucidate the American experience in all its complexity. It is too easy to assume what it means to be an American. Suffice it to say that nation-states employ numerous mechanisms to inculcate values in daily life both formally and informally. Yet the adoption of those values and attendant duties does not confer citizenship unilaterally, nor do all migrants wholly embrace them.

The permeability of national boundaries has fluctuated to coincide with the economic need for cheap labor. With the birth of our nation in the eighteenth century, newcomers were welcomed so long as they were willing to swear allegiance, fulfill their patriotic duties, and adopt the practices of white Anglo-Protestants, with few exceptions. In their public lives, immigrants often acquiesced in exchange for a chance at economic mobility—the American dream.

My maternal grandfather, Antoun Donato, was among the huddled masses welcomed at Ellis Island in the early 1920s. After obtaining naturalized citizenship in 1926, he returned home to his native Aleppo (Syria) to find a wife to accompany him back to America. He was among the last wave of Syrian immigrants to America before more stringent immigration policies were enacted. As with many migrants who attained citizenship after adulthood, he lived a dual life committed to being American yet maintaining many Old World practices as he redefined what it meant to be an American. He and thousands of European migrants could claim whiteness as they entered the country and sought its rewards. Despite his outward signs of assimilation, he and my grandmother employed many foreign material objects in religious rituals, food preparation, adornment, and recreational activities. Iron skewers for grilling marinated lamb, copper kettles for brewing "Turkish" coffee, gold bracelets that jangled from my grandmother's wrist signaling her presence, and crystal-clear glass water pipes for smoking aromatic tobacco were some of the most memorable visual, auditory, and olfactory symbols of my family's Syrian-American identity. Yet, many of these vestiges of the old country disappeared in subsequent generations as the light of new institutions and public education taught my parents the civic knowledge deemed important for becoming American.

In *The Archaeology of Citizenship*, Stacey Camp poses questions of central importance to understanding the American experience, namely "who is an American?" and how has America's citizenry shifted over the course of the past three hundred years? Using a diachronic approach to the archaeological record, she demonstrates that citizenship is a process rather than a static, legal state of being. It consists of more than just a simple list of rights and duties; moreover, it has evolved and is always contested. Camp shows how historical archaeology—with its sensitivity to lines of evidence created by the subaltern—challenges accounts of citizenship that privilege and prioritize historical documents and legal case studies over experiences visible in archaeological data and oral histories.

Using theoretically informed models that link citizenship to consumption, Camp convincingly argues that ordinary people can shape ideas about citizenry by using material culture as a medium of social action. Their consumption patterns—what they acquired, used, and discarded— expressed lived experiences through the adoption, reinterpretation, and/ or disregard of materials that find their way into the archaeological record. Individuals from marginalized groups were active agents who recognized that consumption of costly goods would not help them transcend isolation and discrimination. In an effort to develop cultural citizenship, their religious, political, and racial loyalties often took precedence over national identity.

Camp provides a comprehensive overview of the ways in which immigrants to America have been extended and denied citizenship and the ways in which archaeology can be used to monitor that process. She interrogates how the Mt. Lowe Resort and Railway, an early-twentieth-century tourist destination in southern California, conveyed to visitors important elements of a national meta-narrative regarding the appropriation of wilderness, the destruction of indigeneity, technological prowess, and manifest destiny. In the course of absorbing these messages, tourists witnessed toiling Mexican immigrants who were lured across the border and forced to endure company-sponsored "Americanization" campaigns. As her research illustrates, such assimilation attempts were not conducted with the intention of extending equal citizenship to Mexican immigrants. Rather, these programs sought to reproduce extant structures of inequality in American society along racial, class, and gender lines. For example, Mexican Americans were taught to fill low-paying jobs that Anglo-Americans refused. Efforts to assimilate and embrace our neighbors from the south were forgotten when their labor was no longer needed at the onset of the Great Depression.

The plight of these Mexican immigrants and their liminal status both in the United States and back in their homeland is made clear, raising important questions about citizenship in a multinational, globalized world. The issues of inclusion and exclusion are beyond mere academic interest; they fuel a national debate in which politicians and policy makers are actively embroiled, from the ways in which contemporary men of color are excluded from citizenship due to incarceration to transnational flows along the U.S.-Mexico border, the focus of this work. Camp shows how historical archaeology can make a contribution to the existing literature on the contested nature of American citizenship and national belonging. Her analyses demonstrate that marginalized peoples created parallel and alternate visions by imposing new meanings on the material world, effectively redefining what it meant to be American. By providing a clearer understanding of how material culture is implicated in the process of forging an American identity, she illuminates an essential dimension of the American experience.

Michael S. Nassaney
Series Editor

Preface and Acknowledgments

In one of my most memorable experiences as a Southern California high school student, our social studies instructor decided to tackle what was then and what continues to be a politically loaded topic: immigration policy in the United States. Because we were Southern California residents living close to the border, this subject matter hit close to home for many students in my classroom. This was especially true for me; my Anglo-American mother married my Hispanic stepfather when I was six years old. As part of my teacher's lesson plan for the day, he carefully laid out a thick, tan line of masking tape across the front of the classroom. He then told students who supported the construction of a massive wall along the U.S.–Mexico border to stand at the far right of the tape, and instructed students who believed in unrestricted immigration between borders to stand at the far left end of the tape. Students who fell somewhere between these two viewpoints were told to stand in the middle of the tape.

Nearly my entire class, with the exception of a few of my close friends, chose to stand at the far right end of the tape. With more than thirty students glaring at us from the other side of the tape and the opposite side of the room, my friends and I felt both socially and politically isolated in our classroom as well as at our high school. This experience, among many others growing up in the nearly all Anglo-American community of Villa Park, California, ignited a curiosity in me to understand why people harbored such deep-seated feelings about immigration in the United States. Why has our country transformed from a somewhat welcoming place for certain types of immigrants, a nation to which my Austrian great-grandmother and German great-grandfather immigrated in search of a better life for their children, to a place of selective restriction? And how have immigrants fought back and redefined what it means to be an American citizen?

The disciplines of history and law offer robust bodies of scholarship that provide partial answers to my questions. Yet this literature frequently lacks the bottom-up perspective that historical archaeological research elicits. This book therefore seeks to place historical archaeological data in dialogue with interdisciplinary commentaries on the history of citizenship and attempts to delineate the practices and attributes unique to American citizens. It does so by first examining in chapter 1, "Who Is an American?," how American citizenship has been defined (and policed) from historical and legal perspectives. As we will discover, from the founding of the American empire by British subjects dissatisfied with the parameters of citizenship back in their home country, what it means to be an American has frequently gone hand in hand with the acquisition and display of specific types of goods and commodities.

This point—that goods have come to define American citizenship—should resonate with those familiar with contemporary America, a country now known for its rampant and, as some would argue, frightening obsession with mass consumption. The introductory chapter of this book briefly explores the historical foundations of this consumer ethic by once again drawing upon interdisciplinary research on how consumption has been equated with being an American citizen. In tracing the lineage of and linkages between consumption and American citizenship, this book shows how historical archaeology can intervene in multidisciplinary debates on the subject matter.

Historical archaeology is unique in that its practitioners encounter firsthand the history of consumer practices through the excavation and laboratory analysis of goods acquired by communities, households, families, and individuals. Historical archaeology, I argue, thus provides yet another lens through which we can understand how quotidian practices—such as purchasing an exotic vase made in China—became equated with being an American, and a specific type of American at that; in the case of an African American family living in early twentieth century Oakland, California, this purchase conveyed that they were an upper-class American family knowledgeable of goods that communicated their affluence and nationality (Mullins 2001).

The most crucial chapters in this book are those that map out historical archaeological research on how everyday people living in America consumed or chose not to consume in order to lay claims to citizenship—a citizenship some already had as naturalized citizens yet they did not get to experience due to their class, race, or gender. Chapter 2, "Historical Archaeologies of Citizenship," and chapter 4, "The Archaeology of Citizenship," demonstrate the utility and theoretical weight of the discipline. They show that historical archaeology contributes a material-centric vantage point from which scholars can understand how citizenship policies have developed over time and how these policies have been experienced by those subjected to them. Importantly, these case studies show how individuals and communities have worked to shape their own notions of "Americanness," a point often lost in historical and legal accounts of citizenship that privilege and prioritize historical documents and legal case studies over individual and communal experiences visible in archaeological data and oral histories.

Although composing this book has answered many pressing personal and academic questions that had been on my mind since my youth, it took the assistance and encouragement of a "village" to finish. Toward this end, many thanks are owed to my colleagues, family members, and friends who inspired this book or made the composition of it attainable. Most of this book was written while I was pregnant or had a small child under foot. My husband, mother-in-law, and mother deserve much credit for watching my two-year-old daughter, Lana, and my newborn son, Ty, while I wrote. My mother-in-law, Brenda, has been especially generous, leaving a lucrative job and the beautiful climate of Oahu to live in Moscow, Idaho, and be a permanent nanny to our children. My husband's steadfast commitment to my career and our children has also aided in getting this book through the publication stage. My childhood and now adulthood best friends Gina Lee and Tracy Clifton, both of whom attended the high school discussed at the beginning of this preface, have likewise provided the emotional nourishment needed to survive late nights of writing despite being states and time zones apart.

The Mount Lowe Archaeology Project, which is discussed in chapters 3 and 4, would never have managed to get off the ground without assistance from the staff of Angeles National Forest. District archaeologist Mike McIntyre (now forest archaeology supervisor) was instrumental in this project, sharing maps and archaeological reports associated with the site, providing office space for public outreach events, offering up equipment for the project, and finding curatorial space for artifacts generated from my research. Darrell Vance, forest archaeologist and Heritage Program manager, was also quick to respond to requests and support my research.

David Pebbles of Angeles National Forest similarly shared GIS base maps of Echo Mountain with me.

Data discussed in chapters 3 and 4 were recovered with the help of many friends, students, family members, and colleagues. At Stanford University, Barbara Voss, Ian Hodder, Paulla Ebron, and Lynn Meskell provided me with the archaeological training and advice needed to run my own archaeological field project. Barb was a model mentor during my time at Stanford, taking time out of her busy schedule to travel to, hike to, and help excavate my dissertation research site in 115-degree weather. Barb's resolute commitment to descendent communities and to the preservation of histories often unmentioned in or that run counter to popular historical accounts and her infallible work ethic have inspired me from the first day we met. I am forever thankful to Barb for taking me in, teaching me the ropes of historical archaeology, and encouraging me to have the confidence to run my own projects and trust my own archaeological instincts. Sam Wineburg in the Department of Education similarly encouraged me to think outside the boundaries of my own discipline and exposed me to interdisciplinary literature from which I continue to draw inspiration. Fellow graduate student and laboratory colleague Bryn Williams's penchant for and ability to wade through and translate cutting-edge interdisciplinary theory led to countless conversations about race, historical archaeology, archaeological theory, and gender that have driven much of my research and writing. The staff and administration in Stanford University's Department of Anthropology, especially department manager Ellen Christensen and student services officer Shelly Coughlan, are the backbone of the graduate program, providing unwavering emotional and logistical support needed to navigate the doctoral program.

My research would not have been possible without the assistance of stakeholder communities and community members. Those who are invested in Mount Lowe's history immediately made me feel welcome as an outsider and researcher, and the community surrounding the historical resort treated me like a local after only a short period of time residing there. I am forever indebted to Brian Marcroft of the Scenic Mount Lowe Historical Railway Committee, a friend whose tireless passion for Mount Lowe endeared the site of Mount Lowe to me and motivated me to finish my research project for future generations of Mount Lowe enthusiasts to read. I am also grateful for Brian's lovely family, who not only let me "borrow" Brian on the weekends to hike out to Mount Lowe and page through all of his documents related to the site at their home but who also frequently came along for the ride. John Harrigan also spent a great deal of time surveying the site and passing along both archival maps of the site and maps he had drawn himself. His book, *Mount Lowe Power* (2000), was a source of inspiration. Paul Ayers, another local historian, has always been willing to share rare photographs of the resort from his private collection as well as take me on a survey of the site. Paul sparked my interest in labor relations at the site thanks to several newspaper articles he gave me as I first began my project. Michele Zack, an Altadena local and noted author of award-winners *Altadena: Between Wilderness and City* (2004) and *Southern California Story: Seeking the Better Life in Sierra Madre* (2009), always made me feel at home while I was working in and visiting Southern California. The late charismatic Robert Wilde animated Mount Lowe for me when he recounted hiking around what was left of Mount Lowe as a teenager. Conversations with Mike Manning, Paul Rippens, and Michael Patris similarly helped give shape to my dissertation project.

Reconstructing the events that took place at Mount Lowe Resort and Railway required extensive archival research at libraries, museums, and historical societies in Northern and Southern California between 2004 and 2009. Gratitude is extended to the curators and archivists who aided me in what often turned out to be quite an elusive, demanding, and time-consuming search for the documentary trail of Mount Lowe's labor history. These museum professionals include Peter Blodgett (H. Russell Smith Foundation curator of western historical manuscripts, The Huntington Library), Marva Felchin (director of the Autry Library, Autry Museum of Western History), Jennifer Allan Goldman (associate curator and institutional archivist, The Huntington Library), David Kessler (Bancroft Special Collections, University of California, Berkeley's Bancroft Library), Dan Lewis (curator of science, technology, and transportation, The Huntington Library), Manola Madrid (Southwest Museum), Liza Posas (reference librarian, Southwest Museum), Deirdre del Re (Altadena Historical Society), Kim Walters (director of the Braun Research Library, Southwest Museum), and Jennifer Watts (curator of photographs, The Huntington Library). Bill Deverell (professor of history at the University of Southern California and director of the Huntington-USC Institute on California and the West) also directed me to pertinent resources while I researched at the Huntington Library and has always found time in his busy schedule to correspond with me about all things Southern California.

Funds to support research detailed in this book as well as the completion of this manuscript were provided by a number of public and private institutions: a Stanford University School of Humanities and Social Sciences Graduate Research Opportunities Grant to support multiyear archival research; the Altadena Historical Society for funding to present my findings on Mount Lowe Resort and Railway to the community; two predissertation Mellon Summer Field Grants to initiate the preliminary stages of field work at Mount Lowe; a grant from the Historical Society of Southern California for archaeobotanical analysis related to the project; a visiting scholar fellowship from the Autry National Center for the Study of the American West that allowed me to complete archival research related to my dissertation project; and numerous grants from Stanford Archaeology Center to support travel to conferences and other forms of public dissemination of my findings between 2006 and 2008. Grants received in 2009, 2011, and 2012 from the National Park Service's Japanese American Confinement Sites Grant program, a Faculty SEED Grant from the University of Idaho Research Council, and financial support from my department have made preliminary archaeological research at the Kooskia Internment Camp possible. Finally, the University of Idaho's Department of Sociology and Anthropology and the University Press of Florida helped offset reproduction costs associated with figures in this book.

Mount Lowe Resort and Railway was excavated and interpreted with the help of many archaeological field school students, volunteers, and staff. Excavations at Mount Lowe were intense and physically challenging; the section house landscape was difficult to access by foot, had no restroom or access to water, featured temperatures that would often reach 115 degrees Fahrenheit by 10 or 11 a.m., and was accessible only on foot along a steep, dangerous trail that was once part of Mount Lowe's railway grade. Despite the many obstacles faced on that perilous project, I look back on it fondly due to the first-rate crews with which I had the pleasure of working in 2005 and 2006.

Marisa Solórzano deserves special note, as she worked alongside me for both of Mount Lowe's field seasons, surviving poisonous spider bites and enduring nearly an entire field season excavating the section house's cesspool. Her humor, diligence, brilliant archaeological drawings and cartoons, and steadfast commitment to the project will always be remembered. In the summer of 2005 at Mount Lowe, my volunteers and students included Marisa Solórzano, Nicole Adelle Rich, Whitney Jacobs, Emily Burt, Scott Mathers, Illana Ruth Lohr-Schmidt, Laura Alvarenga Ortiz, Gianni Sami, Alicia Boswell, Paula Wegner, and Zack Wegner. The summer of 2005's staff included Stacy Kozakavich, Joanne Grant, Bryn Williams, and Barbara Voss. In the summer of 2006, volunteers and students included Jamie Kistner, Sonia Sifuentes, John Colgrove, Melanie Rudolph, Denise Brown, Claire Rich, Kristin Lynn Nado, Laura Ng, Koji Ozawa, Cailee Mellen, Zack Wegner, Jonathan Harvey, Kaitlyn Rich, Paula Wegner, Amy Amberger, and Christine Hajek. The summer of 2006's staff included Marisa Solórzano (lead crew chief), Stacy Kozakavich, Barbara Voss, and Joanne Grant. Once the fieldwork had ceased, several students volunteered to help me clean, photograph, identify, analyze, catalog, and curate my artifact assemblage; Rachel Engmann, Adrian Meyers, Andrew Nicchitta, and Christian Maltbaek assisted with the laboratory process. Mike Stoyka of Sonoma State University analyzed faunal remains from Mount Lowe and Virginia Popper of the University of Massachusetts at Boston analyzed and interpreted archaeobotanical remains recovered from the resort.

Professional support within the discipline of historical archaeology as well as at my current institution aided in the production of this manuscript. My colleagues in the Department of Sociology and Anthropology at the University of Idaho have provided both the intellectual support and friendship necessary to undertake this writing project. Departmental colleagues Mark Warner and John Mihelich have provided additional encouragement that made the completion of this manuscript possible. Paul Mullins provided thoughtful commentary on portions of this manuscript, and Michael Nassaney offered the encouragement and feedback needed to finish a final draft of the book. Finally, I am indebted to my students at the University of Idaho who continually challenge my thinking on historical archaeology and force me to clarify its important role in contemporary American culture in and outside of the classroom.

Abbreviations

DREAM Act	Development, Relief, and Education for Alien Minors Act
MLRR	Mount Lowe Resort and Railway
PERC	The Pacific Electric Railway Corporation

Introduction

Citizenship has been a defining element of American life from colonial times to the present. As with one's class, sexuality, gender, and race, an individual's citizenship standing has been a meaningful vector of identity in America. The right to work, the right to vote, the right to travel, the right to free speech, and the right to an education are just a sliver of the many freedoms historically predicated upon one's naturalization status in the United States.

In the nation's earliest days, citizenship was a fluid, free-floating idea, one that had yet to be cemented into law. Citizenship instead referred to the cultural practices expected of individuals inhabiting the geopolitical boundaries of the United States. At that time, central to the concept of citizenship was the freedom for "all individuals to pursue their actions and activities without risk or arbitrary or unjust political interference" (Hall and Held 1989, 177). At best, citizenship was ambiguous, with "members of the founding generation" leaving "few explicit definitions of what they meant by citizenship" (Kerber 1997, 834). In more recent times, citizenship has not only connoted certain beliefs and behaviors peculiar to those residing in America; it has also transformed into a legal condition determined by a complex nexus of economic and social interests of the American empire. The 1882 Chinese Exclusion Act, the first legal provision that explicitly forbade a group of people from entering the United States based on their racial and ethnic identity that was passed after Chinese immigrants were no longer desired for their labor, is a good example of how politics and culture are intertwined. And while the legal and cultural expectations of American citizens have been historically unstable, one thing has remained constant: people and groups occupying all echelons of society—from state institutions to individual noncitizens desiring social and legal inclusion—have always contested citizenship.

This book promises a fresh attempt at teasing out these multiple meanings by looking at how different groups residing in America have constituted and articulated what it means to be an American using material culture as a medium of social action. I oscillate back and forth from the institutions imparting ideals about American citizenship to the individuals on the receiving end of such ideological instruction. As I assert in later chapters, the vantage point that historical archaeology affords permits a reading of citizenship that is multiscalar in methodology, nuancing previous studies of American citizenship that prioritize historical documents and court rulings over individual and communal responses. Inspired by globalization and transnationalist studies that look at how local identities and practices are informed by the global and the local, this mutually constitutive approach captures how national and regional Americanization and citizenship efforts enacted by corporate and federal entities were negotiated and retooled by, to use Scott's (1994) oft-cited phrase, "those of little note."

One might wonder how historical archaeology can intervene in debates on what has constituted American citizenship, a subject that tends to be dominated by documentary data. This book etches out a route to employing an archaeology of citizenship by showing how archaeological data can be elicited to explore how multiple interest groups have defined citizenship in the past. Throughout the course of American history, what people do and do not purchase and consume has served as a cornerstone of citizenship and marker of American identity. Archaeologists see the residues of these consumer transactions in their assemblages, permitting an unrivaled perspective from which we can discuss how goods were used by historic peoples to express their feelings regarding American nationality and citizenship.

With the exception of a few groundbreaking studies (e.g., Mullins 1999a, 1999b, 2001, 2011a, 2011b), historical archaeologists have understated the novel role citizenship played in shaping American consumption patterns. This book takes seriously the social and legal category of citizenship by looking at how it has historically and recently impacted the lives of nonnaturalized and naturalized Americans. As I argue throughout this work, because consumption has been linked with one's display of patriotism and national identity, citizenship should be framed as a lens through which we can theorize and interpret the consumer decisions historic Americans made.

Theorizing Citizenship

What constitutes citizenship and who counts as a citizen? This is perhaps one of the most contested questions in contemporary America, with many of today's politicians calling for the selective, intentional exclusion of Mexican nationals while conversely ignoring Pacific, Atlantic, and Canadian borders that surely welcome "illegal" immigrants as well. Although political pundits are currently making public arguments that citizenship should be unilaterally restricted, the United States continues to sustain "corporate interests that exploit the cheap labor of vulnerable immigrants" (Ong 1999, 9). The H-2 guest worker program is a prime example of this form of state-sanctioned "illegal" immigration, where Mexican nationals are imported into the United States and held captive by the American employers who hire them. Likened to a modern form of slavery, this program allows companies to treat employees as they see fit, forcing them to work long hours and placing them in harsh and what most would consider uninhabitable housing. Workers objecting to these conditions "face deportation, blacklisting, or other retaliation" (Southern Poverty Law Center 2007, 1). Hence, state and federal policies are rife with social contradiction, making the regulation of immigration much more a cultural project than a legal or economic one.

The exclusion of specific groups via legal means is certainly not understudied, with a canon of work branching across nearly all academic disciplines that trace the lineage of racially and ethnically based exclusionary laws, acts, and statutes. Rather, the lacuna in citizenship studies lies in its failure to grasp how legal measures were actualized, enforced, and experienced beyond their legal meanings. This book sees citizenship as a process rather than a static, legal state of being with which we have come to associate "citizenship." It aims to capture how people choose or choose not to adopt certain behaviors and goods expected of American citizens. Unlike other fields, historical archaeology unveils these choices by calling upon archaeological data anchored to discrete periods of time. The discipline can attend to "vernacular notions of citizenship" (Rosaldo 1999, 260) constructed by marginalized populations frequently left out of or invisible in the historical records. Archaeology's diachronic emphasis is needed in citizenship studies because it illustrates that a group or individual's decision to partake in consumption can vacillate over time depending on a pastiche of sociopolitical and socioeconomic factors.

This book also strives to promote a more inclusive vision of citizenship: one that considers how American identities have been defined not only legally but also culturally by citizens and noncitizens alike. Supporting my thesis is a sophisticated body of scholarship in cultural anthropology that theorizes how citizenship is experienced on the ground, in the private lives of communities and individuals subjected to the legalities of citizenship. Most important to readers of this book, this literature forms a solid foundation for comprehending how citizens are made as well as how citizens choose to align or unalign themselves with American nationality. This work stresses the cultural construction of the commonplace, taken-for-granted terms "nation" and "citizen"; whereas "nation" refers to a place whose sovereignty is artificially bound by political or cultural groups, or both, "citizen" denotes an individual who is considered or considers himself a member of this geopolitical and geocultural territory. Given these definitions, the nation and its citizens are fictions of our modern time, reinforced by the collective experience of "reading books, pamphlets, newspapers, maps, and other modern texts" that make mention of nation-states; "the modern nation-state, in this view, grows less out of natural facts—such as language, blood, soil, and race—but is a quintessential cultural product, a product of the collective imagination" (Appadurai 1993, 414). Citizens and nations equally rely upon each other to maintain this illusion of their authenticity, and material culture is the catalyst often called upon to sustain this façade.

Take, for example, the Colonial Revival movement in turn-of-the-twentieth-century America. Ignited by their growing discomfort with momentous changes in technology and the diversification of America's citizenry, Anglo-Americans fled to the safety of what they called old America and imagined it as a place of comfort and solace (Denenberg 2003, 3). Wallace Nutting profited off of these fears by designing and selling goods, such as "a hand-tinted photograph, a reproduction Windsor chair, an illustrated book, or a chest of drawers just like Grandmother's," that evoked a "soothing, idealized American history" absent of "staggering social change" (3). These representations of America's yesteryears could be found in middle-class parlors, bedrooms, and kitchens, conjuring up an idyllic, depoliticized, quaint, and simple America weightless of the historical baggage of modern times. The nation and its value system were now part and parcel with the growth of commercialism in America. Patriotism and nationalism were neatly bundled with the rhetoric of commercialism and free enterprise. Before we follow this train of thought to its logical conclusion and stipulate that consumers were duped by consumerism's messages, we must also acknowledge that the nation needs citizens to buy into this consumer logic and nostalgia for the past. Americans were not automatons; they held their own citizenship aspirations that sometimes radically departed from those of the nation-state and the entrenched consumer culture that took flight in early-twentieth-century America.

If we are to hold steadfast to the contemporary definition of citizenship, then we conceptualize it as a legally binding state of being that places an individual under the umbrella of a nation. But if we are to follow the creative lead of cultural anthropologists (Appadurai 1990; Kearney 1995; Ong 1996, 1999; Rosaldo 1994, 1999, 2003), then we see that citizenship is not just a legal standing but also a category of belonging regardless of an individual's naturalization status. Framed in this manner, citizenship becomes fluid and versatile: a self- or group-fashioned condition of existence not entirely subject to state intervention and demarcation. Cast in this light, citizens are not blindly supporting the nation's goals and intentions; citizens instead are people with their own diverse interests and motivations.

Rosaldo invigorated anthropological debates concerning immigrant personhood and identity by introducing the concept of "cultural citizenship" in 1993. Based on his research among Latino immigrants in San Jose, California, Rosaldo discovered that Latinos saw citizenship as a highly mediated status; legal standing was merely one of the many reference points his informants' associated with national belonging and American citizenship. An original concept fueled by Rosaldo's ethnographic fieldwork, "cultural citizenship" reframes citizenship by extending the definition of it "beyond the dichotomous categories of legal documents, which one either has or does not have, to encompass a range of gradations in the qualities of citizenship" (Rosaldo 1994, 57). Key to this book is Rosaldo's assertion that the "micropolitics" of everyday life within Latino "communities—neighborhoods, workplaces, churches, and activist groups" ignite and inspire new definitions of citizenship that "may very well affect a renegotiation of the basic social contract of America" (1994, 61, 62). As Rosaldo therefore sees it, those legally excluded from full citizenship pioneer and formulate new collectivities in spite of the state. These coalitions demand inclusion within and benefits from the state. California's recently passed DREAM (Development, Relief, and Education for Alien Minors)

Act, where noncitizen minors can attend public universities and receive in-state tuition rates, shows how the state can concurrently embrace a particular collective for the sake of a nation's growing need for a labor force while still excluding the same individuals from other citizenship privileges by citing legal grounds.

Ong revisits (1996, 1999) Rosaldo's "cultural citizenship" by attending to the conditions that contour a state's decision to embrace or deny a community or individual's request for legal and social inclusion in the nation. Ong's formulation of citizenship departs from Rosaldo in several meaningful ways. First and foremost, she refracts citizenship through the lens of political economy, in the process adeptly highlighting how the economic imperatives and needs of a nation determine "subjects' location within the nation-state" and "the construction of their citizenship" (Ong 1996, 737). This point is made especially clear in chapters 4 and 5 of my book, which detail how Mexican immigrants were brought across the border by American-owned railway companies and forced to endure company-sponsored "Americanization" campaigns. As my research illustrates, such assimilation attempts were not carried out with the intention of crafting Mexican immigrants into American citizens who would be treated as equals to Anglo-American citizens. Rather, these programs sought to replicate preexisting structures of inequality in American society that stratified citizens based upon their race, class, and gender. Mexican immigrants, for example, received instruction in skills and trades associated with low-paying and ill-respected professions that middle- and upper-class Anglo-Americans had little interest in occupying. When their labor was no longer needed at the onset of the Great Depression, efforts to assimilate and embrace Mexican immigrants were forgotten, thus demonstrating Ong's point that the economic needs of nation-states govern citizenship policies and procedures.

To capture this elasticity exercised by both nation-states and immigrants, Ong devises the phrase "flexible citizenship" in her later works (e.g., 1999). Flexible citizenship deviates from "cultural citizenship" in that it acknowledges that citizenship policies are negotiated not only by subordinated groups as Rosaldo urges but also by nations who formulate courses of action based on their economic demands (Ong 1999, 17). She also contends that these flexible approaches to citizenship, where the state simultaneously supports restricting and importing noncitizens, inform immigrant national loyalties and desires for citizenship. Couched between immigrants and nations are state-sponsored and private institutions, such as churches, orphanages, almshouses, and prisons, that also mediate and contour nations, noncitizens, and citizens' decisions regarding the parameters of citizenship.

This idea—that citizenship is mediated across all strata of society but not in equal ways—is a critique Ong levels at Rosaldo. As she aptly points out, citizenship rights are unevenly distributed, for states and corporations have more leverage to legally deny or approve of noncitizens in ways unfathomable by immigrants themselves. Ong thus feels that Rosaldo mistakenly "gives the erroneous impression that cultural citizenship can be unilaterally constructed and that immigrant or minority groups can escape the cultural inscription of state power and other forms of regulation that define the different modalities of belonging" (1996, 73). At the same time, Ong does not discard Rosaldo's emphasis on how subordinated groups, such as Latinos, remake and lay claim to a citizenship denied to them on both cultural and legal grounds or deny the associated social power such organization and collaboration can have.

Globalization and transnationalist scholars have also considered the meaning of citizenship to those socially or legally excluded from it. They provide productive ways of thinking about how allegiances and collectivities are formed in support of as well as in opposition to the nation. Holston and Appadurai (1996), for example, assert that citizenship can be concurrently emancipatory and exclusionary. On the one hand, citizenship can erase "local hierarchies, statuses, and privileges in favor of national jurisdictions and contractual relations based in principle on an equality of rights" (Holston and Appadurai 1996, 187). On the other, those who choose to align themselves with a nation can sometimes also choose to discriminate against those who are of other nationalities. This discrimination can take many dangerous forms, including exclusion based on imagined racial and ethnic differences. This is why Anderson (1983) has correctly observed that "national identity" is rooted in the idea of an "imagined community," one that is based on perceived rather than "real" differences since members of a national community are initially anchored to that landscape solely based on superficial, geographical terms.

A common thread that runs through much of this book is the idea that groups who disagree with the parameters of citizenship or do not subscribe to the philosophies and convictions of the American nation can shape ideas about the nation's citizenry. Historical archaeological studies show that ordinary people shaped national discourses regarding citizenship and formed their own "imagined communities" that, in turn, informed state and federal citizenship policies. From female reformers hired by a railway company to supposedly transform Mexican immigrant railway workers into "good American citizens" to the intentional communities seeking to redefine gender and class roles in American society, historical archaeological research highlights the agency exerted by ordinary citizens and noncitizens to forge new definitions of community belonging outside of the sometimes narrow parameters of nationality.

A prime example of this, chapter 4, "The Archaeology of Citizenship," investigates how immigrants to the United States and the companies who recruited and hired them concocted their own versions of "imagined communities." In early-twentieth-century Southern California, companies such as the Pacific Electric Railway Corporation (PERC) sought out cheap labor from Mexico. Enticed by the promise of better living conditions, higher wages, and free transportation to America from Mexico by prospective American employers such as PERC, Mexican nationals migrated to the United States en masse in the early twentieth century. Once across the border, Mexican immigrants encountered discrimination based on their racial classification and class standing within American society. PERC required that all employees of Mexican heritage endure "Americanization" instruction, providing insight into the role American companies envisioned Mexican immigrants occupying in American society. Americanization instruction involved demoralizing lessons in proper bathing, hygiene, dress, child-rearing, and house cleaning for Mexican girls and women, and training in lower-class trade- and service-oriented professions for Mexican boys and men. Dreams dashed, many Mexican migrants headed home only to endure additional marginalization from Mexican nationals who took issue with "Americanized" Mexicans or who saw Mexicans who migrated back to Mexico from America as disloyal to the Mexican nation. Data mined from archaeological research at one site of Americanization instruction, a Mexican railway workers' household owned by PERC, along with oral history and archival studies illuminate how Mexican immigrants formed their own opinions about citizenship and national identity in light of social alienation in their homeland and in their nation of migration.

Several of the case studies presented in this book add theoretical weight to globalization theorists' point that not all immigrants aspire to citizenship or to belong to one particular nation (c.f., Holston and Appadurai 1996, 190; Tsing 1993; Spiro 2008) or any nation, for that matter, especially in countries where an individual or group's legal citizenship is trumped by a society unwilling to embrace legal citizens who are of a particular racial, socioeconomic, or ethnic group. This is especially true in countries where the economic disparities between "residents have become too gross and the areas of commonality too few to sustain" liberal ideologies of citizenship (Holston and Appadurai 1996, 192). During the early twentieth century, the concept of citizenship began to unravel due to border crossings enacted not merely by individuals but also by nations themselves. First-world countries such as the United States sought out the labor of noncitizens to mass produce products and work in sectors considered undesirable to middle- and upper-class Americans. In this sense, then, nation-states have also become "de-territorialized" in that they require third-world foreign labor to buoy their first-world economy (Kearney 1995, 553; Gupta and Ferguson 2002). Ironically, many nations' frequent border crossings for and dependency upon other nations' labor, services, and goods unravel the notion of a nation-state as a bounded, independent community and "'natural' marker of cultural and social difference" (Gupta 2003, 321).

Some scholars therefore go as far as to speculate that the nation as we know it today will fade from memory, inspiring new possibilities of belonging and community building independent of a geopolitical terrain. Chapter 5, "The Future of Citizenship," looks at specific examples of how the latter scenario is at work in our modern world. It provides evidence that individuals weave together communities outside of nation-states, especially when individuals or entire groups of people are disenfranchised. Archaeological studies of wartime internment camps—institutions where individuals are stripped of their citizenship but not deported back to their nation of origin—allow archaeologists to see how this process unfolds. Do individuals in these settings use materiality to fight for citizenship, do they long for their country of origin, or do their citizenship aspirations form a hybrid of the latter and former sentiments? As the case studies presented in this book demonstrate, the answer is not straightforward but is rather complex, with individuals' choices determined by their ages, classes, and genders and visible in the archaeological record.

This finding—that citizenship is not a legal or social category of belonging to which everyone aspires—has serious implications for historical

archaeological research and consumption studies. As historical archaeological and, for the most part, consumption studies on citizenship stand,
materiality is read as a tool marginalized peoples inhabiting historic
America used to demand social or legal inclusion as American citizens.
Interdisciplinary literature on consumption in America postulates that
both nonconsumption and consumption have been perceived as an expression of one's citizenship and allegiance to the American nation (Rydell
1984; Cohen 1990, 2003; Rydell and Kroes 2005; Banet-Weiser 2007; Hoganson 2007). This literature, however, is predominantly rooted in the
documentary record or media (although see Chin 2001 for the exception
to the rule); what results from a heavy reliance on this form of data is
that all consumer decisions are painted with a broad brush, particularly
when it comes to understanding historically disenfranchised Americans'
consumerism. Their purchasing patterns—especially the discovery of
high-status goods in low-status households—are frequently interpreted
as an attempt to puncture an all-Anglo-American, middle-class consumer
sphere.

But, as we will see in this book's archaeological case studies, not all individuals on the margins of American society saw consumption as paving
a pathway toward social and legal acceptance in America. Rather, many
marginalized groups were well aware that the consumption of middle-
and upper-class goods would not help them transcend the social and legal isolation and discrimination they faced in America. Chapter 2, "Historical Archaeologies of Citizenship," similarly details communities that
emerged within the borders of America but that abandoned the cultural
beliefs associated with their nationality. Historic intentional and utopian
communities in America conjure up alternative visions of civic belonging, with religious, political, and ethnic/racial loyalties taking precedence
over national identity. In situations where individuals are deliberately opting out of membership within a national community, archaeological data
adds a new and needed portrait of what belonging can look like outside
of a political territory. Chapter 2 captures the multiplicity and plasticity
of definitions of American citizenship and nationality by outlining how
people in all walks of life have fought to demarcate what an American citizen looks like, acts like, and, most pertinent to archaeologists, consumes
and discards. As historical archaeological case studies show, American
citizenship has always been mediated by people of all backgrounds despite
its more recent definition as a legal category.

Chapter 2 shows that the buying, displaying, owning, and acquisition of goods have historically been linked with the expression of one's loyalty and adherence to American nationality. Material culture thus acts as interlocutor, mediating the relationship between the nation and corporations, communities, families, and individuals. At different moments in American history, groups and individuals have consumed to symbolize their loyalty to the nation. Consumption patterns are made transparent during excavations, which in turn allow archaeologists to surmise a site occupant's relationship to the American nation. Did the site residents, for instance, forgo or embrace a nation-state?

Before speculating, an archaeologist must be acutely aware of who was considered a citizen during the time period in which their site was occupied. They should also have a general understanding of the politics of consumption at that particular moment in time. This book provides broad summaries of both the legal parameters of citizenship over the course of American history and the historic fastening of consumption to American identity. Chapter 1, "Who Is an American?," and chapter 2, "Historical Archaeologies of Citizenship," are therefore literature reviews, and they identify fundamental publications on these topics.

Consumption and Citizenship

The gnarly, tangled relationship between citizenship aspirations and consumption has been exhaustively probed on a number of interdisciplinary fronts, with scholars working in the fields of history, material culture studies, sociology, anthropology, and cultural studies. Copious and exhaustive, this literature historicizes the meaningful role consumption has played in American culture, one that some argue stems back to the American Revolution (Breen 2004).

Mullins, one of the first historical archaeologists to extensively comb this literature, has presented the most compelling argument for archaeological attention to citizenship aspirations and desires to date. In line with this endeavor, he has successfully placed this copious body of interdisciplinary writing in dialogue with archaeological data recovered from a variety of geographical and temporal contexts. Mullins recently put forth arguments for an archaeology of consumption that acknowledges that goods help individuals to "confirm, display, accent, mask, and imagine who we are and who we wish to be, which breaks from seeing consumption as a largely reflective process that instrumentally displays social status, evokes ethnicity, exhibits gender, or confirms other essential identities" (2011a, 134–35; see also Mullins 2011b). Despite Mullins's work, historical archaeologists have been guarded about framing citizenship and, more broadly, consumption as salient aspects of one's daily life. The archaeology of citizenship falls within the scope of Mullins's consumption framework because it positions materiality as a mode of communication rather than as a passive practice emulative of an individual's personhood or broader societal ideologies. The former model is powerful because it lends agency to the objects people use and acknowledges that goods can be used to transform local, regional, and national politics.

Mullins's work articulates this point well, locating political and citizenship aspirations in goods that initially appear elusive, genteel, or quotidian to the archaeologist's eye. In his earlier work (1999a), he sees consumption as not merely a means to an end but also as a symbolic system that marginalized groups used to initiate dialogue about and, in some instances, gain access to the predominantly Anglo-American consumer space. As he explains, "rich with symbolic possibilities and carrying the tacit promises of citizenship, material goods provided a seemingly innocuous, yet meaningful, mechanism to reposition African Americans in opposition to racialized inequalities" (Mullins 1999a, 18). These desires are evident in the archaeological assemblage of the Maynard-Burgess family's household, which was occupied from 1850 to 1980 in Annapolis, Maryland. Excavations unearthed an unusual assortment of artifacts that speak to the politicization of consumption, including a flask featuring a Whig log cabin motif, an 1852 Franklin Pierce campaign redware pipe, and an 1840 William Henry Harrison campaign medalet (20–24). The latter two artifacts are unexpected because the Maynard-Burgess family members were prohibited from voting during those particular campaigns. Their support of Franklin Pierce is additionally surprising given that Pierce was "a vocal champion of Southern slaveholding interests and a vicious critic of abolitionists" (22). Instead of reading these objects' meanings verbatim (e.g., as evidence of the Maynard-Burgesses' choices of political candidates if they were able to legally vote), Mullins interprets the consumption of these objects as evidence of the family's "desire for American citizenry rights," "genuine nationalism, idealistic identification with the political process, and aspirations to participate as citizens" (24).

Mullins (2001) sees the same potential for social transformation present in objects that are not as politically obvious or interpretively straightforward as campaign ephemera. Mullins argues that the purchase and display of bric-a-brac activated and embodied consumers' hopes and dreams for a future America, momentarily suspending the stigmatization they faced as second-class citizens; it allowed them to think "about who they and their society *could* be" (2001, 164). Recovered from the Maynard-Burgess house, a porcelain figurine of a girl was designed to encourage consumers to recall a romanticized, "peaceful, non-industrial past" that "provided a comforting ideological vision of America's agricultural heritage that contrasted radically to late-nineteenth-century urbanization and social unrest" (161). The artifact is a peculiar find within an African American household in that it recalls a time when slavery still existed. Yet one of the household's occupants, John Maynard, was a "social climber" who displayed other goods and behavior that rivaled Anglo-American standards of gentility and affluence. For Mullins, then, this object is symbolic of social mobility and emblematic of the promise of freedom and equality under Reconstruction—an object consumed by African Americans to negate the structural constraints they encountered as a racialized minority group.

Although Mullins's work has generally focused on the experiences of African Americans, he has also shown that other marginalized groups consumed bric-a-brac to transcend their social position. Neighboring Norwegian and Irish immigrants, for instance, used and displayed a bric-a-brac figurine of Abraham Lincoln. This artifact was found by archaeologists in a West Oakland, California, privy that dates to approximately 1887. The figure of Lincoln had been a popular fixture in parlors after the Civil War, but as racial tensions once again grew between African Americans and Anglo-Americans, the iconography associated with Lincoln memorabilia changed. Gone was any reference to emancipation or African Americans as the Lincoln statue found in the West Oakland privy demonstrates. Mullins explains that the Norwegian and Irish's consumption of this new, modestly dressed, and realistically depicted Lincoln was strategic, especially when it came to the Irish who "were marginalized by racism and often associated with highly stigmatized blackness" (Mullins 2001, 163). These case studies illustrate that goods can be used to undermine exclusionary, pervasive ideologies of who counts as an American citizen and, also interrelated, who can consume. Equally significant, Mullins's work shows that everyday goods—not just artifacts with political slogans—are used by those on the margins of society to counter the racism they faced in their daily lives.

Due to Mullins's meticulous book- and article-length treatments of this literature, some of which is published in *The Archaeology of Consumer Culture* (2011b) in the "American Experience in Archaeological Perspective" series, this book tables extended discussions of it following this chapter. To strengthen my contention that American consumption practices have always been bound up with discourses concerning citizenship and status in America, I offer a snippet of this literature, including a few vignettes that clarify how material culture was used as a vehicle for expressing nationalism and patriotism.

There are two general directions this literature heads that are pertinent to the archaeological study of citizenship. The first body of work looks at how the upper strata of American society, advertising agencies, and businesses collapsed and conflated citizenship with consumption (Lears 1981, 1994; Leach 1993; Cross 2000). Those belonging to the upper crust were aware that the minutiae of one's material existence, including buttons, textiles, and jewelry, were scrutinized by American citizens. As scholars have documented, politicians used goods to communicate political sentiments and nationalist loyalties. John Adams, for instance, found himself walking a fine line between staying faithful to the American republic and bowing to his wife's desire to display her family's upper-class standing. He balanced these conflicting needs by buying clothing and textiles in France for his wife while limiting his own individual consumption of goods to those produced on American soil (Brekke 2006, 235). A politician's fashion misstep could elicit public outcry. John Adams made such a mistake by donning a jacket with "French embroidery," provoking disdain from the American public who viewed Adams's flair for foreign-produced, "effeminate" clothing as evidence of his "monarchist tendencies" (239). George Washington made similar politically inspired fashion statements by procuring and wearing clothing that was modest and made in America (225).

The second strain of this sizeable consumer citizenship literature hones in how ordinary Americans' purchasing habits were constrained by their social position, especially for individuals who were considered property (such as enslaved African Americans) or who were seen as second-class citizens, such as immigrants and blue-collar workers. Part of this body of work argues that women who were legally bound to their husbands found ways around legal exclusion in order to participate in the burgeoning late-eighteenth- and early-nineteenth-centuries' consumer marketplace (Martin 2006). Women sold clothing, butter, and eggs, and concocted other sorts of small-scale domestic and informal economies that allowed them to accumulate funds for their own purchases (Martin 2006, 194). Yet their presence in the broader public sphere, a sphere that was highly gendered and reserved for men during this time period, was subdued, representing a mere 5 percent to 15 percent of purchases in one late-eighteenth-century store in Virginia (194). Engaging in these underground activities afforded women freedom, if fleeting and momentary, from the restrictions placed on their civic activities and behaviors.

Hartigan-O'Connor investigates another dispossessed group of consumers: African American slaves and Anglo-American servants who were working inside the homes of well-to-do Anglo-Americans. These two groups were entrusted with the task of shopping for their employers, which required building a knowledge of popular, affluent styles of clothing and trendy, desired commodities. Through this process, they "realized the potential for self-fashioning that economic autonomy and consumer knowledge provided," becoming "particularly attuned to the role of clothing in declaring or masking identity" (Hartigan-O'Connor 2006, 137). Consequently, some African Americans chose to wear their employer's cast-off clothing rather than outfits that merchants reserved for and sold only to African Americans, such as "negro cloth" that was "coarse" and "sold in bulk" (137). By securing clothing that would otherwise remain unavailable to them due to racist merchants who would not sell such items to them or allow them inside their stores (Hartigan-O'Connor 2006, 142; Martin 2006, 182), African Americans artfully and intentionally maneuvered and manipulated the symbols of Anglo-Americans, subverting and undermining Anglo-Americans' dominance over consumerism and aesthetically pleasing goods.

Historical archaeologists have placed these two approaches in conversation by looking at the interplay and tensions between fashions prescribed by elites and the everyday people who had to live and wrestle with these guidelines. White's study of the minutiae of dress and adornment—buckles, aglets, buttons, and rings, to name a few artifacts—demonstrates the entangled relationship between social status and an individual's body in colonial America. Small finds easy to overlook but frequently found in the archaeological record, such as a buckle used to "fasten shoes, breeches, stocks, hats, swords, collars, girdles, gloves, gallus, and any other kind of clothing that might need fastening" (White 2005, 31), placed one's social standing on display for the world to see. Ornately decorated buckles were a sign of wealth while poorly made, "coarse" buckles were reserved for the destitute, as noted by an order placed by George Washington in 1759 "for his slaves at Mount Vernon" (33). For ordinary people, a vogue, stylish buckle was not merely a status symbol when worn but also a "form of currency" (47) that could be exchanged for clothing or other goods. For the financially strapped or downtrodden, the loss of such a prized object could be devastating. Abner Sanger, a member of the lower class, documented in his diary entry dated November 5, 1778, the loss of a buckle that warranted the formation of a small search party to recover (47–48).

Recognizing the transformative potential contained within one's wardrobe, elites living in colonial America saw the body as a tabula rasa upon which the socioeconomic status, cultural values, and political beliefs could be inscribed. Elites sought to demarcate boundaries between themselves and those living in the American colonies by establishing sumptuary laws that prohibited certain groups from donning specific textiles and styles of clothing. The Massachusetts Bay Colony, for example, passed sumptuary laws that sought to mark and privilege those of English nationality and to make visible the class standing and rank of the colony's residents (Loren 2010, 27–28). Much to the discontent of elites and colonial officials, some nonelites used clothing and bodily adornment as a catalyst for social mobility and change, and as a way to mask their social position and contest sumptuary laws. In Jamestown, Virginia, "colonists were scandalized by the ways their neighbors mixed fashions" (36). Jamestown commoners chose clothing that was reserved for the upper classes, undermining and contesting elites and colony officials' monopoly on luxurious textiles and ornate accoutrements (34–36).

Although comprehensive on the archival front, literature binding acts of consumerism to beliefs about citizenship still lacks a committed archaeological perspective. A ground-up rather than a top-down approach will add further texture to this already nuanced documentary treatment of consumer citizenship in historic America.

Summary

In keeping with the thematic goals and mission of the "American Experience in Archaeological Perspective" series, this book aims to bridge the disciplinary divide between historical, cultural, legal, consumer, and archaeological studies of citizenship and Americanization. This requires that I, as an archaeologist, perform my own academic border crossing of sorts. As with all ventures into unchartered territory, some ideas and concepts in disciplines new to me may be lost in the process or cursory in content. But the goal of this book is not to rewrite the history of citizenship from legal or historical perspectives but rather to give a lay of the scholarly terrain on these subjects and then offer concrete examples of how historical archaeology can intervene in these cross-disciplinary debates.

With this in mind, the book begins by outlining the hegemonic discourses of citizenship firmly rooted in legal restriction. Enacted by both states and the federal government, the move to deny an individual or group's request to enter the United States using the law as justification is a more recent invention. It was only in the twentieth century that the concept of an "illegal alien" became a household phrase, calling into question contemporary efforts to further restrict entrance into the United States. After reviewing the history of citizenship as a legal standing, the book then branches out into historical archaeological case studies that spotlight the role materiality plays in expressing feelings about nationality identity. One case study in particular highlights how decisions regarding national belonging and loyalties are not straightforward. Rather, one's feelings about their nationality and citizenship status can vary not only across time and cultural groups but also within an ethnic or racialized group itself.

This point is missed by scholarly literature that overwhelmingly favors seeing citizenship as a legal construct or imposed status. Here is where archaeologists and anthropologists can intervene, as they observe the lived, on-the-ground realities of citizens and noncitizens. The case studies profiled in this volume offer examples of how individuals have redefined what it means to be an American citizen, forging their own definitions in light of and in spite of federally and corporately imposed measures. In today's turbulent economic times, historical archaeology can provide useful examples of how different groups of people imagined national belonging in

America. In doing so, they have the power to propose new and innovative definitions of citizenship to affect societal change. Noncitizens and citizens alike have fought to define what citizenship should entail and who could partake in the rituals and rights of citizenship, often provoking and demanding alterations to ascriptive, legal measures meant to police and admit individuals inhabiting America. Their failures and successes can help motivate and inspire new formulations of citizenship—ones that challenge the path the nation has been carving out since the 1882 Chinese Exclusion Act, the first legal attempt to limit citizenship based on an individual's racial status—and forge new ones that conceptualize citizenship in more socially and legally inclusive ways.

1

....

Who Is an American?

What does it mean to be an American and who counts as an American citizen? For some it means the right to vote, to observe religious beliefs free from persecution, or the right to bear and carry arms. For others it means enjoying the tripartite but fairly ambiguous luxuries of freedom, equality, and democracy.

Turning to the history books to consider what traits and qualities have been fastened to American identity over time, we find that what it means to be an American has regularly involved exclusion and isolation—conditions that seem unbefitting of and counterintuitive to establishing a free, equal, and democratic nation. We also discover that some Americans have actively worked to limit others' civic participation and citizenship, whether due to an individual's or group's racial, gender, legal, citizenship, or class standing. We see that citizens, such as the ones who will be discussed in chapter 5, have been denied rights promised to them by the Constitution as naturalized citizens. Thus, while some people assume that all American citizens have been treated equally and granted the same privileges over the course of the nation's history, the reality stands that laws and policies have operated on a different and unequal premise, one legal historian Henry Chambers (2007) has described as a system of "tiered personhood," where "the basic humanity of subordinate groups is denied because of their race, ethnicity, or nationality" (McKanders 2010, 172). The unjust imprisonment of nearly 120,000 Japanese American citizens during World War II is just one of many instances in which the legal citizenship of groups has been retracted due to social prejudice (Casella 2007).

Citizenship laws, which are a set of rules and regulations most Americans assume to be set in stone and untouchable that police the boundaries of a nation's citizenry, are in practice malleable and unevenly applied to different groups of people. This reality can be seen as fluid in the sense that laws, especially those that discriminate against individuals based on various aspects of their identity (e.g., gender, sexual orientation, class, race, and ethnicity), can be and have been denounced and made to accommodate more diverse populations. But in more recent times citizenship has erred on the side of exclusion, as made apparent by the internment of innocent Japanese American citizens during World War II and the repatriation of half a million Mexican Americans and Mexican immigrants back to Mexico by the United States government during the Great Depression. Citizenship, then, has been shaped and contoured by both the social and political issues of a particular historical period as well as by previously established freestanding laws, acts, and statutes.

Therefore, the hegemonic sphere of state and federal laws has not solely defined citizenship. Over time, consuming goods has come to be considered a highly politicized move, one that encapsulates an individual's beliefs about citizenship in arguably more socially salient and meaningful ways than one's legal standing and naturalization status. The act of consuming, shopping, displaying, and acquiring goods—what we call "consumption"—has been historically construed as expressing one's relationship to the American nation. Here is where we see Rosaldo's "cultural citizenship" in action. Archaeologists are privy to the results of individuals' and groups' consumption habits, making them especially well positioned to examine how marginalized historic actors used the acquisition of goods to express their beliefs about citizenship and their desire to make it into their own image, as Rosaldo has asserted.

I take this argument a step further later in this book by offering case studies of how citizenship can be pliable in the hands of ordinary Americans, all the while still acknowledging that the law is often powerful and nonnegotiable. These archaeological studies mark the book's transition into more "locally oriented" interpretations of citizenship, where communities and groups exert creativity to force citizenship into casts of their own devices. Mae Ngai acquiesces, asserting that the "liabilities of illegal alienage and alien citizenship may . . . be at least partially offset through individual and collective agency" (2004, 3). Historically, people have used their buying power to negate legal strictures denying them American citizenship. Marginalized individuals thus "pursue social inclusion, making claims of belonging and engaging with society, irrespective of formal status" (3).

This framing of citizenship as something simultaneously desired and retooled by groups dispossessed of it or prohibited from securing it is different from traditional models of citizenship. In these latter scenarios, social and legal inclusion in a nation's citizenry is entirely dependent on a group's ability to render elements of their culture invisible and dissolve into the melting pot of a predominantly Anglo America (Flores and Benmayor 1997, 15). By choosing instead to investigate the diverse expressions of "cultural citizenship" in historic America, this book and the historical archaeological case studies contained within it present a clearer picture of how state and federally enacted citizenship laws, acts, statutes, and structures were experienced and reconceptualized by the communities and individuals subjected to them.

Local expressions of national belonging cannot be understood and interpreted without first considering the legal dimensions of citizenship and how, in recent times, such legal definitions have been tethered to exclusionism. Beginning from this starting point, this chapter inquires how the modern notion of citizenship as a legal, contractual relationship between an individual and the nation emerged. It provides a genealogy of American citizenship policies from the perspective of the nation-state, offering historical context for the groups and historical actors who have had to fight for cultural and legal inclusion.

American Citizenship: A Brief History of the Concept

Although the United States did not gain independence from Britain until 1776, colonists began contemplating what it would mean to be citizens living in a country separate from Britain upon arriving in North America. It was not until the mid- to late 1800s that a firm stance on both citizenship and immigration would begin to take shape. State and federal positions on these hotly debated and controversial topics, however, still fluctuate. America has both opened and closed its doors to immigrants, at times choosing to extend its borders to be more inclusive and later retracting its geopolitical boundaries to craft a more exclusive citizenry. Immigration policies have been influenced by a whole host of factors, including relationships with other nations, economic conditions within the nation, and paranoia over an individual's gender, criminal record, national loyalties, religion, race, or ethnicity, with one's "race" being only the most recent factor in determining who can be admitted into the American nation.

Citizenship in Colonial Times

The first European settlers in North America brought a distinct set of cultural beliefs and values that later helped crystallize their definitions of what the United States was to stand for and what its citizens should believe. British settlers arrived in North America with a fairly strong sense of what the relationship between an individual and his or her nation of origin should resemble. This would change as colonists grew weary of British restrictions on their actions and economic ventures while Britain attempted to transform North America into a "profitable overseas" colony (Smith 1997, 49). Crucial to the subject matter of this book, tensions between colonists and Britain frequently hinged on questions of citizenship, "on who would be full members of the colonial communities and who would instead be subjugated, expelled, or killed" (51), and on consumption as well (Breen 2004).

British colonists brought with them a sense of social hierarchy and stratification, which they believed to be natural and God-given. This was based on their understanding of British subjecthood as well as a firm belief in Manifest Destiny—the notion that God led them to discover North America and that this new land was destined to be a second Holy Land. Colonists did not, however, bring with them a concept of nationality as we know it today, a term that we define as a responsibility or belonging to a geographical territorial unit bound by distinct political, governmental, and cultural beliefs: such a concept did not exist in medieval England (Kettner 1978, 4–5). In medieval England, an individual's class standing and social position were more important than their nationality or ethnicity: "Legally, people were peasants, gentlemen, barons, burghers, laity, or clerics first, and Englishmen, Belgians, or Germans second or third, if at all" (Smith 1997, 42). By the seventeenth century the English developed a more complex definition of British subjecthood; belonging to the English empire could be established through *jus soli* and *jus sanguinis*, the latter of which refers to an individual's heritage or family lineage and the former of which refers to being born on British soil (Kettner 1978, 15). One of the few advantages of being a British subject was the ability to purchase, inherit, and own property, something aliens could not do unless "they did so only at the sufferance of the crown and for the use of the king" (6).

Because British colonists had a well-established vocabulary and knowledge of English notions of subjectship, the colonies lacked many of the formalized provisions aimed at curbing citizenship that became commonplace in nineteenth-, twentieth-, and twenty-first-century America. As time passed and colonists spent more time in North America, however, colonists found that their initial beliefs about the relationship between subjecthood and individuals and groups who did not share their values, whether religious, political, or ideological, were radically changing. The British judged an individual's religious beliefs as a marker of their character, primarily because some Protestants believed "that God had chosen the English to uphold true and free religious beliefs against slavish Catholicism" (Smith 1997, 48). This caused strife between British colonists and British officials back home, the latter of whom were most concerned about creating a well-oiled colony that was profitable for the British Empire (Kerber 1997, 846). As Rogers Smith surmises, "as imperial and colonial leaders each sought naturalization policies serving their own interests, they clashed repeatedly over who should be included and increasingly over what being a British subject really meant" (1997, 55).

This certainly is not to say that ethnic, racial, and religious conflict between European settlers, Native Americans, and African Americans was not present in the colonies' earliest days (Smith 1997, 41). Despite maintaining an amicable stance with certain religious groups, colonists objected to British preference for "policies that officially regarded members of friendly tribes, and even free Africans, as loyal 'overseas' British subjects almost like the colonists themselves" (54). Colonists took offense to this, as they saw African Americans and Native Americans as savages and less "civilized" than Europeans. Thomas Jefferson echoed early colonists' beliefs, seeing Native Americans as "ignorant heathens who might be the equals of whites with proper education" (61).

An ideology that emerged in tangent with European colonialism and imperialism, racism was also present in the colonies' earliest days. British colonists enacted violent and ethnocentric tactics to persecute Native Americans and African Americans. For Native Americans, the proposed solutions involved either assimilating or eradicating them, a policy that was maintained well into the twentieth century. These solutions were motivated by colonists' desires to acquire more land and additional resources for people of their own nationality and imagined race in the New World. When conflict between colonists and Native Americans did take place, strict regulations were imposed on Native Americans in an effort to curtail additional resistance. These included "statutes denying former tribesmen rights to testify in colonial courts, imposing curfews, restricting travel, and requiring observance of Christian practices" (Smith 1997, 60).

The rights of Native Americans and African Americans would continue to be contested as British colonists began to see themselves as a separate group. The need for a great amount of labor to carry out the imperial interests of the colonies took priority over seeing African Americans as human beings deserving of equal rights. As such, African Americans were positioned on an even lower rung of colonial society than Native Americans, one where African Americans were considered incapable of self-governance. As Smith explains, "in terms of the categories of English law, this black chattel slavery amounted to a new kind of subjectship—a subjectship to an individual master so complete that American legal authorities strove, never quite successfully, to ignore the slaves' humanity and to view them simply as property" (1997, 63–64). Not all colonists supported the enslavement of African Americans; some supported abolition and gave slaves the chance to purchase their freedom, though this practice was not the norm in the colonies' early days (64). The precarious social standing and civic responsibilities of Native Americans and African Americans would stay on the forefront of American colonists and politicians' minds as the British colony transformed into the American republic.

The British government and British colonists also held diverging opinions on Catholics living in the colonies. While Catholics were conferred British subjecthood in the New World's colonies, they found themselves declared noncitizens and aliens in Great Britain and Ireland (Smith 1997, 54). British colonists preferred extending citizenship privileges to European Catholics over African Americans and Native Americans, though in the eyes of the British republic, the latter two groups better served imperial interests because they were less likely to cause political strife back in Britain. British officials formalized their contempt of Catholics by creating an American statute in 1609 that "denied naturalization to all non-Protestants, as well as all those unwilling to take an oath of allegiance" (55). Catholics continued to be targeted as unwelcome aliens in the mid- to late-1600s; they were prohibited from holding office in Virginia, priests were not allowed within Massachusetts' borders, and in some colonies Catholics were subjected to forced disarmament, surveillance, and additional taxes for holding different religious convictions than other colonists

(57). Indeed, Roger Williams was banished from the Massachusetts Bay Colony in 1636 for heretical religious beliefs; he established Providence later that year and the Rhode Island Colony soon became a haven for religious heretics such as Anne Hutchinson.

Voting privileges in the colonies were likewise sharply circumscribed by British colonists' worldviews and by colonial officials back home in Britain. Virginia was known to be the most exclusive of all the colonies, with a 1762 statue denying voting privileges to "free blacks, mulattos, Native Americans, women, minors, and all non-Protestants, with Catholics expressly banned" (Smith 1997, 58). In other colonies, suffrage was predominantly set aside for "free, white, Protestant adult native, English-born, or naturalized male property owners" (58). Many of these voting restrictions would not be lifted until the late 1800s and early 1900s. Federal policies introduced during and directly after the American Revolution would continue in this discriminatory vein, restricting entry to certain elements of the public deemed as a threat to the republic as well as denying the status of personhood to African Americans with the passing of the *Dred Scott* decision in 1857.

The Revolutionary and Post-Revolutionary Eras, 1763–1857

Colonists began to flesh out and debate how British subjecthood differed from what would eventually become notions of American allegiance and citizenship during the Revolutionary and post-Revolutionary eras. Because a diverse population of non-British citizens had immigrated or been recruited to populate the New World, British citizens living in North America found themselves abandoning previous ideas of citizenship as posited by English law. In England there existed "a broad distinction between subjects and aliens, reflecting a clear sense that members of the community ought to enjoy a status different than that accorded to outsiders" (Kettner 1974, 208). In the colonies, this division was blurred by colonists wishing to encourage the settlement of North America, leading them to become more open to the notion that "*all* [Kettner's emphasis] subjects had a right to share the same benefits and privileges of membership without distinction or discrimination" (1974, 210).

Colonists also started to reflect upon their relationship with Britain and their national loyalties. This turn inward was partly provoked by colonists' growing dissatisfaction with increased British surveillance and control over the colonies' economic activities and output. As the colonies grew in size and economic productivity, Britain imposed what colonists perceived as stringent and unfair limitations on their ability to profit from the fruits of their labor (Breen 2004). Suddenly colonists found themselves financially strapped due to the "economic regulatory acts of 1764 and 1765, the Townshend Acts of 1767, the 1773 conferral of a tea monopoly on the British East India Company, and the 1774 Coercive Acts" (Smith 1997, 71). Now colonists had to pay more customs fees and additional taxes on goods, and were required to purchase stamps to mail documents (71).

Consequently, colonists began to see allegiance to one's nation as contractual and mutable, meaning that citizenship was something that could be temporary or permanent depending on both the nation's and the citizen's desires. This was a radical departure from British definitions of subjecthood, which held once a citizen, always a citizen (Kettner 1974, 211). The circumstances of the Revolutionary War also prompted this new definition of citizenship and allegiance, as the "founders of new republican states" felt that it "now seemed inconsistent to insist that individuals could be forced against their will to subject themselves to regimes of which they did not approve" (221). Hedged in by British officials who treated colonists as second-class citizens, the concept of an "American" was born by frustrated colonists. Their dissatisfaction prompted the creation of novel notions of national belonging and citizenship unheard of in the imperial world.

It was at this remarkable moment in American history when a more inclusive definition of citizenship than that of British subjecthood developed. British colonists generally agreed that Americans were notably different from British subjects in that Americans, as immigrants and colonists, faced unique obstacles and perils in the New World that made them particularly adept at collaboration and innovation. Unlike British subjecthood, American citizenship was not a product of one's "ethnicity, religion, or national origins" (Smith 1997, 77). Rather, it was an amalgamation of characteristics specific to the environment and social climate in America that transformed "newcomers into industrious, independent, egalitarian free men who loved liberty and were capable of practicing it" (77).

Despite exacting this more liberal philosophy of citizenship, certain groups did not fall under this supposedly inclusive vision of citizenship. With independence, individual states were given free rein to define citizenship and immigration policies. States managed certain aspects of their citizenry, with one of their primary goals being the cessation of "the British policy of penal transportation to America" (Neuman 1993, 1841). After the Revolutionary War, individual states made a concerted effort to abolish this practice. Georgia, for example, "enacted a statute in 1787 directing that felons transported or banished from another state or a foreign country be arrested and removed beyond the limits of the state, not to return on penalty of death" (1842). Other states went even further by not only banning the entry of convicts from abroad but also preventing convict "migration from sister states" (1842). Aware of this, the British "made some attempts to send convicts to the United States secretly, as ordinary indentured servants" (1841). For example, "one shipload . . . successfully landed in Baltimore in December 1783, but a second ship in 1784 was refused permission to enter United States ports, and ended up in British Honduras" (1841–42).

Between the late 1700s and early 1800s, a series of restrictive measures were put in place that sought, for the very first time in American history, to give voice to an ascriptive and uniquely American federal immigration policy. Formed in response to the French Revolution that brought numerous newcomers seeking political asylum to American shores and an increase in the amount of immigrants coming to the United States between 1790 to 1798 from "France, Ireland, and Germany" (Stone 2004, 30), the Naturalization Act of 1798 and, introduced shortly later, the Alien and Sedition Laws were designed to put an end to political upheaval and dissent in the United States. Federalists proposed the Naturalization Act of 1798 because their opposing party, the Democratic Republicans, had historically gained the favor "of the foreign vote" (Smith 1956, 22).

This law was also in response to the XYZ incident, which spawned a "quasi-war" between France and the United States over commerce (Pani 2008, 221). This event sparked American concern over French dissidence within the United States, which American politicians reasoned could lead to another Revolution if immigration remained unregulated. Up until 1795 immigrants could obtain citizenship if they lived in America for a minimum of two years (Stone 2004, 30). In 1795 Federalists expanded this requirement to five years (30). The Naturalization Law of 1798 further extended the amount of time an alien had to spend living in the United States from five years to fourteen years (Smith 1956, 33); this act "established the longest residence requirement for citizenship in the history of the United States" (34). This law also ushered in a new era of immigrant surveillance. All immigrants were processed in the district court "within forty-eight hours of their entry, and resident aliens were to report within six months after the bill became law" (34).

Congress passed additional immigrant restriction and surveillance acts in 1798, including the Alien Friends and Alien Enemies Acts. The latter declared that in a time of war, any immigrant from the country with which the United States was in combat would be considered alien enemies "who could be apprehended, restrained, secured, and removed" (Smith 1956, 47). The act also authorized the president of the United States to devise any additional policies related to enemy aliens that he or she "deemed necessary for public safety" (48). The Alien Friends Act, proposed by Federalists unsatisfied by the Alien Enemies Act, was much more drastic and tyrannical, authorizing the president power to "seize, detain, and deport any noncitizen he deemed dangerous" regardless if the United States was at war with the noncitizen in question's home country (Stone 2004, 31). Even more contested was the Alien Friends Act's disavowal of a noncitizen's "right to a hearing," "to be informed of the charges against him," and ability to "present evidence on his behalf" (31). Seen as the ultimate violation of the Constitution by many scholars of American immigration policy and even by Thomas Jefferson himself (Smith 1995, 229), the ideologies and fear that propelled the Alien Friends Act has continued into modern times.

The Sedition Act of 1798 similarly gave the United States government liberty to persecute and prosecute immigrants, resulting in their imprisonment for two years (Smith 1956, 95) or the imposition of a fine no greater than two thousand dollars (Stone 2004, 36) on any immigrant who made negative statements or speech against the United States government or its leaders. Heftier fines would be levied upon immigrants who conspired against the government, with a penalty of a maximum of five years in prison and a fine of up to five thousand dollars (Smith 1956, 95). Republicans were generally opposed to this act, as many saw it as a violation of the First Amendment. Other politicians feared that newspapers and writers would be hesitant to publish anything that could be perceived as an attack on government officials or as a negative portrayal of the American empire (Stone 2004, 39). Naturalized citizens likewise took issue with the act; for example, "a public meeting in Suffolk County, New York, resolved that the act impaired the right of 'every citizen' to publish his 'opinions respecting the propriety' of government officers and measures" (44).

The Passenger Act of 1819 also came of age during this era of surveillance, a time period in which Aristide Zolberg argues that America sought to enact "remote control" over its citizenry (2006, 110). This form of governance involved weeding out and prohibiting undesirable immigrants from reaching America's ports and borderlands. The Passenger Act of 1819 restricted how many passengers a ship could carry based on the cargo it was transporting. It also required the ship to declare its passengers' "name, occupation, and place of origin" to the United States government upon arrival (Zolberg 2006, 111). This privileged immigrants who came from wealthy nations, such as Britain, and freightliners that could afford to carry large cargo. Furthermore, a limitation on the number of immigrants on ships caused the price of immigration to the United States to rise. In effect, with the passing of this act the United States government was sending a message to the world that they preferred "free immigrants from middling classes of European society" (113).

Although not immigration policy per se, the *Dred Scott v. Sandford* case of 1857 is worth noting because it rendered African Americans ineligible for citizenship, a decision that some say led to the onset of the Civil War (Finkelman 2007, 3). Dred Scott was a slave who, when traveling with his owner through states that prohibited slavery, sued to become a free man and claim citizenship within those states. The Supreme Court's controversial ruling held "that under no circumstances could Scott or any black person—whether born free, formerly enslaved, or then still enslaved—be a citizen of the United States under the Constitution and laws as they then stood" (Chambers 2007, 211). Chambers asserts that this ruling operated under the presumption of a "tiered" notion of citizenship that pervaded this era, where rights were unequally doled out to American citizens. Women, for example, were considered full citizens but were excluded from voting and holding political office. Ranked a rung above African Americans on the ladder of evolution, Native Americans were only eligible for citizenship if they defected from their tribes (219).

Taken together, the acts and laws crafted during the Revolutionary and post-Revolutionary periods demonstrate "a growing distrust not only of aliens but of the people in general" (Smith 1956, 94), setting the tone for how immigrants would be treated in the coming years. Such xenophobia, however, would be tabled, albeit momentarily, ushering in a historically anomalous era that would witness the overturning of *Dred Scott* and the types of racism it engendered.

The Civil War and Reconstruction Eras, 1861–1876

The advent of the Civil War is an especially unusual time period in American history. Marked by a concern for the civil liberties of previously excluded groups that would prove short-lived, politicians of this era drew attention to the civil rights of African Americans and, to a limited extent, the freedoms of others. Starting with the passage of the Thirteenth Amendment in 1865, which ended slavery, citizenship policies of Reconstruction era America radically altered the face of citizenship. In a drastic departure from colonial America, an astounding "three constitutional amendments and six major federal statutes" relating to immigration and civil liberties were introduced into federal law (Smith 1997, 286). Unlike prior and later measures, this legislation envisioned America as a place where some previously excluded groups could enjoy equal liberties. Additionally, it was during this era that the federal government made bold endeavors to usurp states' legislative power over immigration and citizenship. The liberal, civic ideals of this era would go unrealized in forthcoming years, however, leading historian Rogers Smith to remark that Reconstruction politicians crafted a vision of an "America that 'never was'" (1997, 286).

States' rights to determine naturalization and immigration policies exercised in America's earliest days were superseded by the Civil Rights Act of 1866 and the Fourteenth Amendment, both of which guaranteed the "civil rights of all qualified, natural-born, and naturalized Americans, including former slaves and free blacks" (Kaczorowski 1987, 45). Under the provisions of the Fourteenth Amendment, states were forbidden from challenging citizens' "rights to due process and equal protection under the law" (45). Further chipping away at states' control over national citizenship, section two of the Fourteenth Amendment declared that states that violated it faced losing a seat in Congress and representation at the federal level (Smith 1997, 310). The Fourteenth Amendment also granted citizenship privileges to individuals born on American soil, allowing African American slaves, their children, and other historically marginalized groups, such as Chinese emigrants, to become legal citizens (Zolberg 2006, 182; Chambers 2007, 220). But at the same time this provision also disqualified individuals born outside of the country from naturalization, preventing enslaved African Americans "born in Africa or the West Indies" from naturalizing (Daniels 2004, 11; Smith 1997, 310). Although emancipatory for some, the Fourteenth Amendment exempted some groups deemed unqualified or unprepared to be bestowed the honor of citizenship and the privileges it conferred. Women, for instance, were deemed incapable of voting and were effectively excluded from it (Smith 1997, 311).

The Fifteenth Amendment similarly sought to grant many citizens the right to vote regardless of elements of their identity, forbidding "state and local governments from preventing a citizen from voting" (McKanders 2010, 178). Now states found that their jurisdiction over their residents' rights would have to be deferred to national and federal policy. Individual states were given some leeway in terms of determining the extent of their residents' civil liberties, especially with reference to how they applied in terms of an individual's "age, sex, mental capacity, and alienage" (Kaczorowski 1987, 56). States therefore skirted around the liberal philosophies and constitutional amendments of the Reconstruction era. Despite espousing racial equality for African Americans, these amendments were undermined by state-sanctioned racism that came in many forms. Such discrimination included discouraging African Americans from seeking political office or preventing African Americans from entering towns at sundown (Loewen 2006). The Civil Rights Act of 1866 provided an umbrella for citizens who felt unjustly persecuted by state and local officials, with section 2 allowing the latter officials to be tried in federal court if they failed to uphold a citizen's rights and privileges. Section 3 made similar allowances, with local and state courts facing replacement by federal courts should a citizen who felt his or her civil rights were being violated prefer to be tried by a nonpartisan federal court (Kaczorowski 1987, 58).

Although a major step toward securing equal rights for all American citizens, the Civil Rights Act of 1866 did not go unchallenged. Former Confederates were especially uneasy with the notion that states should share decision making with the federal government (Kaczorowski 1987, 67). The Civil Rights Act gave African Americans citizenship and economic privileges, such as the ability to own, sell, and purchase property, freedoms white supremacists found unacceptable. Southerners often refused to defer to federal authority on these issues, choosing instead to continue to see African Americans as slaves and to treat any supporters of emancipation and the extension of civil rights to all citizens as enemies of the state. In protest, they engaged in acts of violence and "economic in-timidation" (50–51) against African Americans. Contrary to what federal law now required, Southern states frequently neglected to prosecute the individuals who instigated or partook in hate crimes and instead became beacons of support for them. Southern states, too, "refused to recognize that blacks were citizens possessing the natural rights of free people" (51). They turned a blind eye to state officers and officials who failed to safe-guard the "personal safety and property of blacks" (51).

In a sign of things to come, the Immigration Act of 1875 mandated that "contracting to supply Chinese laborers" would be considered a felony and punishable by law (Smith 1995, 230). The Immigration Act of 1875 would go down in the history books as the first immigration policy de-signed to exclude individuals based on their ethnic or racial designation. The Gilded Age would see an expansion of this act, what would become known as the 1882 Chinese Exclusion Act, along with a handful of restric-tive acts aimed at groups deemed morally and intellectually inferior to whites.

The Gilded Age (1876–1900) and the Progressive Era (1900–1940)

The liberal tides of citizenship that washed over the Reconstruction-era America would prove temporary and short-lived. The door to opportu-nity and equal citizenship that was swung open during the Reconstruc-tion era would be shut. Between 1880 and 1924 acts and laws that made citizenship unattainable for a larger group of individuals than seen in pre-vious years were proposed and state-sanctioned. It was also during this era that the census would begin to note an immigrant's nationality and race as well as track and analyze the percentage of immigrants arriving in America by national origin, the former beginning in 1899 and the latter in 1909 (Ngai 2004, 25). Although some have argued that the intensification of anti-immigrant rhetoric was due to an exponential growth in the diver-sity and number of immigrants coming into the United States during this time period, Daniels has shown that this increase was actually gradual and "remarkably stable," and that the diversity of immigrants coming into the country was comparable to other eras in American history (2004, 4).

Several scholars choose instead to blame this era's impassioned Ameri-can exceptionalism and nativism on a growing acceptance of racism that was endorsed by members of academic and scientific communities, a racism that placed white Americans at the pinnacle of evolution (Orser 2007). Uniquely American, this racist nativism encompassed "every type and level of antipathy toward aliens, their institutions, and their ideas," a nativism some assert mounted and grew in strength from first European and Native American contact (Higham 1963, 3). As a consequence, a considerably large group of people from all walks of life and diverse backgrounds would be prevented from migrating to the United States, including

> aliens hired under labor contracts (1885), paupers, polygamists, the insane and diseased (1891), anarchists or subversives (1903), the disabled (1907), stowaways, illiterates over age 16, alcoholics and psychotics (1917), persons ineligible to become citizens (most Asians) and non-immigrants without proper documentation (1924), drug addicts, immoral sex offenders, laborers not in demand in the United States, those previously deported for any reason and those aiding illegal aliens (1952). (Smith 1995, 231)

It would not be an overstatement to say that the exclusion of others from citizenship became the norm and inclusion the exception.

Fervent anti-immigrant campaigns were largely fueled by the scientific and anthropological communities of the time (Horsman 1981; Stocking 1987). These schools of thought took Darwin's models of evolutionary development designed to explain the survival and extinction of animal and plant species and applied them to humankind. One of these scholars, Herbert Spencer, coined the phrase "survival of the fittest" to explain how Darwinian evolution was at work in Western society (Jackson and Weidman 2004, 80). Spencer subscribed to the philosophy of unilinear evolution, which posited that all cultures progress through the same evolutionary sequence. Spencer argued that some cultural groups, such as Native Americans, Africans, and Polynesians, were frozen in time and arrested in earlier states of development. In his opinion, these cultural groups lacked many of the features of Western society, such as a written language, an expansive government, and monumental architecture. These facets of Western life, he asserted, were irrefutable signs of an evolved society that were remiss in evolutionarily inferior societies.

Spencer took his argument one step further by claiming that "less evolved" humans existed within Western society. Spencer considered the poor, the destitute, the orphaned, the widowed, the mentally ill, the criminal, and the divorced "less fit" to survive in Western society. His statements provided intellectual fodder for politicians and governmental officials wishing to deny welfare, charity, and an education to such groups. A self-made man, Spencer also held fast to the idea that a free-market economy moved individuals to compete against one another, an action that strengthened the human race (Jackson and Weidman 2004, 82). Government intervention in any aspect of life, including charity and control of the market, was therefore seen as a hindrance to the evolution of Western society.

Spenserian beliefs had a direct impact on citizenship and immigration policies penned during this period of time. Women, seen as biologically predisposed to "maternal" and homemaking tasks, found that they would remain ineligible to vote. Infuriated by their inability to take part in the political process, some women joined the suffrage movement and furthered its platform by embracing the gender roles handed to them by American society (Smith 1997, 285). Women took on positions that reinforced and passed on this ideological domestic order, such as reformers, teachers, and educators of disadvantaged women and children, in order to assert that they were deserving of voting rights. While many politicians were comfortable with the idea that women were citizens of the American nation, their civic responsibilities and rights as citizens were seen as separate issues. Women suffragists would not be considered equal citizens until the 1920 passing of the Nineteenth Amendment, which would validate women's rightful place in the American political system by conferring voting privileges.

A woman's citizenship could also be compromised by her choice in spouse. An American woman's citizenship hinged on whom she chose to marry while a man, on the other hand, could marry as he saw fit and not risk losing his citizenship (Cott 1998, 1441). According to the Expatriation Act of 1907, American women were legally required to adopt the citizenship standing and nationality of their partners upon marriage (Nicolosi 2001). This form of citizenship, derivative citizenship, made women entirely dependent upon men for their nationality. This act was designed to prevent Anglo-American women from mixing with individuals deemed racially undesirable and "was certainly in keeping with concerns over racial purity as evidenced by the growing number of state miscegenation laws" (Nicolosi 2001, 5). Men's citizenship, in contrast, was both stable and empowering; men could confer citizenship privileges to noncitizen women through the rite of marriage, a statute passed by Congress in 1855 (Cott 1998, 1457).

Scientific racism also contributed to dwindling stateside support of the freedoms that the Reconstruction amendments—the Thirteenth, Fourteenth, and Fifteenth—promised to African Americans. Jim Crow laws passed and enacted by states ignored constitutional amendments that gave African Americans certain freedoms. The federal government ignored the passage of state laws that included segregation "in public accommodations such as railroads, jails, health care facilities, hotels, and restaurants" (McKanders 2010, 180). Mexican Americans similarly experienced discrimination on racial grounds that came in the form of segregation. Like African Americans, Mexican Americans encountered signs in public places that read "Mexicans and Niggers Stay Out," "Mexicans and Dogs not Allowed in Restaurants," and "No Mexicans Served" (182). So while the Thirteenth, Fourteenth, and Fifteenth Amendments granted basic human and civil rights to African Americans and other persecuted ethnic groups, those constitutional liberties were not always upheld in practice. The supposedly emancipatory amendments of the 1860s meant to grant equality to many groups—not just citizens—inhabiting the American nation were thus forgotten and ignored, only to be replaced by laws and legislation that widened the gap between ethnic and racial groups.

Theories purported to pinpoint the differences between cultures, genders, and ethnic groups were introduced by both self-proclaimed and academically trained scholars, which helped xenophobic sentiments gain traction in American society (Desmond 1999, 6). Polygenic thought took root in the Western world during the 1850s and helped to cement notions of racial difference. In contrast to monogenists, polygenists believed that different "races" of the human species sprouted up across the world rather than at one moment of "creation" (such as the Biblical story of Adam and Eve). Some sought to characterize and typologize the racial groups of the world by looking for physiological, cultural, and emotional traits unique to different "races." Their work was highly subjective, reflecting racial biases of the time more than the real attributes of the cultures they were studying. Samuel George Morton, for instance, was a highly regarded and influential scholar who believed that the history of humankind's evolution could be seen by studying human skulls. Under duplicitous conditions, he collected more than one thousand crania from cultures spanning the entire globe (Thomas 2000, 42). He then measured the cranium capacity and volume of skulls from different "races." His analysis led him to conclude that Caucasians were of a superior stock due to their large cranial cavity while Chinese and Africans were the lowest races, so low that they were more "like other animals" than humans (42).

Out of this "scientific racism" grew the early-twentieth-century eugenics movement, a move toward altering the supposed "races" of humankind through both biological and cultural means. Dovetailing off Darwinian thought that theorized how maladaptive traits were weeded out of animal and plant species, reformers claimed that the same ideology could be applied to races deemed less "fit" by Western standards. Eugenicists could not agree upon how to implement social Darwinism, though. Supporters of scientist Francis Galton, for example, argued that the government must prevent "lower" races from intermarrying or interbreeding with more "evolved" races because the former may muddy and taint the "superior" stock's gene pool (Jackson and Weidman 2004, 101). Others applied Gregor Mendel's theory of blending inheritance to racial groups, asserting that advantageous traits could be passed down from a less evolved to a more evolved race through breeding offspring (Jackson and Weidman 2004, 103).

Because of the diversity of opinions on immigration and race within the scientific community, the American government did not adopt a uniform policy on how to manage and handle previously established immigrant communities within the United States. At times, though, the American government supported and funded programs to assimilate immigrants into Anglo-American culture or provided reform instruction to impoverished American citizens with the intention of getting them back on their feet. But given the bountiful cornucopia of federally sanctioned acts and laws passed during this landmark era aimed at curtailing certain groups of immigrants seeking admittance into the United States, it appears as though politicians shared a unified belief that specific nationalities, races, and ethnicities were unfit for citizenship.

One of the first immigration policies passed during this burgeoning age of restriction, the Immigration Act of 1882, prohibited "entry to persons likely to become public charges, such as convicts, 'lunatics,' and 'idiots'" (Smith 1997, 359). Those who passed the requirements of admission into the United States were charged a fifty-cent tax (359). Following the push to federalize and diminish states' judicial control over the nation's citizenry, the Immigration Act of 1882 also delegated oversight of immigration to the secretary of the treasury (Higham 1963, 44).

With an economic depression looming, Americans looked for a group to blame for the nation's financial woes. Chinese immigrants became the targets of this anger, with whites arguing that Chinese immigrants had stolen jobs that should have rightfully belonged to Anglo-Americans. Politicians cited scholarship concerning the racial fitness of individuals of Chinese heritage to support their position that the Chinese were undeserving and ill suited for American citizenship. The 1882 Chinese Exclusion Act is considered by immigration scholars to be a landmark ruling because it represents the federal government's first attempt to restrict a group of people based on their racial status (Orser 2007, 150–51; Smith 1995, 230; Smith 1997, 359). Besides enacting a ten-year hiatus on Chinese migration, the act also issued "a head tax on all immigrants (except Canadians and Mexicans) to defray the cost of regulating immigration and caring for immigrants" that gave the government permission to deport nonnaturalized Chinese immigrants and prevented Chinese migrants from obtaining citizenship (Smith 1995, 230). In 1892 the Geary Act was passed, which denied entry to Chinese immigrants for another ten years as well as required that Chinese residents living in the United States register their presence with the Internal Revenue Service. Chinese immigrants' registration had to be officiated by "at least one 'white' witness," "reflecting the widespread conviction that the Chinese were natural liars" (Smith 1997, 363).

World War I likewise triggered fear among nativists who worried that America's shores would be bombarded by individuals who, displaced from their homelands due to the war, would seek political asylum and citizenship. The Immigration Act of 1917 broadened the 1882 Chinese Exclusion Act by extending its reach to "Asian Indians and all other native inhabitants of a 'barred Asiatic zone' that ran from Afghanistan to the Pacific" (Ngai 2004, 18). In addition, it required a literacy examination for all immigrants who desired to enter the country. A contentious policy that was passed "after four presidential vetoes," the literacy requirement was "an important symbolic victory for those nativist groups who favored a more restrictionist policy" (Smith 1995, 231).

The National Origins Act of 1924, also known as the Johnson-Reed Immigration Act, was another measure taken to secure America's borders and prevent World War I refugees from immigrating to the United States.

The act initiated a racially based quota system that determined how many immigrants would be permitted to naturalize based on the country's ethnic and racial composition in 1890 (Ngai 2004, 22). Southern and Eastern Europeans—undesirable groups by Anglo-American racial preferences—found that their quota was reduced from 44 percent to 12 percent (Smith 1995, 232) while those occupying "the Western Hemisphere remained exempt" (233). The latter provision enabled America to maintain a steady flow of predominantly Western European immigrants. The National Origins Act of 1924 would not be overturned for more than forty years. The Immigration Act of 1965 would significantly rewrite its terms and the overall conditions of American immigration policy. No longer would immigration and naturalization lean in favor of Western Europeans. Rather, all countries would be granted the same number of outbound immigrants who desired American citizenship. Potential citizens would also have to fill a gap or a need in the labor pool (Smith 1995, 234).

Starting with the 1882 Chinese Exclusion Act, the late nineteenth and early twentieth centuries witnessed a tightening of immigration, especially when it came to immigrants deemed racially undesirable by the scientific community of the time. These restrictions were retracted only when the economic needs of the American nation called for cheap labor, as we have seen with modern immigration policies that support the importation of foreign labor without extending the benefits of citizenship to such workers.

Summary

The story of citizenship and immigration policy in America starts out as one of ambiguity and, with some exceptions to the rule, collectivity and inclusion. Yet this inclusion was motivated by the newly established republic's need for a population to work and produce goods and food for the British Empire. In more recent years the story of citizenship has taken a different turn, with the whole-scale exclusion of socially or racially undesirable groups becoming characteristic of American immigration policy rather than an isolated event. Contemporary immigration and citizenship policies have made entry into and gaining access to civic duties within the United States increasingly difficult.

But, by the same token, some laws have been annulled, overturned, or passed to extend civil liberties denied to those previously excluded. In a sense this tension between opening and closing the gateways to American citizenship can be productive. At times this force gains so much traction that it inspires new formulations to emerge. The *Dred Scott* ruling, a court case that dismissed an African American man's plea for citizenship but, more importantly, denounced his very humanity by declaring him nothing more than property, inspired three revolutionary constitutional amendments and, some would argue, the Civil War. In the right hands, citizenship measures can be made malleable, molded by politicians and ordinary American citizens alike to mirror the civil liberties that a democratic nation by definition necessitates.

What impels these changes? And what compels individuals to seek or choose not to seek out citizenship, be it cultural or legal? The answer is multipronged and is best tackled with an interdisciplinary approach. Historical archaeology offers one of the many vantage points from which we can begin to tease out citizenship longings. This book looks at how people have expressed their beliefs about national belonging and American citizenship with material culture. Although historical archaeology is one of many disciplines that can offer considerable insight into citizenship studies, its contributions are currently inconspicuous and understated. Importantly, the forthcoming chapters feature alternative models of citizenship as introduced by American citizens and noncitizens themselves, offering new ways of conceptualizing national belonging outside the scope of the law.

2

....

Historical Archaeologies of Citizenship

Since the age of global expansionism and European colonization, humans have been forced to organize communities within the geopolitical spaces we call "nations." Besides eliminating opportunities for cross-cultural interaction and community formation across borders, nation-states have also constructed boundaries within their own borders. Barriers between groups of people are erected within nation-states to naturalize divisions between genders, races, and classes, often with the ultimate intent of preventing socially transgressive coalitions from taking shape and destabilizing the objectives and legislative power of the nation-state.

Globalization studies have shown, however, that boundaries between nations can be superficial and have been fluidly lived by the subjects inhabiting them (Appadurai 1990, 1993, 2001, 2003; Holston and Appadurai 1996). Borders can mask the complex relationships that can be forged between people regardless of national identity and citizenship standing. These studies have also demonstrated that an individual or group can seek acceptance as a cultural citizen without desiring to secure legal citizenship. The concept of cultural citizenship discussed in this book's introduction draws attention to all of these points. The crucial thrust of this chapter, then, is that citizens are not just made, and states do not harbor sole authorship over the conferral of citizenship or national belonging; people can cross legal and cultural borders as well as make themselves into citizens.

Within the historical archaeological case studies presented in this chapter, we see groups making claims for social inclusion without pursuing avenues that necessitate judicial inclusion. So while the United States has become less welcoming to immigrants in the late nineteenth, twentieth, and twenty-first centuries, its political system and founding principles, ones that celebrate difference, still make way for the existence of diverse communities who sometimes hold views and aspirations that radically depart from those of the nation. From an archaeological standpoint, this rich assortment and pastiche of people, belief systems, and cultures is what makes the study of the American experience so compelling. This chapter parades a caravan of cultures that have fashioned American citizenship to their liking, many of which would be invisible without historical archaeological research.

This continual refashioning of "Americanness" can be witnessed through the archaeological data recovered from historical sites, as Americans have exercised their use or avoidance of material culture to express their beliefs about citizenship and national belonging. Two photographs taken during the height of early-twentieth-century immigration restriction make this fact evident. The first photograph was taken in 1908 at Los Angeles, California's Mount Lowe Resort and Railway (MLRR). In it, several families sit at a table on what appears to be a veranda or porch while collectively eating a meal. They wear neatly pressed white cotton clothes and dine at a table dressed with matching tablewares, the image conveying an air of middle-class respectability. But their stark, sullen faces communicate a different message, one of discontent marked with a hint of defiance. The historical and archaeological data recovered from the pictured family, which are discussed in depth in the following two chapters, provide additional layers of information required to properly interpret the photograph.

The individuals in the photograph were Mexican immigrants hired to work on and repair a railway at a famous tourist destination, MLRR. To keep their jobs, workers and their families were expected to participate in the company's Americanization program, an initiative that was aimed solely at employees of Mexican heritage. The adoption of "western" material culture, including clothing, housing decor, and tablewares, was a central component of this program, with some items provided to workers by their employers. Failure to follow the company's prescriptive guidelines would result in a loss of one's job and potential deportation back to Mexico. So while this family visibly embraced some symbols of white middle-class culture, their faces and the oral histories collected from immigrants in similar historical and geographical contexts tell a story of material assimilation without ideological conversion. To put it more precisely, MLRR's workers consumed and used goods that would allow them to keep their jobs, but they likely contested the meanings behind them.

The second image comes from a 1905 edition of *Sunset Magazine*. Here a man is dressed in attire typically associated with Mexican immigrants—a serape draped across his chest and a sombrero shading his face from the hot sun. But as the text accompanying the article shows, his dress is a ruse (Camp and Williams, forthcoming). As the caption below the image explains, he is a "coolie dressed as a Mexican Peon to be smuggled unto the United States." This man was born in China, which made him ineligible for citizenship or admission into any American ports of entry beginning in 1882. Like other Chinese migrants seeking work or hoping to reunite with family in America—Erika Lee estimates the number of people to be somewhere in the ballpark of 17,300 (2002, 55)—this man used the symbols of another ethnic group—Mexican nationals—to gain entry into the United States, a group who would ironically be prohibited from entering the United States in the coming years. It was only through the conduit of material culture—clothing in this case—that Chinese immigrants reinscribed and reinvented their nationality to foil American immigration officials.

These two photographs show that the desire for citizenship comes in many forms. It can be superficial, a material practice enacted to gain admission into a nation in order to labor, reunite with family, or seek some other form of political, social, or economic asylum. It can also be fundamental to one's welfare, with the rejection of such material goods resulting in a loss of one's job and immediate deportation. For some, the impulse to be a member of a nation-state cannot be overstated. It can be a deeply meaningful relationship, not simply one that is about securing admission into the country for ulterior or personal motives, but one where an individual or group develops an unwavering and genuine faith in a nation's political, religious, or other cultural system. The wrapping of a fallen soldier or veteran's body with an American flag is emblematic of this type of relationship, where the individual and state are profoundly interwoven and inextricable.

In the absence of photographic and documentary evidence such as the images detailed earlier, historical archaeologists are privy to these material symbols of national belonging through the excavation of artifacts. Artifacts, especially in the case of minority, marginalized, and immigrant communities, frequently provide the only method of accessing responses to immigrant assimilation campaigns, Americanization efforts, and citizenship laws, statutes, and acts. This chapter will thus demonstrate the discipline of historical archaeology's substantial contribution to the existing literature on the contested nature of American citizenship and national belonging.

The chapter begins by taking a look at the archaeology of institutions, places where an individual or group's citizenship is stripped, forced upon, or made conditional, dependent on a subject's adherence to and acceptance of behavior expected of citizens. The chapter then looks at how citizenship practices have been codified, policed, and reinforced by the middle and upper classes, paying particular attention to how mundane, quotidian material habits, such as dining, dressing, and decorating one's home, became encoded as normative practices expected of good American citizens. The last section of the chapter illustrates that people on the margins of American society mediated and selectively embraced these codes of conduct. The chapter thus concludes with a look at how disenfranchised groups—such as immigrants, marginalized groups, and utopian and intentional communities—set themselves apart from the upper echelons of American society and other nativists by proposing their own interpretations of American citizenship.

Institutional Settings

Attention to a citizen's allegiance is especially heightened when an individual's patriotism is tested, taught, or questioned or in historical settings where one's citizenship is temporarily or completely retracted. An institution's goal, whether federal, private, or nonprofit, is to transform their residents into proper citizens, and the ultimate plan is to relinquish control over them and assimilate them back into the broader American society. In recent years, historical archaeologists (e.g., Casella 2007) have made significant strides in the archaeology of such institutions, including schools, prisons, asylums, almshouses, churches, orphanages, boarding schools, intentional and utopian communities, and prisons and internment camps (the latter institution will be discussed in chapter 5). These data reveal complex, multilayered stories regarding how individuals confined or subjected to these institutions responded to the regulations imposed upon them, regulations that were frequently related to the expectations conferred upon American citizens. They open up a window through which we can understand both the individual's and the institution's definitions of American citizenship and how these visions were material in nature.

Schools

American schools began as institutions where pupils were taught not only writing and arithmetic but also proper civic habits as budding young American citizens. Historically, pedagogical techniques used in the classroom varied across gender, class, racial, and ethnic lines, which reveal the ways in which certain groups of people were envisioned (or not envisioned) to be part of the American citizenry. What was (and was not) taught to specific groups of students gives us insight into the people that teachers and the United States government deemed as fit for American citizenship.

Many schools were specifically established by the state for political reasons—to create educated voters (Gibb and Beisaw 2000, 126) and "as a necessary foundation on which to create and amass wealth" (112). Simply one's access to schools can therefore reveal who was considered worthy of citizenship. Along these lines, Rotman (2009), Gibb and Beisaw (2000), and Beisaw (2009) have argued that renovations and modifications to schoolhouses—often solely noticeable through the archaeological record—can illuminate community attitudes toward national civic education efforts and the federal government's attempt to universalize and democratize education for the betterment of certain citizens. American schoolhouses and boarding schools excavated by historical archaeologists have documented federal, regional, local, group, and individual responses to civic education, in some cases capturing attitudes unmentioned in the documentary record.

Deborah Rotman's archaeological investigation of the Wea View Schoolhouse in Indiana, which was constructed in 1862, exposes some of these responses. According to the local school board, the objective of the Wea View Schoolhouse was to transform students into "better citizens" (Hooker 1917, 106, quoted in Rotman 2009, 77). Better citizenship meant, to the school's teachers and board, following Victorian gender roles. This was made apparent through the excavation of privies that were separated by sex. The women's privy contained objects that encouraged girls to prepare for their role as domestic help or as wives who would be the caretakers of their children, homes, and husbands. These artifacts included ceramic vessels, metal and glass container fragments, and silverware. In contrast, artifacts recovered from the men's privy taught boys that their place was outside of the home, with pocketknives, rubber balls, marbles, hex nuts, and a bicycle license plate discovered. In addition, "several straight pins, a needle, and a safety pin were found concentrated in association with buttons" (Rotman 2009, 81) in one of the corners of the schoolhouse's foundation, further suggesting that girls were being taught gender-specific activities. Rotman, however, points out that the latter objects could have been simultaneously or alternatively used in community gatherings that took place at the schoolhouse, as evidenced by artifacts such as "a pressed-glass punch cup, fancy serving spoons, a cake knife, and tobacco pipe bowls" (80).

Rural schools such as Schoolhouse 12 in LeRay, New York, similarly served the dual function of being a community center and an educational facility for students of mixed age groups (Peña 1992). Although the excavated archaeological data was scant, when paired with historical and architectural information, the site reveals that not all schools followed stringent Victorian ideologies. This seems especially true of rural American schoolhouses, where communities lacked the financial resources and population to support several teachers to teach multiple grade levels. This issue is archaeologically visible at LeRay, where the physical structure of a large schoolhouse was found instead of several buildings that could accommodate different grades and genders. Whereas prescriptive literature demanded separate playgrounds, privies, and even "entrances to the classroom for boys and girls," rural schoolhouses such as LeRay's Schoolhouse 12 featured "open, rectangular plans" that "allowed for flexibility," permitting "access to education for a large segment of the rural population" with no visible architectural features that partitioned genders (Peña 1992, 17). These limitations resulted in an education that sharply deviated from that which prevailed during the Victorian era, perhaps leading its non-gender-segregated pupils to craft different visions of citizenship.

Some schools also operated to eradicate and rob their students of their ethnic heritage by replacing it with an Anglo-American value system that was seen as central to gaining full citizenship. This was particularly the case among Native American boarding schools that were established in the late nineteenth century across the western United States. Between 1891 and 1990 Arizona's Phoenix Indian School served to equip Native American primary and secondary students with skills that Anglo-Americans perceived as necessary for their transition from reservation to urban life or from noncitizens to American citizens. Not only were boarders taught the prescriptive gender roles instilled in the Wea View Schoolhouse's students, but they were also instructed in trade-oriented work that would keep Native Americans on the lower rung of the ladder of the American class structure. Trades that Anglo-American instructors deemed fit for Native Americans included carpentry, blacksmithing, wagon making, tin working, and shoe, harness, and cabinet making (Lindauer 2009, 86; 1996; 1997). Half of the school day involved training in these trade skills while the other half was reserved for academics.

As part of the boarding school campaign, many Native American children were forcibly removed from their homes and families and placed into these institutions against their parents' will. The reasoning behind these forced relocations was to assimilate Native American pupils into western culture; this was seen as a national imperative because these children were legally conferred citizenship upon their birth on American soil. The younger the child, the better, because this would mean the child would have less interaction and exposure to familial traditions and cultural beliefs that worked in opposition to Anglo-American ideals. For instance, boarding school teachers stressed the importance of independence and the accumulation of wealth, while on tribal lands "children were continuously conditioned by their mother's extended family to the importance of interdependence" that emphasized sharing one's good fortune (such as an overly productive crop) with others (Lindauer 2009, 91). Discipline was unnecessarily harsh within the doors of boarding schools and threatened not only the emotional but also the physical well-being of Native American students. Students were isolated and placed in community jails for resisting Americanization instruction; in other cases, corporal punishment was used by teachers, prompting some students to flee schools and run away, an action that sometimes resulted in a child's death due to inclement weather (Lindauer 2009, 93; Brunson 2012).

Traces of assimilation attempts and Native American children's responses to it have been found in the archaeological record of the Phoenix Indian School. Evidence of instruction in individuality and independence was found in the form of personalized combs and toothbrushes inscribed with students' names (Lindauer 2009, 96). Covert resistance to this tutelage was also recovered from the Phoenix Indian School in the form of objects traditionally associated with Native American culture: a projectile point and two clay artifacts that appear to resemble a bird and four-legged animal (99, 101). Possession of these artifacts would have been kept secret from boarding school officials and instructors since they likely "provided a sense of security and connection to the customs and traditions of home" (99): the exact types of memories and beliefs that boarding schools were designed to eradicate.

Orphanages and Almshouses

The Schuyler Mansion, an orphanage built in 1761 just outside of Albany, New York, provides another opportunity to examine how proper class and gender roles expected of American citizens were passed on to youths. As in boarding schools and schoolhouses, instruction was catered toward reaffirming popular ideas about gender-appropriate skills. When girls at the mansion turned approximately twelve years old, they had the option of continuing their education at a local high school or attending an industrial school "where they were taught domestic skills such as sewing, child care, and cooking" (Feister 2009, 107).

Training on how to act as an adult and as a proper American citizen began much earlier than high school or college, though (Feister 2009, 109). The spatial distribution of child-related artifacts found at the Schuyler Mansion shows that children engaged in gender-segregated play, with "93 percent of the play items traditionally associated with young girls" discovered in a garden close to the mansion. In contrast, 40 percent of boy-related artifacts were found in "areas farther from the house, mainly near the carriage barn located on the far edge of the property" (113). Girls were thus expected to stay close to the mansion under the watchful eye of their overseers while boys were allowed a more expansive and less policed area to play. Some children resisted being kept in the orphanage by running away from its premises but were frequently returned to institutions because they lacked the families to whom the children in schoolhouses or boarding schools could return.

Other institutions similarly sought to eliminate aspects of an individual's life and beliefs that did not conform to the standards expected of American citizens. As a nation built on the principle that all citizens have an equal chance to excel and prosper in the United States regardless of their heritage, ethnicity, class standing, or gender, failure to prosper in America has historically been interpreted as a reflection of the ineptitude of the individual rather than as a structural issue and an inherent function of capitalism, the latter of which requires a lower class to support middle- and upper-class members of society. Downtrodden members of

American society have consequently been subjected to reform campaigns that have come in a variety of forms and harbored diverse intentions; nevertheless, they shared the goal of teaching instituted individuals to be productive citizens and not rely on their state or nation for financial support.

Because their citizenship was dependent upon their husband's naturalization standing, women who were single, were unwed mothers, or were widowed found that society was unwilling to grant them the full privileges of citizenship that men enjoyed. Additionally, women who did not conform to "Victorian ideals of female piety and purity could be incarcerated as immoral or insane" (Spencer-Wood 2009a, 117). Women without male partners or husbands hence found it difficult to support themselves because American culture had clearly delineated roles for women that placed them squarely within the home and domestic sphere rather than in public places or in jobs outside of the home. This belief, known as the separate spheres ideology (Wall 1994), permeated the social milieu of nineteenth- and early-twentieth-century American culture, making it difficult for women who did not fit the mold of domestic housewife and caretaker of children to establish themselves professionally, although Rotman (2006) argues this ideology was not as pervasive, uniformly adopted, or easily received as scholars initially envisioned.

Almshouses offered a refuge for women unable to find employment or in need of childcare. Although the aims, scope, and intentions of these institutions varied based on the individuals or groups running them, the ultimate goal crosscut these institutions: to transform women into productive, self-sustaining American citizens who were not dependent on the system for aid and assistance (Baugher 2009). Sadly, the reality of this goal was that it was unattainable for most women who faced gender discrimination in the workplace, especially in times of economic recessions and depressions. As Spencer-Wood explains, "the predominance of women and girls at many almshouses was the result of the gender ideology associating women with domesticity, which justified inequalities such as lower pay and a sexual double standard, ultimately resulting in women's poverty" (2009a, 135). Thus, more women and children found themselves in almshouses than men (Spencer-Wood 2009a, 117; 2010).

Because prescriptive guidelines for treating the poor and homeless are often invisible in the documentary record and were frequently outlined by the proprietors of institutions, archaeologists have paid special attention to how institutions, the people held within them, and the people operating them followed such rules and regulations. Besides revealing how citizenship often rested on one's economic position, the study of these particular manifestations of institutions can also tell us how American concepts of citizenship deviated from that of the British. Spencer-Wood (2001, 2009a, 2009b), for example, details how the English segregated the poor into two different groups: the "worthy" and "unworthy," with worthy paupers deserving of support "because they could not work due to acts of God, such as accident, illness, infirmity, or old age," and unworthy paupers considered "able-bodied paupers" who were seen as "lazy, profligate, vicious criminals for not working" (2009a, 118).

Spencer-Wood looks at how these English conceptions of poverty, which arose in the fifteenth century, materialized in Massachusetts' Falmouth Almshouse. Built around 1824, the Falmouth Almshouse housed needy women, men, and children. Its architecture reflected the English classification of worthy and unworthy paupers by segregating the two groups, although the house's layout did not further divide its occupants by gender and age, as was done in England (Spencer-Wood 2009a, 127–28). To offset the costs of the almshouse as well as to teach residents the all-important Protestant work ethic that they were assumed to lack (hence resulting in their institutionalization), the institutionalized were expected to pick oakum, manufacture clothing, care for and tend to farm animals, and produce crops (131).

In the Old World, the English forced the poor to engage in physically demanding labor as punishment for the poor's perceived lack of independence (Spencer-Wood 2009a, 130). Although it is unclear from archaeological and historical data if this took place at Falmouth Almshouse, there is evidence that several women left the grounds of institutions. One woman left to stay with a friend and was later "brought back to the workhouse with her baby" (133). Another woman took her child and went to stay with her mother (133). "Both cases show that some unwed mothers resisted stigmatization and incarceration, providing for their infants with relatives or friends rather than raising them in the workhouse" (133).

Although nineteenth-century almshouses inflicted social shame and humiliation on their residents, these forms of stigmatization were not comparable to earlier colonial methods of handling the poor, ill, or orphaned. In colonial Virginia, the Anglican Church was deemed responsible for the impoverished; the cost of caring for them fell upon each parish, causing tension between the government, church, and colonists in need of help. As in England, workhouses were established for these individuals in order "to furnish employment and residential care" (McCartney 1987, 288). When Virginia's poor grew in size by the late seventeenth and early eighteenth centuries, parishes and Virginia politicians decided to pass a 1755 act that amplified the poor's already precarious social standing. The passing of this act required paupers to wear badges on their right sleeve that were "made of blue, red, or green cloth, as dictated by the vestry, and printed with the name of the parish to which the poor person belonged" (292). If the individual failed to wear their badge in public, they could be denied food, and they faced up to a five-year prison sentence. Their status as infirm, orphaned, or impoverished thus transformed fully fledged British subjects into second-class citizens.

Residents of the New York's Municipal Almshouse Complex, which was in operation from 1736 to 1797, enjoyed more freedom than those housed at almshouses in Virginia and Massachusetts (Baugher 2001, 199). A diversity in ceramic-ware types, forms, and patterns and the lack of numerous matching vessels suggests that individuals were not forced or expected to comply with middle- and upper-class modes of behavior, which encouraged the use of ceramic wares uniform in make, appearance, and design (186). The intentions behind the almshouse complex, however, paralleled later reform efforts, as evidenced by the requirement that the institutionalized had to engage in productive labor such as clothing and button manufacturing; this would teach the institutionalized how to behave like proper American citizens who upheld the industrious principles of the Protestant work ethic (Baugher 2009, 190). Evidence of button production and a wide assortment of buttons found in the archaeological collection also supports Baugher's conclusion that residents at the Municipal Almshouse Complex were not required to wear uniforms and could instead enjoy "freedom of choice in their dress" (2001, 199). Residents tended a colonial garden that shared similarities with "typical forms found within middle class and elite colonial gardens," an activity that supposedly taught them how to garden and theoretically equipped them with training desired by potential employers (Baugher 2001, 194).

Should one successfully navigate or work their way out of an institution and join middle-class America, the formerly impoverished would still find that their social position would require constant maintenance. Membership in middle-class America involved an awareness of and an eagerness to attend to the latest fashions in ceramics, clothing, and home decor. The middle class dictated the behaviors, materials, morals, and roles expected of Americans because they constituted "a significant portion of the urban residential population" during the mid-nineteenth century, and they consumed and foisted their expectations and prescriptive guides and manuals to the American public (Praetzellis, Praetzellis, and Brown 1988, 193). Collectively they formed a worldview that would come to stand for American citizenship and America as a nation, a vision that still holds weight in our modern American society.

Middle- and Upper-Class Communities

Starting in the 1800s the attainment of wealth and affluence epitomized the American dream. As the narrative at the time went, lower-class Americans were to aspire to the lifestyle of middle and upper classes; by copying and replicating the latter's behaviors and material practices, lower-class Americans might eventually attain full acceptance as citizens of the American nation. Those who relied upon the nation's government to supply items necessary to survive were not counted as full-fledged citizens. Lower-class Americans were expected to emulate the actions, beliefs, and practices of middle and upper classes, the latter of whom were seen as ideal American citizens.

Out of the middle and upper echelons of the American class system emerged "ideologies which distinguished them from both the working class and elites," a worldview that was likewise grounded in materiality (Fitts 1999, 39). This philosophy required much work on the part of its adherents to maintain, involving a complete restructuring of everyday life in America. With this in mind, historical archaeologists have charted the emergence of a distinct set of middle- and upper-class American values that permeated every aspect of Americans' lives from the mid-1800s to the early twentieth century. These values became equated with good citizenship and the enactment of American nationality. In more specific terms, historical archaeologists have considered how this ideology manifested itself in the archaeological record of middle- and upper-class American households and communities.

Diana DiZerega Wall was one of the first historical archaeologists to examine at length how this ideology developed over time and how it played out in the lives of ordinary Americans. She investigates material culture's pivotal role in the increasing segmentation of gender-specific tasks for women and men, which began in the 1830s, a process that went hand in hand with the transformation of America from a country of producers to one of consumers. At the crux of this transition from a rural to industrial economy was the reorganization of the American family structure. Prior to this restructuring of American life, women, men, and children were expected to work both within and outside of the home. Domestic responsibilities did not solely fall upon women, and the financial welfare of the household was not entirely at the disposal of men. Rather, women were charged with the task of handling both the economic and domestic aspects of supporting a family, which involved "producing items for household use (like food, candles, clothes, and even yarn and cloth) and sometimes for market, bearing children and caring for infants, . . . running the day-to-day operations of the household," and helping to operate her husband's business or trade in the event of his absence" (Wall 1994, 5).

By the mid-nineteenth century, however, women were presumed to be incapable of handling the financial affairs of their households and were told that they were best suited to serve as the moral guardian and caretaker of their home and offspring. Women found that their position as Americans became one entirely consumed with domesticity, with their place as citizens in the exterior, public world virtually invisible. Now men were the only ones responsible for working and producing an income to support their wives and children. This time period is marked by a gendering of tasks where women were assumed to be biologically predisposed to caring for the home and children while men were seen as fit for work outside of it. This essentialist rhetoric was inflamed by prescriptive literature that provided a compass for how women should go about their role as moral guardian of the home. Wall's influential work (1991, 1994) has addressed this separation of genders by looking at the role women had in perpetuating the ideologies coinciding with this remarkable shift in American mindsets.

By comparing the ceramic assemblages of eleven late-eighteenth- and early-nineteenth-century households in New York, Wall discovered that women contributed to the social differentiation between genders taking place across the nation (1994, 136). It is apparent from her data that women began to adopt ritualized dining practices much earlier than previously thought, practices scholars assumed were imposed upon women by men. Thus, women did not passively accept their new role in American culture but rather welcomed it, reworking it and making it their own. This involved intentionally selecting matching dishwares, using individualized place settings, and practicing elaborate dining rituals.

Prior to the 1830s food, not the styles and arrangement of dishes, was the focal point of a meal (Wall 1994, 148). This changed after the mid-nineteenth century when communally designed vessels replaced wares that served individuals and suited the shape and form of the specific food that was being served. Examples of these dining wares included "covered serving dishes, open serving dishes, bakers, a butter dish, a pitcher, . . . a gravy boat, . . . cups, saucers, a tea pot, a slop bowl, a sugar, a creamer, . . . [and] muffin plates" (Fitts 1999, 53). Today Americans are familiar with this serving style, with each individual using their own plate, fork, spoon, knife, and cup to eat. Wall therefore concludes that women constructed new formations of citizenship that revolved around these ornate eating and dining rituals and attendant ceramic and glasswares as their citizenship opportunities were severely circumscribed outside of their household. If women were going to be denied citizenship outside of their homes, they were certainly going to find a way to be considered proper citizens inside of it.

Women interpreted and communicated their interest in this ideology through their consumption and display of goods. Matching vessels composed of undecorated pure white granite were particularly sought after by the middle classes because they embodied purity, "thrift, . . . morality, . . . modesty, . . . [and] Christianity" (Fitts 1999, 58). These principles were reified and further articulated through household architecture. Gothic-style decor reminiscent of Christian churches, such as door frames, sideboards, mantels, furniture, and clocks, have been archaeologically recovered inside middle-class homes from this era. Such decor reminded women of their God-given role as protectors of the home (47). Plants and flowers adorned wallpaper, light fixtures, drape pullbacks, furniture, glass, and ceramics and were grown inside the home; the archaeological remnants of many of these naturalistic objects have confirmed their prevalence in middle-class homes. Women engaged in such decorative practices to assert their innate connection to the natural world created by God (48).

To ensure that their offspring would attain the same material abundance they had acquired, middle-class parents limited the number of children they birthed by practicing sexual abstinence (Fitts 1999, 46). Toward the same end, children were showered with attention and were granted an extended amount of time to act as "children" than that allowed by previous generations, with many children living in their parents' home well past the age of twenty and "only 35.3% of native-born middle-class males" marrying "before their 29th year" (46). Out of these newly established attitudes about childhood was born a philosophy known today as the "cult of domesticity" (46). The household was depicted as a sanctuary for children to flourish and grow into good, God-fearing, productive, industrious, and financially secure American citizens. Within their homes, children were taught the skills necessary to reproduce their parents' middle-class standing. For instance, ritualized dining practices, such as giving a child his or her own place setting at the table and corresponding silverware, or, if the child was a girl, giving her "toy table settings and toy tea sets" to instill within them "the appropriate manners and domestic skills," conveyed the ideals of middle-class domesticity (50).

One of the pressing questions that has arisen out of Wall's work is whether this ideology was commonplace within American society and, to be more specific, how lower classes felt about its stringent behavioral and material requirements, standards most difficult to achieve and maintain for those lacking in wealth. Fitts addresses this question by looking at how the cult of domesticity was interpreted by white-collar workers in 1860s New York. From his investigation Fitts discovers that middle-class Americans living in Brooklyn consciously used goods to communicate their class standing to others of the same economic position, and they passed on these values to their children. Of the families Fitts studied, all six of them owned matching white granite tea wares and dinnerwares and an impressive five out of six owned additional sets of these wares (Fitts 1999, 52). Families also selected specialized dishes for each type of food, vessels that would be placed on display for visitors and children dining at their tables. Numerous miniature tea sets were also recovered from the middle-class homes, including three collections featuring matching vessels that contained specialized vessels such as "pitchers, soup tureens, or serving dishes" (54). These findings suggest that middle-class Americans, at least in the case of Fitts's Brooklyn households, listened closely to prescriptive literature on genteel behavior, following its orders when it came time to buy toys and ceramics for their families.

Although pervasive, other historical archaeological studies have shown that the "separate spheres" ideology was not all encompassing. LouAnn

Wurst, wary of the overdeterministic manner in which this ideology has been employed, questions the life span of this dichotomous gender system that pitted men against women. Rather than painting households as complacent loci where men and women simply acted out their prescribed gender roles, Wurst reconceptualizes the home as a site of struggle, a place where gender was hammered out and contested on a day-to-day basis (2003, 233). Rotman finds this to be the case in Deerfield, Massachusetts, a village where women sophisticatedly undermined the prevailing separate spheres ideology. Massachusetts property laws prevented women from inheriting property, effectively making women second-class citizens in their own communities. Male benefactors were the only citizens granted the right to inherit property up until 1864 (Rotman 2006, 668). The women of Deerfield contested their second-tier citizenship by blurring the lines between the supposed separation of the public and private spheres. This was done by engaging in economically viable and successful craft-related work outside of their homes, such as manufacturing "traditional rugs, embroidery, and jewelry for market sale as part of the Arts and Crafts movement" (670). Men in the village also took part in work that was at that historical moment associated with women, including weaving, pottery, and furniture making. Deerfield's men, then, also purposefully chose to defy the binary gender system imposed upon mid- to late-nineteenth-century American domestic and economic life (670).

Hadley Kruczek-Aaron (2002) also discovers evidence of struggles over gender norms and expectations at the home of New York's Gerrit Smith, an elite nineteenth-century politician, religious leader, and reformer. From her close reading of archives and archaeological data associated with Smith's estate, Kruczek-Aaron found that traditional gender ideologies were hotly contested by the residents of Smith's estate and were the subject of disagreement between Smith, his wife, and his daughter. Smith believed in restrained consumption and supported the temperance and abolitionist movements by making his estate "home to a Temperance Hotel and his mansion and barn . . . a popular safe haven for numerous African Americans fleeing from slavery" (Kruczek-Aaron 2002, 176). He stressed these values in his political addresses, in his religious teachings, and in his conversations with his family. One would therefore expect to find that the archaeology of his homestead would conform to his publicly professed beliefs. Transfer-printed pearlware vessels associated with the mansion's debris found during excavations along with extensive renovations of Smith's mansion documented in the archives show that his family did not exercise the moral restraint publicly professed by Smith. Correspondence between Smith and his daughter and wife also document internal conflict within the Smith family over conspicuous consumption and ornate household decor; in line with his writings, Smith preferred simplicity while his wife and daughter chose goods that communicated their upper-class standing. Gerrit Smith was so dismayed with his wife's spending habits that he called her actions a "disease," one that "caused repeated stress within the Smith household" (179).

If middle- and upper-class communities contested consumption habits, then we might assume that these prescriptive behaviors were met with equal disdain in communities that had limited economic or cultural access to goods and the cultural capital needed to purchase such products.

Marginalized Communities

Although middle- and upper-class behaviors served as the norm against which an individual's citizenship aspirations could be measured, marginalized and oppressed communities did not always blindly adhere to this value system. The archaeological case studies presented in this section shed light on how both individuals on the margins of society, whether due to their class standing, immigration history, religious beliefs, or gender status, dealt with imposed and voluntary types of Americanization and civic reform. As we will see, communities who viewed themselves as oppressed citizens created parallel and alternative visions of American belonging and citizenship.

Immigrants

How did the material practices of the upper and middle classes trickle down to masses? Were they, as Wall asks of working-class immigrants living in nineteenth-century New York, accepted unquestioned "to gain entry to the bourgeoisie society so that either they or their children could partake of its power" (Wall 1999, 105)? Were the boundaries of social standing easily transgressed in execution, with class permeable and capable of being transferred from one hand to another with the careful assembling and use of middle-class clothing, goods, and ceramics as well as an acquisition of the knowledge needed to use these items? Acquiring the latter knowledge was just as important as the ownership of goods to express it, so important that "although wealth affects the ability to purchase the correct symbols, it is the lack of appropriate symbolic behavior rather than wealth which precludes membership in a particular class" (Fitts 1999, 40). Did they instead construct an alternative material world, one where goods and behaviors were imbued with meaning best understood within their own class, religious, ethnic, or racial group? Or did a combination of the two occur, with lower classes consciously manipulating material culture when needed (to satisfy employers' wishes, for instance) while also sustaining connections to their communities? How were these material expectations lived and experienced by individuals inhabiting the margins of society?

Wall looks at this from the point of view of working-class immigrants in nineteenth-century New York. She juxtaposes four ceramic assemblages recovered from middle- and working-class families. Middle-class assemblages markedly differed from those belonging to working-class women in that middle-class women chose ironstone plates that featured matching Gothic patterns (Wall 1999, 113). Working classes, in contrast, selected dishes that featured a wide variety of nonmatching Gothic patterns and patterns that were different from those found within middle-class New York women's homes. Working-class women, Wall asserts, were therefore not interested in emulating and aspiring to the material practices of middle-class women. Stylistic differences among dishware patterns, she believes, could be indicative of a symbolic system that communicated meanings indecipherable to middle-class women. Although the provenience information does not allow for such analysis, Wall believes that there may have been differences not only across class divides but also within working and middle classes. Perhaps working-class "women from the Irish families preferred china in one molded style while those from the German families preferred china in another pattern" (114), a difference only visible if one were able to associate refuse with a particular family or ethnic group. While not supported by the data at hand, Wall's supposition prompts scholars to remember that working- and middle-class women were not homogenous groups who mechanically adopted the material practices of women within the same socioeconomic status.

Other archaeological studies have documented the formation of a distinctly American working-class identity with its own corresponding material culture that departed from middle-class standards. In the early-nineteenth-century company town of Lowell, Massachusetts, employees and their employers simultaneously manipulated their material worlds, albeit for divergent purposes. A planned community, Lowell was an experiment in creating an effective, productive, and moral workforce and citizenry. A worker's every move was meticulously scripted and choreographed, with "a series of zones through which workers moved on their way to work, to church, to shops and so on" (Beaudry and Mrozowski 2001, 120). Town architects believed that they could shepherd worker efficiency by relegating bars and other restaurants that sold alcohol to the outskirts of Lowell (121). Behavior was also closely monitored because "any expression of working-class culture, working-class identity, posed a threat to the carefully constructed bourgeois facade" of Lowell (121).

Predictably, these attempts fell short in execution. Working-class employees casually smoked "cheap white ball clay pipes" (Beaudry and Mrozowski 2001, 126–27), pipes that were different from those used by the middle and upper classes. Significantly, lower-class Irish employees smoked pipes that featured Irish slogans, thus making it known that they had little desire to be a part of the American citizenry. Some pipes "bore political legends, Home Rule being the most common, while others displayed shamrocks and the name of the great Irish republican martyr Wolf Tone" (123). The very practice of smoking a pipe emblazoned with political and nationalist slogans can be read as a mode of opting out of American culture and the citizenship such involvement might confer.

As one would expect, the economic disparities that existed between Irish workers and mill workers in better-paid positions were visible in their material lives. The housing of company agents, individuals who were ranked higher and receiving higher wages than other mill employees, was equipped with indoor plumbing years before the homes of mid-level employees. In turn, lower-class workers would have to continue to use unsanitary privies and wells even though "this was nearly thirty years after the companies were instructed to rid themselves of these vestiges of a bygone era" (Beaudry and Mrozowski 2001, 125). This may partially explain the apathy and outright disinterest Irish workers expressed toward American citizenship. Interestingly, Grace Ziesing interprets the presence of costume jewelry, some of which were near exact replicas of expensive pieces considered fashionable by the middle classes, in working-class housing at Boott Mills as evidence of working-class "aspirations to middle-class status" (quoted in Beaudry and Mrozowski 2001, 125). Yet Beaudry and

Mrozowski's analysis of Lowell takes the interpretation of this site in a different direction, cautioning that class mobility is simply one of the many aspirations to which immigrants held fast.

Although it appears that Lowell's lower-class Irish workers were disinterested in belonging to America's civic body due to the shared experience of marginalization, patriotic and nationalist beliefs can vary across ethnic groups as well as within their membership. Excavations at New York's Five Points neighborhood encapsulate this diversity of national longings, where newly arrived Irish and German immigrants lived side by side. Clay pipe analysis helps archaeologists understand their feelings about citizenship and their place within American society. Clay pipes set working-class immigrants and day laborers apart from the middle and upper classes who preferred "a pipe of briar wood or meerschaum" (Reckner 2001, 105). A large percentage, 20 percent, of the pipes recovered from German households dating to the mid-1800s feature American patriotic symbols that included the Great Seal of the United States (fig. 2.1) (Reckner 2001, 105). Patriotic motifs were significantly less common in the Irish assemblage dating to the same time period, where only "6% show any nationalistic theme in their design" (105). The Irish assemblage also contained both American and Irish nationalistic themes, including one pipe "with a harp and shamrock motif" (105). German immigrants were able to weave seamlessly into the fabric of America while Irish immigrants were greeted with hostility due to their religious beliefs and their perceived racial traits (Orser 2007). Restrictions were placed on Irish immigrants' civic duties while Germans were allowed to move freely about society.

This differential treatment, Reckner claims, manifests itself in the pipe assemblages whereby the Irish, as outcasts in America, still clung to symbols reminiscent of their homeland. Germans, in contrast, selected pipes that celebrated their new nationality by displaying American iconography. A mere twenty to thirty years later, pipes unearthed from the same Irish neighborhood reveal a new pattern. Twenty-three percent of the newly unearthed pipe assemblage consisted of Irish nationalist propaganda. The growth of these pipes' popularity demonstrates the emergence of collective organizations and the formation of unions to represent and protect their interests. The pipe assemblage is a reflection of this united stance as well as the development of Irish nationalism in response to the persistent racism and persecution Irish immigrants faced in America.

Other artifacts recovered from Irish households in Five Points show

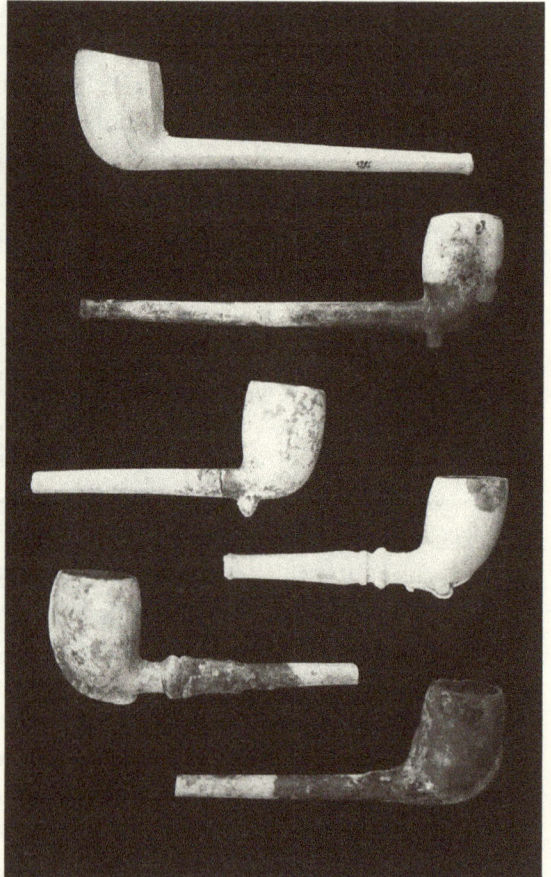

Figure 2.1. Pipes recovered from German immigrant households featuring the Great Seal of the United States. Image courtesy of Paul Reckner.

how the Irish refracted discrimination through their material world. The Irish community of Five Points lived in crowded, unsanitary tenements where twenty-two families would occupy a space built to house up to ten families, and privies would spill over "into the rear courtyards and basement apartments" (Brighton 2008, 24). A teacup recovered from Five Points shows that despite their living conditions, Irish immigrants purchased symbols popular among middle-class American citizens while also putting a uniquely Irish spin on middle-class gentility. On the teacup's exterior is Father Theobald Mathew while the interior rim features a beehive, bees, and the phrases "Temperance and Industry" and "Industry Pays Debt" (24–25). Father Mathew was a prominent member of the temperance movement, one who believed that the working classes could uplift themselves by abstaining from alcohol (25). Brighton places this teacup within the context of a contemporaneous Irish movement to negate, manage, and refute persistent, discriminatory depictions of the Irish by American politicians and the media. So while they consumed materials familiar among middle-class American citizens, the Irish still made it known that they would remain tied to their homeland and its religious practices by embracing what Brighton calls a "dual national consciousness" (2011, 40).

With the passing of time, Irish immigrants became more adept with and conscious of their manipulation of the materials symbolizing citizenship in the United States. Diachronic analysis, a methodological approach few outside of the discipline of historical archaeology can employ that allows scholars to examine how cultural groups and their consumer habits change over time, has been used by Brighton in his research on Irish communities in America and Ireland. Of particular significance is Brighton's concern with the material shifts that take place from the Irish's point of departure in Ireland to their movement upward from working- to middle-class Irish American communities. To confront these transformations, he considers two temporally distinct glass and ceramic assemblages from an early lower-class Irish immigrant community in Five Points, New York, dating between 1850 and 1860 and a later middle-class Irish immigrant community in Paterson, New Jersey, dating between 1880 and 1910. The Five Points community owned mismatched and low-cost ceramics, a pattern that mirrors that of "rural poor classes in Ireland" (Brighton 2011, 41). Such wares were visual signposts to middle-class Americans, helping to uphold the belief among middle-class Americans that the "Irish poor were uncivilized" (41). Socially and financially alienated from consuming goods, Five Points' Irish immigrants failed to pass the test of American respectability, one that would preclude them "from gaining the benefits of American citizenship" (42). After years of living in America, the Irish maintained some elements of their culture brought over from rural Ireland. Mismatched ceramics are still commonly found inside Irish immigrants' homes, but the diversity and complexity of vessel forms becomes more pronounced in second-generation or well-established Irish immigrant communities (42–43).

Italian immigrants also used a suite of material culture to express their views on citizenship. Michael Fette, an Italian immigrant who came to the United States in the 1880s, smartly navigated the nineteenth-century world of Harlem, New York. Beginning as a scavenger, Fette was able to climb the ladder of corporate America to become a law clerk and real estate agent (Fitts 2002, 4). He became a respected leader and figurehead of the Italian community, achieving quick ascent into the American political realm. In the process, he befriended important political leaders and "even Teddy Roosevelt" (4–5). He learned English by reading newspapers daily and became fluent in the language shortly upon arriving in the United States (6).

Fette struck a harmonious balance between his American and Italian identities by carefully selecting a patchwork of material goods that expressed this dualism. Although a staunch supporter of naturalization for Italians who came to America's shores, Fette still maintained that Italians must continue to celebrate their Italian culture (Fitts 2002, 5). His parlor merged religious ideologies popular in Italian culture with decor that showcased his knowledge of middle- to upper-class Victorian fashions. A porcelain crucifix commonly found in other Italian immigrants' homes hung on the parlor wall of Fette's house, which was tempered by knick-knacks, a mantel clock, and potted plants found in most middle- to upper-class American homes (6). Upon his first successful real estate transaction, Fette added a piano to his parlor, a commodity that was "a symbol of assimilation, announcing both a family's refinement and desire to be American" (6). Considered as a collection, the goods in Fette's parlor "showed that he understood aspects of American middle-class values and desired to be a 'respectable citizen' even if his parlor had a distinctive Italian flair" (8).

Fette also drew inspiration from both cultures to make choices about his food and the wares on which he would eat it. He owned several sets of matching tablewares, including formal and everyday ceramic sets. Some of the wares' decorations were typical of a middle-class American family while other patterns subtly expressed Italian preferences. Majolica wares, in particular, were stylistically similar to those used in Italy. He owned a comparatively large set of tea wares, six to be exact, that also conveyed an air of sophistication. Interestingly, it was somewhat unusual for Italians to consume tea; coffee was their drink of choice. Fitts speculates that tea wares may have allowed Fette to entertain both Italians and Americans, serving coffee in the wares to the former while serving tea to the latter (2002, 9). With a home decked out in what was in vogue for middle-class Americans and tablewares that would be the envy of good American citizens, Fette still made time for a few Italian diversions, some of which substantially departed from the middle-class value system he was emulating in other contexts. In his spare time, Fette consumed hard liquor, wine, and beer, all of which were found in his archaeological assemblage. This was consistent with Italian tradition where alcohol was routinely consumed at meals within the home as well as drunk in public places such as "local saloons" and "beer halls" (11).

Chinese migrants also resourcefully "mangled" symbols and icons of Anglo-American Victorian gentility to expand their businesses and gain economic footing within nineteenth century California (Praetzellis and Praetzellis 2001). Dissatisfied with the notion that Victorian ideologies and the material practices associated with Victorian refinement were adopted wholesale and uniformly, Praetzellis and Praetzellis argue that Chinese migrants, such as Chinese immigrant Yee Ah Tye, engaged in a game of "impression management" of their own design "not merely to imitate the Victorian upper crust in some nervous attempt at social advancement" (Praetzellis and Praetzellis 2001, 647). Fluent in English, Yee Ah Tye was a well-respected community leader both in his own Chinese community and by Anglo-Americans in Sacramento's business district. Artifacts recovered from the association over which Yee Ah Tye presided, the Sze Yud District Association, yielded a mixture of Anglo-American and Chinese manufactured objects, including "Staffordshire bowls, a basin, soup plates, and dinner plates" featuring Chinese marks of ownership (648).

Instead of interpreting this set of artifacts as proof of assimilation efforts, Praetzellis and Praetzellis place the artifacts within the local context of nineteenth-century Chinese merchant affairs and business relationships. According to the documentary record, Chinese businessmen "regularly held open houses and banquets for influential members of Sacramento's establishment" (649). At these events, a carefully orchestrated mixture of both Chinese- and American-produced goods, including a "dining table set with a cloth, knives, forks, and celery glasses" that conveyed Yee's knowledge of Victorian behaviors, helped him gain the favor of Anglo-American businessmen who equated these material practices with morality and gentility (649).

As these examples have shown, immigrants in nineteenth- and early-twentieth-century America used mass-produced material culture not merely to appease Americans occupying the upper echelon of society but instead fused the material practices of their culture of origin with that of their new nation. This was not necessarily a straightforward or linear process, nor was it one that happened immediately upon their migration. Much like many cultural transitions and changes, it could take years for migrants to achieve a happy medium that paid homage to both cultures and nationalities. Immigrants did not submissively submit to the desires of those making more than them or who had achieved full citizenship standing. Rather, they creativity and strategically merged material practices gleaned from both cultures into a collage, in effect redefining American citizenship on their own terms and for the diversification of American society. These points are important to commit to memory as we sort through the mass-produced bits of glass and ceramics that seem overwhelmingly alike from site to site and try to make sense of what these objects meant to the people who owned them.

But not all cultures existing on the outskirts of American society were open to merging their belief systems with those of middle-class America. And not all cultures were accepted with open arms by middle- and upper-class America. Those exiled from American society exerted creative force to craft new visions of community and citizenship. The study of intentional and utopian communities provides alternative forms of community building, ones that can potentially inform future imaginings of community belonging outside of national origins.

Intentional and Utopian Communities

In recent years historical archaeologists have paid special attention to intentional and utopian communities, groups formed with specific plans, behaviors, and actions in mind. The planning and implementation of intentional communities required much foresight and thought, which involved extensive documentation and resulted in a watershed of documentary records, including written records, manifestos, ledgers, diaries, books detailing the community's philosophies and ideologies, and newsletters. Historical archaeologists have then juxtaposed these materials against the archaeological data they have excavated to determine if the communities lived up to their idealized behaviors and intentions. For example, in the case of the late-nineteenth-century Socialist community of Kaweah, archaeologists have pursued answers to questions that the archaeological record can sometimes solely reveal (Kozakavich 2007), such as did residents actually follow the community manifesto's prohibition on the consumption of mass market items?

While archaeology can address how residents and community leaders bridged the gap between their everyday experiences and their settlement's expected and idealized practices, the historical archaeology of intentionally developed communities also offers sustained and critical commentary on how American ideals and civic duties were contested. Utopian communities provide exceptional insight into how groups saw American citizenship because such communities were usually formed by those disaffected or disenfranchised by citizenship legislation or by individuals indifferent to "specific dominant culture forms and moral imperatives" (Van Bueren 2006, 133). Those attracted to utopian communities tended to hold the belief that "the only obstacles that impede the expression of . . . human traits concern the ordering of society" such as the formation of national boundaries (Tarlow 2002, 301).

Utopian and intentional communities flourished in America during the late nineteenth and early twentieth centuries, a time when federal policies concerning who could immigrate to and naturalize in America were legalized (see chapter 1). Although the communities explored in this final section "failed" in the sense that they were short-lived and, in the case of some communities, defeated by the forces of capitalism and the power of the state, they offer alternative visions of citizenship and community belonging for those currently dissatisfied with American culture. At the same time, community members still struggled with the trappings of their former life as American citizens, sometimes choosing to consume emblems of their socioeconomic standing or remaining prejudiced against certain types of American citizens due to their race, ethnicity, class, or gender. Nonetheless, there is much to learn from intentional communities beyond "what did not work"; rather, we should be asking "what did work and why" (Van Bueren 2006, 148). The lessons learned from these communities' failures and successes can perhaps help us generate new iterations of American citizenship and national identity. Finally, the mere existence of these communities highlights the fact that America has tolerated and, to a certain extent, been a safe harbor for diverse settlements. Their presence speaks to the nation's historic ability to be tolerant of others and of other definitions of American citizenship, though not always legally permissive.

Intentional communities thus capture the fluidity and elasticity of American identity, an identity of contestation, with idealized communities seeking to critique aspects of American society that have failed them and left them yearning for more. Most intentional communities developed during America's industrial age of the late nineteenth and early twentieth centuries, although utopian groups such as the Shakers have called America home since colonial times (Starbuck 2004; Tarlow 2002, 309). Turn-of-the-century America was a time when the country and its citizens' personal and private lives were undergoing radical transformations due to industrialization and urbanization. Secular, religious, and political intentional communities challenged the very foundation of an American citizen's life during this era: a time when some men sought to escape the banality of industrial work that demanded nearly all of their week for little pay and when some women felt "trapped in or threatened by unhappy marriages, relentless childbirth, or domestic slavery" that the cult of domesticity demanded (Tarlow 2002, 302).

Tomaso and colleagues' (2006) study of New Jersey's Feltville, a mid-nineteenth-century industrial village named after its owner, looks at how its owner, David Felt, responded to these monumental changes in Americans' lives. Built "to solve practical problems experienced by laborers during the industrial revolution—such as poor housing, lack of access to community facilities, and an urban environment that was increasingly seen as unhealthy and demoralizing" (Tomaso et al. 2006, 23), Feltville challenged working class conditions that presented formidable obstacles for social mobility in America. A well-to-do printer and publisher, Felt offered single women and married men with families the chance to labor at his factory in the community from 1845 to 1860, the entire duration of Feltville's existence. His vision of equality for all American citizens is evident in the archaeological signatures of the community, which document Felt's attention to his workers' needs. Town residents and employees "had fresh air, a quiet neighborhood, house gardens, and relatively clean water because of the well-built and carefully placed wells and privies" (28). Eight of the workers' cottages are still standing today because of Felt's concern with detail and use of durable building materials (29). Children were forbidden from working in his factory and instead were allowed to attend a school built by Felt on Feltville's premises. Felt gave his workers' children the chance to advance in the world beyond the lower-class standing of their parents.

The intentional community of San Diego, California's Theosophical Society, which was in operation from ca. 1900 to 1920, similarly sought to improve American society through the education of children, though with different goals in mind. Developed and run by Katherine Tingley, the Theosophical Society had a towering boarding school on its premises to cater to children. Half of the society's five hundred residents were children who were under the charge of Tingley. Paralleling the Socialist communes of the time, Tingley taught them how to be "free men and women" in order to "achieve a universal brotherhood of man" as well as how to share and to have "self-reliance, love for all people, altruism, mutual clarity, and, more than anything else, to think and reason for themselves" (Van Wormer and Gross 2006, 101).

The archaeology of the Theosophical Society shows that these beliefs were not superficial but rather a deeply ingrained philosophy that was enacted through the daily denial of certain forms of material culture. Unlike most American citizens who saw mass consumption as one's civic duty, material culture was seen as a hindrance to an individual's spiritual and moral development. This attitude is reflected in the recovery of a "low percentage of consumer items and beverage bottles in the assemblage and lower economic index value of the ceramic assemblage," an especially reduced number of mass market goods when compared to other contemporaneous, local archaeological assemblages (Van Wormer and Gross 2006, 112).

Other communes sought not only to improve the lives of their work-ers' children but also to confront commonly held ideas about gender and class. Informed by Marxist thought that held "society would be best served if workers owned the means of production, thus thwarting exploi-tation of their labor by capitalists" (Van Bueren 2006, 135), Los Angeles, California's early-twentieth-century Llano del Rio Cooperative Colony was founded by American Socialist Party member and politician Job Har-riman. He proposed a drastic alternative to American gender roles, espe-cially as they pertained to a woman's civic duties such as women's right to vote. Dovetailing off of East Coast reform movements that reframed domestic interior work as meaningful labor worthy of pay, Llano's women were allowed to labor outside of the home, were paid for their work, and were encouraged to pursue trades that were historically associated with men (135). To allow time for work outside of the home, women's tradi-tional work inside the home, such as child-rearing and housekeeping, was minimized through time-saving plans; such innovative ideas included de-signing Llano households that required minimal cleaning and allowed for complete surveillance of children (136).

According to archival records and archaeological data associated with Llano, community members tried to evenly distribute activities across the entire community rather than leave them to individual families or specific genders. A community Montessori kindergarten relieved women of some childcare duties at Llano, and it demanded that this "domestic function" be counted as a "public profession" (Van Bueren 2006, 147). Dining also appears to have been a collective effort, with a "communal steam laun-dry and a bake oven" noted in archival records associated with the site (147). Modifications to Llano's landscape, which included the planting of non-native trees and the arrangement of rocks in shared community areas as well as the placement of privies in communal rather than individual homes, likewise appear to emphasize collectivity and a shared social iden-tity (147).

In a time when the law declared that American women were second-class citizens who were not allowed to vote, Llano's belief that women and men were equally valuable members of society worthy of full citizenship privileges was progressive. But utopian planners' reconsideration of com-munity belonging and citizenship within their borders was not always more inclusive than that of the United States' government, its institutions, its corporations, or its cultural values. In some cases, policies determining Llano's citizens and membership were more exclusive than those of the federal government. Llano's members expressly forbade "Negroes, Hindus, Mongolians, and Malays" from joining the community to avoid interracial mixing, which they deemed a threat to the Anglo-American race (Van Bueren 2006, 138). The economic disparities between Llano residents—class differences they claimed to be working toward minimizing—may have persisted, too, as objects that connoted one's middle-class standing in American society, such as expensive imported Asian ceramics, have been found at the site in select homes (148).

Like members of Llano, members of a nineteenth-century Shaker utopian community that was comprised of "19 communities extending from Maine to Kentucky and a membership of over 6000 by the 1850s" used the built environment and material culture to undo what they saw as unequal gender hierarchies in American culture (Savulis 1992, 196). Opting instead to see men *and* women as equally contributing citizens, Shakers reordered their lives around this ethos by allowing women to be community leaders in their political and religious spheres. Despite professing a life of equality for women and men, the Shakers still subscribed to some aspects of the separate spheres ideology popular in the nineteenth-century American society surrounding them. For example, Shakers believed that women's activities should be confined to the domestic sphere while men should be involved with work outside of the home. This is observable in the materials used and symbology employed by male and female community members to depict their belief system. "Men produced detailed maps of communities, whereas women wrote poetry describing building interiors and painted spiritual landscapes and dwellings" (197).

Despite some of the highlighted failures and disappointments, intentional communities offer the promise of new ways of building community outside of the hegemonic sphere of the nation-state.

Summary

Much of the research presented in this chapter does not explicitly frame itself as the historical archaeology of citizenship. But given the important social distinctions that citizenship and noncitizenship connoted throughout American history and the significant relationship between consumption and expressions of citizenship, historical archaeologists must become more attuned to how the materiality they excavate is connected and in response to naturalization policies, aspirations, and regulations.

Although some marginalized groups used consumption to express their desire to be treated as fully naturalized American citizens, not all individuals harbored the same feelings about consumption and citizenship. Beliefs regarding citizenship and consumption vacillated just as much as the parameters of citizenship shifted over the course of American history; consumption practices hence changed across time periods, regions, and even within the same cultures, ethnic groups, genders, households, and classes. The next two chapters look at this variability in citizenship desires by exploring the archaeology and documentary history of a Mexican immigrant community living in early-twentieth-century Los Angeles, California. Living on the margins of two nations, these immigrants were subjected to a forced assimilation program by their employers, the Pacific Electric Railway Corporation (PERC). Carried out by Anglo-American female reformers, this movement sought to transform nearly every aspect of Mexican immigrants' lives to meet Anglo-American standards and sensibilities. However, as these immigrants discovered, adherence to such prescriptive rules would not help them advance in Anglo-American society. This finding made citizenship for lower-class immigrants a status unworthy of pursuing, as those who had obtained it repeatedly encountered various forms of discrimination in America.

Chapter 3 examines another process of citizen-making under way in early-twentieth-century America by studying the setting in which these immigrants labored, Mount Lowe Resort and Railway (MLRR). While the resort's immigrants were repairing and maintaining its internationally renowned railway under the hot, burning Southern California sun, the tourists who visited and took a ride on Mount Lowe's railway were also expressing their ambitions for citizenship. At this particular juncture in American history, the ritual of tourism was perceived as one of the ways to support the nation. Tourist destinations such as Mount Lowe helped the middle and upper classes, people who could afford the luxury of touring, celebrate and physically perform this requirement of citizenship by designing amusements that reminded tourists of the nation's greatness.

Chapters 3 and 4 reinforce the importance of giving weight to the historical and cultural factors that drive consumer behavior and interrogate consumer-choice models that universalize consumer actions and behavior. Some of these studies tend to predict a consumer's likelihood of purchasing objects solely based on their income and class standing (things that can easily be subverted through such practices as buying objects in second-hand stores, bartering, dumpster diving, or the passing down of heirlooms from one generation to the next), or the studies assume that consumers can exercise an unfettered free will and purchase whatever they desire irrelevant of their economic condition, citizenship status, or racial and gender identity. The next two chapters explore some of the fallacies inherent in both assumptions, adding a new perspective and voice to debates within historical archaeology concerning what conditions and colors consumer decisions and actions. Equally important, these chapters stress citizenship as an influential vector of one's identity. In acknowledgment, these chapters place citizenship alongside and at the intersection of more traditionally accepted forms of personhood through which archaeological data has been interpreted, including one's race, class, and gender.

3

....

Tourism and Citizenship

At the dawn of the twentieth century, the diversity of America's citizenry was increasing exponentially. With the exception of the relatively recent exclusion of individuals of Chinese heritage in 1882, people from all parts of the world were entering the United States in search of equality, freedom, and all that the "American dream" embodied. American politicians languished over the nation's new citizenry and expressed xenophobic fears about their new multicultural empire. No longer able to routinely massacre or displace large populations of non-Anglo ethnicities, pundits proposed and initiated methods of cultural assimilation as a solution to turning a heterogeneous population into a homogeneous one. Many twentieth-century thinkers postulated that a diverse citizenry would lead to political strife and social upheaval. Native American boarding schools as well as orphanages and almshouses for the poor were just a few of the many Americanization initiatives enacted during the Progressive Era to quell and subdue what were perceived as troubling cultural and social differences.

This chapter and the next profile two citizen-crafting processes at work during this time period. This chapter takes the first of these processes, tourism, seriously by seeing it, as a number of scholars have argued, as an expression of American nationality, exceptionalism, and a love for one's nation. Tourism initially began as an "expensive status marker" (Bruner 2005, 196) for upper-class Anglo-Americans that served to naturalize their class status and remind others that the right to tour was restricted to a select, wealthy few. But as resorts and tourist destinations grew in size and numbers and the practice of touring became more popular, tourism started to be seen as a unique facet of American identity and citizenship irrespective of one's economic position. Yet in reality not all could afford to partake in leisure, which meant that not all American citizens could fulfill their civic responsibilities as tourists.

This chapter looks at how one of the most popular tourist sites in the western United States, Mount Lowe Resort and Railway (MLRR), provided object lessons on what constitutes American citizenship and identity. At MLRR, middle- and upper-class tourists visiting the resort learned behavior expected of American citizens who shared their socioeconomic standing. Following the lead of other tourism theorists, I liken the practice of tourism to a ritual. Rituals remove members from their culture and place them in a temporary state of being that anthropologists have termed "liminality." This liminal existence has "few or none of the attributes of the past or coming state" (Turner 1969, 94), meaning that the activities, environments, and expected behaviors differ vastly from the previous state of being to which those undergoing a ritual are accustomed. Individuals who partake in rituals together form an "intense comradeship," which reinforces cohort membership, the formation of a collective thinking and class solidarity, and the emergence of a shared set of values and beliefs (94). By seeing tourism as a ritual that encourages the development of a group consciousness among individuals involved in the ritual, the practice of tourism becomes a vehicle through which certain classes of society form an identity separate from those excluded from the ritual.

The ritual of tourism in historic America served to divide and segregate Americans into different classes of citizens. Tourists repeatedly viewed exhibits that affirmed widely held beliefs about biological differences between whites and nonwhites. Native Americans and other castigated racial and ethnic groups were placed on display in exhibits at tourist sites and World's Fairs that highlighted physiological differences between the toured and the touring (Burton 1983; Rydell 1984). By repeatedly encountering these displays of difference, white tourists developed a sense of cultural superiority over those who were not able to tour or were being toured. Noted tourism theorist Dean MacCannell chooses to describe the process of "sightseeing" as a "ritual performed to the differentiation of society," where "the totality of differences between social classes, life-styles, racial and ethnic groups, age grades (the youth, the aged)," and "political and professional groups" is made evident to tourists (1999, 11, 13).

The following chapter, "The Archaeology of Citizenship," looks at a very different citizen-making ritual underway at the resort, a process that targeted the resort's Mexican immigrant employees. Although lessons in proper citizenship for employees and guests took place simultaneously at the resort, the lessons were not equal or evenhanded in their content, structure, or implementation. For MLRR's Mexican immigrant workers, citizenship was not achieved by touring or working at the resort. Rather, it was made nearly unattainable by resort owners who placed their poorly paid employees in a filthy, overcrowded homestead that failed county health inspections on multiple occasions. Rather ironically, the company expected its workers to listen to hired reformers who instructed them in "proper" hygiene, household and landscape maintenance, shopping, dress, child-rearing, bathing, eating, household decor, and dining.

As I argue in chapter 4, some Mexican immigrants recognized the impossibility of following through with these expectations of citizenship and expressed little desire to become members of American society. In contrast, middle- and upper-class tourists eagerly adopted the language of the resort and the messages it conveyed about their superior relationship to other classes of citizens in America. These two contrasting case studies thus bolster cultural anthropologists' contention that cultural forces mediate citizenship, which often requires social inclusion for legal inclusion to be meaningful and worth seeking for marginalized groups such as MLRR's workers (Ong 1996, 1999; Rosaldo 1994, 1999, 2003).

Tourism and American Citizenship

Even in its earliest incarnations, the act of touring a site was linked with cultural betterment and self improvement. When the verb "tour" and the noun "tourist" came into the English language in the mid-seventeenth century, a tourist was defined as "one who travels for pleasure or culture, visiting a number of places for their objects of interest, scenery, or the like" (Shaffer 2001, 11). Initial attempts at tourism were not, however, explicitly linked to expressing one's affiliation with or membership within a nation-state. English tourists in the mid-seventeenth century instead used it to assert their class position in society. At this time, tourism involved gazing upon nature and observing landscapes. Middle- and upper-class English tourists demonstrated their social standing and exhibited their knowledge of tourist practices by identifying elements in natural landscapes that represented the "sublime, the beautiful, and the picturesque" (12). Grand Tours across Europe involved observing these elements in the landscapes, which were supposed to evoke enjoyment and personal enlightenment among tourists. One's competency of these terms and their ability to recite them to describe the natural environment was read by other tourists on the Grand Tour as evidence of their affluence and cultural competency.

When it crossed the Atlantic, tourism conveyed a very different message. While those who first engaged in the practice in the late 1790s were affluent, the American version of the European Grand Tour was not merely about personal fulfillment or performing one's class status. American tourism celebrated America's greatness and was a vehicle for patriotism among American citizens. Early tourist sites such as Saratoga Springs, the Catskill Mountains, the White Mountains, Sulphur Springs, and Niagara Falls opened in the 1820s and became part of what was marketed as the American Grand Tour. These sites capitalized on European ideas of nature to entice tourists and prevent them from traveling to Britain (Brown 1995, 18). Tourists pilgrimaged to these sites at a time when Americans still needed confirmation that God ordained their separation from Britain's rule. On the West Coast, towering rock formations and waterfalls of Yosemite and gushing geysers of Yellowstone provided visual confirmation of the United States' greatness (Sears 1989, 6). Visiting early-American tourist sites allowed individuals to both "stake a claim in elite society" by harboring elite-controlled knowledge of sites as well as emphasize the distinctive character and supposedly superior quality of American landscapes and American culture (Brown 1995, 5).

The association of tourism with performing American citizenship was made more explicit during the Progressive Era when vacationing was proposed as an answer to increasing blue-collar workers' productivity on the job (Aron 1999, 191). In the 1910s and 1920s social reformers, social scientists, and businessmen agreed that the working class needed vacations to become better employees. The same argument was made for poor and destitute women and children. Lower-class women were transported from the hot, crowded, and polluted streets of big, urban cities to quaint, cooler countryside homes run by middle- and upper-class female reformers. Reformers saw it as their moral duty to protect lower-class women, arguing that "female workers were more delicate and frail than their male counterparts and that, as potential mothers, they needed and deserved special provisions, protection, and services" (188).

The recommended vacation for lower-class women and their families did not mirror that of a typical middle- or upper-class Anglo-American tourist. Rather, working-class women found their vacations to be more work than pleasure, with reformers teaching them how to be "an efficient and productive workforce" (Aron 1999, 201). One settlement house operated a vacation facility on Lake Michigan for working-class children. There, reformers taught girls and boys gender-specific behaviors, with the former learning how to care for the home and the latter learning how to perform ground maintenance work for the camp (187). These lessons aimed to siphon lower-class children into blue-collar professions while at the same time imparting a middle-class set of values and behaviors required to work for the middle classes.

Although tourism opportunities expanded for stigmatized groups during the Progressive Era, some groups were still excluded from partaking in the ritual of tourism. Prevented from performing their citizenship duties, groups excluded based on their ethnicity or race received the message that they were second-class citizens. African Americans and Jews who wished to travel found themselves banned from hotels or forbidden from staying in the same buildings as white tourists. In response, they built their own places of leisure.

Prevented from visiting and staying at Catskill mountain resorts outside of New York, the Jewish community constructed the Park Inn and Fleischer Hotel for individuals of Jewish heritage. Although the facilities were considered low-end by Catskill resort standards, they provided the environment needed to unite and grow an ethnic group regularly excluded from equal treatment in urban and rural America. The Catskills became "a place where Jews could celebrate who and what they were and what they had become, where they could take pride in their accomplishments, and that proclaimed their cultural power" (O'Donovan 2011, 277). African Americans did the same, opting to build and operate hotels in popular white tourist places such as Atlantic City, Cape May, and Niagara Falls (Aron 1999, 158). In these places African Americans could enjoy the sights and locales of whites during the daytime while retiring to all-black lodging in the evening without "fear of discrimination" (214). By fighting for and occupying spaces where they were once forbidden, Jewish and African American communities exercised the rights promised to them as American citizens, including the right to tour.

Tourism in the western United States, especially in California, played a formative role in the minds of white tourists. Marketed as "wonderlands for whiteness" (Wrobel 2002, 176), tourist sites in Southern California drew upon booster rhetoric and widely accepted American discourses regarding the fate of the West. Californian attractions, such as MLRR, relegated the West's diverse peoples and history to a thing of the past, instead choosing to highlight the technological achievements of Anglo-Americans. Undesirable ethnic groups who had occupied the prehistoric and historic West were depicted as a dying race, a group of people who would not play a part in the West's white future. Western boosters wove what a number of scholars have termed a "Spanish Fantasy Past" (Deverell 1997, 236), one that explained away the disappearance of Spaniards, Native Americans, and Mexican Americans as predestined (Deverell and Flamming 1999, 120; Wrobel 2002; Deverell 2004; DeLyser 2003; Kropp 2006). As the master narrative went, "genetic and racial primacy, Yankee entrepreneurism, and the master plan of Manifest Destiny" were to blame for the failure of these ethnic and racial groups to persist, not the American colonization of the western frontier (Deverell 1997, 236).

Replacing the region's history of diverse peoples was a past that romanticized the yesteryears of California, emphasizing and falsely painting its Spanish-colonial period as an idyllic, pastoral time when Native Americans and the Spaniards coexisted in peace and harmony (McWilliams 1973; Deverell 2004). Tourist attractions, such as Southern California playwright John Steven McGroarty's "The Mission Play," reappropriated the region's Spanish heritage to further the white belief that they were destined to own and dominate western landscapes (Sánchez 1993, 71). McGroarty's play orchestrated a story that attributed the "disappearance of Native Californios, the Spaniards, and Mexican Americans" to "natural selection, an idea substantiated by anthropologists of the time" (Camp 2011b, 283). The play stands as a prime example of what Sánchez "calls the 'mission myth,'" an ideology created to diminish and eventually erase from memory the region's "Mexican heritage" and Mexican present (Sánchez 1993, 71).

Southern California's MLRR similarly reinscribed its western landscape with a tale that privileged white accomplishments and the destruction of western ethnic groups, wildlife, and the environment in the name of "American progress." Like other attempts to wipe the West's slate clean of its undesirable ethnic heritage, MLRR provided lessons on the proper citizenry of the nation. The resort did so by socially marginalizing those deemed unfit for full citizenship privileges, whether tourists or workers. As a result, the resort enticed whites to migrate West, to a landscape depicted by boosters as far away from the crowded, busy, and multiethnic eastern cities (McWilliams 1973, 143). MLRR's reimagining of Southern California's landscape, peoples, and history left a lasting impression on the region, a place that remains internationally known for its attractions (e.g., Disneyland, Sea World, and Knott's Berry Farm) rather than the diverse peoples who occupied its past and currently occupy it in the present.

Case Study: Mount Lowe Resort and Railway

California's MLRR was one of the most popular tourist attractions in the late-nineteenth- and early-twentieth-century western United States, and, "after San Francisco and Los Angeles, probably the most recognizable geographic name in the state" (Seims 1992). Located in Angeles National Forest just above Altadena, California (map 3.1 and fig. 3.1), MLRR featured four large hotels (fig. 3.2), a zoo, a bowling alley, a post office, a miniature golf course, a fox farm, an observatory with a full-time astronomer, the world's largest searchlight, and an extensive railway system that included one of the world's steepest railway inclines at the time (Hoehling

Map 3.1. Location of Mount Lowe Resort and Railway.

Figure 3.1. Mount Lowe Resort and Railway prior to the destruction of Lowe Observatory (*right*) and Echo Mountain House (*left*), no date. Image courtesy of the Los Angeles Public Library Photo Collection.

Figure 3.2. Echo Mountain House, date unknown. Image courtesy of the Los Angeles Public Library Photo Collection.

1958; Manning 2005; Robinson 1977; Seims 1976; Zack 2004: 81). It lured visitors from far and wide, as evidenced by postcards mailed to Asia and Europe that today sit in archives associated with the site. In total, more than three million tourists visited MLRR during its years of operation.

The resort was built in the early 1890s and opened for business in 1893 by Thaddeus Lowe, a wealthy inventor who gave himself the title "Professor." Lowe has been extensively studied (Hoehling 1958; Manning 2005; Robinson 1977; Seims 1976, 1992, 1999) because he was the first man to suggest and then use a gas air balloon to spy on the South during the Civil War (Manning 2005). He made a substantial fortune by inventing one of the first ice-making machines, and he authored and held a number of patents, all of which helped fund construction on MLRR. Lowe's vision was too lofty for his pocketbooks, however, resulting in his bankruptcy and the transfer of MLRR to Valentine Peyton for $190,000. Peyton then sold the resort to the Pacific Electric Railway Corporation (PERC), which continued to operate it as a tourist attraction.

Research on MLRR commenced in 2004 when a collaborative partnership was formed between Angeles National Forest and Stanford University's Department of Anthropology. The research later became known as the Mount Lowe Archaeology Project and involved two consecutive archaeological field seasons held in 2005 and 2006 (Camp 2009). Initially, the goals were to recover data from two sites located at the resort's worker housing: one area that was occupied by railway workers of Mexican heritage and the other occupied by Anglo-American railway workers. The intention of this methodology was to compare the treatment and consumption patterns of workers of different racial and class standings. Unfortunately, the site associated with Anglo-American workers had been cleared to make way for a picnic area, resulting in the recovery of very few artifacts. As a consequence, intrasite comparison could not be performed.

However, the data recovered from a household associated with the resort's Mexican immigrant railway workers was rich in quality and quantity. Furthermore, as was discovered during archival research performed between 2004 and 2009, this site is also the only known household associated with PERC's Americanization movement to be excavated in the western United States. PERC developed this program to teach its workers of Mexican heritage about "proper" ways of "American" living as defined by middle- and upper-class Anglo-American women hired by the company to work as reformers and teachers. Data recovered from this household yields significant insight into how Mexican immigrant workers felt about citizenship; was it something to which they aspired or was it something they had little interest in securing? This movement and the archaeological remnants recovered from the household associated with it will be discussed in further detail in chapter 4.

Before moving on to the results of this archaeological and archival research, it is crucial to understand how tourists experienced the landscape. The resort's amenities, layout, and attractions offer information into how PERC envisioned the relationship between tourists and workers. By drawing upon historic photographs, maps, documents, and other ephemera related to the resort, I consider the lessons tourists were taught as they moved about and traveled through the space of MLRR. The next chapter then investigates how workers experienced the landscape in ways that dramatically departed from the experience of tourists. Importantly, I employ a diachronic approach to considering how the landscape of the resort and its offerings changed over time. I link these changes to broader social ideologies circulating among the American public regarding the proper constitution of their nation's citizenry.

Destroying Nature and Praising Technology, 1870–1910

Unlike late-seventeenth- and eighteenth-century tourism on the East Coast where the practice communicated a national identity separate from England, late-nineteenth- and early-twentieth-century travel to the West conveyed an altogether different message. Leisure and recreation on the East Coast was no longer viewed as a meaningful symbol of American ingenuity and nationality. The forced removal of Native Americans from the West required that Americans author a narrative to explain away the violence and terror that colonization incurred. The ideology of "Manifest Destiny" served this purpose, which posited that Anglo-Americans were a "separate, innately superior people who were destined to bring good government, commercial prosperity, and Christianity to the American continents and to the world" (Horsman 1981, 1–2). This philosophy held that Anglo-Americans in particular were "a superior race" while non-white, "inferior races were doomed to subordinate status or extinction" (1–2).

Transcontinental travel was "understood as an extension" of the doctrine of Manifest Destiny (Rothman 1998, 23; Shaffer 2001, 20), drawing clear lines between Anglo-Americans and travelers of other ethnicities and racial groups. The acquisition of California from Mexico in 1848 bolstered Anglo-Americans' faith in their God-given right to the North American continent. Deverell explains this train of thought: "The 1846–48 war against the Republic of Mexico—a nasty, brutal affair—drove home Manifest Destiny's darkest assumption that racial and national supremacy went hand in glove" (2004, 12). California was both "geographically and psychologically" the "ultimate frontier," and travel to the state became a part of the "American Dream" (Starr 1973, 46; Jakle 1985, 244). As famed western historian Frederick Jackson Turner proclaimed in 1893, the year MLRR first opened, "The true point of view in the history of this nation is not the Atlantic coast, it is the Great West" (Turner 1992).

The West's wilderness and its creatures sat in the way of easterners' occupation of the frontier. Depicted as "a moral vacuum, a cursed and chaotic wasteland," the "wilderness was the villain" and "the pioneer, as hero, relished its destruction" (Nash 1967, 24). Tourists especially feared bears and mountain lions. To pave the way for tourists, then, wildlife in Southern California was exterminated en masse. Grizzly bears, whose image adorns the California state flag, were trapped and killed in Angeles National Forest—where MLRR was located—and the San Bernardino National Forest. So many bears were slaughtered, in fact, that an entire "distinctive California subspecies" became extinct (Davis 1998, 218).

Tourists were encouraged to engage in wildlife extermination campaigns that allowed them to reenact the "taming" of the western frontier. The mountain ranges engulfing MLRR were "regarded as a local frontier" (Vernon 1952, 116) where frontier fantasies could be acted out. Carefully selected caged animals were placed on exhibit in the resort's "Menagerie of Native Animals" (James 1894), animals that might compromise their visitors' well-being. These animals included bears, civet cats, raccoons, and other animals local to the San Gabriel Mountains (Seims 1992, 7). In the mountain ranges surrounding the resort, trout were dynamited by the ton by commercial fisherman while deer, lizards, and tarantulas were killed and sold to tourists as souvenirs (Davis 1998, 220–21). Capturing, displaying, and selling these animals assured tourists at the resort that the forest was no longer "wild" but instead captive to human desires.

Other neighboring resorts, such as Santa Catalina Island, gave tourists the opportunity to reenact the mythical heroism of the frontier's earliest

Figure 3.3. Children "riding" fish at Santa Catalina Island, 1901. Image courtesy of the Archives, Pasadena Museum of History.

days in a safe, leisurely setting; these activities included sport fishing, cattle hunting, and quail and wild goat shooting (Culver 2004, 101; *Pasadena Daily Evening Star* 1895a; *Pasadena Daily Evening Star* 1895b; *Pasadena Daily Evening Star* 1895c). These activities reassured tourists that western landscapes were no longer exotic and dangerous but instead controlled by humans and scientific interests. A photograph dating to 1901 discovered in a tourist's scrapbook reveals these attitudes (fig. 3.3). It depicts two children "riding" fish on Santa Catalina Island as an amusement, fish that were perhaps killed for the sake of the photograph. One might write off this photograph as an oddity at the most, but it makes ideological sense when understood as a spectacle of western expansionism and imperialism.

The theme of man's dominance over nature figured prominently in the resort's marketing materials and attractions. A bear pit, for instance, where resort employees, including public relations manager and well-known booster George Wharton James, play-wrestled a real living and breathing bear, intrigued MLRR tourists. Bear pits were common in late-nineteenth- and early-twentieth-century zoos and resorts in the West because the bear, an animal that "had long been associated with fear, the woods, and aristocratic hunting privileges" (Rothfels 2002, 22), stood as a visual symbol of humankind's command over the West's wild and untrammeled frontier.

On MLRR's property also stood a fox farm. Although operated independent of MLRR, the fox farm was only accessible by the resort's railway and therefore catered solely to MLRR's visitors. At the farm, visitors could view more than two hundred captive foxes. Visitors could choose a fox to be skinned, which would then be turned into a fur coat or boa, the latter being popular garments of well-to-do women (Owen 1961; *Los Angeles Times* 1891; *Pasadena Daily Evening Star* 1895d). As promotional literature from the farm suggests, some visitors were frightened of foxes. Their safety was promised by fox farm owners who wrote, "The foxes grown on farms are not like wild animals any more. For many generations they have been reared in captivity and so they are tame enough and look for their victuals regularly served instead of prowling around somebody's hen roost" (*Los Angeles Times* 1891).

Although animals were certainly a focal point at the resort, its real claim to fame was its technological achievements and scientific advancements. To access one of the resort's four hotels in Los Angeles's San Gabriel Mountains, tourists boarded MLRR's "Incline Railway" at the base of Echo Mountain in Altadena, California, or at one of the many transfer stations along the PERC's interurban line. The 59 percent grade of MLRR's Incline Railway set a world record, and its supporting cable, which was "one and one-half inches thick" and weighed "more than six tons," was powered by electricity, "the first ever of its kind in history" (Will H. Thrall Collection). This line was accessible from nearly all of the PERC's stops in Los Angeles.

From the day it opened until around 1910, the Incline Railway was the most commonly featured image on the resort's promotional materials and weekly newsletters (fig. 3.4) (Pacific Electric Railway 1903a, 1903b, 1910a, 1910b). The elevation of the resort's hotels and attractions—a height only attainable via the railway—was detailed on nearly every form of ephemera put out by the resort during this time period. MLRR's railway conductor also reiterated mundane, exacting details about the railway's mechanical marvels. Winthrop H. Owen, a railway conductor who worked for the resort, recalled the scripted narrative that he was instructed to recite while taking tourists up to the resort: "Now we approach Horse Shoe Curve. It is a 120 degree curve, which means that for each 100 feet of the

Figure 3.4. Photograph at the top of Mount Lowe's Incline, 1905. Note the signage to the right that states the elevations of one of the resort's hotels, Ye Alpine Tavern. Image courtesy of the Archives, Pasadena Museum of History.

curve, we pass around 120 degrees or 1/3 of a circle" (1961). Brochures similarly praised the Incline Railway as one of the most powerful displays of Americans' triumph over the natural world and the West. One 1903 brochure exuberantly explained, "This [Incline Railway] great product of science and genius, seems at first an impossible fact, but as we ascend and seemingly leave the earth a broader and better view of the valley, the cities, and the achievements of science and the glorious scenes about us" (Pacific Electric Railway 1903b). Tourists readily adopted this language, describing the railway in the same terms on the backs of postcards. On a 1909 postcard depicting Mt. Lowe's Circular Bridge, "Mother" writes, "I am up here in the clouds. We came up this afternoon going back at 4:30. It is 3,000 ft high . . . I wasn't scared."

Two additional technological feats lured tourists to MLRR: the Lowe Observatory and a searchlight acquired by Thaddeus Lowe at the 1893 World's Columbian Exposition in Chicago (Seims 1976, 80). Famous for its "3,000,000 candle power" that made its "beam of light . . . so powerful that a newspaper" could be read from thirty-five miles away (James 1904, 47), the searchlight was used by MLRR's tourists and employees to spy on outlying communities below the mountain and on Santa Catalina Island's tourist activities as well. The Lowe Observatory was another ocular device overseen by astronomers Dr. Lewis Swift and Dr. Edgar Larkin (James, 1894; James 1904, 35). Costing more than fifty thousand dollars in parts alone, the Lowe Observatory gave tourists an otherworldly experience by allowing them to gaze into the sky and observe and locate stars and planets in the solar system. Likewise, Santa Catalina Island's "glass-bottom boats" used to view the island's underwater resources were heralded as great technological accomplishments. These boats drew millions of tourists to the island and "proved to be among the most popular attractions on the island and perhaps the best-known beyond Southern California" (Culver 2004, 112).

To Americans, the invention and possession of these technologies was proof that their nation was at the "apex of an evolutionary framework" because "only the most advanced societies had electrified machines and lighting" (Nye 1990, 35–36). The railroad itself was a potent icon of western expansion and American imperialism; with the sounding of the railroad's roar, people from the eastern United States made their way to, settled in, and brutally destroyed the West. Once the West was occupied, however, American sentiments shifted, prompting dramatic changes in the practice of tourism.

Nature and Nostalgia, 1910–1940

By 1910 the frontier was no longer viewed by Anglo-Americans as a dangerous terrain wrought with aggressive wildlife and social strife. With the frontier's wildlife eradicated and its ethnic heritage erased or romanticized, tourists were instructed to gaze nostalgically upon the landscapes, animals, resources, and peoples that westward expansion had ameliorated. Renato Rosaldo has termed this backward-looking, Janus-faced longing as "imperialist nostalgia," one that "uses a pose of 'innocent yearning' both to capture people's imaginations and to conceal its complicity with often brutal domination" (Rosaldo 1989, 108). It was only after MLRR's wildlife had been captured and imprisoned in its menagerie and its railroad had carved a permanent pathway into the natural landscape still visible today that tourists and resort owners started to express a desire to recapture that which was destroyed in the process of building MLRR.

This sentiment was not only apparent at the resort or in the region; it was also expressed on a national level, arising at a time when the once-open western frontier was subsumed by development and urbanization and its native peoples displaced, forcibly removed, or murdered. The touring of "natural," "untouched" wilderness became popular, provoking theorists who studied this turn in western tourism to call this period the "Great Hiking Era." It was at this time that landscapes were designated "nature only" zones by the federal government as well as by states. California's first national parks—Sequoia, Yosemite, and Grant—were inaugurated in 1890, the same year Congress declared that the frontier was closed. The National Park Service was formed in 1916 and the United States Forest Service in 1905, with both organizations aimed at protecting, conserving, and managing "nature."

Not all elements of the former frontier were desired, though. In the name of nature preservation, efforts to recoup the wide, open, and un-peopled landscapes of the frontier and the persecution of Native Americans continued. At Yellowstone National Park, the U.S. Army chased the park's Native American inhabitants off of what was once their ancestral homeland but what was now federally owned land. "Stone boundary

markers" placed "every half mile along Yellowstone's perimeter" by surveyors reminded Native Americans that they were no longer welcome in
the park (Jacoby 2001, 107). Native Americans were also removed from
their native land when Yosemite became a federally owned national park.
Their presence, park officials argued, jeopardized the image of the park
as a nature preserve (Spence 1999). Native Americans who wished to remain in Yosemite, Glacier, and Yellowstone National Parks were painted
as "trespassers" or criminalized by park and military officials brought in
by the U.S. government to "protect" America's precious resources (Grusin
2004; Jacoby 2001). Native Americans' continued presence and use of the
land "seemed only to demonstrate a marked inability to appreciate natural
beauty" to Anglo-Americans (Spence 1999, 4).

During the Progressive Era, social reformers, politicians, and religious
leaders lambasted industrialization, blaming it for all of the country's
problems. Nature was seen as a place devoid of all of these issues. Millions of Americans headed out to campsites and hiking trails in the hope
that they could somehow reclaim their "nature," "essence," or health that
had been compromised by long work hours and polluted industrialized
cities. MLRR immediately lost its appeal during this phase of American
tourism. Once prized for its technological feats, MLRR was now viewed
as having a hand in the diminishment of America's natural resources. Fueled by the burgeoning conservation movement of the time, tourists now
sought wide, open, untouched, "natural"-looking landscapes, landscapes
that, in MLRR's case, had been destroyed to make way for its abundant
attractions, luxurious hotels, and an expansive railway system.

Numerous work orders, construction blueprints, and renovation pro-
posals from this era document the resort's desperate attempts to modernize its buildings and attractions to suit the new tourist ethic. These records
reveal the resort's intentions to keep up with current tourist expectations
that were contoured by the nature conservation movement. Attractions
that no longer appealed to tourist sentimentalities were abandoned. The
once-famed Incline Railway that had been the centerpiece in nearly every
promotional handout from the resort was now curiously downplayed in
marketing materials and advertisements. Gone, too, were the Lowe Observatory and the World's Fair searchlight.

In their place were animals and landscapes. In a 1913 brochure, for instance, tourists observe frolicking deer, animals that had once been hunted

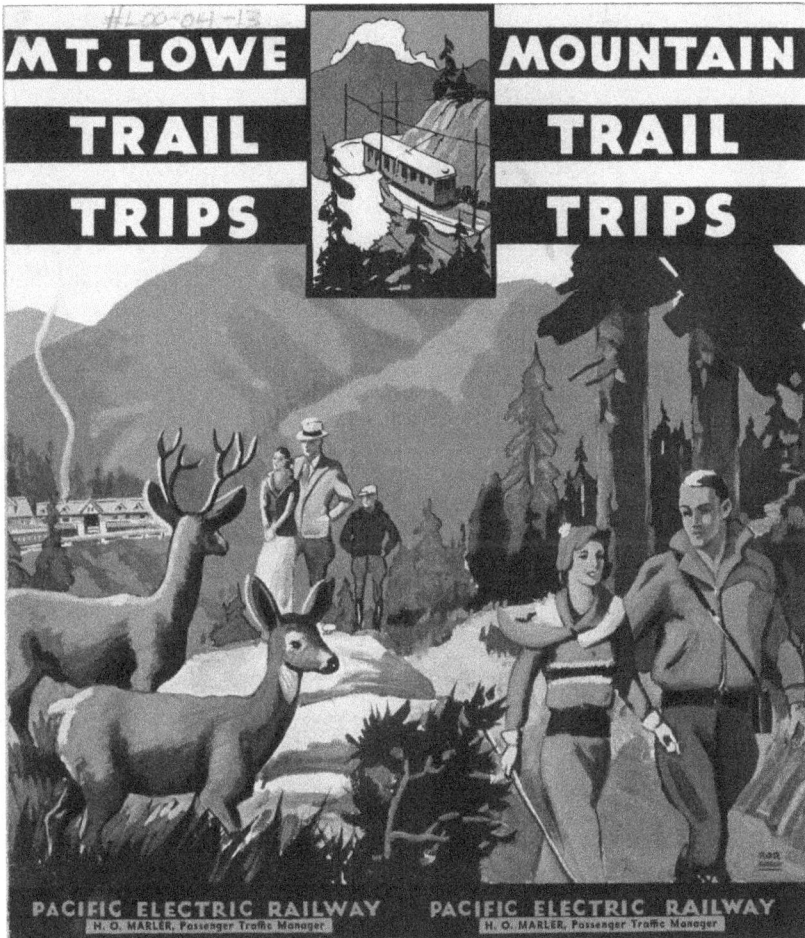

Figure 3.5. Mount Lowe Resort and Railway brochure with deer in the foreground, 1913. The Incline Railway and Lowe Observatory are absent. Image courtesy of the Archives, Pasadena Museum of History.

down and served for dinner at the resort (fig. 3.5). Titled "Mt. Lowe Trail Trips—Mountain Trail Trips," the brochure highlights the natural resources surrounding the resort as well as dozens of hiking trails where tourists could see "magnificent views of rugged" landscapes and witness the untouched "grandeur" of nature. The cover of a March 5, 1922, edition of the *Mount Lowe Daily News*, a souvenir newspaper handed out to tourists visiting the resort, depicts a woman hiking near MLRR with the text, "To the Portals of Hiker's Land via Pacific Electric Railway" (PERC 1922).

Advertisements in local newspapers now used the moniker "Mount Lowe Resort: Ye Alpine Tavern and Cottages," focusing on everything but the resort's once-renowned attractions. Details on the railway, its grade, and the resort's elevation that had previously showered the resort's marketing materials were replaced with images of nature (Camp 2009). The railway was now seen as merely a vehicle used to access nature, not conquer it.

Because of this, the resort owners worked hard to divert tourists' attention away from the attraction's former selling points. To do so, they provided a narrative for the entire tourist experience, instructing tourists what to view and giving them the vocabulary and language necessary to describe these views. In MLRR's earlier heyday, the Incline Railway was one of the primary highlights of a tourist's trip. Tourists would board the Incline at the base of Echo Mountain and ride it to the mountain's peak. This trip, for many tourists, was the only attraction they had traveled to experience. The peak of Echo Mountain was where the tourist experience began. As a June 6, 1936, brochure explained, "At the crest of Echo Mountain you alight from the cable car. Here begins perhaps the most exciting and thrilling part of the trip. For three and a half miles, an open car, built especially to afford an obstructed view in all directions, winds in and around ravines and cliffs and crags . . . slowly making its way through shady forests of towering evergreens. . . . Hospitable Mt. Lowe Tavern, picturesque and spacious, welcomes you at the end of your journey" (PERC 1936). From Echo Mountain, tourists would travel to Ye Alpine Tavern on Mount Lowe, a landscape tucked deep into the heart of the San Gabriel Mountains. To divert tourists' attention away from the Incline Railway, brochures and promotional books composed by the company and handed out to tourists described mundane details about the nature surrounding them. Tourists would presumably read these materials on their way up to Ye Alpine Tavern. The railway conductor would also provide a narrative that reinforced what tourists should be examining. Directing tourists' views was therefore done to obstruct and cancel out the old, undesirable elements of the resort's landscapes.

Horse and burro rides, which had once been used by tourists to explore and reenact the exploration of the western frontier in the forest encompassing MLRR, were now seen as inhumane and were discontinued on March 1, 1935 (PERC Collection WO #35002). Trash that visitors and employees had once casually tossed off the side of railway cars was now systematically collected and removed from the "pristine" natural landscape around the railroad. Tourists well versed in the environmentalist movement sweeping across the nation were quick to point out rubbish that had been missed during routine trash pick-ups (PERC Collection WO #26270).

Given the drastic drop in the number of visitors to the resort in its later years, it appears as though tourists struggled to reconcile the resort's former history with its more modern efforts to be a destination for nature tourism. Marketing the resort to meet new tourist sensibilities was complicated by the presence of the train—the instrument that destroyed much of the West's natural landscape—that tourists had to board to reach the resort's hotels and attractions. In a last-ditch effort to resuscitate the resort, the PERC gave up their intentions to make it more "nature-friendly" and instead marketed it as an upscale urban resort despite its location in the forest. An abundant amount of both fulfilled and unfulfilled work orders at the resort from this period show that its owners did everything in their power to rebrand their resort, even if it meant giving up its appeal to tourists seeking "nature" (*Los Angeles Times* 1924; PERC Collection WO #35002, WO #26270, WO #10730, WO #15487, WO #17089, WO #24156, WO #24898, WO #24157, WO #26467, WO #30489). These attempts failed as well, with the resort closing for business after a fire ravaged its biggest hotel, Ye Alpine Tavern, in 1936.

Directing tourists to gaze upon nature may seem a somewhat innocuous practice. But this attempt to exclude some of the resort's aging technologies from view—technologies that no longer aligned well with tourist expectations and demands—also conveyed messages about the citizenship standing of people who were living in the resort's "natural" landscape. Living in plain view of tourists were some of the resort's workers while other employees were kept out of sight. As I will argue in the next chapter, the layout of the resort's worker housing reveals that workers of marginal ethnicities, races, and genders were unable to escape tourists' line of sight. Their lives, their homes, and their families became part of the attraction for tourists to consume and for their employers to police. Placing marginalized groups in parts of the resort marketed as "nature" zones was a not-so-subtle nod to late-nineteenth- and early-twentieth-century anthropological discourses that argued that racially and socially inferior groups were closer to nature and lower on the evolutionary pyramid of humankind. Liminal workers also found that job placement and advancement was conditional, limited to the few workers who physically and culturally resembled the "ideal" Anglo-American citizen.

Summary

From sanctioning and encouraging tourists to mimic Eastern expansion into the western frontier to then expecting tourists to nostalgically reflect upon this process, the advent and evolution of American tourism served to reinforce notions of cultural and social difference between groups of Americans, further splintering interclass and interracial unions. A photograph from the resort's "White Chariot," a train car that took tourists up to the resort, captures this process of social segregation (fig. 3.6). In figure 3.6, we see that the White Chariot's seating arrangements appears to mirror commonly understood divisions between class and racial groups. In the first top row of the White Chariot sits Anglo-American tourists who are encased in a glass-paneled box that shields them from the heat and

Figure 3.6. White Chariot railway car heading up Echo Mountain's famous Incline Railway. Image courtesy of Paul Ayers.

elements of the natural environment. The next row of tourists is exposed to the outdoors, with the railway car's conductor standing to the side of them. Seated Anglo-American tourists occupy the third and last row of actual seats. And on the last partition of the White Chariot—a place for tourists' luggage—sits several people who are presumably the resort's Mexican immigrant employees, including one of the employee's children. They sit on top of the tourists' luggage, likely charged with the task of carrying it to the tourists' rooms. The White Chariot's segmentation of people based on their racial categorization and class standing echoes the way in which the resort treated its workers. This is merely one of the many instances in which notions of social difference were etched into MLRR's landscape and present in its materiality, giving insight into how citizenship privileges fractured along cultural, class, gender, and racial lines.

4

....

The Archaeology of Citizenship

While tourists were riding the Incline Railway; hiking in the lush, green canyons embracing the resort; and playing astronomer while peering into the Lowe Observatory's magnificent magnifying lens, the resort's workers were repairing and maintaining the railroad, cleaning guest rooms, and burning piles of waste and trash in the resort's incinerators. As the end of the day neared, Mount Lowe's tourists would head back to and rest comfortably in their clean, Craftsman-style cabins and rooms while the resort's railroad workers of Mexican heritage would retire to a mountain far from the tourists where they would share a hot, cramped household with two to three families of similar ethnicity. In the morning the workers would awake and return to work, repairing tracks in a pit located above their homestead and burning the tourists' trash in incinerators that the resort owners strategically placed next to the laborers' home. At the same time, tourists passed overhead on the railroad train and observed the Mexican immigrants' work and activities from above. Placed in a "section house"—a phrase used by railroad companies to refer to houses where workers who repaired "sections" of the railway lived, Mount Lowe's Mexican immigrant workers were situated in a visible, panoptic landscape that allowed every action and behavior to be monitored by their employers and tourists traveling on the railway above their homestead. This surveillance was not limited to activities performed on the public, exterior landscape of the section house, which were witnessed by tourists and managers at the resort. The railway workers' indoor and private lives were also placed under intense surveillance by reformers and inspectors hired by the resort.

This chapter examines several competing processes of citizen-making at work at Mount Lowe. The resort's reformers and owners held conflicting beliefs about Mexican immigrants, selecting material culture and imparting behaviors they saw as fitting of a Mexican immigrant living in American society and working at the resort. The reformers, who were typically young, single Anglo-American women who worked as volunteers, also engaged in voluntary reform with the hope of securing pay for their work, respect outside of the domestic sphere of the home (Camp 2012, 2011c), and to be considered equal citizens and counterparts to men. At the same time, Mexican immigrants voiced their own beliefs about citizenship in songs and in oral histories collected from this region, commentaries that often ran counter to the expectations of Mount Lowe's reformers.

This chapter looks at how these competing discourses and tensions about consumption and citizenship were expressed materially at the resort. I begin by reviewing the scope and intentions behind Mount Lowe's Americanization program and the reformers who carried it out. I also explore the reformers' citizenship aspirations and how such aspirations determined their willingness to see Mexican immigrants as fellow American citizens. Finally, I turn to archaeological data recovered from Mount Lowe's railway workers' household as well as associated documentary and oral history resources to assess how workers responded to their company's definition of what it meant to be a Mexican American citizen.

Reform at Mount Lowe Resort and Railway

When thousands of Mexican immigrants entered the United States during the early 1900s, Americanization instruction was proposed as a solution to quell cultural diversity and reinforce Anglo-American hegemony (McClymer 1991; Barrett 1992; Sánchez 1994; Van Nuys 2002; González 2004). The Pacific Electric Railway Corporation (PERC) contributed to this racial panic by hiring female teachers, camp managers, nurses, and reformers to impart American "ways" to its employees of Mexican descent (Camp 2012; Lewthwaite 2007). The PERC's Americanization program was designed to, in their own words, "educate these immigrants in cleanliness and right living" so that they could "become good American citizens" (PERC 1928). Becoming a "good citizen" in early-twentieth-century America meant consuming the right products, having a tidy and properly decorated home that emulated middle-class fashion sensibilities, eating "American" foods, and wearing American fashions. Toward this end,

PERC claimed to provide training in "English, reading, writing, domestic science, thrift, economy, and marketing" (Elliott 1918, 152).

To ensure compliance with Americanization efforts, PERC's staff policed and inspected its employees' homes as well as provided demeaning demonstrations on "proper" bathing and bed-making (Carr 1919, 1921). To encourage Mexican immigrants to adopt Americanization standards, model "American"-style homes were set up for them to emulate (PERC 1928). Mexican immigrants who chose to follow company policies were granted "special" privileges. For example, women and children whose households met a "certain standard of cleanliness each week" were "rewarded with free passes to Los Angeles for shopping and pleasure trips" (Elliott 1918, 152). Prizes were also awarded to "those women who had learned the most English and finished the greatest number of blocks for their quilts" (Carr 1919). These privileges could be retracted if a woman or child disregarded Americanization standards. If employees or their family members were "careless about observing the rules," wrote PERC engineer Clifford Elliott, they were "disqualified from receiving any such free transportation" (1918, 152).

Some elements of the company's Americanization program initially appear innocuous, but other facets of it were racist in nature. First, PERC singled out its employees of Mexican heritage for Americanization instruction. All other employees were not subjected to such tutelage. Second, the types of instruction offered to Mexican immigrants suggest that Americanization instruction was geared toward replicating and reaffirming the existing class and racial structures of American society. The movement did so by limiting employees' training to domestic-, service- and trade-related skills, skills that constrained their ability to attain professional advancement. A last but equally important goal of Americanization at Mount Lowe was to teach Mexican immigrants proper consumer behavior, for as we learned earlier in this book, consumption was seen as quintessentially American. This was done by giving them matching improved whiteware for the table, clothing, and other material accoutrements found in contemporaneous lower- and middle-class Anglo-American households.

Reformers hired by PERC expressed mixed feelings about their work and their charges. Some blamed Mexican immigrants for their impoverished, downtrodden state rather than the companies who brought them across the U.S.-Mexico border and then paid them substandard wages. For example, Viva Carr, who worked as a reformer and nurse in charge of PERC's Americanization program, believed that individuals of Mexican heritage were intellectually and morally inferior to Anglo-Americans, an idea that was supported by the scientific racism of the time (Horsman 1981; Stocking 1987). In an article published in the company's monthly publication, *Pacific Electric Magazine*, Carr articulated this strain of racist thought by outlining the different "types" of Mexican employees she encountered in her reform work: "It is interesting to note the varying types of Mexican, as one travels from door to door, from camp to camp. The stupid, sullen Mexican of the lower type is our problem and a very discouraging problem it is. From this type on up we have many different grades, all more or less pliable, some naturally clean and some naturally dirty" (Carr 1921). Reflecting this ideology, she blamed the food choices of the company's Mexican immigrants rather than poverty on the high rate of infant mortality among the company's Mexican children, a strategy popular among Anglo-American reformers working in the region at that time (Molina 2006, 97). Discontent with the situation, Carr penned an article about it in the company's magazine, writing, "Under-nourished children are our greatest difficulty, for it is very hard to get the parents to see where the diet is at fault. If we succeed in this, they will tell us that they cannot buy the proper food, thus adding to our difficulties" (1921).

Other reformers were concerned by the poverty and inequality faced by their Mexican students and felt a "true affinity with immigrants since, like these new arrivals, they too were just beginning to gain full citizenship as equal voting members of society" (Garcia 2001, 66). Arletta Kelly, a teacher and reform instructor who worked in neighboring Southern California labor camps in the 1920s and 1930s, disagreed with popular racial thought, stating "you cannot convince me that they are any stupider than any of the others . . . and I used to maintain that so violently . . . that our I.Q. tests are never, were never fair to Mexican students. Because they [Mexican immigrants] just didn't have the vocabulary and the cultural background was entirely different from that. And all of our I.Q. tests were based on an Anglo background, an Anglo culture, and not a Latin culture" (Kelly n.d.). She was also quick to condemn the racism expressed by fellow reformers who worked alongside her. At a meeting held on the subject of reforming Mexican immigrants in Pomona, California, Kelly was offended by an elementary school teacher's comment that "Mexicans were so poor in arithmetic" (Kelly n.d.). She recounts the incident, explaining:

> I took him up on that. I said I didn't think they were. . . . And he said, but they're so slow. And I said, well you stop and think probably the last thing you learn when you learn a foreign language is to think numbers. I said they've got to stop and translate: six and six then becomes seis y seis. I mean it just takes two more steps to do it. And really, I think Mexicans as a whole are very good in math. And I said well, I think there's a problem of translation. (Kelly n.d.)

Why would women like Viva Carr join the Americanization movement when they held such strong convictions about the racial inferiority of the individuals for which they were responsible? And why would women like Arletta Kelly stay in the campaign when she was surrounded by people who did not share her belief that Mexican immigrants were equally as intelligent as Anglo-Americans? For women like Carr and Kelly living in early-twentieth-century America, working outside of the home and in what was typically considered a male-dominated space of the public sphere was a political act, with the very presence of women in work camps (even as volunteers) challenging the association of men with labor. Carr and Kelly voluntarily worked as reformers in an effort to achieve equal citizenship standing and "joined the Americanization movement because the fundamental question of that campaign, defining American citizenship, merged with the basic issue they sought to resolve: how to transform women's citizenship" (Gullet 1995, 72).

To gain access to a formerly all-male space and assert that women were best suited to take on public, labor-oriented work, female reformers recycled essentialist thought that asserted women were biologically predisposed to domestic work, such as raising children, taking care of their husbands, cooking, cleaning, decorating, and tending to the home (McClymer 1991, 4). They argued that jobs such as childcare, textile and clothing production, teaching, and professional cleaning should be left to women, since women were innately skilled at these tasks. By doing voluntary work for companies such as PERC, Carr and Kelly hoped to secure permanent, stable work for future generations of women. But, ironically, this involved claiming that others, such as the Mexican immigrants they were serving, were less deserving of professional work and were in need of Americanization instruction to become, in the words of Carr, "all better citizens" (1921). In the process of seeking their own freedom from the gender biases of their time that made them second-class citizens, reformers were denying such citizenship privileges to Mexican women who were taught by reformers to act as the "moral guardian" of the home (McBane 2006, 82) and expected to stay within its walls to, in the words of a 1918 PERC article, sew and cook (Elliott 1918, 152).

PERC publicized their Americanization work in regional newspapers and in their own publications. Like some of the reformers working for the company, PERC's motivations were fueled by self-interest. Part of the Americanization instruction was inspired by a "welfare capitalist" ethic (McClymer 1991), a logic that rationalized companies providing free provisions (such as housing, food, clothing, and other goods) as a means of maintaining an efficient, stable workforce that would benefit the company. The company's repeated discussions of their "charity" work with their employees of Mexican heritage in local newspapers and in publications were also an image-management tactic meant to downplay complaints filed by residents of towns where the company built its railway worker camps and by state health inspectors. A July 10, 1928, article subtly references this problem, writing, "Thriving communities did not look favorably upon the housing of these people within their city confines, and citizens of many communities exercised much effort to prevent their becoming established" (PERC 1928). In one instance, residents of the town of Alhambra, which was near Mount Lowe Resort and Railway, protested the construction of Pacific Electric's "Ramona Camp" for railway workers (PERC 1929). According to *Pacific Electric Magazine*, Alhambra residents changed their mind when the company landscaped the camp.

In 1927 the company launched a new public relations campaign where members of the public were invited to witness firsthand the company's supposed benevolent work that it was doing for its Mexican employees. PERC held the event to show how, in their words, "the company has given freely to build up these Mexican Camps to their present high standard and is justly proud of the results obtained" (PERC 1927). During the week long "open-house," visitors and tourists were accompanied by guides who elaborated upon "the methods employed in caring for the needs peculiar to such an establishment" (PERC 1927). This article also claimed that this particular "camp was pointed out as a model of cleanliness and well-kept surroundings that could well be patterned after" by a Pasadena city health inspector by the name of "Fox" (PERC 1927).

Public relations materials spoke of the clean, hygienic work camps that were neatly maintained by their Mexican workers who were well versed in such maintenance courtesy of Pacific Electric's Americanization instruction (fig. 4.1, fig. 4.2). But county and state health inspection records as well as oral histories collected from individuals living near or visiting railway workers' camps show that companies such as Pacific Electric failed to maintain sanitary environments in which their workers would labor and live. In some cases the company altogether ignored repeated requests from officials to modernize or sanitize their camps.

The company's failure to uphold the promises it made in official literature was noted by the reformers themselves. Carr made subtle reference to her dissatisfaction with the lack of reformers hired by Pacific Electric, which hindered Americanization goals and objectives and her ability to carry out the job. Equally evident in the following commentary is Carr's belief that her social work should be rewarded with pay, wages that male citizens performing similar labor would have received. As she writes, "It would be a dream to have a teacher for every camp, but as there is no remuneration for service rendered, it is difficult to obtain them" (1919). Two years later, it appears as though Carr's words went unnoticed, much to her chagrin. In a 1921 article, she wrote about the limited time she could devote to tutoring the company's Mexican employees in the English language, lamenting, "We would like to teach our people the English language, but time is limited and it is not possible to do so" (1921).

Articles published in the company's magazine also hinted at PERC's disinterest in investing time and money into their Americanization efforts. Nearly every November and December leading up to Christmas, the magazine made mention of an annual toy-, clothing-, and food-drive that they hosted to help their Mexican employees. A close reading of articles published after the Christmas holiday reveals that the proceeds and gifts donated to the company were not always dispensed to employees. In a 1925 edition of the magazine, a reformer writes that the 624 gifts collected in 1924 "were not distributed" to the families of Mexican employees because there were too many in need and "the supply" was too "limited" to accommodate them (PERC 1925). With the Great Depression on the horizon, it appears as though what little effort was expended on the

HOW COMPANY HAS AIDED MEXICAN WORKER

Types of quarters and surroundings, together with group of women and children residents, and a visiting nurse, at one of our Mexican Camps, of which there are twenty-two. Note the pleasant atmosphere and tidiness which prevails.

Above: Figure 4.1. Pacific Electric Railway Corporation article depicting Mexican immigrant children and section camps, 1928. Courtesy of PERC, Huntington Library, photo source unknown.

Left: Figure 4.2. Pacific Electric Railway Corporation article illustrating camp nurses and inspectors, 1921. Courtesy of PERC, Huntington Library, photo source unknown.

company's Americanization program was scaled back and now directed toward helping the company's middle-class Anglo-American management (Camp 2009, 2012).

The company's failure to live up to the promises made in promotional literature is also apparent in its hiring practices, in its placement of workers on the landscape, and in the goods that were discovered during excavations of the section house and its associated landscape.

Hiring Practices at Mount Lowe Resort and Railway

Although Mount Lowe Resort and Railway spanned hundreds of acres of forested land, tourist activity was contained and managed on two ecologically and culturally distinct landscapes. Echo Mountain was the first stop along the resort's railway line, which in its earlier years (1893–1905) was home to two hotels, an observatory, a zoo, tennis courts, and hiking trails. Mount Lowe became a focal point of tourist activity in 1895, when well-known architect Louis F. Kwiatkowski designed and constructed the C-shaped Craftsman-style Ye Alpine Tavern hotel for the resort (fig. 4.3). A few years after Ye Alpine Tavern was built, a miniature golf course and children's playground were added to the landscape to attract more tourists.

After two fires destroyed its hotels and a windstorm left its observatory roofless, Echo Mountain became a transfer station for tourists to board another train to visit Ye Alpine Tavern. Devoid of tourist attractions by 1905, Echo Mountain (see fig. 3.2) was used to house workers of marginal backgrounds. This reduced the amount of opportunities for marginal workers and tourists to interact and also guaranteed that workers on Mount Lowe and workers on Echo Mountain would not be able to socialize or regularly interact (Camp 2011b).

The section house (fig. 4.4) was built during January and February 1910 to house eight Mexican immigrant railway laborers and their families, costing the company only $533.03. Another railway laborer, Thomas J. Walsh, and the railroad foreman, James J. Goggins, shared a structure of similar size known as a "cottage" on historic maps. One explanation for why Walsh and Goggins were assigned better, larger housing is because of their ethnicity (see table 4.1). Both Walsh and Goggins were Irish, and although Irish immigrants were historically discriminated against in the United States, many eventually made what George Lipsitz terms a

Figure 4.3. Ye Alpine Tavern, date unknown. Image courtesy of the Los Angeles Public Library Photo Collection.

Figure 4.4. Only known photograph of the section house, with the section house in the far left corner of the image, Walsh and Goggins's "cottage" in the middle, and Lowe Observatory in the far right corner. Date unknown. Image courtesy of the Los Angeles Public Library Photo Collection.

Table 4.1. Employees at Echo Mountain

Census Date	Name	Naturalized?	What Year?
1910	James B. McNeil	Yes	1888
	Catherine Robertson	Unknown	—
	Dillivan M. Surker	N/A	—
	Joseph Thorson	N/A	—
	Henry J. Schlermann	No (emigrated in 1902)	—
	Rachel Schlermann	N/A	—
	Edgar L. Larkin	N/A	—
	Charles S. Lawrence	N/A	—
	Frederick Studer	Yes	1869
	William B. Wilsoy	N/A	—
	William H. Hoael	N/A	—
	James J. Goggins	N/A	—
	Thomas J. Walsh	N/A	—
	Pedros Tarios	No	—
	Francisco Gonzales	No	—
	Jose Gomez	No	—
	Garmon Navarro	No (emigrated ca. 1903)	—
	Antonio Acarta	No	—
1920	James J. Goggins	N/A	—
	Thomas J. Walsh	Yes	1888
	Pedro Hernandez	No (emigrated in 1912)	—
	Joseph Hernandez	No (emigrated in 1917)	—
	Sontenes Alba	No (emigrated in 1892)	—
	Angel Moreno	No (emigrated in 1919)	—
1930	Thomas J. Walsh	Unknown	—
	Vivian Alfred	N/A	—
	Jesus O. Villanueva	No (emigrated in 1925)	—
	Joe Marneo	Unknown	—

Place of Birth	Sex	Age	Ethnicity	Trade
Scotland	M	42	White	Dispatcher
Canada	F	57	White	Cook
Michigan	M	31	White	Conductor
Utah	M	23	White	Laborer
Germany	M	24	White	Carpenter
California	F	23	White	Cook
Illinois	M	63	White	Astronomer
Ohio	M	44	White	Photographer
Switzerland	M	44	White	Engineer
Delaware	M	37	White	Motorman
New York	M	31	White	Conductor
California	M	54	White	Section Foreman
New York	M	34	White	Laborer
Mexico	M	26	White	Laborer
Mexico	M	23	White	Laborer
Mexico	M	21	White	Laborer
Mexico	M	25	White	Laborer
Mexico	M	50	White	Laborer
California	M	65	White	Section Foreman
Ireland	M	44	White	Laborer
Mexico	M	23	White	Laborer
Mexico	M	26	White	Laborer
Mexico	M	45	White	Laborer
Mexico	M	22	White	Laborer
Ireland	M	54	White	Laborer
Texas	M	46	White	Foreman
Mexico	M	26	Mexican	Laborer
Texas	M	23	Mexican	Laborer

"possessive investment in whiteness" by asserting their rights as individuals with "white" colored skin to climb up the ladder of railway employment and to obtain better benefits (1998).

Segregating workers based on their ethnicity and naturalization status appears to have occurred across the macrolandscape of Mount Lowe Resort and Railway as well. Starting in 1910 the majority of workers, who tended to be naturalized Anglo-Americans, lived on Mount Lowe. By 1920 a total of twenty-six workers lived on Mount Lowe while only nine individuals resided on Echo Mountain (table 4.1). Most of the workers on Mount Lowe were single or divorced and lived in a large dormitory that resembled Ye Alpine Tavern, while married Mexican men and their families were recruited to live in the section house on Echo Mountain. Four married Mexican immigrant couples lived in the section house in 1910, four in 1920, and four in 1930. Only one single male Mexican immigrant worked on the railway at Echo Mountain in 1910, two single Mexican immigrants in 1920, and none in 1930.

PERC makes special mention of this hiring strategy in several publications, including a 1918 article that notes, "The Mexican is of a migratory nature, so that men with families have always been given preference over single men in employment. In addition, attractions have been provided constantly to hold them in service. The married Mexican is a lover of his home and environment" (Elliott 1918, 150). By recycling commonly held stereotypes about Mexicans that claimed they were migratory in nature and thus unstable when single, PERC masked the real reason behind selecting married Mexican men to live in the section house: if a man brought his entire family across the border to work for the company and was provided housing by a company, he was more hesitant to abandon his work for better pay elsewhere or return back to Mexico.

While census data from the section house's years of occupation (1910, 1920, and 1930) does not make mention of children living in the section house, a 1908 photograph taken of the section house residents documents six children dining under an ivy-lined veranda. The photograph of the "White Chariot" discussed in the previous chapter also provides visual evidence of children. Archaeological data in the form of miniature tea sets (fig. 4.5), marbles, and porcelain dolls (fig. 4.6) also verifies the presence of children on the section house landscape.

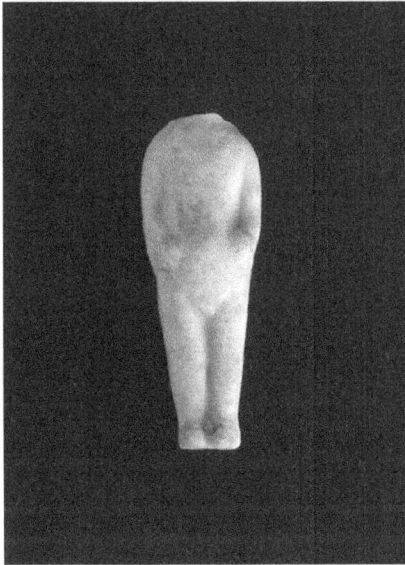

Above: Figure 4.5. Lid to a child's miniature porcelain tea set.

Left: Figure 4.6. Frozen Charlotte doll found during 2006 excavations of the section house.

Reform or Rhetoric? Sanitation in Worker Housing

Despite the fact that medically vulnerable infants and young children occupied the landscape, disparities existed between landscape maintenance
and types of sanitation at the "cottage" occupied by Irish railway workers
and in the "section house" occupied by Mexican railway laborers and their
families. In October 12, 1920, a work order made by the resort requested
that sanitary plumbing and a septic tank be installed in the section house
and in the cottage due to a complaint made by county health inspectors.
The request for the cottage was filled on August 21, 1921, while the request
for the section house went unacknowledged until 1928. Besides their lack
of sanitary plumbing, the section house residents also found themselves
placed next to the two incinerators that burned all of the resort's trash,
and were situated next to a pigpen. Between the 1920s and 1930s Mexican and Irish Americans became the only employees to be housed on
the isolated and desolate Echo Mountain. The resort closed for business
in 1938 when a fire ravaged Ye Alpine Tavern and burned it down to its
foundation.

California Commission on Immigration and Housing inspection records relating to PERC's section camps also suggest that conditions were
not as pristine as they appeared in company photographs (fig. 4.1) and
magazines. One of the company's section camps, located only a few miles
away from Mount Lowe in the city of Arcadia (named the "Arcadia Mexican Section Camp," linking railroad work with individuals of Mexican
descent), and where all of the camp's fifty men, ten women, and eleven
children were Mexican immigrants, was written up by the California
Commission of Immigration and Housing for neglecting to meet the
standards laid out in the Labor Camp Sanitation Act. The California legislature passed the Labor Camp Sanitation Act in 1913, which required
that a number of provisions be made for work camps in California, including "bunkhouses or other sleeping quarters sufficient to protect the
occupants from the elements, kept cleanly, and located on clean and properly situated camp grounds"; "beds or bunks"; "screened and otherwise
sanitary dining quarters and rooms for storage and preparation of food";
"adequate and sanitary toilet facilities"; "sanitary facilities for garbage disposal"; "adequate bathing facilities"; and a caretaker for keeping the camp
clean (Miller 1921, 700). In a letter dated October 24, 1922, inspector M.
E. Edwards condemned PERC for allowing camp occupants to "cook and

sleep in the same room" and sleep in "wooden bunks" that were "in bad condition" (California Department of Industrial Relations 1912–1929).

Of the worst offenses noted by the state health inspector was the camp's lack of bathing facilities; as the report explains, "Bathing facilities should be provided. In this connection we recommend that a community shower bath house be erected. Separate quarters to be provided for men and women. Drainage from the showers to be connected up to your present sewer system. Some provision should be made to heat the water for the showers" (California Department of Industrial Relations 1912–1929). State inspectors required a number of additional improvements, which included installing a sink in all camp kitchens with a drain that would connect to their sewer system, replacing the decrepit wooden bunks with "iron cots or some other sanitary cots," and providing separate dining and sleeping areas (California Department of Industrial Relations 1912–1929).

Historian Carey McWilliams discussed the hiring and treatment of Mexican immigrants by PERC and its subsidiary, Southern Pacific, in his canonical 1948 account of the subject matter (reprinted in 1968). He was an eyewitness to the company's treatment of its Mexican employees as he visited a number of their section camps. During his tour of a PERC camp at the intersection of San Vicente and Santa Monica, he was appalled to discover "forty Mexican families" who lived "as they might live in a village in Jalisco" (1968, 225). At this particular camp, hot water was limited to three days a week, only four outdoor showers for 120 residents were provided, and only one outdoor communal sink was available for the entire camp to wash dishes, clothes, and other items (225). As McWilliams' 1948 account demonstrates, PERC still kept their camps in squalid conditions nearly thirty years after claiming in a 1918 article that they provided "toilets separately maintained for men and women," "hot water during the daytime for the women at the camp," and a room for "family washings" complete with hot water, cold water, and "tables and benches" (Elliott 1918, 151).

Despite these published statements, the aforementioned amenities were not found on the section house's physical landscape or in the archives associated with the site, supporting McWilliams's firsthand account of PERC camps. Work orders from Mount Lowe similarly document the resort's failure to comply with state sanitation regulations and the Labor Camp Sanitation Act, despite their claims to the contrary. PERC was aware of these regulations as evidenced by their publicity releases and marketing materials. A 1918 article written by the company described their compliance at section camps: "More modern toilet facilities, less crowded quarters, fresh air privileges, and shower baths were provided. Washrooms with concrete floors, drains, storm sewer and cesspool connections were installed. . . . The arrangements were strictly in accordance with the legal requirements of the California State Commission of Immigration and Housing" (Elliott 1918, 151). Yet a work order request written on October 12, 1920, documents the company's violation of county health standards at Mount Lowe's section house and the railway foreman's residence on Echo Mountain. According to the work order, the railway workers' bathing facilities and toilets were "very unsanitary" to the point that county health officers requested that the company "make such facilities more sanitary, to install septic tanks and sanitary plumbing" (PERC Collection WO #21352). This work order appears to have been ignored, as another one was placed on August 21, 1921, for the section foreman's house.

It was not until the Los Angeles County Health Department filed another complaint against the company seven years later that changes were made to the railway foreman and section house residents' landscape. And in July 1928 the section house occupants could finally enjoy sanitary plumbing and basic amenities found in nearly all middle-class homes in Southern California, which included a combination toilet, a shower, and a heater. According to the work order, the request was filled to "provide improvement necessary for the general sanitary conditions of track laborers quarters at Echo Mountain, as the present facilities are inadequate in this respect. Los Angeles County Health Department, after an inspection, has requested that this improvement be accomplished promptly" (PERC Collection WO #28457).

Archaeological evidence of these repairs was recovered during the Mount Lowe Archaeology Project, which will be discussed shortly. A cement foundation of a bathroom that appeared to feature a sink, shower, and a toilet was discovered during surface survey at the site of the section house. Ceramic pipes, one of which was manufactured by Gladding, McBean & Company (fig. 4.7), and a cement-lined cesspool were also encountered during excavations (fig. 4.8). Artifacts recovered from the cesspool date to the 1910s and 1920s, also placing the sanitation-related construction work to the late 1920s (Camp 2009). These findings stand in stark contrast to published statements made by the company in 1918, where they blamed Mexican immigrants' lack of hygiene for an outbreak

Figure 4.7. Gladding, McBean & Company pipe found during 2006 excavations of the section house.

Figure 4.8. Cement-lined cesspool associated with section house.

of typhus in PERC camps (Elliott 1918, 151) rather than crowding within the camps' housing units and the company's failure to follow state sanitation regulations:

> The company, on its own initiative, undertook to teach sanitation to the Mexican track laborers and their families, as it realized that sanitary camps meant an increase in intelligence and efficiency. More modern toilet facilities, less crowded quarters, fresh air privileges and shower baths were provided. Washrooms with concrete floors, drains, storm sewer and cesspool connections were installed. The houses were screened and a general sanitation program was carried out, which in time pleased the Mexicans and won the hearty approval of the State, County, and city health authorities. The arrangements were strictly in accordance with the legal requirements of the California State Commission of Immigration and Housing. (Elliott 1918, 151)

PERC continued to praise themselves for a job well done in an article published ten years later, where they reiterated their camps' cleanliness and "wholesomeness" (PERC 1928).

PERC's decision to place its employees of Mexican heritage in landscapes that were dangerous, unsanitary, and uninhabitable from a health inspector's perspective appears to have been intentional, since they repeatedly ignored citations by state and city health officials to modernize and maintain their camps. Other archaeological studies of company-owned landscapes and towns also show that the health and welfare of the working classes were systematically neglected. Archaeological data offers arguably the best and most balanced line of evidence to examine sanitation and worker health issues in a company town because of the biases inherent in corporate archives associated with company towns. For example, Cowie explores the disproportionate treatment of economically vulnerable employees in the nineteenth-century town of Fayette, Michigan. Fayette's blue-collar workers were the victims of "environmental classism" (Cowie 2011, 108), evidenced by high concentrations of industrial waste (slag and charcoal) recovered from the town's working-class neighborhood. In contrast, minimal, "light scatters of slag" were found in Fayette's middle- and upper-class neighborhoods (106). Human-generated waste and trash was likewise densest in working-class yards. Privies were abundant and spaced far away from households in middle- and upper-class neighborhoods while Cowie's team was unable to locate privies in the working-class neighborhood. This, she argues, may suggest that privies were "shallow" and placed on a beach near the neighborhood, causing human excrement to be "incidentally mixed with yard trash" (106).

Mrozowski and colleagues uncovered similar sanitation and public health issues in their noted study of corporate paternalism at Lowell, Massachusetts' Boott Mills boardinghouses. Like Cowie, they compare and contrast if the company's stated goal of establishing a "total, planned industrial community" that would "deter the growth of crowded, unsanitary slums" was put into practice (Mrozowski et al. 1996, 2). As with Fayette and Mount Lowe, Boott Mills delayed repairs and alterations to its working-class boardinghouses that were requisite to maintaining minimal public health standards. Privies associated with the boardinghouses, for instance, were in use through approximately 1910 despite an 1890 request by the Board of Health of the City of Lowell "that all privies be abandoned and replaced by water closets hooked up to sewer lines" (52–53). The boardinghouse residents drank contaminated water until the 1890s, although the city of Lowell offered piped, hygienic water beginning in the 1870s. Rats, evident in the form of faunal remains, gnawed animal bones, and archaeobotanicals, also roamed the trash-infested boardinghouse landscapes (53).

Although PERC's poor treatment of its racially and socioeconomically marginalized workers was therefore not unique for companies operating during this time period, their neglect of the section house workers and their homestead was especially appalling given the public context of the site. As a tourist attraction visited by more than three million people over the course of its existence, Mount Lowe Resort and Railway provided visual proof of Mexican immigrants' innate predilection for disease and filth each time someone boarded the railway and viewed the incinerators puffing billowing smoke onto the section house's landscape. Archaeological work on the section camp's landscape offers additional evidence that what PERC officially stated and published tended to be propaganda that masked their neglect of the section house residents. This data also demonstrates that the company did not see Americanization as a process that would end in Mexican immigrants' legal and social inclusion within the American citizenry. Rather, it was a process with no end in sight, one that was designed to keep Mexican immigrants and their children as second-class noncitizens.

Archaeological Methodologies

The archaeological and landscape data recovered from Mount Lowe's section house represents a panoply of citizenship aspirations: those of the reformers and their Americanization efforts, those of the resort, and those of the Mexican immigrant railway workers' community. The Mount Lowe Archaeology Project began as a collaborative partnership between Angeles National Forest and Stanford University in 2005 and was initially formed to document, catalog, and interpret the breadth of resources associated with Mount Lowe Resort and Railway. The Scenic Mount Lowe Railway Historical Committee and Brian Marcroft, a local historian and one of the founding members of the committee, also assisted with the project. These data included ephemera; cultural resources; archaeological sites associated with the resort; documentary, photographic, and other archival data; and ethnographic interviews with stakeholder groups. As with most archaeological projects, the research questions narrowed as archival data revealed that the resort had built separate housing for its Mexican railway workers and that the workers were subjected to the company's Americanization program. From thereon the research agenda shifted to explore the goals, intentions, and scope of the Americanization movement and how the company's Mexican immigrant railway workers coped and adjusted to the movement's directives and initiatives.

The Mount Lowe Archaeology Project involved two field seasons that were held in 2005 and 2006. The first season in 2005 involved GIS mapping, surface survey and collection, and archaeological testing at Echo Mountain (fig. 4.9), one of several mountains associated with Mount Lowe Resort and Railway. During routine brush removal in conjunction with surface survey, the extant foundations of the section house were revealed (fig. 4.10). Two 1 × 1 m test units in the corner and middle of the section house were excavated to identify the extent and integrity of the deposits. The placement of these test units was determined using a PERC historic map detailing the "ideal" layout of section houses built by the company (map 4.1, map 4.2). This map, which was discovered by local historian Brian Marcroft, played a crucial role in the study of the section house and its residents because it outlined the expected function of each space in the section house (e.g., "kitchen"). Artifacts found in these two units suggest that the section house residents were following prescriptive guidelines by performing certain activities in their proper spaces (e.g.,

Figure 4.9. Excavated section house seen from above.

cooking in the kitchen). This discovery along with the identification of a cesspool and garden associated with the section house led to more extensive archaeological investigations held in the summer of 2006.

Excavations in 2006 focused on four distinct zones connected with the section house as denoted on historic maps (map 4.2): a mixed activity area that served numerous roles—a trash dump, garden, horse corral, and pig

Figure 4.10. Partial aerial view of excavation areas in 2006.

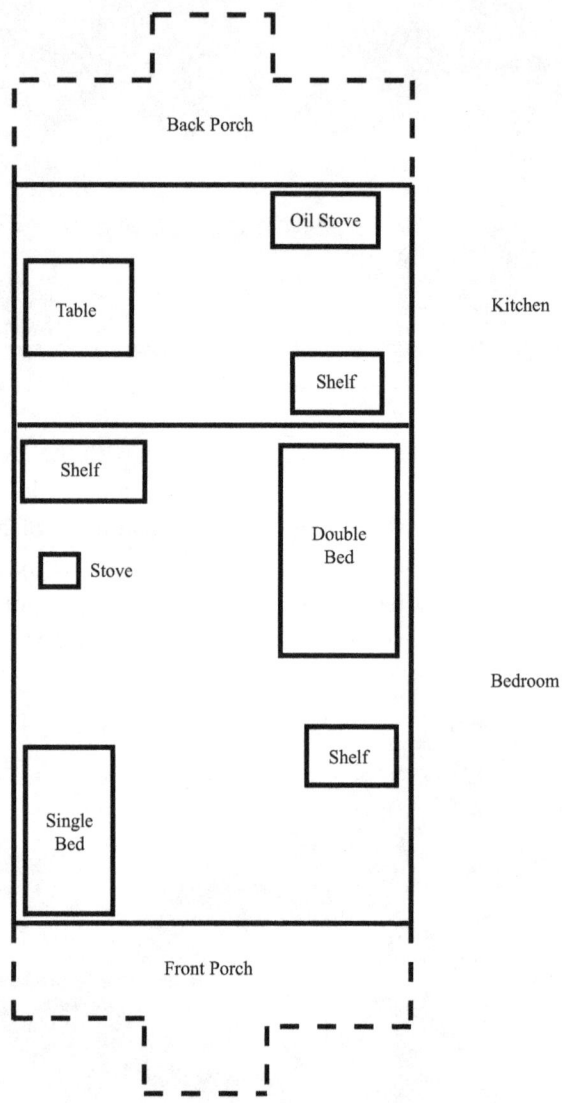

Map 4.1. Reconstruction of 1924 Pacific Electric Railway Corporation map denoting activity areas inside an ideal section house.

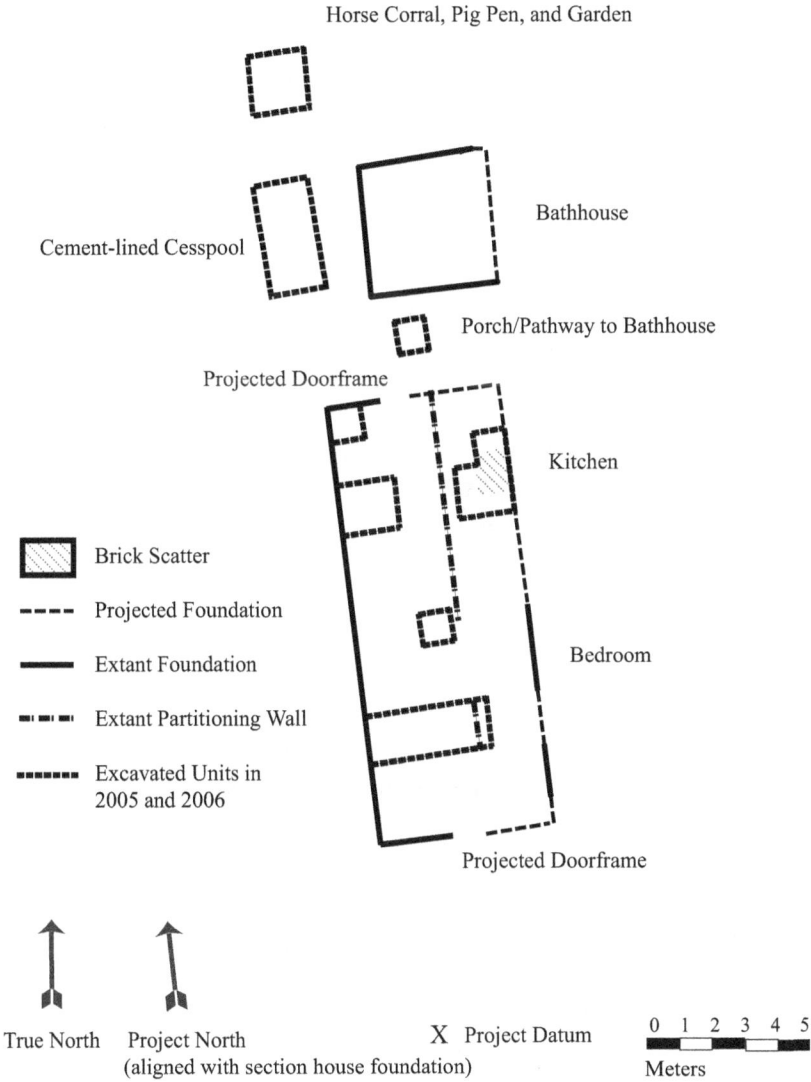

X Project Backsite

Horse Corral, Pig Pen, and Garden

Bathhouse

Cement-lined Cesspool

Porch/Pathway to Bathhouse

Projected Doorframe

Kitchen

Brick Scatter

Projected Foundation

Extant Foundation

Bedroom

Extant Partitioning Wall

Excavated Units in 2005 and 2006

Projected Doorframe

True North   Project North   X Project Datum
(aligned with section house foundation)

0 1 2 3 4 5
Meters

Map 4.2. Location of excavated features and units in section house during the 2005 and 2006 Mount Lowe Archaeology Project.

pen—at different points in time; a cesspool next to the section house's bathroom where trash was dumped; the interior of the section house as delineated by extant foundations; and an outdoor pathway leading from the section house to the bathroom. A 2 × 2 m unit was placed in the mixed activity area, a 1 × 1 m was excavated in the outdoor pathway, and the contours of the cement-lined cesspool determined the extent of the cesspool excavations. Excavations that took place inside the section house's interior comprised of three discrete activity zones noted by a historic map (Map 4.2); these areas included a bedroom (1 × 3 m unit), kitchen (2 × 2 m unit), and dining room (2 × 2 m unit). The results of this more extensive field season, the preliminary field season in 2005, and the associated archival research are discussed and interpreted in what follows. The archaeological findings confront stereotypes and caricatures of Mexican immigrants, provide a snapshot of the challenges Mount Lowe's Mexican workers faced living on the section house landscape, and, crucial to this book, show that national loyalties and citizenship aspirations varied within the Mexican community itself, destabilizing "assumptions central to racist thought that groups such as . . . 'Mexicans' are homogenous races who act in a similar manner due to their shared ethnic background" (Camp 2011c, 15).

Writing, Literacy, and Education

Publications written by PERC describe hiring reformers to teach Mexican immigrants because they were illiterate and only fluent in Spanish. A July 1918 article on Americanization work being performed in PERC's camps, for example, claimed that "about 99 percent of the Mexicans in the camps are ignorant, being unable to read and write" (Elliott 1918, 151). But early-twentieth-century sociological and anthropological accounts of Southern California's Mexican immigrant population suggest that some of them actively sought to improve their reading and language skills.

Social scientist Manuel Gamio conducted a survey of migrant literacy while employed by the Social Science Research Council, which resulted in several book-length publications (Gamio 1930, 1931). He discovered that most Mexican immigrants were either bilingual or literate in at least one language. Additionally, he noted that Mexican immigrants in the United States dedicated more time to reading in America than in Mexico because there were "more Mexican newspapers in the United States than in Mexico" (1931, 120). When financially possible, some Mexican immigrants also invested a great deal of energy into their children's education. To bolster his claims, Gamio interviewed numerous Mexican immigrants, including Elías Gonzáles, who arrived in the United States in 1911 at the age of twelve. Gonzáles recounted how his father "sacrificed himself all he could" so that his son could be educated in America (1931, 123–24). Yet all the schooling in the world could not counter the racism that Gonzáles encountered outside of the educational system. Consequently, Gonzáles could only find work in the trade sector, explaining: "I learned English well but I can almost say that it hasn't done me any good. What was wrong was that I wasn't able to learn any trade and I have had to work very hard where I have found work, whether it was on the railroad, in the cotton fields or beet fields, in the hotels as a waiter, as an elevator man, or in the asphalt" (1931, 124).

The section house archaeological assemblage provides a counternarrative to the image of Mexican immigrants put forth by PERC. Twenty-one artifacts associated with language acquisition, reading, and writing were recovered, suggesting that some of the house's residents could read English and were literate in Spanish, English, or both. A piece of paper ripped from what seems to be a mail-order catalog published in English appears to be an advertisement for leather tools. Another piece of paper, which reads "Wednes[day]," looks to be part of an English calendar or time schedule for the railroad. Pencil lead, wood pencil fragments, metal pencil caps, ink pen fragments, and an ink bottle cap manufactured by Milwaukee's Diamond Chemical Inks were also found. The ink bottle cap dates from the late 1890s to the early 1920s, the period in which the section house was occupied. Together these objects capture the hopes of the section house's occupants, aspirations invisible and outrightly dismissed in the company's narrative accounts of their Mexican employees.

Dining and Foodways

The food that Mexican immigrants ate and the vessels in which they consumed their meals were intensely scrutinized by reformers. Mexican immigrants—Mexican women in particular—were schooled in laying out and using matching vessels and individual utensils and wares at their dining tables. Women and children were specifically targeted for this instruction because the former were the literal and metaphorical reproducers of culture inside the home (for further discussion of the gendered aspects of reform at Mount Lowe, see Camp 2012) while the latter would be the bearers of it in years to come.

The section house residents seem to have embraced some aspects of these genteel behaviors. The ceramic collection is dominated by what appears to be one complete set of plain molded and unmolded whiteware and improved whiteware, which make up 59 percent of the assemblage. In contrast, only 4 percent of the ceramic collection (six vessels) featured either molded or painted flower and vine designs. Close to half of the identifiable glass tableware (44 percent) had at least two matching vessels. The abundance of matching glassware and identical plain improved whiteware present in the section house's assemblage may be read as a deliberate attempt on the part of the section house's residents to counter reformers' insinuation that Mexican immigrants were naturally unclean and unfit for American citizenship. For reformers, the color white was symbolically laden, representing "purity and virtue, just the values a mother adhering to the ideology of domesticity would want to emphasize to her family" (Fitts 1999, 58). Anne McClintock similarly asserts that Victorians' fixated on white because of their fascination with "clean, white bodies and clean, white clothing" (1995, 211).

Plates were the most commonly identifiable vessel in the ceramics assemblage next to identifiable hollowware. A 1908 photograph taken of the section house occupants dining beneath an ivy-draped porch suggests that they dined communally. In the photograph two adult men, three adult women, two female children, two male children, and a baby sitting on a man's lap eat a meal together, suggesting that two or three section house families would share food. Communal dining, which could lower the expense of food, has also been documented at other early-twentieth-century western U.S. work camps. An abundance of "plates with deep centers and broad rims" nearly identical to those recovered at Mount Lowe were found in the housing quarters of miners of varying ethnic affiliations in Ludlow, Colorado (Saitta 2007, 79–80). These ceramics were flexible and could function as both bowls and plates.

Jars and containers make up 17 percent of the glass vessel assemblage, suggesting that food storage was a regular part of the section house residents' daily lives and another money-saving strategy. California's Kern's Glass Manufacturing Company, which opened for business in the early 1920s, manufactured three out of the four identifiable jars in the collection. Hazel-Atlas produced the other identifiable jar, which dates between

1923 and 1964. Since Hazel-Atlas produced a wide variety of glass vessels, it is unclear what was stored in this particular jar. The reliance on local foods may denote the presence of reformers at the site, as other historical archaeological studies of marginalized groups document their resistance to local foodways. For example, Mullins's (1999a) analysis of late-nineteenth-century African American communities living in Annapolis, Maryland, shows that African Americans intentionally ordered products from mass-market catalogs to circumvent racism they encountered in local markets and businesses. They chose instead to pay more for items by ordering out of mass-market catalogs.

Cowie's work on the company town of Fayette, Michigan, also supports the interpretation of jars as evidence of the reformers' presence on the section house landscape. By sampling archaeological deposits in three distinct neighborhoods separated by their class standing and socioeconomic status, she finds that canning jars were absent in assemblages associated with Fayette's upper- and working-class residents while they were ubiquitous in middle-class households. One explanation she offers for this unexpected finding is that middle-class residents were financially stable enough to afford jars, "as their middling situation provided both sufficient funding and cultural education to purchase and experiment with the new technology" (Cowie 2011, 100). In contrast, she argues that canning jars may have been financially out of reach for the working classes, who may have instead recycled and reused bottles and packing jars to can and preserve goods (99–100).

Faunal and archaeobotanical data also suggest that the section house residents were frugal and, at times, hungry for food. A total of 17 cows, 18 sheep, 12 pigs, 2 cottontail rabbits, 1 turkey, 18 chicken, 5 large ducks, and 1 trout were identified out of the 697 identifiable bones. With the exception of cottontail rabbits, all of these species were served at the resort. Reformers gave chickens to the section house residents to raise. Diagnostic ammunition found at the site implies that the section house residents sought out resources of their own. The section house residents may have also procured the unidentified small mammals and rodents in the faunal assemblage on their own. For example, the remains of a ground squirrel, jackrabbits, and cottontail rabbits recovered from a contemporaneous (1898–1933) section house occupied in the same region exhibit evidence of human processing or cooking (Nettles and Hamilton 2005). The majority of the meat cuts found in the section house assemblage came from the head (pork), hind and fore-shank, feet, and neck (Stoyka 2009). These particular cuts were commonly used in stews and soups that were not served at the resort. Soups and stews could be easily consumed in a communal setting because they offered a quick solution to feeding a large number of workers and their families in a short amount of time and did not require tending, a luxury for workers.

Gardening went hand in hand with food preservation and canning, and it was framed in literature published by PERC as a means to overcome poverty. Teaching Mexican immigrants the practice of gardening (as if they had not learned such a skill back in Mexico) was also discussed in this literature as a mechanism for imparting western beliefs about landscaping and keeping one's exterior environment clean. According to a March 30, 1931, edition of *Pacific Electric Magazine*, two hundred trees were planted on the hillside near the section house that year in order to "improve watersheds," "prevent erosion," and "increase the beauties of our famous Mt. Lowe journey" (PERC 1931). A total of nine tar-paper seedling cases were discovered in the garden unit during excavations in 2006 that appear to be the result of these beautification and slope stabilization processes. Trees may have also been planted to prevent tourists riding on the railway from viewing the section house and its incinerators in later years. Archaeobotanical evidence demonstrates that the section house residents also gardened, but they did so to supplement the foods they acquired from the resort. Although the data was scant, a few seeds from cultivated plants were identified that appear remarkably similar to a neighboring section house's archaeobotanical collection. At both Mount Lowe's section camp and Southern Pacific's Honda section camp (ca. 1898–1933), the remains of a fig, common bean, blackberry, and grape were identified, with the common bean being a staple of Mexican immigrants' diet (Nettles and Hamilton 2005). In addition, wild elderberry and chili pepper were found at Mount Lowe, the latter find also commonly consumed by Mexican immigrants (Popper 2007, 380).

Considered together, the lack of tin cans, the finding of sizeable serving vessels designed to accommodate a large dinner party, the cuts of meat, the archaeobotanical evidence, the presence of ammunition manufactured to hunt small game, and the diversity of animals, birds, and fish discovered at the site imply that the section house residents collectively and intentionally pooled resources and sought out all possible food sources in the mountains surrounding them. This may have strengthened bonds among workers and their families, sparking the emergence of a class- and ethnicity-based group consciousness. This seems evident in songs and oral histories from working-class Mexican immigrants that are discussed later in this chapter.

Spatial Distribution of Artifacts

Following standard archaeological procedures, the provenience information for each artifact recovered at Mount Lowe Resort and Railway was recorded. This data was then used to track the distribution of artifacts across the landscape using a total station, a handheld GPS unit, and GIS software (ArcView) to map and project data. Mapping from the 2005 field season verified that the section house closely aligned to that which was depicted in an historic PERC map. Surface collection scatters mapped in 2005 also suggested that the section house residents adhered to the idealized behaviors (e.g., cooking in the "kitchen" portion of the section house) noted on the historic map. The 2006 field season substantiated these discoveries by examining discrete activity areas (the kitchen, the dining room, the bedroom) within the section house's interior.

Cleanliness of one's interior and exterior landscapes was a common theme in PERC's reform literature. The tidiness of the landscape was assessed by placing a 1 × 1 m excavation unit in a space that served as an outdoor pathway leading from the back door of the section house to the bathroom. Fewer artifacts were recovered in this unit than in the interior section house units of the same size (1 × 1 m), providing evidence that the section house residents sought to clean what they could of their crowded landscape. For example, among the minimum number of identifiable glass and ceramic vessels count, only one ceramic vessel and two glass vessels were found in the outdoor excavation unit between the section house and the bathroom. The amount of small finds was equally diminutive in the outdoor pathway unit, with only one button recovered from the unit. The contrast is especially notable when compared to two units of the same size placed inside the section house's interior, where two buttons, two beads, and two clothing fasteners were recovered from one interior 1 × 1 m unit, and six buttons, three beads, one safety pin, and a pencil fragment were found in the other 1 × 1 m unit.

Another method of determining the cleanliness of the section house is to examine the horizontal movement of artifacts across the section house's landscape and taphonomy processes impacting the accumulation of discard across the site through the minimum number of individual vessels analysis. Ceramic and glass fragments recovered in both 2005 and 2006 found in the interior of the section house, the cesspool, and the horse corral, pig pen, and garden units crossmend, which aids in the reconstruction of events that lead to the discard of artifacts. The plausible explanation for this pattern of distribution is that when objects broke inside the section house, the occupants swept up what they could; threw out the broken pieces into the cesspool, pig pen, or garden; and the remaining, smaller fragments fell through the wooden floorboards of the section house for archaeologists to recover seventy to eighty years later.

Despite cramped living quarters with, at times, approximately fourteen people inhabiting the section house, the section house residents appeared to have closely followed other prescriptive expectations outlined by reformers. They did so by performing activities in what Anglo-American reformers considered their "proper places." The number of sewing-, clothing-, and adornment-related artifacts found underneath the section house's floorboards totaled 157 individual objects or 95 percent of the recovered sewing-, clothing-, and adornment-related artifacts. Sixty-three percent (99 artifacts) of those artifacts were recovered in the bedroom units of the section house, demonstrating that bodily adornment and getting dressed was performed in its prescribed space. In contrast, only 9 artifacts associated with clothing were found in outdoor spaces. The majority of glassware pieces were recovered from the cesspool, where large pieces of broken glass were likely deposited upon breaking inside the section house or where entire vessels were discarded after their use. The second largest number of glassware (twenty-seven vessels) were found inside the section house's kitchen. Finally, fifteen out of the twenty-one artifacts (or 71 percent of the collection) associated with writing, education, and literacy were found within the bedroom and sleeping area of the house. This demonstrates that some form of education was taking place within the section house, whether it was through reform instruction or lessons imparted to children by their parents.

The section house residents may have followed these spatial rules as an impression-management tactic done to deter and avert reformers' and their employer's gaze. Mullins (1999b) has described a similar pattern of behavior in his study of another marginalized group, African Americans who lived in historic Annapolis, Maryland. Between 1870 and 1905, he discovered that African Americans purposely decreased their consumption of fish to distance themselves from "racial caricatures" drawn by Anglo-Americans. These illustrations used African Americans' preference for fish as a rationale for their supposed racial inferiority. In adhering to prescriptive literature, Mexican immigrants may have sought to counter stereotypes that painted them as inherently unfit for citizenship. Oral histories collected from Mexican immigrants living and working in Southern California during the section house's period of occupation suggest that their compliance was not ideological; it was a strategy enacted to avoid deportation or loss of employment that could result in deportation.

Interpreting the Section House Assemblage

Excavations conducted at Mount Lowe Resort and Railway's section house have unearthed the voices, albeit muted, of its formerly invisible Mexican immigrant railway workers. Although it was not possible to locate direct descendents of Mount Lowe's workers, oral histories collected from Southern California's Mexican immigrant population offer another perspective on how they dealt with and perceived education and Americanization instruction. Did they envision it as a pathway toward achieving equal rights and American citizenship? Or did they see it as a marketing and public relations ploy devised to suppress public outcry regarding railway companies' treatment of its workers and unsanitary camps that could easily leach into neighboring communities' soil and underground water?

The answer to these questions splintered along class lines within the Mexican immigrant and Mexican American communities of the early-twentieth-century western United States. Well-to-do middle-class Mexican Americans who had lived in the United States for many years expressed animosity toward newly arrived Mexican immigrants who could not afford the symbols of a middle-class Anglo-American lifestyle (Camp 2011a). This intragroup hostility took many forms, including Mexican Americans' support of the repatriation or Americanization of newly arrived Mexican immigrants (Sánchez 1993, 119). Established Mexican Americans were especially put off by Mexican immigrants' consumption behaviors or, rather, their lack thereof. One Mexican American newspaper reporter complained: "We Mexicans, or rather our ignorant and foolish countrymen, are to blame for being treated badly in some of the counties of Texas. The poor Mexican who comes from Mexico without money, without clothes and looking for work accepts all the humiliations which he is made to suffer and even when he has been able to earn something he doesn't try to better his condition" (Gamio 1931, 119). This reporter's scathing critique of his Mexican brethren replicated the widely held stereotypes about Mexican immigrants, including some held by PERC's reformers. Mexican immigrants were well aware that Mexican Americans accepted and repeated these typecasts that posited Mexican immigrants as lazy, uneducated, and irrevocably stuck in an unending cycle of poverty. A Mexican immigrant living in Los Angeles expressed his frustration with this internal class system of the Mexican American community in a *corrido* (song) that became popular among first generation immigrants:

You go along showing off
In a big automobile.
You call me a pauper
And dead with hunger
And what you don't remember is
That on my farm
You went around almost naked
And without sandals.
This happens to many
That I know here
When they learn a little
American
And dress up like dudes,
And go to the dance.
But he who denies his race
Is the most miserable creature.
There is nothing in the world
So vile as he
The mean figure of the renegade
And although far from you,
Dear Fatherland,
Continual revolutions
Have cast me out—
A good Mexican
Never disowns

The dear fatherland
Of his affections.

(McWilliams [1948]1968: 210)

Here the songwriter chastises Mexican Americans for their consumption of American clothing and for their use of the English language. He also mentions the discrimination Mexican immigrants faced if they chose to return back to their homeland of Mexico.

Mexican immigrants such as Emilia Castaneda de Valenciana were subjected to a different form of discrimination when they migrated back to Mexico after encountering racism in the United States. De Valenciana describes her exceedingly difficult transition from living in the United States to living in Mexico because her family was considered foreigners there. They abandoned their homes in the United States after her father tired of "being on relief" and desired to find employment elsewhere. As she recalled, Mexico was unkind to Mexican immigrants who had left and then returned: "A lot of people did discriminate against us because we were Americans. We didn't belong there. Isn't it strange? Here, the Anglos discriminate against us because we're Mexican. They belong in Europe, don't they? . . . We're all foreigners. People used to discriminate against us because we were American citizens and didn't belong in that country" (de Valenciana 1972). Mexican immigrants thus found themselves in an unusual and unfortunate predicament. If they chose to stay within the United States, they would experience discrimination from both Mexican Americans and Anglo-Americans. And if they chose to go back home to Mexico, they would also be seen as outsiders who, in the words of de Valenciana, "didn't belong" there.

Cast aside by Mexican nationals in their homeland, demonized by Anglo-Americans in the United States, and castigated by Mexican Americans in their own neighborhoods, these oral histories and songs demonstrate that Mexican immigrants were cognizant of the fact that citizenship was unattainable no matter what activities in which they engaged or objects they consumed. Scholars writing during the era in which the section house was occupied also observed such feelings among Mexican immigrants. Emory Bogardus wrote in 1934, "Citizenship is disappointing to him [Mexican citizens], for he is still likely to be treated as a Mexican and a foreigner. Citizens of the United States as a rule do not distinguish between naturalized and unnaturalized Mexicans" (1934, 78). Another historian of Mexican immigration similarly remarked, "Hedged in by group hostility, the immigrants long ago lost interest in citizenship. Lack of funds, the language difficulty, and illiteracy were important factors but not nearly as influential as segregation and discrimination" (McWilliams 1968, 220).

This scenario reminds archaeologists that marginalized groups are heterogeneous, harbor divergent desires, and act in unpredictable ways. Dynamic and multilayered, citizenship aspirations varied across ethnic groups as well as within them. Archaeologists should therefore exercise caution in automatically ascribing Anglo-American values and citizenship aspirations to racialized or marginalized communities and households when objects associated with "middle-class" culture are recovered via excavation (Praetzellis and Praetzellis 2001). An uncritical reading of PERC's documents and publications would lead one to believe that the company's Mexican immigrant employees desired and benefitted from Americanization instruction, which archaeological data and associated archival materials prove to be false.

Summary

The section house residents appear to have conformed to many aspects of the reform guidelines outlined by PERC; they adhered to the spatial guidelines and used matching tableware when they could afford it, but Mexican immigrants did not passively accept the philosophies that undergirded Americanization instruction. Sarah Deutsch's study of Protestant missionaries' work in New Mexico's Mexican American communities has made this point clear. Deutsch shows that while Anglo-American "missionaries tended to count their moral victories by tables 'set with American dishes,' 'tablecloths,' 'cooking utensils and furniture,'" Mexican immigrants' adoption of Anglo-American material culture and domestic practices did not result in philosophical conversion (1987, 77). Missionaries, Deutsch argues, thus conflated Mexican immigrants' desire for these goods with an "enthusiasm for their entire cultural complex" of Americanization instruction and consumption (77). Although reformers believed "deeply in the power of material culture" as a mode of acculturating non-Anglo-Americans, the recipients of reform instruction separated the ideological underpinnings of Americanization instruction from the materiality associated with it (86).

This, too, appears to be the case for Mount Lowe's section house residents. They used the products and goods provided to them by the resort and reformers while concurrently rejecting reformers' racist stereotypes by consuming objects that directly confronted them. The presence of education- and literacy-related artifacts is a prime example of this; such objects counter archival statements that describe Mexican immigrants as illiterate and uninterested in social and economic advancement in American society through education. Workers did not consume reformer-issued goods with the intention of gaining their favor or finding acceptance as consumer citizens in a country that equated goods with American citizenship. Goods reminded Mexican immigrants that the principle of universal citizenship did not apply to them, even if they were citizens by law. Barred from enjoying the inclusivity of a well-established middle- and upper-class Mexican American community in Southern California and forced to "reform" their behaviors by the Anglo-Americans who frequently brought them across the border and hired them, goods offered little consolation in a society that constantly reminded them of their second-class citizenship standing.

This is an important case study for historical archaeologists because it shows that not all individuals on the margins of American society equated consumption with citizenship. Instead, they formed a class- and ethnicity-based communal identity that denied the power of consumption as a force that could help marginalized groups transcend the social barriers they faced in American society. This crucial lesson teaches us alternative models of community formation and community building, one that questions shopping and consumption as a unifying trait that can bridge differences across Americans. This leads us to the most pressing question we now face in modern America: what are the qualities we wish to see as inherent in American citizenship? The final chapter of this book looks at how we have moved away from earlier democratic and nonascriptive notions of American citizenship. What lessons about American citizenship can archaeologies of the recent past teach us?

5

....

The Future of Citizenship

What are the next steps toward pursuing an archaeology of citizenship? What should it look like, and how might it contribute to historical archaeology's goal of revealing inequality and confronting racism in our modern, global world (c.f. Orser 1996, 1999; Funari, Jones, and Hall 1999; Buchli and Lucas 2001)? For this author, the answer can be found in the hot, arid desert of Arizona where the University of Michigan's Jason De León and his crew of archaeological field students have collected more than six tons of artifacts left by undocumented Mexican migrants who had been seeking refuge and work in the United States.

Risking dehydration, sunstroke, and death, it is estimated that more than a half-million Mexican migrants cross the U.S.-Mexico border each year. De León seeks to "humanize" the migrant's journey, which has been framed as a legal rather than human rights issue in the United States, by studying the trash migrants leave behind: children's and women's shoes, water bottles, and first-aid kits (Drake 2011). At present, the exact number of migrants who cross the U.S.-Mexico border is unclear because it is vast body of land that makes policing its entirety nearly impossible. By employing archaeological methodologies such as mapping and artifact collection, De León has located new migration routes initiated by migrants. He has discovered that migrants have taken "more remote and dangerous" routes to the United States due to "stricter border controls—such as increased patrols or fences," and "enforcement strategies" that have resulted in more "suffering and death" among migrants (Drake 2011).

The artifacts De León collects are important not only because they put a human face to and soften the image of Mexican migrants who are often painted as dangerous "criminals" or "terrorists" by the American media but also because they capture the undocumented's responses and

challenges to United States immigration policy and enforcement: practices invisible to the naked eye if one were to examine immigration laws
and legislature of the time. Furthermore, as De León's archaeological research has shown, American border patrol and law enforcement agencies'
policing tactics have increased the number of undocumented migrants'
deaths. His project stands as an example of how archaeological studies of
the historic and recent past can be called upon to raise questions about
contemporary citizenship laws and the surveillance employed to enforce
them.

Although sometimes bleak, the case studies presented in this volume
encourage scholars to retreat back to a question that the country's earliest settlers pondered: what do we want America's civic body to look like
in the next ten, twenty, or even one hundred years? Only in the past one
hundred years have immigrant restrictions based on nationality, men-
tality, and criminality been cemented into law. Historical archaeological
data presented in this book have demonstrated the power of communities
and individuals to undermine, mediate, and transform these structures,
in turn penning their own commentaries on American citizenship.

The work featured in this concluding chapter is activist-oriented
scholarship that expands on this idea, research that makes direct linkages
between the archaeological data recovered and current or more recent
attempts to circumscribe, circumvent, or revoke group and individuals'
citizenship privileges. As American historical archaeologists and academics working in a time of dwindling economic resources, we are regularly
pressured to demonstrate the relevance of our work to modern issues. The
archaeology of citizenship gives scholars an opportunity to address these
questions by generating and contributing fresh, new, and vital data that
can impact public perceptions on contemporary immigration and citizenship laws.

Archaeologies of Modern Citizenship

As we witnessed in chapter 4, legal citizenship does not automatically
lend itself to inclusion and acceptance within American society. Although Renato Rosaldo (1994) devised the concept of "cultural citizenship" to explain how those marginalized by citizenship laws seek inclusion
within the broader national community, this term can also be applied to

situations where individuals remains excluded from the national community even though they are naturalized citizens. This was the case for some Mexican Americans living in late-nineteenth- and early-twentieth-century California, many of whom had been granted legal citizenship after the Mexican-American War of 1848. But, as discussed in chapter 4, for many Mexican immigrants legal citizenship did not translate into social acceptance. In this instance, then, the "cultural" conditions of a racist, anti–Mexican American nation overturned and negated the citizenship privileges and national membership promised by the law.

Since the late nineteenth and early twentieth centuries, the door to citizenship has become increasingly narrow, with its parameters defined by the racial, economic, and imperial objectives of the American nation. The onset of World War II ignited unfounded mass hysteria in the United States and sparked xenophobia against Japanese American citizens and Japanese immigrants. In what is arguably one of the most grossly unjust events in American history, nearly 120,000 individuals of Japanese heritage were imprisoned in dilapidated, barely inhabitable internment camps and falsely accused of committing treason and acts of sabotage against the United States during World War II. Although relatively new, the archaeology of Japanese American internment is gaining traction and momentum within academia (c.f., Branton 2004; Clark et al. 2008; Clark 2012; Farrell and Burton 2004; Skiles 2008; Skiles and Clark 2010; Slaughter 2006; Shew 2010; Kamp-Whittaker 2010). Up until recent years, archaeological publications on the topic were generated by federal agencies seeking to locate, document, and manage internment-era structures and other associated archaeological deposits, which in turn produced an impressive number of site reports documenting such cultural resources (Burton 1996, 1998, 2005a, 2005b, 2006; Burton and Farrell 2001, 2006, 2007, Burton et al. 2003; Burton et al. 2002, Burton et al. 2001; Tamir et al. 1993).

As we move into a post-9/11 America and into an era not unlike that which followed the onset of World War II, the internment of Japanese Americans and Japanese immigrants is important to recall lest we let history repeat itself. Ongoing research at Colorado's Amache Internment Camp (also known as the Granada Relocation Center) under the direction of the University of Denver's Bonnie Clark has been instrumental in documenting how archaeological data can illuminate citizenship aspirations in the most dire of circumstances. By working closely with stakeholder groups, former internees, and descendent communities, Clark and her students have animated a history that lay deeply buried and hidden within the remote desert canvassing Amache Internment Camp.

Clark's collaborative project has bred several masters' theses, including Shew's (2010) "Feminine Identity Confined: The Archaeology of Japanese American Women at Amache, a World War II Internment Camp." This exceptional piece of scholarship examines how the structure of internment camps altered Japanese American standards of femininity as well as incited different philosophies of femininity across generational lines. Shew attends to the generational differences present within Japanese American women's responses to internment, and she considers how women coped with losing control over and being denied power over aspects of family life that were traditionally spearheaded by women (2010, 53). Shew argues that first-generation (issei) and second-generation (nisei) women's notions of gender contrasted sharply, with the latter adopting opulent "Americanized" beauty rituals in defiance of the former's more reserved, modest styles of dress and cosmetics. These differences show up in the material record of Amache, where objects such as beauty supplies that were marketed during the war are found in deposits associated with nisei women. During World War II, the consumption of American beauty products was one of the ways citizens were instructed to support the war. Beauty stores would hold "Defense Sales," which "inferred that maintaining feminine beauty was a patriotic contribution to the war effort" (Shew 2010, 136). Shew asserts that the presence of nail polish bottles, brass lipstick tubes, and a makeup compact (137–39) found at Amache indicates that second-generation Japanese Americans were swayed by such rhetoric and, accordingly, emulated Anglo-American beauty ideals (137).

Kamp-Whittaker's master's thesis on children at Amache also takes note of seemingly innocuous "American" activities and material practices adopted by nisei, including becoming members of the Boy Scouts of America, playing with wartime associated toys, buying wartime associated goods, and planting and growing "Victory gardens" to further wartime efforts (2010, 142). These practices are lumped together by Kamp-Whittaker, but they are best considered within the context in which they were enacted. Victory gardens, for instance, were grown during school time at camps, a time in which children were taught Anglo-American standards of behavior. School was seen as a place where Anglo-American teachers could instill Anglo-American principles and material practices into Japanese children. The school day was valued by camp authorities as a time in the day in which they could both control Japanese American children and attempt to erase perceived "Japanese" elements of their identity in a setting removed from the children's Japanese parents.

Other less public activities, such as playing with toys after school on the perimeter of the camp, bringing objects to the camp from home, buying objects from the camp store or from businesses local to Amache, and the ordering of goods from catalogs, were more covert and reflective of families' and children's perspectives on what it meant to be a Japanese American citizen. Toys and goods associated with war, including colorless glass candy containers in the shape of military vehicles (Kamp-Whittaker 2010, 126), toy battleships (125), and a bomber military jacket that Tooru Nakahira received for his birthday after walking "with his grandmother to Lamar, about 15 miles from camp" to purchase it (137) facilitate our understanding of how nisei fused their dual Japanese and American identities. Considered alongside the knowledge that many Japanese Americans voluntarily joined the American military during World War II, it seems that part of the Japanese American community still remained committed to maintaining the "American" half of their dual identity, even in the midst of being unjustly imprisoned and persecuted. That portions of the Japanese American community continued to support the American government speaks to the incredibly powerful role citizenship standing and nationality plays in forming community: a role so important that injustices can be overlooked in favor of staying within a nation's boundaries and waiting for the nation's principles of democracy and equality for all to be eventually realized—principles temporarily suspended during Japanese American internment.

Although not archaeological in the strict sense of the word, Jane Dusselier's (2005, 2008) research examines the material practices of Japanese American internees and how such activities relate to American citizenship. Dussilier argues that through the process of transforming barracks into homes, barren landscapes into ornate gardens (also discussed at length in Helphand 2006; Tamura 2004) and playgrounds, and scraps of wood and stones into pieces of artwork, furniture, toys, and jewelry, Japanese Americans were engaging in intentional, political practices to "reterritorialize" American soil. This behavior, Dusselier says, is an expression of some Japanese Americans' desire to belong to the nation even as they were simultaneously excluded from it; their actions were done not only to recall their Japanese heritage, ancestry, and their former homeland of Japan but also to remind camp overseers of their dual Japanese American status by transforming American-grown elements of the environment and geography into familiar landscapes and cultural forms.

Importantly, Dusselier urges scholars to consider how these national loyalties and allegiances splintered along generational, gender, class, and religious lines (2005, 195), a suggestion I have taken to heart in my research at Idaho's Kooskia Internment Camp. The Kooskia Internment Camp was a World War II internment camp inhabited by 265 Japanese men. By placing the findings at Kooskia in dialogue with previously excavated and analyzed internment camps occupied by multigenerational and gendered populations, I intend to continue to examine the diverse ways racialized minorities, such as the Mexican immigrants discussed in this book, communicated their feelings about American citizenship using material culture. Although only one archaeological field season has been completed, preliminary finds from 2010 already reveal the textured and nuanced relationships Japanese and Japanese American men had with Japan and with the United States. This project will also contribute to an already flourishing scholarship of the archaeology of masculinity, which is not necessarily a study of men, per se, but rather a materially grounded examination of masculinity and its various iterations within and across "cultural groups" (Williams 2008, 53; Brashler 1991; Knapp 1998a, 1998b; Joyce 2000, 2004, 2005; Alberti 2006; Wilkie 2010). This body of scholarship seeks to challenge the assumption that gender roles have been static across time and cultures by looking at discrete geographical and temporal moments in history where gender ideologies were formed and preformed (Gutmann 1997).

The case study of Kooskia's all-male and predominantly first-generation Japanese internees contributes to this philosophical project by considering how citizenship aspirations differed across generations, classes, and genders. Elena Creef's survey of media and literature addressing issei men's experiences in internment camps leads her to conclude that "one of the most consistently unexplored themes of the internment experience has been an examination of the impact of this history on Japanese American masculine identity" (2004, 53). Along with Creef, Lon Kurashige argues that internment was a profoundly transformative event in issei men's lives, with their traditional role as a patriarch and financial head of the household eclipsed and lessened by the U.S. government, which "assumed his role as provider of his family's food, shelter, and clothing" (2002, 95). David Eng (2000) and Creef (2004) liken internment to racial castration in that many Japanese men were "rendered impotent in their ability to protect both their property and their families" (Creef 2004, 55). Women, too, found that their "traditional submissive position" in the Japanese family home was impossible to replicate in the setting of an internment camp, with some women, especially nisei, taking advantage of "this opportunity to explore new social roles outside their traditional submissive position" (Branton 2004, 133–34).

Historical archaeological studies at Kooskia can add to both citizenship and masculinity studies given the intensely material ways Japanese internees dealt with isolation and imprisonment (e.g., growing gardens, engaging in woodworking, creating flower arrangements and other crafts, erecting landscaping such as bridges, small pond features, and pathways, etc.). Scholars generally agree that issei and nisei experiences and relationships to the United States and Japan fundamentally departed from one another. Some, like Shew, assert that nisei, who were automatically granted citizenship upon their birth on American soil, sought to break free of traditional Japanese culture by consuming American goods and media as well as by changing their physical appearance by adopting and keeping current on the latest American hairstyles, makeup, and styles of dress.

Although only one field season has been conducted thus far and laboratory research is preliminary, when placed in dialogue with archaeological assemblages collected from multigenerational and multigendered camps such as Amache, a few unique findings from the camp seem to suggest that first-generation Japanese men experienced internment in different ways. Take, for example, figure 5.1, artwork found during a surface survey of a trash midden across from the internees' barracks. Figure 5.1 is a piece of artwork that was pieced together from scraps of sediment and stone found in the landscape surrounding Kooskia, a hybrid form of art merging modern and ancient stoneworking traditions that extend into the deep past of Japanese art history. Archival sources note that internees went "stone hunting" and engaged in "stonecrafting," both of which "had been a popular activity at Fort Missoula" (Wegars 2010, 101). A photograph taken of male internees at Montana's Fort Missoula Internment Camp documents this form of art as the men display it for the photographer

Figure 5.1. Artwork recovered from Idaho's Kooskia Internment Camp, a World War II Japanese American internment camp. Image courtesy of Mary Petrich-Guy.

(Van Valkenburg 1996, 55). Similar forms of Japanese internee art made out of rock and sediment have also been featured in museum exhibits, with pieces serving both artistic and functional roles ranging from rock-decorated pencil holders to vases (Hirasuna 2005). Did this artwork tradition begin there as a form of resistance, as Dusselier suggests, becoming mobile when one or several of the men who engaged in it transferred to Kooskia and shared it with internees there?

Gaming pieces (fig. 5.2) cobbled together from stone and construction materials found during the 2010 excavations of the Kooskia Internment Camp also seem to be indicative of the internees' generational status and class standing. According to Nishimoto, *hana*, a game that originated in Japan, was reserved for lower-class, first-generation Japanese American men and popular among lower-class gardeners, fishermen, older produce men, farmers, and migratory farm laborers (1995, 8). Nishimoto argues that playing games such as *hana* and *mah-jongg* allowed issei men to protest internment and racism in America:

> For the Issei, the ideal was to strike it rich and return to Japan to live a life of leisure. Gambling must have seemed like an easy way to achieve this dream to those who worked so hard, often for little return. What is more, for the Issei and the older Nisei, whose upward social and occupational mobility was typically blocked by racial prejudice and discrimination, especially before World War II, gambling was not only a form of entertainment and a social activity, it was also a form of resistance to constraint. (1995, 87)

Other artifacts recovered in 2010 also seem to support the idea that Japanese men used Japanese goods to recreate a semblance of Japan. These finds include a gastrointestinal supplement manufactured in Japan by the Wakamoto Pharmaceutical Company from 1929 to 1936 and banned from importation into the United States during World War II (Wakamoto 2012; Oliver 2012), a vase featuring a raised clay dragon relief manufactured in Japan during the Nippon era (1891–1921) (McDaniel 2012) (in a decorative style known as "moriage"; Stitt 1974, 126), and fragments of a Fukizumi porcelain bowl manufactured in Japan (Workman 2012). While a more robust data set will be collected in future field seasons to substantiate our interpretations, Kooskia's archaeological assemblage seems to support scholars' claims that issei immigrants' loyalties were with Japan.

By the same token, what are we to make of a pillow cover featuring a bold red, white, and blue American flag with "U.S.A." emblazoned above it hand-sewn by a Japanese internee held at Kooskia (Wegars 2010, 100)? Was this pillow intentionally crafted to convince camp officials that Japanese Americans were equally deserving of American citizenship? Sometimes migration and border crossings entangle national alliances, sparking altogether new allegiances that converge in unexpected and messy ways. For example, Miasato (2002) found that second-generation Japanese women living in Peru who divorced their partners or who worked full-time outside of the home saw themselves as Peruvian citizens rather than of Japanese ethnicity. They sought acceptance within the native Peruvian community rather than from their Japanese peers who shunned such nontraditional behavior. Peruvian society thus allowed women of Japanese ethnicity to take on new roles in society. Diving deep into the toolbox of historical archaeology, the Kooskia Internment Camp Archaeological

Figure 5.2. Gaming pieces crafted out of stone and sediment found at the Kooskia Internment Camp, a World War II Japanese American internment camp. Image courtesy of Mary Petrich-Guy.

Project (http://www.uidaho.edu/class/kicap) continues to pursue more information on these artifacts and the meanings underlying them, with oral histories planned and documentary research underway in the coming years. Time will tell; we have just begun to scrape the surface of the copious oral histories, correspondence penned by internees and camp officials, and artifactual history waiting to be excavated at Kooskia during future field seasons.

Citizenship in Modern America

Historical archaeologists frequently juggle three different temporalities, eyeing the past and present with the future in mind; they spend hours researching in libraries, museums, and archives to learn more about the people who lived at their sites, they reach deep into the ground beneath their feet and dig through layers of dirt to see what people in the past consumed and ate, and they seek to make their work relevant to living people by talking to descendent communities and stakeholder groups who are invested in or connected to a site's history. The study of citizenship necessitates a complementary approach because beliefs about the nation's citizenry have "been neither inevitable nor linear" (Thelen 2000, 551) and require that scholars track back and forth between different nodes in time. A case in point is the history of African American men's relationship to the American nation; they "won the right to vote, then lost it, and then regained it in different places in struggles that stretched across a century" (551). Historical archaeology's methodological attention to the *longue durée*—what has happened in the past, how it has impacted the present, and how it might shape the future—makes the field well positioned to tackle the topic of American citizenship.

The history of citizenship is paradoxical, and the symbols associated with national belonging express circuitous and ambiguous ideas about American citizenship. The Statue of Liberty, which has been considered an emblem of American identity, stands on America's eastern coast, welcoming "the homeless," the "tired," and the "poor." An icon of hope for immigrants, the words inscribed on the Statue of Liberty promise to shelter and protect those who have just arrived on America's shores: "Give me your tired, your poor, / Your huddled masses, yearning to breathe free, / The wretched refuse of your teeming shore, / Send these, the homeless, tempest-tost to me, / I lift my lamp beside the golden door." Contrast the Statue of Liberty's message with that of the phrase "melting pot," a term used to describe the demographical composition of the United States' citizenry. Made famous by playwright Israel Zangwill, the metaphor of the melting pot conjures up images of immigrants sacrificing and shedding aspects of their ethnicity and heritage to become "Americans" (Gleason 1964, 25).

These two popular symbols of American citizenship and nationality fail to capture the breadth of citizenship desires and beliefs expressed by groups and individuals living in historic and contemporary America, including those documented within this book. For instance, Italian immigrant Michael Fette slowly became entrenched in the American way of life the longer he lived in the United States, although he still clung to certain aspects of his Italian identity (Fitts 2002). The same is true of the German immigrants in Reckner's (2001) study, who came to the United States with hardly anything in their pockets. As they moved up the ladder of American society, they purchased clay pipes with American motifs, celebrating their new homeland and newfound social standing. When the nation turns against certain groups of immigrants, such as the Irish in New York's Five Points neighborhood, some turn toward their roots for sustenance. Facing repeated discrimination and marginalization in historic New York, the Irish formed a collective anchored in their Irish heritage. They purchased and smoked pipes that honored their nation of origin, with harps and Irish slogans etched into their clay bodies.

The study of citizenship from a historical archaeological perspective therefore paints a multidimensional picture of life in historic America, canvassing the diversity of citizenship aspirations and desires over the course of American history, an individual's life span, or an ethnic group's time in the United States. Diana DiPaolo Loren and Mary Beaudry express similar sentiments, arguing that "becoming American" is a process rather than a sharp transition in a group or individual's life, one archaeologists can witness in the small things past Americans left behind visible in the stratigraphic record (2006). Citizenship longings can change and evolve over the course of one's life, illustrating that American citizenship evokes a wide spectrum of conflicting longings, desires, and ambitions.

As witnessed in this book, although American citizenship holds the promise of equal treatment in the United States, naturalized citizens' experiences in America have been and are unequal. In America today, for instance, gay couples are unable to partake in the ritual of marriage in most states (Adam 2003). Their sexuality precludes them from accessing the rights extended to heterosexual American citizens who are allowed to form a marital union. With marriage comes "tangible and intangible benefits that are linked to and support psychological health," including "spousal benefits, such as social security and public pensions; income tax benefits; inheritance, insurance, and survivorship rights including estate tax benefits; health insurance in spouses' group plans; the right to sue for wrongful death of a spouse; and power to make medical decisions on behalf of a spouse"; these rights are inaccessible to gays and lesbians (Herdt and Kertzner 2006, 36). Another example of the unequal distribution of citizenship rights is the United States' "don't ask, don't tell" policy, which prevented openly gay individuals from serving in the military. It was only recently overturned in 2010 even though "evidence from studies on foreign militaries . . . suggests that lifting bans on homosexual personnel does not threaten unit cohesion or undermine military effectiveness" (Belkin 2003, 174). Once again, this confirms that American citizenship in and of itself does not guarantee fair treatment while living within the geopolitical boundaries of the United States.

Racial categorization, like sexuality, has also predetermined each person's range of opportunities as an American citizen. A more extreme example of the denial of citizenship privileges due to an individual's perceived race was the proposed Senate Bill 1070 (S.B. 1070) that Arizona governor Jan Brewer signed on April 23, 2010 (Martinez 2012, 176). Among many other contentious things, S.B. 1070 gives Arizona law enforcement agencies the right to request and "determine the immigration status of the person" during "any lawful stop" if there exists "reasonable suspicion" (177). Governor Brewer also went after the state's ethnic studies program, preventing school districts from teaching courses on ethnic or racial histories. Although S.B. 1070 was later ruled unconstitutional in a lawsuit between Arizona and the federal government, Mexican immigrants continue to be unjustly targeted as the primary source of crime and economic instability in the United States' southwestern and western regions.

States continue to take matters into their own hands when it comes to citizenship and immigration. Texas has gone as far as to involve citizens in surveillance operations from the safety of their homes; the Texas Virtual Border Watch Program, which can elicit "a dangerous and unproductive attitude with private citizens seeking to draw rather uncompromising lines between who is worthy of inclusion in a society and who is not," allows citizens to watch the border and report any unauthorized crossings from the comfort of their homes (Koskela 2010, 108). Since the 1990s the federal government has invested an unprecedented amount of funds into supporting Operation Gatekeeper in the name of "securing the border" (Purcell and Nevins 2005, 220); between 1993 and 1997 alone, the U.S. Immigration and Naturalization Service budget for border enforcement rose from $400 million to $800 million (220). Mark Purcell and Joseph Nevins point out the irony in such policing, where the U.S. supports "growing economic integration between the U.S. and Mexico" despite parading out a barrage of policing technologies on the border (220). Mexican immigrants thus continue to cross the border seeking work because there are American employers who will hire them, yet the U.S. government has been lenient toward the latter group while criminalizing and incarcerating the racially marginalized former group.

Historical archaeology can trace these changing belief systems about membership within the national community of the United States. Although many Americans celebrate the nation's contract that promises equality and democracy for all, the study of citizenship suggests that the nation makes decisions on a case-by-case basis, and people who exhibit what are deemed "marginal" characteristics are unable to enjoy the full scope of American citizenship. This captures what McKanders has termed "tiered personhood" (2010, 172), where a certain group of citizens experiences American citizenship in categorically different ways due to their sexuality, class, gender, or race. By studying past inconsistencies and injustices in the doctrines of American citizenship, we may begin to "imagine the directions citizenship may take in the future—as well as the obstacles it may encounter" (Thelen 2000, 551).

The eras of internment, confinement, and exclusion based on one's ethnic and racial identity continue to haunt us in the present. Lawful citizens as well as individuals who consider themselves "cultural" citizens continue to face unjust harassment and persecution in modern America, making archaeologies of historical instances in which citizenship was denied or retracted all the more important to document, analyze, and share with the American public. The recent passing of Arizona's Support Our Law Enforcement and Safe Neighborhoods Act (Arizona S.B. 1070), which gives law enforcement personnel the right to request legal forms of identification from individuals who resemble "illegal aliens," is just one of the many instances where American history is repeating itself, giving police officers free rein to persecute individuals based on their physiological characteristics. Archaeological research can bring these injustices to light by recalling historical instances in which similar events occurred, reminding us that the archaeological remnants of citizenship laws and beliefs are present among us everywhere in the detritus of the more recent American past.

References

Newspapers and Archival Resources

California Department of Industrial Relations. 1912–1929. Division of Immigration and Housing Records, Carton 77—Pacific Electric Railway Labor Camp Reports, BANC MSS C-A 194. Berkeley: University of California, Berkeley, Bancroft Library—Special Collections.

Los Angeles Times. 1891. "Fox Fur Farming," November 3, p. G6.

———. 1924. "Mount Lowe Resort: Ye Alpine Tavern and Cottages," May 28.

Pacific Electric Railway Company (PERC) Collection. n.d. Work Orders, WO #10730, Envelope #7, The Huntington Library, San Marino, CA.

———. n.d. Work Orders, WO #15487, Envelope #8, The Huntington Library, San Marino, CA.

———. n.d. Work Orders, WO #17089, Envelope #10, The Huntington Library, San Marino, CA.

———. n.d. Work Orders, WO #21352, Envelope #13, The Huntington Library, San Marino, CA.

———. n.d. Work Orders, WO #24156, Envelope #16, The Huntington Library, San Marino, CA.

———. n.d. Work Orders, WO #24157, Envelope #16, The Huntington Library, San Marino, CA.

———. n.d. Work Orders, WO #24898, Envelope #16, The Huntington Library, San Marino, CA.

———. n.d. Work Orders, WO #26270, Envelope #17, The Huntington Library, San Marino, CA.

———. n.d. Work Orders, WO #26467, Envelope #17, The Huntington Library, San Marino, CA.

———. n.d. Work Orders, WO #28457, Envelope #18, The Huntington Library, San Marino, CA.

———. n.d. Work Orders, WO #30489, Envelope #19, The Huntington Library, San Marino, CA.

———. n.d. Work Orders, WO #35002, Envelope #19, The Huntington Library, San Marino, CA.

———. 1903a. "Mount Lowe: A Trip of Surpassing Grandeur." Bancroft F868.L8.67.M6

1903. Berkeley: University of California, Berkeley, Bancroft Library—Special Collections.

———. 1903b. "Mount Lowe: A Way up Trip." Berkeley: University of California, Berkeley, Bancroft Library—Special Collections.

———. 1910a. "Mt. Lowe: 6011 Feet Altitude." Bancroft F868.L8.67.M8 1910z. Berkeley: University of California, Berkeley, Bancroft Library—Special Collections.

———. 1910b. "Mt. Lowe: The Famous Mountain Trolley Trip." Bancroft F868.L8.67.M85 1910. Berkeley: University of California, Berkeley, Bancroft Library—Special Collections.

———. 1922. "To the Portals of Hiker's Land via Pacific Electric Railway," *Mount Lowe Daily News*, March 5.

———. 1936. "Mt. Lowe Tavern and Cottages." Pasadena: Pasadena Museum of History—Special Collections.

Pasadena Daily Evening Star. 1895a. "Santa Catalina: Island the Popular Resort," January 30.

———. 1895b. Advertisement, June 15.

———. 1895c. "Santa Catalina Island! Ever Grand, Ever Attractive, Always Unique: The Season of 1895," June 15.

———. 1895d. "Echo Mountain House—Mount Lowe Railway, 3500 Feet above the Level of the Sea," January 29.

Oral Histories

de Valenciana, Emilie Castaneda. 1972. Interview by Christine Valenciana. Transcription of tape recorded interview. Oral history #700. Center for Oral and Public History at Pollak Library, California State University, Fullerton.

Kelly, Arletta. n.d. Interview by Fred Zunig. Transcription of tape recorded interview. Oral history #48b. Center for Oral and Public History at Pollak Library, California State University, Fullerton.

Owen, Winthrop. 1961. Trolley driver oral history. Pasadena Museum of History.

Thrall, Will H. Collection. n.d. Huntington Library, San Marino, CA.

Secondary Sources

Adam, Barry D. 2003. "The Defense of Marriage Act and American Exceptionalism: The 'Gay Marriage' Panic in the United States." *Journal of the History of Sexuality* 12, no. 2: 259–76.

Alberti, Benjamin. 2006. "Archaeology, Men, and Masculinities." In *Handbook of Gender in Archaeology*, edited by Sarah Milledge Nelson, 400–34. Lanham, Md.: AltaMira Press.

Anderson, Benedict. 1983. *Imagined Communities: Reflections on the Origin and Spread of Nationalism*. London: Verso.

Appadurai, Arjun. 1990. "Disjuncture and Difference in the Global Cultural Economy." In *Global Change: Nationalism, Globalization, and Modernity*, edited by Mike Featherstone, 295–310. London: Sage Publications Ltd.

———. 1993. "Patriotism and Its Futures." *Public Culture* 5, no. 3: 411–29.

———, ed. 2001. *Globalization*. Durham, N.C.: Duke University Press.

———. 2003. "Sovereignty without Territoriality: Notes for a Postnational Geography." In *The Anthropology of Space and Place: Locating Culture*, edited by Setha M. Lowe and Denise Lawrence-Zúñiga, 337–49. Oxford: Blackwell Publishing.

Aron, Cindy S. 1999. *Working at Play: A History of Vacations in the United States*. Oxford: Oxford University Press.

Banet-Weiser, Sarah. 2007. *Kids Rule! Nickelodeon and Consumer Citizenship*. Durham, N.C.: Duke University Press.

Barrett, James R. 1992. "Americanization from the Bottom Up: Immigration and the Remaking of the Working Class in the United States, 1880–1920." *Journal of American History* 79, no. 3: 996–1020.

Baugher, Sherene. 2001. "Visible Charity: The Archaeology, Material Culture, and Landscape Design of New York City's Municipal Almshouse Complex, 1736–1797." *International Journal of Historical Archaeology* 5, no. 2: 175–202.

———. 2009. "Historical Overview of the Archaeology of Institutional Life." In *The Archaeology of Institutional Life*, edited by April M. Beisaw and James G. Gibb, 5–13. Tuscaloosa: University of Alabama Press.

Beaudry, Mary C., and Stephen A. Mrozowski. 2001. "Cultural Space and Worker Identity in the Company City: Nineteenth-Century Lowell, Massachusetts." In *The Archaeology of Urban Landscapes: Explorations in Slumland*, edited by Alan Mayne and Tim Murray, 118–31. Cambridge: Cambridge University Press.

Beisaw, April M. 2009. "Constructing Institution-Specific Site Formation Models." In *The Archaeology of Institutional Life*, edited by April M. Beisaw and James G. Gibb, 49–66. Tuscaloosa: University of Alabama Press.

Belkin, Aaron. 2003. "Don't Ask, Don't Tell: Is the Gay Ban Based on Military Necessity?" *Parameters* 40, no. 4: 173–83.

Bogardus, Emory S. 1934. *The Mexican in the United States*. Los Angeles: University of Southern California, School of Research Studies Number Five, Social Science Series Number Eight.

Branton, Nicole Louise. 2004. "Drawing the Line: Places of Power in the Japanese-American Internment Eventscape." Doctoral thesis, Department of Anthropology, University of Arizona.

Brashler, Janet. 1991. "When Daddy Was a Shanty Boy: The Role of Gender in the Organization of the Logging Industry in Highland West Virginia." *Historical Archaeology* 25, no. 4: 54–69.

Breen, T. H. 2004. *The Marketplace of Revolution: How Consumer Politics Shaped American Independence*. Oxford: Oxford University Press.

Brekke, Linzy. 2006. "'To Make a Figure': Clothing and the Politics of Male Identity in Eighteenth-Century America." In *Gender, Taste, and Material Culture in Britain and North America, 1700–1830*, edited by John Styles and Amanda Vickery, 225–46. New Haven, Conn.: Yale University Press.

Brighton, Stephen A. 2008. "Catholic Identities, the Catholic Temperance Movement, and Father Matthew: The Social History of a Teacup." *Northeast Historical Archaeology* 37:21–37.

———. 2011. "Middle-Class Ideologies and American Respectability: Archaeology and the Irish Immigrant Experience." *International Journal of Historical Archaeology* 15:30–50.

Brown, Dona. 1995. *Inventing New England: Regional Tourism in the Nineteenth Century*. Washington, D.C.: Smithsonian Institution Press.

Bruner, Edward M. 2005. *Culture on Tour: Ethnographies of Travel*. Chicago: University of Chicago Press.

Brunson, Tiffany. 2012. "What Boys and Girls Are Made of: Social Identity and Gender at the Fort Spokane Indian Boarding School, Fort Spokane, Washington." Master's thesis, Department of Sociology and Anthropology, University of Idaho.

Buchli, Victor, and Gavin Lucas, eds. 2001. *Archaeologies of the Contemporary Past*. London: Routledge.

Burton, Benedict. 1983. *The Anthropology of World's Fairs: San Francisco's Panama Pacific International Exhibition of 1915*. London: Scholar Press.

Burton, Jeffrey F. 1996. "Three Farewells to Manzanar: The Archaeology of Manzanar National Historic Site, California." *Publications in Anthropology* 67. Tucson: Western Archaeological and Conservation Center, National Park Service, U.S. Department of the Interior.

———. 1998. "The Archaeology of Somewhere: Archaeological Testing along U.S. Highway 395, Manzanar National Historic Site, California." *Publications in Anthropology* 72. Tucson: Western Archaeological and Conservation Center, National Park Service, U.S. Department of the Interior.

———. 2005a. *Tule Lake Segregation Center, Modoc County, California*. Tucson: Western Archaeological and Conservation Center, National Park Service, U.S. Department of the Interior.

———. 2005b. "The Fate of Things: Archaeological Investigations at the Minidoka Relocation Center Dump, Jerome County, Idaho." *Publications in Anthropology* 90. Tucson: Western Archaeological and Conservation Center, National Park Service, U.S. Department of the Interior.

———. 2006. *Poston Relocation Center, La Paz County, Arizona*. Tucson: Western Archaeological and Conservation Center, National Park Service, U.S. Department of the Interior.

Burton, Jeffrey F., and Mary M. Farrell. 2001. "This Is Minidoka: An Archaeological Survey of Minidoka Internment National Monument, Idaho." *Western Archaeological and Conservation Center Publications in Anthropology* 80. Tucson: National Park Service.

———. 2006. "An Archaeological Survey of the John Herrmann 'Farm-in-a-Day' Property, Jerome County, Idaho." *Publications in Anthropology* 95. Tucson: Western Archaeological Conservation Center, National Park Service, U.S. Department of the Interior.

———. 2007. "World War II Japanese American Internment Sites in Hawai'i." Trans-Sierran Archaeological Research, Tucson, AZ, in Cooperation with Japanese Cultural Center of Hawai'i Research Center, Honolulu, HI.

Burton, Jeffrey F., Laura Bergstresser, and Anna Tamura. 2003. "Archaeology at the Gate: Archaeological Investigations at the Entrance of the Minidoka Relocation Center." Tucson: Western Archaeological and Conservation Center, National Park Service, U.S. Department of the Interior.

Burton, Jeffrey F., Jeremy Haines, and Mary Farrell. 2001. "I Rei To: Archaeological Investigations at the Manzanar Relocation Center Cemetery, Manzanar National Historic Site, California." *Publications in Anthropology* 79. Tucson: Western Archaeological and Conservation Center, National Park Service, U.S. Department of the Interior.

Burton, Jeffrey F., Mary Farrell, Florence Lord, and Richard Lord. 2002. *Confinement and Ethnicity: An Overview of World War II Japanese American Relocation Sites*. Seattle: University of Washington Press.

Camp, Stacey L. 2009. "Materializing Inequality: The Archaeology of Citizenship and Race in Early 20th Century Los Angeles." Doctoral thesis, Department of Anthropology, Stanford University, Stanford, CA.

———. 2011a. "Consuming Citizenship? The Archaeology of Mexican Immigrant Ambivalence in Early 20th Century Los Angeles," *International Journal of Historical Archaeology* 15, no. 3: 305–28.

———. 2011b. "Materializing Inequality: The Archaeology of Tourism Laborers in Turn-of-the-Century Los Angeles." *International Journal of Historical Archaeology* 15:279–97.

———. 2011c. "The Utility of Comparative Research in Historical Archaeology." In *The Importance of Material Things*, vol. 2, edited by Julie M. Schablitsky and Mark P. Leone, 13–28. Rockville, Md.: Society for Historical Archaeology, Special Publication 9.

———. 2012. "From Reform to Repatriation: Gendering an Americanization Movement in Early 20th Century California." In *Historical and Archaeological Perspectives on Gender Transformations*, edited by Suzanne Spencer-Wood. New York: Springer.

Camp, Stacey L., and Bryn Williams. Forthcoming. "Beyond Ethnicity: Archaeologies of Race in Historic California." In *Archaeologies of the American West*, edited by Mark Warner and Margaret Purser. Norman: University of Oklahoma Press.

Carr, Viva M. 1919. "Welfare Work among Mexican Employees." *Pacific Electric Magazine* 4, no. 1 (June 10).

———. 1921. "Camp Welfare." *Pacific Electric Magazine* 5, no. 8 (January 10).

Casella, Eleanor Conlin. 2007. *The Archaeology of Institutional Confinement*. Gainesville: University Press of Florida.

Chambers, Henry L., Jr. 2007. "*Dred Scott*: Tiered Citizenship and Tiered Personhood." *Chicago-Kent Law Review* 82:209–32.

Chin, Elizabeth. 2001. *Purchasing Power: Black Kids and American Consumer Culture*. Minneapolis: University of Minnesota Press.

Clark, Bonnie J. 2012. "The Tangible History of Amache: Archaeology Research Design and Methodology for Field Investigation," Summer 2012. Denver, Colo.: University of Denver.

Clark, Bonnie J., April Kamp-Whittaker, and Dana Ogo Shew. 2008. "The Tangible History of Amache: Archaeology Research Design and Methodologies for Field Investigations," Summer. Denver, Colo.: University of Denver.

Cohen, Lizabeth. 1990. *Making a New Deal: Industrial Workers in Chicago, 1919–1939.* Cambridge: Cambridge University Press.

———. 2003. *A Consumers' Republic: The Politics of Mass Consumption in Postwar America.* New York: Vintage Books.

Cott, Nancy F. 1998. "Marriage and Women's Citizenship in the United States, 1830–1934." *American Historical Review* 103, no. 5: 1440–74.

Cowie, Sarah E. 2011. *The Plurality of Power: An Archaeology of Industrial Capitalism.* New York: Springer.

Creef, Elena Tajima. 2004. *Imaging Japanese America: The Visual Construction of Citizenship, Nation, and the Body.* New York: New York University Press.

Cross, Gary. 2000. *An All-Consuming Century: Why Commercialism Won in Modern America.* New York: Columbia University Press.

Culver, Milton Lawrence, Jr. 2004. "The Island, the Oasis, and the City: Santa Catalina, Palm Springs, Los Angeles, and Southern California's Shaping of American Life and Leisure." Doctoral thesis. Department of History, University of California, Los Angeles.

Daniels, Roger. 2004. *Guarding the Golden Door: American Immigration Policy and Immigrants since 1882.* New York: Hill and Wage.

Davis, Mike. 1998. *Ecology of Fear: Los Angeles and the Imagination of Disaster.* New York: Vintage Books.

DeLyser, Dydia. 2003. "Ramona Memories: Fiction, Tourist Practices, and Placing the Past in Southern California." *Annals of the Association of American Geographers* 93, no. 4: 886–908.

Denenberg, Thomas Andrew. 2003. *Wallace Nutting and the Invention of Old America.* New Haven, Conn.: Yale University Press.

Desmond, Jane C. 1999. *Staging Tourism: Bodies on Display from Waikiki to Sea World.* Chicago: University of Chicago Press.

Deutsch, Sarah. 1987. *No Separate Refuge: Culture, Class, and Gender on an Anglo-Hispanic Frontier in the American Southwest, 1880–1940.* Oxford: Oxford University Press.

Deverell, William. 1997. "Privileging the Mission over the Mexican: The Rise of Regional Identity in Southern California." In *Over the Edge: Remapping the American West,* edited by Valerie Matsumoto and Blake Allmendinger, 172–200. Berkeley: University of California Press.

———. 2004. *Whitewashed Adobe: The Rise of Los Angeles and the Remaking of its Mexican Past.* Berkeley: University of California Press.

Deverell, William, and Douglas Flamming. 1999. "Race, Rhetoric, and Regional Identity: Boosting Los Angeles, 1880–1930." In *Power and Place in the North American West,* edited by Richard White and John M. Findlay, 117–43. Seattle: University of Washington Press.

Drake, Nadia. 2011. "Immigration Tracked through Desert Detritus." *Nature,* April 11.

Dusselier, Jane E. 2005. "Gendering Resistance and Remaking Place: Art in Japanese

American Concentration Camps." *Peace and Change: A Journal of Peace Research* 30, no. 2: 171–204.

———. 2008. *Artifacts of Loss: Crafting Survival in Japanese American Concentration Camps.* New Brunswick, N.J.: Rutgers University Press.

Elliott, Clifford A. 1918. "Home Attractions Keep Track Laborers Satisfied—Solving the Labor Problem by Providing Free Section Houses with All Conveniences, Land for Gardens and Chicken Raising as Well as Free Transportation to Amusement Places for Their Employees and Families." *Pacific Electric Magazine,* July 27, 150–52.

Eng, David. 2000. *Racial Castration: Managing Masculinity in Asian America.* Durham, N.C.: Duke University Press.

Farrell, Mary M., and Jeffrey F. Burton. 2004. "Civil Rights and Moral Wrongs: World War II Japanese American Relocation Sites." *SAA Archaeological Record* 4, no. 5: 22–28.

Feister, Lois M. 2009. "The Orphanage at Schuyler Mansion." In *The Archaeology of Institutional Life,* edited by April M. Beisaw and James G. Gibb, 105–16. Tuscaloosa: University of Alabama Press.

Finkelman, Paul. 2007. "*Scott v. Sandford*: The Court's Most Dreadful Case and How It Changed History." *Chicago-Kent Law Review* 82:3–48.

Fitts, Robert K. 1999. "The Archaeology of Middle-Class Domesticity and Gentility in Victorian Brooklyn." *Historical Archaeology* 33, no. 1: 39–62.

———. 2002. "Becoming American: The Archaeology of an Italian Immigrant." *Historical Archaeology* 36, no. 2: 1–17.

Flores, William V., and Rina Benmayor. 1997. "Constructing Cultural Citizenship." In *Latino Cultural Citizenship: Claiming Identity, Space, and Rights,* edited by William V. Flores and Rina Benmayor, 1–23. Boston: Beacon Press.

Funari, Pedro Paulo A., Siân Jones, and Martin Hall, ed. 1999. *Historical Archaeology: Back from the Edge.* One World Archaeology, vol. 31. London: Routledge.

Gamio, Manuel. 1930. *Mexican Immigration to the United States: A Study of Human Migration and Adjustment.* Chicago: University of Chicago Press.

———. 1931. *The Mexican Immigrant: His Life-Story.* Chicago: University of Chicago Press.

Garcia, Matt. 2001. *A World of Its Own: Race, Labor, and Citrus in the Making of Greater Los Angeles, 1900–1970.* Chapel Hill: University of North Carolina Press.

Gibb, James G., and April M. Beisaw. 2000. "Learning Cast Up from the Mire: Archaeological Investigations of Schoolhouses in the Northeastern United States." *Northeast Historical Archaeology* 29:107–29.

Gleason, Phillip. 1964. "The Melting Pot: Fusion or Confusion." *American Quarterly* 16, no. 1: 20–46.

González, Gilbert G. 2004. *Culture of Empire: American Writers, Mexico, and Mexican Immigrants, 1880–1930.* Austin: University of Texas Press.

Grusin, Richard. 2004. *Culture, Technology, and the Creation of America's National Parks.* Cambridge: Cambridge University Press.

Gullet, Gayle. 1995. "Women Progressives and the Politics of Americanization in California, 1915–1920." *Pacific Historical Review* 64, no. 1: 71–94.

Gupta, Akhil. 2003. "The Song of the Nonaligned World: Transnational Identities and the Reinscription of Space in Late Capitalism." In *The Anthropology of Space and Place: Locating Culture*, edited by Setha M. Low and Denise Lawrence-Zúñiga, 321–36. Oxford: Blackwell Publishing.

Gupta, Akhil, and James Ferguson. 2002. "Beyond 'Culture': Space, Identity, and the Politics of Difference." In *The Anthropology of Globalization: A Reader*, edited by Jonathan Xavier Inda and Renato Rosaldo, 65–80. Oxford: Blackwell Publishing.

Gutmann, Matthew C. 1997. "Trafficking in Men: The Anthropology of Masculinity." *Annual Review of Anthropology* 26:385–409.

Hall, Stuart, and David Held. 1989. "Citizens and Citizenship." In *New Times: The Changing Face of Politics in the 1990s*, edited by Stuart Hall and Martin Jacques, 173–88. London: Lawrence & Wishart.

Harrigan, John. 2000. *Mount Lowe Power*. Self published.

Hartigan-O'Connor, Ellen. 2006. "Collaborative Consumption and the Politics of Choice in Early American Port Cities." In *Gender, Taste, and Material Culture in Britain and North America, 1700–1830*, edited by John Styles and Amanda Vickery, 125–49. New Haven, Conn.: Yale University Press.

Helphand, Kenneth I. 2006. *Defiant Gardens: Making Gardens in Wartime*. San Antonio, Tex.: Trinity University Press.

Herdt, Gilbert, and Robert Kertzner. 2006. "I Do, but I Can't: The Impact of Marriage Denial on the Mental Health and Sexual Citizenship of Lesbians and Gay Men in the United States." *Sexuality Research & Social Policy* 3, no. 1: 33–49.

Higham, John. 1963. *Strangers in the Land: Patterns of American Nativism, 1860–1925*, 2nd ed. New York: Atheneum.

Hirasuna, Delphine. 2005. *The Art of Gaman: Arts and Crafts from the Japanese American Internment Camps, 1942–1946*. Berkeley, Calif.: Speed Press.

Hoehling, Mary. 1958. *Thaddeus Lowe, America's One-Man Corps*. New York: Julian Messner, Inc.

Hoganson, Kristin L. 2007. *Consumers' Imperium: The Global Production of American Domesticity, 1865–1920*. Chapel Hill: University of North Carolina Press.

Holston, James, and Arjun Appadurai. 1996. "Cities and Citizenship." *Public Culture* 8, no. 2: 187–204.

Horsman, Reginald. 1981. *Race and Manifest Destiny: The Origins of American Racial Anglo-Saxonism*. Cambridge, Mass.: Harvard University Press.

Jackson, John P., Jr., and Nadine M. Weidman. 2004. *Race, Racism, and Science: Social Impact and Interaction*. New Brunswick, N.J.: Rutgers University Press.

Jacoby, Karl. 2001. *Crimes against Nature: Squatters, Poachers, Thieves, and the Hidden History of American Conservation*. Berkeley: University of California Press.

Jakle, John A. 1985. *The Tourist: Travel in Twentieth-Century North America*. Lincoln: University of Nebraska Press.

James, George Wharton. 1894. *Photographic Scenes along the Line of the Mount Lowe Railway*. Echo Mountain, Calif.: Mount Lowe Railway—Mountain Office.

———. 1904. *The Grandest Railway in the World: Scenic Mount Lowe and Its Wonderful Railway*. Los Angeles: Pacific Electric Railway.

Joyce, Rosemary A. 2000. "A Precolumbian Gaze: Male Sexuality among the Ancient Maya." In *Archaeologies of Sexuality*, edited by Robert A. Schmidt and Barbara L. Voss, 263–83. London: Routledge.

———. 2004. "Embodied Subjectivity: Gender, Femininity, Masculinity, Sexuality." In *A Companion to Social Archaeology*, edited by Lynn Meskell and Robert Preucel, 82–95. Oxford: Blackwell.

———. 2005. Archaeology of the Body. *Annual Review of Anthropology* 34:139–58.

Kaczorowski, Robert J. 1987. "To Begin the Nation Anew: Congress, Citizenship, and Civil Rights after the Civil War." *American Historical Review* 92, no. 1: 45–68.

Kamp-Whittaker, April. 2010. "Through the Eyes of a Child: The Archaeology of WWII Japanese American Internment at Amache." Master's thesis, Department of Anthropology, University of Denver.

Kearney, Michael. 1995. "The Local and the Global: The Anthropology of Globalization and Transnationalism." *Annual Review of Anthropology* 24:547–65.

Kerber, Linda K. 1997. "The Meanings of Citizenship." *Journal of American History* 84, no. 3: 833–54.

Kettner, James H. 1974. "The Development of American Citizenship in the Revolutionary Era: The Idea of Volitional Allegiance." *American Journal of Legal History* 18, no. 3: 208–42.

———. 1978. *The Development of American Citizenship, 1608–1870*. Chapel Hill: University of North Carolina Press.

Knapp, Bernard A. 1998a. "Boys Will Be Boys: Masculinist Approaches to a Gendered Archaeology." In *Reader in Gender Archaeology*, edited by Kelly Hays-Gilpin and David S. Whitley, 365–73. London: Routledge.

———. 1998b. "Who's Come a Long Way, Baby?" *Archaeological Dialogues* 5, no. 2: 91–125.

Koskela, Hille. 2010. "Did You Spot an Alien? Voluntary Vigilance, Borderwork and the Texas Virtual Border Watch Program." *Space and Polity* 14, no. 2: 103–21.

Kozakavich, Stacy Colleen. 2007. "The Center of Civilization: Archaeology and History of the Kaweah Co-operative Commonwealth." Doctoral diss., Department of Anthropology, University of California, Berkeley.

Kropp, Phoebe S. 2006. *California Vieja: Culture and Memory in a Modern Place*. Berkeley: University of California Press.

Kruczek-Aaron, Hadley. 2002. "Choice Flowers and Well-Ordered Tables: Struggling over Gender in a Nineteenth-Century Household." *International Journal of Historical Archaeology* 6, no. 3: 173–85.

Kurashige, Lon. 2002. *Japanese American Celebration and Conflict: A History of Ethnic Identity and Festival, 1934–1990*. Berkeley: University of California Press.

Leach, William. 1993. *Land of Desire: Merchants, Power, and the Rise of a New American Culture*. New York: Vintage Books.

Lears, T. J. Jackson. 1981. *No Place of Grace: Antimodernism and the Transformation of American Culture, 1880–1920*. New York: Pantheon Books.

———. 1994. *Fables of Abundance: A Cultural History of Advertising in America*. New York: Basic Books.

Lee, Erika. 2002. "Enforcing the Borders: Chinese Exclusion along the U.S. Borders with Canada and Mexico, 1882–1924." *Journal of American History* 89, no. 1: 54–86.

Lewthwaite, Stephanie. 2007. "'Writing Reform' in Early Twentieth-Century Los Angeles: The Sonoratown Anthologies." *Journal of American Studies* 41, no. 2: 331–64.

Lindauer, Owen. 1996. "Historical Archaeology of the United States Industrial Indian School at Phoenix: Investigations of a Turn of the Century Trash Dump." *Anthropological Field Studies Number 42*. Department of Anthropology, Arizona State University, Tempe.

———. 1997. "Not for School, but for Life: Lessons from the Historical Archaeology of the Phoenix Indian School." Office of Cultural Resource Management, Arizona State University, Tempe.

———. 2009. "Individual Struggles and Institutional Goals: Small Voices from the Phoenix Indian School Track Site." In *The Archaeology of Institutional Life*, edited by April M. Beisaw and James G. Gibb, 86–102. Tuscaloosa: University of Alabama Press.

Lipsitz, George. 1998. *The Possessive Investment in Whiteness: How White People Profit from Identity Politics*. Philadelphia: Temple University Press.

Loewen, James W. 2006. *Sundown Towns: A Hidden Dimension of American Racism*. New York: Simon & Schuster.

Loren, Diana DiPaolo. 2010. *The Archaeology of Clothing and Bodily Adornment*. Gainesville: University Press of Florida.

Loren, Diana DiPaolo, and Mary C. Beaudry. 2006. "Becoming American: Small Things Remembered." In *Historical Archaeology*, edited by Martin Hall and Stephen W. Silliman, 251–71. Oxford: Blackwell Publishing.

MacCannell, Dean. 1999. *The Tourist: A New Theory of the Leisure Class*. Berkeley: University of California Press.

Manning, Mike. 2005. *Intrepid: An Account of Professor T.S.C. Lowe, Civil War Aeronaut and Hero*. Self published.

Martin, Ann Smart. 2006. "Ribbons of Desire: Gendered Stories in the World of Goods." In *Gender, Taste, and Material Culture in Britain and North America, 1700–1830*, edited by John Styles and Amanda Vickery, 179–200. New Haven, Conn.: Yale University Press.

Martinez, George A. 2012. "Arizona, Immigration, and Latinos: The Epistemology of Whiteness, the Geography of Race, Interest Convergence, and the View from the Perspective of Critical Theory." *Arizona State Law Journal* 44: 175–211.

McBane, Margo. 2006. "Culture Vultures: White New Womanhood's Preserving and Reinterpreting of California's 'Primitive' Heritage of Native Americans, Mexicans, and the Wilderness, 1800s to 1930s." In *Considering America from Inside and Out: A San José/Ostrava Dialogue Sharing Perspectives*, 81–97. Ostrava, Czechoslovakia: Universitas Ostraviensis.

McCartney, Martha W. 1987. "Virginia's Workhouse for the Poor: Care for 'Divers Idle and Disorderly Persons.'" *North American Archaeologist* 8, no. 4: 287–303.

McClintock, Anne. 1995. *Imperial Leather: Race, Gender, and Sexuality in Colonial Conquest*. New York: Routledge.

McClymer, John F. 1991. "Gender and the 'American Way of Life': Women in the Americanization Movement." *Journal of American Ethnic History* 10, no. 3: 3–18.

McDaniel, Olivia. 2012. "For the Man: Traditional Decor," March 20. http://www.uidaho.edu/class/kicap/updates.

McKanders, Karla Mari. 2010. "Sustaining Tiered Personhood: Jim Crow and Anti-Immigrant Laws." *Harvard Journal on Race & Ethnic Justice* 26, no. 1: 163–210.

McWilliams, Carey. 1968. *North from Mexico: The Spanish-Speaking People of the United States*. New York: Greenwood Press. First published in 1948.

———. 1973. *Southern California: An Island on the Land*. Santa Barbara, Calif.: Peregrine Smith. First published in 1946 by Duell, Sloan, & Pearce.

Miasato, Doris Moromisato. 2002. "I Woman, I Man, I Nikkei." In *New Worlds, New Lives: Globalization and People of Japanese Descent in the Americas and from Latin America in Japan*, edited by Lane Ryo Hirabayashi, Akemi Kikumura-Yano, and James A. Hirabayashi, 187–207. Stanford, Calif.: Stanford University Press.

Miller, R. Justin. 1921. "Labor Camp Sanitation—A Basis for Education and Citizenship." *American Journal of Public Health* 11, no. 8: 697–702.

Molina, Natalia. 2006. *Fit to be Citizens? Public Health and Race in Los Angeles, 1897–1939*. Berkeley: University of California Press.

Mrozowski, Stephen A., Grace H. Ziesing, and Mary C. Beaudry. 1996. *Living on the Boott: Historical Archaeology at the Boott Mills Boardinghouses, Lowell, Massachusetts*. Amherst: University of Massachusetts Press.

Mullins, Paul. 1999a. *Race and Affluence: An Archaeology of African America and Consumer Culture*. New York: Kluwer Academic/Plenum Publishers.

———. 1999b. "Race and the Genteel Consumer: Class and African-American Consumption, 1850–1930." *Historical Archaeology* 33, no. 1: 22–38.

———. 2001. "Racializing the Parlor: Race and Victorian Bric-a-Brac Consumption." In *Race and the Archaeology of Identity*, edited by Charles E. Orser Jr., 158–76. Salt Lake City: University of Utah Press.

———. 2011a. "The Archaeology of Consumption." *Annual Review of Anthropology* 40:133–44.

———. 2011b. *The Archaeology of Consumer Culture*. Gainesville: University Press of Florida.

Nash, Roderick Frazier. 1967. *Wilderness & the American Mind*. New Haven, Conn.: Yale University Press.

Nettles, Wendy M., and M. Colleen Hamilton. 2005. "Life at a Remote Railroad Section House Revealed through Material Culture." Paper presented at the Society for California Archaeology Annual Meeting, Sacramento, April.

Neuman, Gerald L. 1993. "The Lost Century of American Immigration Law (1776–1875)." *Columbia Law Review* 93, no. 3: 1833–1901.

Nevins, Joseph. 2002. *Operation Gatekeeper: The Rise of the "Illegal Alien" and the Making of the U.S.-Mexico Boundary*. New York: Routledge.

Ngai, Mae M. 2004. *Impossible Subjects: Illegal Aliens and the Making of Modern America*. Princeton, N.J.: Princeton University Press.

Nicolosi, Ann Marie. 2001. "'We Do Not Want Our Girls to Marry Foreigners': Gender, Race, and American Citizenship." *NWSA Journal* 13, no. 3: 1–21.

Nishimoto, Richard S. 1995. *Inside an American Concentration Camp: Japanese American Resistance at Poston, Arizona*. Edited by Lane Ryo Hirabayashi. Tucson: University of Arizona Press.

Nye, David Edwin. 1990. *Electrifying America: Social Meanings of a New Technology, 1880–1940*. Cambridge, Mass.: MIT Press.

O'Donovan, Maria. 2011. "A Trip to the Mountains: Travel and Social Relations in the Catskill Mountains of New York." *International Journal of Historical Archaeology* 15:267–78.

Oliver, Kali D. V. 2012. "Traditional Health: Wakamoto Bottle." March 20. http://www.uidaho.edu/class/kicap/updates.

Ong, Aihwa. 1996. "Cultural Citizenship as Subject-Making: Immigrants Negotiate Racial and Cultural Boundaries in the United States." *Current Anthropology* 37, no. 5: 737–62.

———. 1999. *Flexible Citizenship: The Cultural Logics of Transnationality*. Durham, N.C.: Duke University Press.

Orser, Charles E., Jr. 1996. *A Historical Archaeology of the Modern World*. New York: Plenum Press.

———. 1999. "Negotiating Our 'Familiar' Pasts." In *The Familiar Past? Archaeologies of Later Historical Britain*, edited by Sarah Tarlow and Susie West, 273–85. London: Routledge.

———. 2007. *The Archaeology of Race and Racialization*. Gainesville: University Press of Florida.

Pacific Electric Railway Corporation (PERC). 1925. "Annual Visit of Santa Claus: Supplies Many Kiddies in Our Company with Christmas Cheer." *Pacific Electric Magazine* 9, no. 8 (January 10).

———. 1927. "Mexican Camp at Pasadena Held as a Model One." *Pacific Electric Magazine* 11, no. 11 (April 10).

———. 1928. "How Company Has Aided Mexican Worker." *Pacific Electric Magazine*, July 10, 3.

———. 1929. "Picnic Lures Largest Crowd: Attendance, Reflected by Concession Tickets, Shows Greatest Number at Last Gathering." *Pacific Electric Magazine*, 14, no. 4 (September 10).

———. 1931. "Two Hundred Trees Planted on Route on Mt. Lowe." *Pacific Electric Magazine*, 10, no. 5 (March 10): 5.

Pani, Erika. 2008. "Saving the Nation through Exclusion: Alien Laws in the Early Republic in the United States and Mexico." *Americas* 65, no. 2: 217–46.

Peña, Elizabeth S. 1992. "Educational Archaeology: Historical Archaeological Investigations at Schoolhouse 12 in the Town of LeRay, Jefferson County." *The Bulletin: Journal of the New York State Archaeological Association* 103:10–19.

Popper, Virginia S. 2007. "Macrobotanical Analysis of Soil Samples from a 'Section House' on Echo Mountain (ANF ECHO 2006), Los Angeles County, California." Fullerton, Calif.: South Central Coastal Information Center.

Praetzellis, Adrian, and Mary Praetzellis. 2001. "Mangling Symbols of Gentility in the Wild West: Case Studies in Interpretive Archaeology." *American Anthropologist* 103, no. 3: 645–54.

Praetzellis, Mary, Adrian Praetzellis, and Marley R. Brown, II. 1988. "What Happened to the Silent Majority? Research Strategies for Studying Dominant Group Material Culture in Late Nineteenth-Century California." In *Documentary Archaeology in the New World*, edited by Mary C. Beaudry, 192–202. Cambridge: Cambridge University Press.

Purcell, Mark, and Joseph Nevins. 2005. "Pushing the Boundary: State Restructuring, State Theory, and the Case of U.S.-Mexico Border Enforcement in the 1990s." *Political Geography* 24:211–35.

Reckner, Paul E. 2001. "Negotiating Patriotism at the Five Points: Clay Tobacco Pipes and Patriotic Imagery among Trade Unionists and Nativists in a Nineteenth-Century New York Neighborhood." *Historical Archaeology* 35, no. 3: 103–14.

Robinson, John W. 1977. *The San Gabriels: Southern California Mountain Country*. San Marino, Calif.: Golden West Books.

Rosaldo, Renato. 1994. "Cultural Citizenship in San Jose, California." *PoLAR* 17, no. 2: 57–64.

———. 1999. "Cultural Citizenship, Inequality, and Multiculturalism." In *Race, Identity, and Citizenship*, edited by Rodolfo D. Torres, Louis F. Mirón, and Jonathan Xavier Inda, 253–61. Oxford: Blackwell Publishers.

———. 2003. "The Borders of Belonging: Nation and Citizen in the Hinterlands." In *Cultural Citizenship in Island Southeast Asia: Nation and Belonging in the Hinterlands*, edited by Renato Rosaldo, 1–15. Berkeley: University of California Press.

Rothfels, Nigel. 2002. *Savages and Beasts: The Birth of the Modern Zoo*. Baltimore: John Hopkins University Press.

Rothman, Hal K. 1998. *Devil's Bargains: Tourism in the Twentieth-Century American West*. Lawrence: University Press of Kansas.

Rotman, Deborah. 2006. "Separate Spheres? Beyond the Dichotomies of Domesticity." *Current Anthropology* 47, no. 4: 666–73.

———. 2009. "Rural Education and Community Social Relations: Historical Archaeology of the Wea View Schoolhouse No. 9, Wabash Township, Tippecanoe County, Indiana." In *The Archaeology of Institutional Life*, edited by April M. Beisaw and James G. Gibb, 69–85. Tuscaloosa: University of Alabama Press.

Rydell, Robert W. 1984. *All the World's a Fair: Visions of Empire at the American International Exposition, 1876–1916*. Chicago: University of Chicago Press.

Rydell, Robert W., and Rob Kroes. 2005. *Buffalo Bill in Bologna: The Americanization of the World, 1869–1922*. Chicago: University of Chicago Press.

Saitta, Dean. 2007. *The Archaeology of Collective Action*. Gainesville: University Press of Florida.

Sánchez, George J. 1993. *Becoming Mexican American: Ethnicity, Culture, and Identity in Chicago Los Angeles, 1900–1945*. Oxford: Oxford University Press.

———. 1994. "'Go after the Women': Americanization and the Mexican Immigrant

Woman, 1915–1929." In *Unequal Sisters: A Multicultural Reader in U.S. Women's History*, edited by Vicki L. Ruiz and Ellen Carol DuBois, 284–97. New York: Routledge.

Savulis, Ellen-Rose. 1992. "Alternative Visions and Landscapes: Archaeology of the Shaker Social Order and Built Environment." In *Text-Aided Archaeology*, edited by Barbara J. Little, 195–203. Boca Raton, Fla.: CRC Press.

Scott, Elizabeth M. 1994. "Through the Lens of Gender: Archaeology, Inequality, and Those of Little Note." In *Those of Little Note: Gender, Race, and Class in Historical Archaeology*, edited by Elizabeth M. Scott, 3–24. Tucson and London: University of Arizona Press.

Sears, John F. 1989. *Sacred Places: American Tourist Attractions in the Nineteenth Century*. Amherst: University of Massachusetts Press.

Seims, Charles. 1976. *Mount Lowe: Railway in the Clouds*. San Marino, Calif.: Golden West Books.

———. 1992. "National Register of Historic Places Registration Form. Property Name: Mount Lowe Railway, Angeles National Forest." Gresham: United States Department of the Interior, National Park Service.

———. 1999. *World's Wonder: Marvelous Mount Lowe—Last Days of Mount Lowe*. Los Angeles: Pacific Electric Railway Historical Society.

Shaffer, Marguerite S. 2001. *See America First: Tourism and National Identity, 1880–1940*. Washington, D.C.: Smithsonian Institution Press.

Shew, Dana Ogo. 2010. "Feminine Identity Confined: The Archaeology of Japanese Women at Amache, a World War II Internment Camp." Master's thesis, Department of Anthropology, University of Denver.

Skiles, Stephanie. 2008. "Confined Cuisine: An Archaeological and Historical Examination of Culinary Practices at Amache, Colorado's WWII Japanese Internment Camp." Master's thesis, Department of Anthropology, University of Denver.

Skiles, Stephanie, and Bonnie J. Clark. 2010. "When the Foreign Is Not Exotic: Ceramics and Colorado's WWII Japanese Internment Camp." In *Trade and Exchange: Archaeological Studies from History and Prehistory*, edited by Carolyn D. Dillian and Carolyn L. White, 179–92. New York: Springer.

Slaughter, Michelle Ann. 2006. "An Archaeological and Ethnographic Examination of the Presence, Acquisition, and Consumption of Sake at Camp Amache, a World War II Japanese Internment Camp." Master's thesis, Department of Anthropology, University of Colorado at Denver.

Smith, James F. 1995. "A Nation That Welcomes Immigrants? An Historical Examination of United States Immigration Policy." *U.C. Davis Journal of International Law & Policy* 1, no. 2: 227–47.

Smith, James Morton. 1956. *Freedom's Fetters: The Alien and Sedition Laws and American Civil Liberties*. Ithaca, N.Y.: Cornell University Press.

Smith, Rogers M. 1997. *Civic Ideals: Conflicting Visions of Citizenship in U.S. History*. New Haven, Conn.: Yale University Press.

Southern Poverty Law Center. 2007. *Close to Slavery: Guestworker Programs in the United States*. Montgomery, Ala.: Southern Poverty Law Center.

Spence, Mark David. 1999. *Dispossessing the Wilderness: Indian Removal and the Making of the National Parks*. Oxford: Oxford University Press.

Spencer-Wood, Suzanne M. 2001. "Introduction and Historical Context to the Archaeology of Seventeenth and Eighteenth Century Almshouses." *International Journal of Historical Archaeology* 5, no. 2:115–22.

———. 2009a. "A Feminist Approach to European Ideologies of Poverty and the Institutionalization of the Poor in Falmouth, Massachusetts." In *The Archaeology of Institutional Life*, edited by April M. Beisaw and James G. Gibb, 117–36. Tuscaloosa: University of Alabama Press.

———. 2009b. "Feminist Theory and the Historical Archaeology of Institutions." In *The Archaeology of Institutional Life*, edited by April M. Beisaw and James G. Gibb, 33–49. Tuscaloosa: University of Alabama Press.

———. 2010. "Feminist Theoretical Perspectives on the Archaeology of Poverty: Gendering Institutional Lifeways in the Northeastern United States from the Eighteenth Century through the Nineteenth Century." *Historical Archaeology* 44, no. 4: 110–35.

Spiro, Peter J. 2008. *Beyond Citizenship: American Identity After Globalization*. Oxford: Oxford University Press.

Starbuck, David. 2004. *Neither Plain nor Simple: New Perspectives on the Canterbury Shakers*. Lebanon, N.H.: University Press of New England.

Starr, Kevin. 1973. *Americans and the California Dream: 1850–1915*. Oxford: Oxford University Press.

Stitt, Irene. 1974. *Japanese Ceramics of the Last 100 Years*. New York: Crown Publishers.

Stocking, George W. 1987. *Victorian Anthropology*. New York: Free Press.

Stone, Geoffrey R. 2004. *Perilous Times: Free Speech in Wartime from the Sedition Act of 1798 to the War on Terrorism*. New York: W. W. Norton.

Stoyka, Michael. 2009. "Mount Lowe Archaeological Project Faunal Analysis." Fullerton, Calif.: South Central Coastal Information Center.

Tamir, Orit, Scott C. Russell, Karolyn Jensen, and Shereen Lerner. 1993. "Return to Butte Camp: A Japanese-American World War II Relocation Center." Prepared for the Bureau of Reclamation, Arizona Projects Office.

Tamura, Anna H. 2004. "Gardens below the Watchtower: Gardens and Meaning in World War II Japanese Incarceration Camps." *Landscape Journal* 21:1–21.

Tarlow, Sarah. 2002. "Excavating Utopia: Why Archaeologists Should Study 'Ideal' Communities of the Nineteenth Century." *International Journal of Historical Archaeology* 6, no. 4: 299–23.

Thelen, David. 2000. "How Natural Are National and Transnational Citizenship? A Historical Perspective." *Indiana Journal of Global Legal Studies* 7, no. 2: 549–65.

Thomas, David Hurst. 2000. *Skull Wars: Kennewick Man, Archaeology, and the Battle for Native American Identity*. New York: Basic Books.

Tomaso, Matthew S., Richard F. Veit, Carissa A. DeRooy, and Stanley L. Walling. 2006. "Social Status and Landscape in a Nineteenth-Century Planned Industrial Alternative Community: Archaeology and Geography of Feltville, New Jersey." *Historical Archaeology* 40, no. 1: 20–36.

Tsing, Anna Lowenhaupt. 1993. *In the Realm of the Diamond Queen: Marginality in an Out-of-the-Way-Place*. Princeton, N.J.: Princeton University Press.

Turner, Frederick Jackson. 1992. *The Frontier in American History*. First published in 1921 by Henry Holt. Tucson: University of Arizona Press.

Turner, Victor. 1969. *Liminality and Communitas: The Ritual Process*. Ithaca, N.J.: Cornell University Press.

Van Bueren, Thad M. 2006. "Between Vision and Practice: Archaeological Perspectives on the Llano del Rio Cooperative." *Historical Archaeology* 40, no. 1: 133–51.

Van Nuys, Frank. 2002. *Americanizing the West: Race, Immigrants, and Citizenship, 1890–1930*. Lawrence: University Press of Kansas.

Van Valkenburg, Carol Bulger. 1996. *An Alien Place: The Fort Missoula Detention Camp, 1941–1944*. Missoula, Mont.: Pictorial Histories Publishing Co.

Van Wormer, Stephen, and G. Timothy Gross. 2006. "Archaeological Identification of an Idiosyncratic Lifestyle: Excavation and Analysis of the Theosophical Society Dump, San Diego, California." *Historical Archaeology* 40, no. 1: 100–118.

Vernon, Charles Clark. 1952. "A History of the San Gabriel Mountains." Master's thesis, Occidental College, Los Angeles.

Wakamoto, Company, LLC. Electronic Communication. 26 February 2012.

Wall, Diana DiZerega. 1991. "Sacred Dinners and Secular Teas: Constructing Domesticity in Mid-19th-Century New York." *Historical Archaeology* 25, no. 4: 69–81.

———. 1994. *The Archaeology of Gender: Separating the Spheres in Urban America*. New York: Plenum Press.

———. 1999. "Examining Gender, Class, and Ethnicity in Nineteenth-Century New York." *Historical Archaeology* 33, no. 1: 102–17.

Wegars, Priscilla. 2010. *Imprisoned in Paradise: Japanese Internee Road Workers at the World War II Kooskia Internment Camp*. Moscow: University of Idaho, Asian American Comparative Collection.

White, Carolyn L. 2005. *American Artifacts of Personal Adornment, 1680–1820: A Guide to Identification and Interpretation*. Lanham, Md.: Rowman & Littlefield.

Wilkie, Laurie. 2010. *The Lost Boys of Zeta Psi: A Historical Archaeology of Masculinity in a University Fraternity*. Berkeley: University of California Press.

Williams, Bryn. 2008. "Chinese Masculinities and Material Culture." *Historical Archaeology* 42, no. 3: 53–67.

Workman, Jessica. 2012. "Japanese Pottery: Dear to Our Hearts." March 20. http://www.uidaho.edu/class/kicap/updates

Wrobel, David M. 2002. *Promised Lands: Promotion, Memory, and the Creation of the American West*. Lawrence: University of Kansas.

Wurst, LouAnn. 2003. "The Legacy of Separate Spheres." In *Shared Spaces and Divided Places: Material Dimensions of Gender Relations on the American Historical Landscape*, edited by Deborah Rotman and Ellen-Rose Savulis, 225–37. Knoxville: University of Tennessee Press.

Zack, Michele. 2004. *Altadena: Between Wilderness and City*. Altadena, Calif.: Altadena Historical Society.

———. 2009. *Southern California Story: Seeking the Better Life in Sierra Madre*. Sierra Madre: Sierra Madre Historical Preservation Society.

Zolberg, Aristide R. 2006. *A Nation by Design: Immigration Policy in the Fashioning of America*. New York: Russell Sage Foundation.

Index

Page numbers in italics refer to illustrations

Acarta, Antonio, 104–5
Adams, Abigail, 14
Adams, John, 14
African Americans: and class, 24; and clothing, 15; diet of, 124–25; and European settlers, 23; during Gilded Age and Progressive Era, 35; and intentional and utopian communities, 69; legal status of, 24, 25, 29, 30–31, 32, 35; material culture of, 12–13; public perceptions of, 125; purchasing practices of, 121; during Reconstruction, 13, 30–32; and slavery, 24; and tourism, 76; and voting rights, 12, 25, 140
Africans, 33, 36
Ah Tye, Yee, 63–64
Alba, Sontenes, 104–5
Albany, N.Y., 47
Alfred, Vivian, 104–5
Alhambra, Calif., 99
Alien and Sedition Laws, 27
Alien Enemies Acts (1798), 28
Alien Friends Act (1798), 28
Almshouses, 7, 43, 48, 49, 50
Altadena, Calif., 78, 84
Amache Internment Camp (Colo.), 132–34
Americanization programs: and class, 125; components of, 8, 41, 74, 95–96, 119–20, 122; effectiveness of, 128; female reformers and, 8, 70, 74, 95, 96–99, 100, 120; purposes of, 6, 70, 99
American Socialist Party, 68
Anderson, Benedict, 7
Angeles National Forest, 78, 80, 82, 114
Anglican Church, 49–50

Animals, 82–84, 88–89, 121
Annapolis, Md., 12, 121, 124
Appadurai, Arjun, 7
Arcadia, Calif., 108
Archaeology of Consumer Culture, The (Mullins), 14
Arizona, 45, 130, 142, 143
Arizona Senate Bill 1070, 142, 143
Artifacts: from African American sites, 12–13; from almshouses, 50; from Amache Internment Camp, 133, 134, 136; associated with Chinese immigrants, 63; associated with German immigrants, 59–60; associated with intentional and utopian communities, 67, 69; associated with Irish immigrants, 59–62; associated with Italian immigrants, 63; associated with Ludlow, Colo., miners, 120; associated with twenty-first-century Mexican immigrants, 130–31; from boarding houses, 113; and class, 55, 57, 58, 59–62, 112–13, 121; from Fayette, Mich., 112–13, 121; and gender roles, 44–45, 47; from Kooskia Internment Camp, 136, 137, 138, *139*; from Mount Lowe Resort and Railway, 106–*7*, 110, *111*, 114–15, 119, 120–24, 129; Native American, 46; political, 12, 13, 58; from schools, 44–45, 46
Asylums, 43
Atlantic City, N.J., 76

Baltimore, Md., 27
Baugher, Sherene, 50
Beaudry, Mary C., 58–59, 141
Beisaw, April M., 44
Board of Health, City of Lowell (Mass.), 113

Bogardus, Emory, 127
Boott Mills (Lowell, Mass.), 58, 113
Brewer, Jan, 142
Brighton, Stephen A., 61
British, 22–25, 49, 74–75
British East India Company, 26
British Honduras, 27
Brooklyn, N.Y., 54
Buckles, 16
Buttons, 14

California, 5–6, 8, 63, 76–77, 78, 82. *See also*
    Mount Lowe Resort and Railway (MLRR)
California Commission on Immigration and
    Housing, 108–9, 110, 112
Cape May, N.J., 76
Carr, Viva, 97, 98, 99, 100
Catholics and Catholicism, 23, 24–25
Catskill Mountains, 75, 76
Chambers, Henry L., 19, 29
Children: and almshouses, 48, 49; and
    education, 44–45, 67, 68, 119; and gender
    roles, 8, 44–45, 47, 54; and infant mortal-
    ity, 97; at intentional and utopian com-
    munities, 67, 68; at Mount Lowe Resort
    and Railway, 92; Native American, 45–47;
    in rural economy, 52; and tourism, 75, *83*;
    U.S.-born, 8, 46; in WWII internment
    camps, 133–34
Chinese, 36, 69. *See also* Immigrants:
    Chinese
Churches, 7, 43
Citizenship: and age, 9; during Civil War
    and Reconstruction eras, 30–32; and
    class, 6, 9, 20, 49, 51, 143; during colonial
    era, 21–25; components of, 1, 23–24; and
    consumption, 2, 20; cultural or flexible,
    4, 5–7, 40–41, 131–32; definitions of, 19;
    and economy, 6; and ethnicity, 9, 19, 20;
    forms of desire for, 42; and gender, 6, 9,
    20, 34–35, 143; during Gilded Age and
    Progressive Era, 32–38; and historical
    archaeology, 139–40, 141, 142–43; historical
    evidence of, 2, 3, 8; and inequality, 6, 7,
    19; influences on, 7–8; laws governing,
    19–20, 24–25, 27–29, 30–31, 32, 34–35; and
    nationality, 19; and national origin, 25; and
    race, 6, 9, 19, 20, 143; during Revolutionary

and post-Revolutionary periods, 25–30;
    scholarship on, 2, 3–4, 5–10, 17; and sexual
    orientation, 20, 141, 143; traditional models
    of, 21
Civil Rights Act of 1866, 30, 31
Clark, Bonnie, 132–33
Class: and Americanization programs, 96;
    and citizenship, 51; and clothing, 14, 15–16,
    41, 84; Herbert Spencer on, 33–34; at
    intentional and utopian communities, 69;
    and material culture, 41, 50–51; middle, 41;
    movement between levels of, 56–57; and
    race, 73; resistance to, 68; and tourism,
    72–73, 74–75. *See also* Lower class; Middle
    class
Coercive Acts, 26
Colonial Revival movement, 4–5
Constitution, U.S., 28
Consumption: and Americanization pro-
    grams, 95, 96, 128; and class, 10, 14, 15–16,
    51, 125–26; during colonial era, 20; and
    Colonial Revival movement, 4–5; and
    gender, 15, 52–53, 55–56; and identity, 2;
    influences on, 3; marginalized groups and,
    10, 12–14, 15, 41, 56–64, 70, 95, 125–26, 129,
    136; and patriotism, 11, 67, 133; and poli-
    tics, 12, 14, 20; and race, 12–13; scholarship
    on, 2, 10–16, 70–71. *See also* Artifacts
Cowie, Sarah E., 112, 121
Creef, Elena, 135, 136

Daniels, Roger, 32
Deerfield, Mass., 55
De León, Jason, 130–31
Democratic Republicans, 27, 28
Deutsch, Sarah, 128
De Valenciana, Emilia Castaneda, 127
Deverell, William, 82
Diamond Chemical Inks, 119
Disneyland, 78
DREAM (Development, Relief, and Educa-
    tion for Alien Minors) Act (Calif.), 5–6
Dred Scott v. Sandford (1857), 25, 29, 30, 39
Dusselier, Jane, 134–35

Echo Mountain. *See* Mount Lowe Resort and
    Railway (MLRR)
Edwards, M. E., 108

1882 Chinese Exclusion Act, 1, 18, 32, 37, 38
Elliott, Clifford, 96
Eng, David, 136
England and Great Britain, 22, 24, 25, 26, 49
Expatriation Act of 1907, 34

Falmouth Almshouse (Mass.), 49
Fayette, Mich., 112–13, 121
Federalists, 27, 28
Felt, David, 66, 67
Feltsville, N.J., 66–67
"Feminine Identity Confined: The Archae-
ology of Japanese American Women at
Amache, A World War II Internment
Camp" (Shew), 133
Fette, Michael, 62–63, 140
Fifteenth Amendment, 31, 35
First Amendment, 28
Fishing, 83
Fitts, Robert K., 54
Five Points neighborhood (New York, N.Y.),
59–62
Fleischer Hotel, 76
Fort Missoula Internment Camp (Mont.),
136–37
Fourteenth Amendment, 30–31, 35
France, 27
Franchise. See Voting rights
French Revolution, 27

Galton, Francis, 36
Gamio, Manuel, 118–19
Geary Act, 37
Gender roles: children and, 8, 44–45, 47, 54;
development of, 52, 55–56, 135; in inten-
tional and utopian communities, 68, 69;
material culture associated with, 44–45,
53, 54; resistance to, 55, 66, 68, 69, 98–99;
and tourism, 75; in WWII internment
camps, 133, 136
Georgia, 27
Gibb, James G., 44
Glacier National Park, 88
Gladding, McBean, & Company, 110, 111
Goggins, James J., 102, 103, 104–5
Gomez, Jose, 104–5
Gonzáles, Elías, 119
Gonzales, Francisco, 104–5

Granada Relocation Center (Colo.), 132–34
Grand Tour, 74–75
Grant National Park, 87
Great Britain. See England and Great
Britain
Great Depression, 6, 20, 100

Harlem, N.Y., 62
Harriman, Job, 68
Harrison, William Henry, 12
Hartigan-O'Connor, Ellen, 15
Hazel-Atlas, 120–21
Hernandez, Joseph, 104–5
Hernandez, Pedro, 104–5
Hoael, William H., 104–5
Holston, James, 7
Hunting, 82, 83
Hutchinson, Anne, 25

Idaho, 135
Immigrants: Asian, 37; aspirations of, 8–9;
Canadian, 37, 104–5; Chinese, 1, 30, 32,
37, 42, 63–64; and class, 9, 14; clothing associated with, 42; convicts as,
27; Eastern European, 38; and ethnicity, 9; French, 27; German, 27, 59–60,
104–5, 140; Irish, 13, 27, 58, 59–62, 102–6,
140–41; Italian, 62–63, 140; Japanese,
132; and labor, 1, 3, 6, 9; Latino, 5, 7; and
material culture, 64; and middle-class
values, 56; Norwegian, 13; and race, 9;
Scottish, 104–5; Southern European,
38; Swiss, 104–5; and U.S. Census, 32;
Western European, 38
Immigrants, Mexican: and Americanization programs, 97–98, 125; and class,
125–26; clothing associated with, 42; and
discrimination, 8, 127–28; and education,
119, 125; and 1882 Chinese Exclusion Act,
37; and exemption from head tax, 37;
and literacy, 118–19, 129; and Mexican
Americans, 125–27; numbers of, 8, 95,
130; public perceptions of, 98–99, 126;
repatriation of, 20, 125, 127; and social
and economic mobility, 70, 129; in the
twenty-first century, 3, 130–31, 142. See
also Mount Lowe Resort and Railway,
Mexican employees of

Immigration: and French Revolution, 27;
during Gilded Age and Progressive Era,
32, 33, 36–38, 72; illegal, 3; laws governing,
27–29, 30, 32, 33, 36–38, 131; restrictions
on, 1, 17, 18; and U.S. economy, 38
Immigration Act of 1875, 32
Immigration Act of 1882, 36–37
Immigration Act of 1917, 37
Immigration Act of 1965, 38
Intentional and utopian communities, 65–69,
67
Ireland, 24

James, George Wharton, 83
Jamestown, Va., 16
Japanese American internment camps, 43,
132–39
Japanese and Japanese Americans, 19, 20,
132–39
Jefferson, Thomas, 23, 28
Jews, 76
Jim Crow laws, 35
Johnson-Reed Immigration Act, 37–38

Kamp-Whittaker, April, 133
Kaweah (Socialist community, Calif.), 65
Kelly, Arletta, 97–98
Kern's Glass Manufacturing Company, 120
Knott's Berry Farm, 78
Kooskia Internment Camp (Idaho), 135, 136,
138–39
Kooskia Internment Camp Archaeological
Project, 138–39
Kruczek-Aaron, Hadley, 55
Kurashige, Lon, 135
Kwiatkowski, Louis F., 102

Labor Camp Sanitation Act, 108, 109
Lake Michigan, 75
Lamar, Colo., 134
Larkin, Edgar L., 86, 104–5
Lawrence, Charles S., 104–5
Lee, Erika, 42
LeRay, N.Y., 45
Lincoln, Abraham, 13
Lipsitz, George, 102
Llano del Rio Cooperative Colony (Los
Angeles, Calif.), 68–69

Loren, Diana DiPaolo, 141
Los Angeles, Calif., 41, 68, 78, 84, 96, 126
Los Angeles County Health Department,
110
Lowe, Thaddeus, 80, 86
Lowell, Mass., 58–59, 113
Lower class: in Great Britain and North
America, 47–50; heterogeneity of, 57;
living conditions of, 58, 66, 67; and material culture, 56–64, 96; and middle and
upper classes, 51; public perceptions of,
47; and reform movements, 47–48; and
tourism, 75–76; and upward mobility,
56–57, 59, 67, 70
Ludlow, Colo., 120

MacCannell, Dean, 73
Manifest Destiny, 22, 77, 81–82
Marcroft, Brian, 114
Marneo, Joe, 104–5
Marxism, 68
Massachusetts, 16, 24, 25, 49, 55
Mathew, Theobald, 61
Maynard, John, 13
Maynard-Burgess family and site, 12, 13
McClintock, Anne, 120
McGroarty, John Steven, 77
McKanders, Karla Mari, 143
McNeil, James B., 104–5
McWilliams, Carey, 109
Mendel, Gregor, 36
Mexican Americans, 20, 35, 77, 125–27, 132.
See also Immigrants, Mexican; Mount
Lowe Resort and Railway, Mexican
employees of
Mexican-American War, 82, 132
Mexico, 8, 82
Middle class: and child rearing, 54; and
family size, 53; heterogeneity of, 57;
influence of, 51; and material culture,
50–51, 53, 54, 55–56, 57, 58, 59, 96; and
tourism, 70, 74–75; worldview of, 51
Milwaukee, Wisc., 119
Misato, Doris Moromisato, 138
"Mission Play, The" (McGroarty), 77
Montana, 136
Moreno, Angel, 104–5
Morton, Samuel George, 35–36

Mount Lowe Archaeology Project, 80–81, 110, 114–18, 123
Mount Lowe Daily News, 89
Mount Lowe Resort and Railway (MLRR): bowling alley at, 78; closing of, 91, 108; and conservation movement, 88–91; dining at, 121, 122; establishment of, 80, 82; fires at, 91, 102, 108; hotels at, 78, *79,* 84, 85, 90, 91, 94, 102, *103;* location of, 78; as middle- and upper-class destination, 73; miniature golf course at, 78; narrative promoted by, 77–78; non-Mexican employees of, 84, 96, 98, 99, 100–106, 108; observatory at, 78, *79,* 86, 88, 89, 94, 102, *103;* ownership of, 80; photos of, *79, 85, 92, 103;* popularity of, 78–80, 88, 91, 102, 113; post office at, 78; railway at, 78, *79,* 84–86, 87, 88, 89, 90, 92–93, 94; searchlight at, 78, 86, 88; size of, 102; tourist activities at, 82, 83, 84, 86, 88–89, 90, 94, 102; wildlife at, 78, 82, 83, 84, 87, 88–89, 102
Mount Lowe Resort and Railway, Mexican employees of: activities of, 70, 94, 104–5, 114–15, 122, 123, 124, 128; and Americanization programs, 6, 8, 41, 70, 74, 95–96, 100, 119, 122, 128; Anglo-American perceptions of, 97, 106, 118, 129; artifacts of, 106–7, 110, *111,* 114–15, 119, 120–24, 129; children of, 97, *101,* 106–7, 108, 113, 119, 120; and class, 6, 113; communal identity of, 129; consumption by, 129; diet of, 97, 122; and discrimination, 8, 96–97, 100, 129; housing for, 74, 80–81, 94, 102, *103,* 106, 114–17, 118, 119, 124; and literacy, 119, 129; living conditions of, 74, 94, 97, 100, 102, 106, 108–12, 113, 124; monitoring of, 94, 96, 119; and occupational training, 6, 8; photos of, 41, *92,* 93, 120; and social and economic mobility, 70; and tourists, 91, 94, 113; typhus outbreak among, 112; wages for, 97. *See also* Immigrants, Mexican; Mexican Americans
Mount Vernon, 16
Mrozowski, Stephen A., 58–59, 113

Mullins, Paul, 11–14, 121, 124
Municipal Almshouse Complex (N.Y.), 50

Nakahira, Tooru, 134
National Origins Act of 1924, 37–38
National Park Service, U.S., 87
Native Americans: and boarding schools, 45–47; and citizenship, 29, 46; and class, 46; display of, 73; and European settlers, 23–24; Herbert Spenser on, 33; and national parks, 87–88; removal of, 81, 87–88; and tourism, 77; and trades, 46; traditional culture of, 46; and voting rights, 25
Naturalization Act of 1798, 27–28
Navarro, Garmon, 104–5
Nevins, Joseph, 142
New Jersey, 66
New Mexico, 128
New York, N.Y., 52–53, 54, 56, 57, 58–62, 140
Ngai, Mae M., 20
Niagara Falls, N.Y., 75, 76
Nineteenth Amendment, 34
Nishimoto, Richard S., 137–38
Nutting, Wallace, 4

Ong, Aihwa, 6–7
Operation Gatekeeper, 142
Orphanages, 7, 43, 47
Owen, Winthrop H., 84

Pacific Electric Magazine, 97, 99, 122
Pacific Electric Railway Corporation (PERC): and Americanization programs, 70, 80, 95–97, 98, 99–102; hiring strategy of, 106, 109; subsidiaries of, 109
Park Inn, 76
Passenger Act of 1819, 29
Paterson, N.J., 61
Peru, 138
Peyton, Valentine, 80
Phoenix Indian School (Ariz.), 45–47
Pierce, Franklin, 12
Polygenists, 35–36
Polynesians, 33
Pomona, Calif., 97
Praetzellis, Adrian, 63
Praetzellis, Mary, 63
Prisons, 7, 43

Progressive Era, 72, 75, 88
Protestants, 23, 24, 25
Protestant work ethic, 49, 50
Providence, R.I., 25
Purcell, Mark, 142

Race and racism: and citizenship, 10; and
 class, 73; in colonial North America,
 23–24; during Gilded Age and Progres-
 sive Era, 32–38, 96, 97; limits imposed by,
 141–42; Samuel George Morton on, 35–36
Reckner, Paul E., 59
Reconstruction, 13, 30–32
Rhode Island Colony, 25
Robertson, Catherine, 104–5
Roosevelt, Teddy, 62
Rosaldo, Renato, 5, 6, 7, 20, 87, 131
Rotman, Deborah, 44, 45, 48, 55

Sacramento, Calif., 63, 64
San Bernardino National Forest, 82
Sánchez, George J., 77
San Diego, Calif., 67
San Francisco, Calif., 78
San Gabriel Mountains, 82, 84, 90
Sanger, Abner, 16
San Jose, Calif., 5
Santa Catalina Island, 82–83, 86
Santa Monica, Calif., 109
San Vicente, Calif., 109
Saratoga Springs, N.Y., 75
Scenic Mount Lowe Railway Historical Com-
 mittee, 114
Schlermann, Henry J., 104–5
Schlermann, Rachel, 104–5
Schoolhouse 12 (LeRay, N.Y.), 45
Schools: as community centers, 45; and
 gender roles, 44–45, 47; in intentional and
 utopian communities, 67, 68; Montessori,
 68; Native Americans and, 45–47; pur-
 poses of, 44; rural, 45; scholarship on, 43;
 in WWII internment camps, 133–34
Schuyler Mansion (Albany, N.Y.), 47
Scott, Dred, 29. See also *Dred Scott v. Sand-
 ford* (1857)
Scott, Elizabeth M., 2
Sea World, 78
Secretary of the Treasury, U.S., 37

Sedition Act of 1798, 28–29
Sequoia National Park, 87
Shakers, 66, 69
Shew, Dana Ogo, 133, 136
Slaves, 15, 16. *See also* African Americans;
 Africans
Smith, Gerrit, 55–56
Smith, Roger, 23, 24, 30
Social Darwinism, 36
Socialists, 65, 67, 68
Southern Pacific Railroad, 109, 122
Spencer, Herbert, 33–34
Spencer-Wood, Suzanne M., 48, 49
Stanford University, 80, 114
Statue of Liberty, 140
Studer, Frederick, 104–5
Suffrage. *See* Voting rights
Suffolk County, N.Y., 28–29
Sulphur Springs, 75
Sunset Magazine, 42
Supreme Court, U.S., 29
Surker, Dillivan M., 104–5
Swift, Lewis, 86
Sze Yud District Association (Sacramento,
 Calif.), 63

Tarios, Pedros, 104–5
Texas, 142
Texas Virtual Border Watch Program, 142
Theosophical Society, 67
Thirteenth Amendment, 30, 35
Thorson, Joseph, 104–5
Tingley, Katherine, 67
Tomaso, Matthew S., 66
Tourism: and American identity, 72–73, 74,
 75, 81; and class, 70, 72–73, 74–75, 92–93;
 and conservation movement, 88; destina-
 tions for, 75, 76–77; English and, 74–75;
 and ethnicity, 76–77; and race, 76–77;
 as ritual, 70, 73; as social reform, 75–76;
 and wilderness, 87; and wildlife, 82–84.
 See also Mount Lowe Resort and Railway
 (MLRR)
Townshend Acts, 26
Turner, Frederick Jackson, 82

University of Denver, 132
University of Michigan, 130

Upper class, 51, 70, 72, 74–75
U.S. Army, 87
U.S. Forest Service, 87
U.S. Immigration and Naturalization Service, 142
U.S. Internal Revenue Service, 37
Utopian and intentional communities, 65–69

Villanueva, Jesus O., 104–5
Virginia, 24, 25, 49–50
Voting rights, 25, 29, 30, 31, 34, 68, 140

Wakamoto Pharmaceutical Company, 138
Wall, Diana DiZerega, 51–53, 56, 57
Walsh, Thomas J., 102, 103, 104–5
Washington, George, 14, 16
Wea View Schoolhouse (Ind.), 44–45
West Oakland, Calif., 13
White, Carolyn L., 15–16
White Mountains, 75
Wildlife, 82–84, 88–89
Williams, Roger, 25
Wilsoy, William B., 104–5
Women: activities of, 44, 52–53, 55, 68, 69, 95, 98–99; and almshouses, 48, 49; and Americanization programs, 95, 98–99; and citizenship, 29, 34; and class, 57, 75–76; and consumer marketplace, 15; and dining rituals, 52–53; and education, 44; and gender roles, 48, 52–53, 55, 66, 98–99; incarceration of, 48; and intentional and utopian communities, 68, 69; legal status of, 55; and marriage, 34; and reform movements, 70; single, 48; and social reform, 34; and tourism, 75–76; as unwed mothers, 48, 49; and voting, 30, 34, 68; widowed, 48; and WWII internment camps, 133
World's Columbian Exposition, 86
World War I, 37
World War II, 19, 20, 132, 133, 134, 138
World War II internment camps, 132–39
Wurst, Lou Ann, 54–55

XYZ incident, 27

Ye Alpine Tavern. See Mount Lowe Resort and Railway (MLRR): hotels at
Yellowstone National Park, 75, 87–88
Yosemite National Park, 75, 87, 88

Zangwill, Israel, 140
Ziesing, Grace, 58
Zolberg, Aristide, 29

Stacey Lynn Camp is associate professor of anthropology at Michigan State University and director of the MSU Campus Archaeology Program.

THE AMERICAN EXPERIENCE IN ARCHAEOLOGICAL PERSPECTIVE
Edited by Michael S. Nassaney

The Archaeology of Collective Action, by Dean J. Saitta (2007)

The Archaeology of Institutional Confinement, by Eleanor Conlin Casella (2007)

The Archaeology of Race and Racialization in Historic America, by Charles E. Orser Jr. (2007)

The Archaeology of North American Farmsteads, by Mark D. Groover (2008)

The Archaeology of Alcohol and Drinking, by Frederick H. Smith (2008)

The Archaeology of American Labor and Working-Class Life, by Paul A. Shackel (2009; first paperback edition, 2011)

The Archaeology of Clothing and Bodily Adornment in Colonial America, by Diana DiPaolo Loren (2010; first paperback edition, 2011)

The Archaeology of American Capitalism, by Christopher N. Matthews (2010; first paperback edition, 2012)

The Archaeology of Forts and Battlefields, by David R. Starbuck (2011; first paperback edition, 2012)

The Archaeology of Consumer Culture, by Paul R. Mullins (2011; first paperback edition, 2012)

The Archaeology of Antislavery Resistance, by Terrance M. Weik (2012; first paperback edition, 2013)

The Archaeology of Citizenship, by Stacey Lynn Camp (2013; first paperback edition, 2019)

The Archaeology of American Cities, by Nan A. Rothschild and Diana diZerega Wall (2014; first paperback edition, 2015)

The Archaeology of American Cemeteries and Gravemarkers, by Sherene Baugher and Richard F. Veit (2014; first paperback edition, 2015)

The Archaeology of Smoking and Tobacco, by Georgia L. Fox (2015; first paperback edition, 2016)

The Archaeology of Gender in Historic America, by Deborah L. Rotman (2015; first paperback edition, 2018)

The Archaeology of the North American Fur Trade, by Michael S. Nassaney (2015; first paperback edition, 2017)

The Archaeology of the Cold War, by Todd A. Hanson (2016)

The Archaeology of American Mining, by Paul J. White (2017)

The Archaeology of Utopian and Intentional Communities, by Stacy C. Kozakavich (2017)

The Archaeology of American Childhood and Adolescence, by Jane Eva Baxter (2019)

The Archaeology of Northern Slavery and Freedom, by James A. Delle (2019)

The Archaeology of Prostitution and Clandestine Pursuits, by Rebecca Yamin and Donna J. Seifert (2019)

The Archaeology of Southeastern Native American Landscapes of the Colonial Era, by Charles R. Cobb (2019)

understanding the past" (Deetz 1982: 724; 1988), including gendered experiences.

Domestic residences were not simply containers for the enactment of the rituals of daily life. Architectural style, the arrangement of rooms, and the meanings assigned to particular household spaces represented active social arenas that shaped and were shaped by the human interactions occurring within them—producing and reproducing social relations (e.g., Barton and Somerville 2012; Fennell 2011; Galle 2010; Gibb and King 1991; Nassaney et al. 2007; Pluckhahn 2010; Rotman 2009a; Smith 2007; Van Buren 2010; Voss 2008e). Furthermore, residences "reflect ideals and realities about relationships between men and women within the family and society" (Moore 1996; Spain 1992: 7). Therefore, the spatial organization of the home expresses attitudes about how the activities of daily life should be ordered (e.g., Barber 1994; Bourdieu 1973; Glassie 1975; M. Johnson 1993). Importantly, however, the idea of the "household" is a western concept projected onto archaeological data, and it may not recognize variations in residential arrangements that vary cross-culturally (Voss 2008e).

Dwellings are designed to accommodate occupants as well as reflect the size and economic status of the social groups that reside there. Significantly too, "the gendered, internal relations of households are . . . a dimension of larger socioeconomic and political processes" (Pluckhahn 2010: 356; see also Brumfiel and Robin 2008; Spencer-Wood 2004). Consequently, domestic residences as dynamic social entities are both the medium and outcome of social practices (Barber 1994; Giddens 1984; Pearson and Richards 1994). In historical archaeology, the largest artifact on a site is often the house, the analysis of which provides insights into the ideologies that structured gendered social relations within the household, including possible variations from proscribed cultural norms (Rotman 2009a: 123–124).

Social relations were (and are) neither universally defined nor operationalized; rather, they were (and are) locally rooted in national discourses and negotiated in lived reality by individual human agents. Thus, they existed in a complex entanglement of multiscalar social relations. The home was "an important locale where institutional policies and practices interfaced with small-scale interpersonal relationships" (Voss 2008a: 209). Home was (and is) the place where the larger social and cultural worlds were negotiated and strategically accepted or rejected (either in whole or in part) to create a meaningful family life (Greenwood and Slawson 2008; Joseph 2004; Rotman 2010: 126, 2012: 34–35). Importantly, households were powerful social loci where children were enculturated into their roles as gendered beings in their particular cultural, temporal, and geographic contexts (Baxter 2005a, 2005b).

Gender and other identities are both personal and collective. They are derived from who we think we are (internal) and who others think we are (external) (Newton 2010; Rotman 2013a). Nassaney (2008: 314) cautions that "interpreting identity is not without its caveats; it always runs the risk of reification and essentialism. We must avoid projecting our own categories onto the past. We also need to beware of facile linkages between material objects and ethnic groups." Identity is shaped by policies, daily practices, and institutional structures that "are continually enacted, reproduced, and transformed in social life" (Voss 2008a: 18). People are inextricably bound together with other people, places, and things (Mintz 1987; Nuttall 2009). Therefore, identities—including gendered identities—are forged through interactions with others at multiple scales, such as households, communities, and institutions.

Gender in Colonial New England

Corporate families, which dominated Anglo-European life in colonial New England, were structured by both ecclesiastical and secular ideologies of patriarchal control (Rotman 2009a). During Deerfield's period of initial settlement (ca. 1665–ca. 1750), the village served as an outpost on the turbulent frontier between the British and the French (Paynter et al. 1987: 6). Household parcels were centered along a main street (known colloquially as "the Street") and surrounded by open agricultural fields (McGowan and Miller 1996), the distribution of which occurred through a system of drawing lots (figure 2.1). At least theoretically, this gave all men an equal chance at acquiring the best property and locations within the village (Melvoin 1989: 61–63; Sheldon 1972, 1983). This system created the sense that there was no socioeconomic differentiation within the community, even though the gentry—known locally as "the River Gods"—controlled the

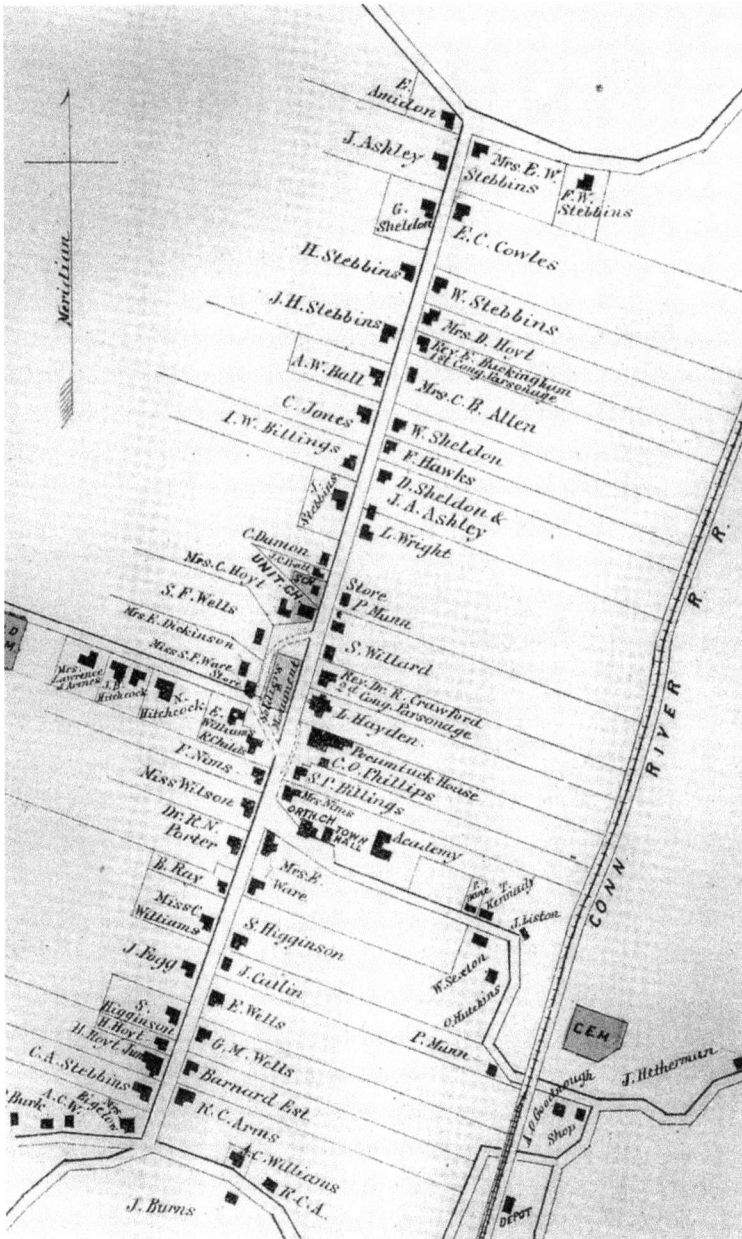

Figure 2.1. Historic Beers map of "the Street" in Deerfield, Massachusetts (Beers 1871).

creation of the village as well as the flow of products and information to and from it (Hood 1996: 139).

The illusion of consensual politics within the community was expressed in individual dwellings, which were fairly diverse and irregularly situated. The original house of the John Nims family (ca. 1740), for example, appears to have been quite small with a cellar measuring only 15 by 20 feet and oriented to magnetic north, rather than parallel to the street (Garrison 1991: 151; McGowan and Miller 1996: 139). The gentry and yeomen farmers alike lived in houses that were similar in basic form, which masked unequal social relations within the community (Paynter 2000; Rotman 2001; St. George 1988). Each household consisted of individuals related by kinship, often multiple generations, and domestic servants. Each corporate family was also linked to other households through kinship, property, and resources. The relative homogeneity of Deerfield during this period was significantly influenced by the equally homogenous Puritan origins of village residents.

Since household authority and community authority were often inseparable, households were neither spatially nor economically isolated entities. Rather, they were part of a larger community system within which goods and services were constantly exchanged (Coontz 1988, 1992; Greven 1970; Nylander 1994: 221; Stewart-Abernathy 1986). Households served as both centers of economic production and loci for social services, education, socialization, work training, and religious instruction (Coontz 1988: 83; M. Johnson 1993; Spain 1992; Wright 1981). Space within individual households was not rigidly delineated along gender lines, and residences often contained only a few rooms, which had multiple functions (Hood 1996: 134; Melvoin 1989: 63; Rotman 2009a).

There was a sexual division of labor, however; men plowed and planted agricultural fields, tended to livestock, and repaired tools, while women processed food and prepared meals, made candles, and did the spinning and weaving (Garrison 1991; Rotman 2006, 2009a; Stewart-Abernathy 1986). This sexual division of labor, however, "did not pull men out into a separate public sphere, distinct from women's household affairs and rewarded on a different basis" (Coontz 1988: 93; Kaestle 1983). Rather, all members of the household contributed to the domestic economy in distinct but complementary ways. The participation of colonial women in vital productive activities resulted in their relatively high status vis-à-vis men (Boserup 1970; Rotman 2006, 2009a). Domestic arrangements similar to those in Deerfield village were also common in the Chesapeake area and elsewhere along the eastern seaboard (Gibb and King 1991).

Corporate families were the economic, social, and political units that tied households to the larger community in a web of interdependence. Patriarchal authority structured order within the village. The materiality of the Street and of individual homes reflected the corporate nature of community life, including hierarchical but complementary gendered social relations. Elsewhere in New England, however, domestic life had different material expressions, particularly for Indigenous peoples, who were one of the primary groups defined by Anglo-Europeans as "other" during the colonial period (Kasper 2012; Nassaney 2004; Silliman and Witt 2010).

As Native peoples adjusted to changing economic, demographic, economic, and social circumstances, new gender roles were negotiated and reconfigured (Nassaney 2004). Among some Indigenous groups, male and female roles were highly interdependent and more flexible than European gender systems. In particular, Narragansett women had greater autonomy vis-à-vis men than European women, in part because they controlled the production of maize, one of the group's principal food sources (Nassaney 2004: 334). They also had greater choice in marriage and family planning, which made them conservative in their responses to Christian conversion in the early colonial period (Bragdon 1996; Kasper 2012). Under colonialism, however, inequalities between Native men and women became increasingly pronounced.

Material practices within Native households, as manifested in tobacco pipes and grinding pestles, elucidated changes to Indigenous gender roles and relations. Among the Huron and other Native American groups of southern New England, smoking traditional pipes was an exclusively male and socially significant activity (Nassaney 2004). Broader dissemination of tobacco in the colonial economic system resulted in increasing use by women and children, which "led to social tensions between men and women by undermining an activity that had once served to reproduce gender relations and ideologies" (Nassaney 2004: 356).

The uncertainty of the changing social world was also expressed in Algonquian society through pestles, cylindrical stones used with wooden

Figure 2.2. Bear effigy pestle of gray slate from Burr's Hill, Warren, Rhode Island. Image drawn by Pamela Rups and provided courtesy of Michael S. Nassaney.

mortars for grinding corn and other grains as part of food preparation. Some pestles were carved with effigies that depicted mythological beings (figure 2.2). Largely associated with women, these effigy pestles were by the mid-seventeenth century clearly symbols through which to communicate with the spirit world. Importantly, in the unsettling conditions under colonialism, "women sought to re-establish the predictability of an earlier social and political order and regain control over their lives and their communities by resisting subordination and connecting to known supernatural life forces in new ways" (Nassaney 2004: 358). Effigy pestles became symbols of biological and cultural survival as well as indicators of women's central roles in the negotiation of a new social order.

The Pequot in Connecticut were also undergoing transformation through culture contact with European American settlers during the colonial period. Although the Pequot held reservation land, it was corruptly managed by colonial overseers (Silliman and Witt 2010). Consequently, Indigenous peoples were increasingly pushed to the literal and metaphorical edges of colonial society, existing on lands of marginal quality and engaging in subsistence agriculture and game hunting. As a result, the Pequot became inextricably bound to colonial settlers through wage labor, exchange, and indebtedness.

George Toney, for instance, moved between the reservation, where his wife, Mary, maintained their residence, and the home of Jonathan Wheeler, a nearby European American farmer and merchant. On the whole, reservation lands were "largely inhabited and strongly guarded by Eastern Pequot women, who saw their male partners, children, siblings, and other relatives depart elsewhere for labor and economic resources" (Silliman and Witt 2010: 57). Importantly, however, both men and women exchanged labor with local merchants in return for credit on food, clothing, or tools. Women often sold baskets, brooms, and other material goods in nearby towns, which took them away from the reservation and traditional spheres of interaction (Silliman and Witt 2010: 53). In addition, these objects were material representations of the displacement Pequot women, men, and families experienced and were symbolic of the renegotiation of the social order under colonial rule in southern New England.

The negotiation of gender roles and relations within this colonial framework found other expressions archaeologically and illustrated the complex economic networks of which Indigenous people were a part. European and locally manufactured ceramics, such as redware, replaced traditional Native-produced vessels, since consumer choices within this context of racism, disenfranchisement, and marginalization were significantly limited (Silliman 2009). Rather than interpret this material change as evidence of acculturation, Silliman (2009: 225) asserts that "when used on the reservation and in Native American community life, *these items become Eastern Pequot objects*" (emphasis in the original). Choosing to buy consumer goods that were both available and affordable "did not translate directly into the dilution of Native cultural practices, attachment to Indigenous communities, or connections to reservation land. These choices represented strategies of survival" (Silliman and Witt 2010: 62).

Whereas ceramic usage changed significantly over time in Pequot households and communities, the archaeobotanical data from reservation homelots illustrate the persistence of traditional ecological knowledge of medicinal plants from the precolonial era, an arena of expertise strongly correlated with women (Kasper 2012; K. McBride 2007). These botanical practices provide further evidence that Indigenous women were central to maintaining households and sustaining the community as well as to "fostering a sense of continuity and managing change" (Kasper 2012: 284). Colonial authorities, guided by patriarchal and ecclesiastical ideals of "proper" gender roles, interacted primarily with Native men. Indigenous women "were rarely acknowledged as actors in the eyes of the male colonial politicians and other observers" (Kasper 2012: 284). Consequently, gendered proscriptions were not imposed upon individual households on the reservation, and Native women remained the community's primary agriculturalists even under colonial rule (Lamb Richmond and Den Ouden

2003: 201–202). So although inequality between Native men and women increased as men participated in colonial economic activities, continuity in some aspects of Indigenous lifeways was actually facilitated by the patriarchal mindset of colonial overseers. At least for the Pequot, traditional ecological knowledge, for example, endured despite other cultural changes under colonialism.

Interestingly, too, in both Indigenous kin groups and European American corporate families, women *and* men contributed to the domestic economy of the household and were integrated into complex webs of social and economic interaction in the colonial world of the northeastern United States. A dialectical analysis reveals, however, that structural similarities belie significant differences in social power and access to resources, especially for women. Furthermore, Silliman's (2009) analysis of ceramics eloquently illustrates the interpenetration of opposites. While similar material culture may have been used in both Indigenous and European American households, the meaning and cultural significance of refined earthenware vessels was by no means identical. Individuals within these households were differentially positioned to not only the material world, but also the complex and interdependent arrangements of which they were a part (see Rubertone 2000).

The racism, disenfranchisement, and cultural persecution of the European American colonial enterprise affected not only Indigenous peoples, but enslaved Africans as well (Fennell 2011; Galle and Young 2004). "Household" and "family" were not coterminous, however, as kinship was not necessarily an organizing principle around which enslaved households were structured. The conditions of slavery generally did not allow for the social configuration of nuclear families. Consequently, gendered social relations were not organized around the ideals of corporate families seen in other colonial settings. Rather, households were social units "that worked cooperatively in production, distribution, and social reproduction activities within the domestic context," such as the pooling of labor and resources (Mrozowski et al. 2008: 707). Enslaved African men and women were often perceived as having different but complementary natures, which were "etched into the spatiality and temporality of daily life" (Wilkie 2004: 77; see also Samford 2004). House compounds were highly gendered, as men and women occupied different household spaces. Exterior areas such as yards, for example, were highly utilized by women collaborating on domestic chores, such as laundry, sewing, and food preparation (Barile 2004; Battle-Baptiste 2011; Fesler 2004; Heath 2004; Stewart-Abernathy 2004; Wilkie 2003). The archaeology of the domestic spaces of slavery, therefore, has yielded material culture associated with these complex households.

By examining dozens of archaeological contexts associated with enslaved Africans on plantations in the Chesapeake region of Virginia, Galle (2010) determined that men and women adopted material strategies that correlated with gender, age, and marital status. Households that consumed large quantities of metal buttons, for example, were those composed of men who were unmarried or perhaps married to women on other plantations; they may have invested in stylish clothing as a display of their personalities and abilities to acquire such goods. Conversely, households with large quantities of refined ceramics were more often "kin-based households anchored by successful enslaved women who worked extraordinarily hard to achieve and maintain an economic position that allowed them to move outside the bounds of their owner's provisioning system" (Galle 2010: 37; Samford 2004). Households with neither buttons nor ceramics appeared to represent individuals who were unable to participate in the market economy, such as women and children separated from husbands or large households for whom all resources were required for survival. Objects of personal adornment and ceramic dishes, therefore, were excellent material expressions of gender, age, ethnicity, and life cycle in these domestic arrangements (Scott 1991a, 1992b; Thomas and Thomas 2004; White 2008).

On the mid-eighteenth-century Rich Neck Plantation in colonial Virginia, foodways, much like buttons and refined earthenwares, were used to mark racial and cultural identity as well as construct and maintain group boundaries (Franklin 2001; Gilchrist 2005). Enslaved African women who cooked in both slave quarters and plantation houses used their resources and knowledge to create novel foodways ("soul food"). In doing so, they demonstrated some measure of autonomous cultural production within the context of slavery as well as their own within-group construction of identity (Franklin 2001: 106).

Foodways were also important on the Saragossa Plantation in Mississippi. Enslaved men made significant dietary contributions through clandestine hunting of deer, opossum, raccoon, and rabbit (Young 2003). This critical supplemental nutrition may have been distributed among households as a way of pooling resources and building solidarity within the community. Furthermore, hunting was an exclusively male activity that would have helped counter "the emasculating effects of the system of slavery" (Young 2003: 128). Knowledge about hunting was transmitted from fathers to sons, which reinforced the role of the father and strengthened both slave families and communities. Through the study of food remnants from archaeological contexts such gendered social relations become visible.

These comparative analyses illustrate that material strategies within households were not influenced solely by gender ideologies. Rather, within plantation contexts in Virginia, "the actions of enslaved women and men, both individually and as members of households, . . . made decisions regarding the allocation of their very limited time, physical energy, and financial resources" (Galle 2010: 36; Young 2004). Furthermore, "an individual's desire and ability to participate in the market economy changed as children were born, as people aged, as spouses or children died, were sold, or ran away" (Galle 2010: 38; also Danforth 2004). Thus, daily life and material practices were structured at the intersection of gender, socioeconomic class, and life cycle, including age and marital status. The dialectical relation of contradiction is also clearly illustrated as interactions within and between these complex units elucidated the *range* of responses and expressions in consumer choices in similar socioeconomic conditions. Furthermore, these highly varied strategies were not mutually supportive of one another. The material worlds of enslaved Africans were selectively mediated according to the needs, desires, and resources of individuals and households.

These gendered human experiences do not represent the sum total of social relations in eastern North America during the colonial period. Other geographic locations had unique social, historical, economic, and political milieus that shaped gender roles and relations within them (e.g., Arkush 2011; Bonine 2004; Clements 2013; Galindo 2004; Loren 2000; Nassaney 2008; Nassaney et al. 2007; Van Buren 2010). Within colonial contexts, however, increasing social inequality was a common feature.

Social Relations of Inequality in the New Republic

Gender roles and relations in Anglo-European society became increasingly hierarchical during the late eighteenth and early nineteenth centuries as emerging economic inequality altered social power within and between families in the newly formed republic (Rotman 2009a). Corporate families were replaced by the modern nuclear family in Anglo-European households as productive activities were increasingly removed from the home and accumulations of surpluses created undeniable class differences within communities (Leone 1999; Leone et al. 1987; Shackel 1993). There was also an increased ideological separation in the roles of men and women with the rise of republican motherhood (Kerber et al. 1989; Leone and Silberman 1995; Porter 1996; Rotman 2009a).

During the second half of the eighteenth century, Deerfield became "a rather well-to-do agricultural periphery of the British world system" (Paynter et al. 1987: 6). The community evolved from "a small, communal village into a more secure, less unified, and more contentious New England town" (Melvoin 1989: 249). The River Gods accumulated surpluses through market sales of grains, animals, timber, and other forest products and began to set themselves apart from other members of the community (Paynter et al. 1987: 6). The illusion of egalitarianism was eschewed in favor of strategies of individual accumulation.

Many elite families in Deerfield renovated or constructed homes in the Georgian style (Stillinger 1992: 79; Sweeney 1986). For example, in 1772, Dr. Thomas and Esther Williams removed the center chimney of their home to create a wide central hall with a main staircase (Blades 1976, 1977; McGowan and Miller 1996: 22) (figure 2.3). Elaborate doorways and gambrel roofs of Georgian architecture became symbols of status and statements of the power of the local gentry; this new house form simultaneously demonstrated the new confidence of the elite class, betrayed their concerns that their social position was weakening, and announced new attitudes regarding privacy and individualism (Garrison 1991; St. George 1988; Sweeney 1984).

Importantly, Georgian architecture transformed previous interior configurations of household space "from organic forms open for public involvement in domestic life to those that regimented and controlled access,

Figure 2.3. Home of Dr. Thomas and Esther Williams (ca. 1750–ca. 1770). Photograph courtesy of Broughton Anderson.

directing visitors and family to portions of the house where certain behaviors were deemed appropriate" (Garrison 1991: 163; see also Deetz 1977; Glassie 1975; M. Johnson 1993). This change had implications for gender relations as the multifunctional and integrated spaces of the colonial period were replaced by floor plans that were rigidly delineated by gender (Coontz 1988: 142; 1992).

A particularly gendered architectural invention—the ell—emerged in the late eighteenth century (Hautaniemi 1999; Spencer 1987). This area almost always contained the kitchen and other spaces for domestic tasks, such as pantries, butteries, woodsheds, and even occasionally a privy (Garrison 1991: 162). Ells emphasized differential perceptions of public and private spaces. Furthermore, relocating female activities to the back of the house was the beginning of a process by which women became increasingly isolated from the community and their labor became differentially valued as public and private spheres diverged (M. Johnson 1993: 137; Rosaldo 1974: 68; Wall 1994: 19; Yentsch 1991: 201). As part of their renovations, Dr. Thomas and Esther Williams constructed a kitchen ell at the rear of their home (McGowan and Miller 1996: 20), signaling their acceptance of an increasing ideological and physical separation of women's and men's roles within their household.

Archaeological excavation at the Williams family homelot revealed the tensions the local gentry were experiencing as other social relations within the village also became increasingly stratified (Blades 1976; Rotman 2001, 2009a, 2009b). Leone and colleagues (1987) observed that disciplined work environments under emerging industrial capitalism found expression through "individual time" in the archaeology of houselots. In addition,

Shackel (1993: 30) asserted that as "behavior became standardized and regimented, it encouraged the development of a modern discipline that allowed for a successful manufacturing process and promoted the consumption of goods, such as ceramics, that reinforced this behavior every day and at special, ritualized meals." In this way, human agents, particularly those belonging to the middle and lower classes, learned to think and conduct themselves according to an emerging social ideal that encouraged individuality and time discipline.

Women—through the very important task of childrearing—were socializing children not only to be good citizens of the republic, but also "to internalize the values of the industrial order" (Coontz 1988: 179–180; Shackel 1996). In this way, the ceramic tableware and teaware that accompanied mealtimes not only instilled the domestic ideals of purity, sanctity, and morality but also taught children about time discipline and etiquette.

The ceramics excavated from a privy associated with Dr. Thomas and Esther Williams (ca. 1750–ca. 1770) in Deerfield did not illustrate the segmentation and standardization expected for elite households of their era (Rotman 2001; 2009a). The juxtaposition of the grand architectural changes to the house to solidify the family's social claim as local gentry and of their apparent rejection of individuality in the ceramic wares (and the new order these represented) illustrated the contradictions extant in the lived experiences of the family (Rotman 2009a: 193). The emerging modern world order may have conflicted with Thomas's very strongly held Tory political convictions, which created interesting social tensions for the family.

Dr. Williams was not only a reputable physician, but also distinguished himself in civil positions. He held seven different political offices between 1746 and his death in 1775: selectman (1746, 1748), town clerk (1748–1751, 1762–1774), moderator of town meetings (nine times between 1754 and 1771), justice of the peace (1754–1765, 1775), representative to the General Court (the provincial legislature) in Boston (1759), special justice of the common plea (1762–1764), and judicial-judge, Court of Common Pleas (1764–1775) (Blades 1976: 8; Sheldon 1972: 853–857). Blades (1976:8) observed, "The respect which Williams commanded as a physician enabled him to assume these numerous political roles. Conversely, his position of power and influence as a civil authority served to reinforce popular respect for him." Williams used his medical training not only in private practice, but in the military as well. During the 1740s and 1750s, he served as a surgeon for the frontier outposts of the militia, for an expedition against France and Canada, and during the French and Indian War (Sheldon 1972: 381, 640, 641).

Williams remained a pivotal figure in the life of the village during the 1760s and 1770s. His political views, however, eventually eroded his social position. As an unrelenting Tory, he became increasingly unpopular as political unrest grew. For example, Williams refused to honor the Whig ban on drinking tea. On May 26, 1775, he received a shipment of tea from Colonel Williams of Great Barrington, Massachusetts, in a package labeled "Monongahela Balsam" (Blades 1976: 9).

As a member of the local gentry during the middle decades of the eighteenth century, Dr. Williams was in a position to assert social, political, and economic influence in Deerfield. His life was even more interesting in light of the difficulties he encountered during his final years due to his unpopular and rebellious political position.

Virtually nothing is known about Thomas's two wives, Anna and Esther, other than they were the mothers to his children (Blades 1976; Rotman 2001). Did they share Thomas's political views? How did they manage their respective households? What roles did these women play in marital and familial relationships? Did they subscribe to the ideals of republican motherhood that were emerging in the larger cultural milieu during their adult lives? As women and spouses in the colonial period, their social status would have been intimately linked to that of their doctor-husband.

The challenges that the Williams family faced signaled, in a way, the beginning of the end for the reigning local gentry in Deerfield and elsewhere in the Connecticut River valley. Not only were political views contested as the Revolution approached, but the economic and social landscape was being reshaped as well through new agricultural practices, technological innovations, and the emergence of wealthy families not tied to the lineages of the village's founding families (Rotman 2001, 2009a).

For wealthy families in the community, the household became less a center of production and more of a locus of social reproduction (Coontz 1988: 83; 1992), often resulting in lower status for women vis-à-vis men in these domestic units. Interestingly, however, women in homes at the lower end of the socioeconomic spectrum were likely to remain involved in productive activities in the home and, therefore, did not experience a similar decline in status (Ember 1983: 304; Rotman and Nassaney 1997).

The gendered uses of space—as well as the lived experiences of individuals—were more complex than simple dichotomies of production/ reproduction, public/private, agricultural/domestic, male/female, elite/ non-elite would suggest (Beaudry 2004; Conkey and Gero 1991; Wurst 2003; Wylie 1991). Although these distinctions had real power, they did not always produce mutually exclusive spaces (Borish 1995: 88; Hautaniemi and Rotman 2003; Rotman 2005, 2013b). In particular, the rural, urban, or suburban context of a household often influenced the degree of rigidity in these social dimensions.

On rural farmsteads, when circumstances demanded, women were involved in outdoor tasks of plowing, planting, and harvesting (Gibb and King 1991: 112–114; McMurry 1988: 61; Stewart-Abernathy 1992). Similarly, men and boys occasionally performed "women's work" in the house, such as cooking, washing dishes, doing laundry, and sewing (McMurry 1988: 61; Osterud 1991: 186; Stine 1991: 498). Women commonly tended the cows and chickens in agricultural spaces, while men were expected to provide firewood to domestic spaces. In addition, when circumstances demanded, both males and females crossed task and space boundaries to get the work done (Hautaniemi and Rotman 2003). Thus, the physical and economic interdependence of home and farm precluded the establishment of rigid boundaries between the spheres of rural men and women, unlike their urban counterparts, who frequently observed a rigid separation (Coontz 1988: 83; McMurry 1988: 57; Nylander 1994: 221). Daily life was guided by kin-based productive relations (Wolf 1997) and reciprocal forms of exchange (Kulikoff 1992). Men *and* women contributed to the domestic economy of the farm and, thus, gendered social relations were hierarchical but complementary (Boserup 1970; Brydon and Chant 1989; Rotman 1995; Rotman and Nassaney 1997).

Over the course of the nineteenth century in particular, farm production became progressively more specialized. Women's role in farm production (such as making butter and cheese for market sale) was economically significant (McMurry 1988: 61; Rotman 2013b). The contribution of farm women to the domestic economy, therefore, granted them relatively high status vis-à-vis men (Rotman 1995: 78, 2013b; Rotman and Nassaney 1997). As butter churning, cheese making, and other activities became more significant to farm revenues, however, tasks formerly completed by women were appropriated by men (McMurry 1988: 61). In addition, as standards of housekeeping rose, women directed their energies away from non-mechanized farmwork and toward fulfilling new ideals of domesticity (Cowan 1982). During the latter half of the nineteenth century, the separation between work and family on specialized farms grew even more pronounced (Halttunen 1982; McMurry 1988: 6). Gender emerged as the defining feature of life after 1850 when men not only monitored women's particular tasks, but supervised the entire process of production and controlled the household coffers partially fed with earnings from women's work (Bruegel 2002: 5). Not only was the entire process of farm production changing, but gender roles were evolving as a consequence (Hautaniemi and Rotman 2003).

Ebenezer Hinsdale and Anna Williams moved to Deerfield during the early period of this transition in western Massachusetts (Rotman 2001, 2009a). The Williamses were part of the wealthy agricultural elite in the village during the first third of the nineteenth century. Their residence was extensively renovated into a grand Federal-style home and was an important material symbol of the family's class and social position (figure 2.4). The construction of a two-story ell with an expansive kitchen at the rear of the house also signaled a separation of gender roles within the household. A trash lens at the top of an abandoned privy was attributed to the Williams's occupation of the site, and the dishes within it likely represented vessels that were broken and discarded while the family moved in circa 1816 (Rotman 2001, 2009a).

Lydia Williams inherited the house and surrounding acreage from her brother, Ebenezer Hinsdale Williams, after his death in 1838 (Rotman 2009a). She rented the house to the family of David and Eliza Barnard. In 1847, Reverend John Moors and his new bride, Esther, joined the Barnards as tenants at the property. No architectural changes were made to the house, but the tenants' occupation was clearly associated with artifacts recovered from a buried land surface. The ceramics from both the privy and the land surface provided glimpses into the gendered social relations operating within the two occupations of the house.

Figure 2.4. Home of Dr. Ebenezer Hinsdale and Anna Williams and later tenants (ca. 1816). Photograph courtesy of Broughton Anderson.

Yentsch (1991) developed a model for color coding refined earthenware vessels as earth-toned or white-toned. The color of ceramic dishes had symbolic associations with male and female activities and, therefore, with separation of men's and women's roles. Yentsch (1991: 225) observed that white-toned vessels were associated with social display and, by extension, the public arena and culture. Earth-toned vessels, in contrast, were relegated to private household spaces dominated by women and distanced from the public spaces. In this way, the roles of men and women were expressed and reproduced through ceramic vessels. The gendered social structure was reinforced daily through the use of different dishes with varied functions and in distinct spaces within the household.

Color coding of ceramics was clearly visible through the dishes from the trash pit associated with Ebenezer Hinsdale and Anna Williams. Vessels for food preparation, processing, and storage were earth-toned, whereas those for food consumption were white-toned. These results were not unexpected since a rigid gender separation was expected among the village's elite. The vessels from the buried land surface (associated with the tenants) revealed less rigid color coding of the ceramics than was true in the earlier occupation of the site. Some of the dishes for food and beverage consumption in this assemblage were earth-toned, rather than white-toned as

Yentsch's model would predict. Given that the artifacts from the land surface represented a period of tenancy rather than ownership, however, the results were also not unexpected. Gender roles in lower-class households were more complementary, with men and women both contributing to the domestic economy and, therefore, not rigidly separated either ideologically or physically (Rotman 2009a; Rotman and Nassaney 1997; Wall 1994).

The architectural data and ceramic assemblages from the Williams site illustrate that house histories were fluid and dynamic and that grand architecture may contradict the social relations within it. The human experiences of the site—along with their attendant material and spatial expressions—were formed at the unique intersection of the historical trajectory of Deerfield and changing agricultural production under industrial capitalism, the rural location of the village, the differing socioeconomic statuses of house residents (landowners versus tenants), and the varied ideals regarding gendered social relations (Rotman 2001, 2009a).

Yet while Deerfield residents were developing links to new markets for their agricultural products, growing commercialization and land speculation resulted in a scarcity of farmland. Consequently, children of farmers were no longer assured of receiving land assets from their parents (Folbre 1985: 202; see also Clark 1982). Children, particularly young men, struck out on their own rather than staying on the family farm, selling their labor power to purchase life's necessities. As household production continued to be subordinated to demands of the market, daughters were likewise displaced from the farm (Abel 1987; Coontz 1988: 149; Temkin-Greener 1979), frequently joining the industrial labor force in places such as the Boott Mills in Lowell, Massachusetts (see Beaudry and Mrozowski 1987a, 1987b). The undisputed patriarchal authority of corporate families was in crisis as economic forces undermined the power of fathers within their households, even though men continued to dominate economic and cultural realms outside the home.

The importance of market economies in shaping social relations of class and gender would become increasingly pronounced in the nineteenth century. The nineteenth century was marked by fluctuating geographical mobility, urbanization, and industrialization. Productive relations were restructured and strategies for social and personal reproduction were questioned (Mrozowski 1991; Paynter 1999; Wurst 2006). As the basis of the economic system became industrial rather than agricultural, "the old ruling class, based on landed and mercantile wealth and exercising power through personal, political, and social ties was challenged by rising sections of a new middle class, whose power was based on the ability to increase productivity and compete in a modern market" (Coontz 1988: 169). Divisions between the spheres of women and those of men continued to increase. These evolving gender ideologies were intimately linked to larger socioeconomic changes.

Increased Social Stratification and Industrial Capitalism

The nineteenth century was an especially dynamic time in historic North America, particularly in the Northeast. An increased dependence upon wage labor transformed work relations and was accompanied by changes in homes and families (Coontz 1988: 189; Hautaniemi 2001; McMurry 1988; Paynter 2000; Rotman 2006, 2009a). Middle-class women were active historical agents in this process. Although women were increasingly excluded from political and economic transactions, new opportunities for education and wage work for young women and new responsibilities in childrearing raised women's aspirations, although not always their status. Female leadership in religion and reform was "an active attempt to claim a distinctive space in American society. Women sought power and influence in religious associations, new family ideologies, and a rearranged domestic order that gave them control over reproduction and moral ascendancy over men" (Coontz 1988: 186; see also Spencer-Wood 1991, 2003, 2004). The cult of domesticity, in particular, emerged as the dominant gender ideal of this time, emphasizing piety, purity, domesticity, and submissiveness while also further elaborating an ideological and physical separation of public and private spheres (Beetham 1996; Rotman 2006; Ryan 1985).

Socioeconomic class was both categorical (linked directly to financial resources) and relational (a position within the social and economic order) (Brighton 2009; Marx and Engels 1972; Weber 1976). The middle class also played an important role in the restructuring and separation of public and private life. Wage labor created a distinction between the class that owned the means of production (the business class) and the class that increasingly had nothing to sell but its own labor power (the working class)

(Coontz 1988: 187; Wurst and Fitts 1999). The middle class—consisting of professionals, small farmers or businessmen, managers, writers, ministers, and in the nineteenth century, clerks—was constantly shaped by the dynamics of capitalist competition and the changing relations between the business and working classes. The middle class had an identity that was distinct from the working class below—since they had been relatively successful in avoiding the worst insecurities and indignities of wage labor—as well as from the capitalists above—since they did not own the means of production (Coontz 1988: 188; Fitts 2001; Wurst 1999). The middle class came into crisis during the economic transition and needed organizational and ideological strategies to survive. Women, in particular, had "a vital role in the elaboration and organization of middle-class values and behavior patterns. . . . [T]hey were specially situated to perceive problems of reproducing class position in a changing society and to develop family strategies that responded to those problems" (Coontz 1988: 190; Fitts 2001; Spain 2001).

By the late nineteenth century, consumption was linked to the emergence of an industrial democracy as well as the spread and significant intensification of mass production, which made conspicuous consumption possible for a larger segment of the socioeconomic spectrum (Mullins 2011; see also Bourdieu 1984; Miller 1987). Rather than representing simply an ideological shift, the material conditions of the working class were also transformed through shorter work days, more leisure time, higher pay, and the extension of credit—all of which facilitated increased consumption by working-class laborers (Mullins 2011) and challenged social ideals of class status.

This rising consumerism was rooted in white racial privilege (Mullins 1999a, 1999b, 2001, 2004). The material disparities of America's consumer culture "were minimized, ignored, and legitimized by pervasive discourses on affluence that trumpeted the accessibility of consumer goods, hyperbolized consumer culture's ever-expanding capacity to provide goods and services, and brazenly heralded the civil and moral benefits of prosaic commodities" (Mullins 1999b: 3). Meanwhile, another ideology was simultaneously emerging. Social Darwinism stressed that "hard work, thrift, intelligence, sobriety, cleanliness, and a little luck guaranteed success, whereas failure resulted from the lack of these characteristics, or, more importantly,

Figure 2.5. Greek Revival home of the Edwin Ware family (ca. 1841). Photograph courtesy of Broughton Anderson.

from their opposites—laziness, extravagance, stupidity, slovenliness, and drunkenness" (McGuire 1988: 460). Consequently, for the marginalized— women, people of color, or working-class individuals and families—consumption may have been a form of empowerment and a means for actively participating in the larger cultural milieu (Mullins 2011).

During the nineteenth century, conspicuous consumption was also visible in domestic architecture. Both the exterior appearance and interior arrangement of homes in Deerfield, for example, were transformed as industrial capitalism increasingly shaped inequality within the village. Architectural styles in the village were inspired by ancient Greek temples and represented rational, public, powerful, and masculine spaces. Houses symbolized "the autonomy and right of the Republican male individual, who had at least been superficially schooled in the classics, to possess and display private property, including personal knowledge" (Leone and Silberman 1995: 128). The Greek Revival's well-delineated, freestanding forms bespoke a fierce individualism (Howard 1989: 92–93). Its other features— cleanliness, order, efficiency, novelty—were also deeply embedded American values. Greek Revival architecture, as illustrated by the home of the Edwin Ware family (figure 2.5), served as "a reminder of the presumed apogee of Old World civilization, [which] had become a grassroots expres-

Figure 2.6. Gothic
Revival home built
by the Reverend
John Farewell Moors
and later owned by
the Arthur Ware Ball
family (ca. 1848).
Photograph by the
author.

sion of American character" (Vlach 1995: 144). The emphasis of the Greek
Revival house as a masculine space devalued or ignored the place of women
within the household.

Conversely, at approximately the same time, the Gothic Revival house
overemphasized the role of women in the family and represented a fundamental shift from Classical to Romantic architectural styles (Downing
1841, 1842; Holly 1878). In Deerfield, a Gothic Revival house was originally constructed by Reverend John Moors circa 1848 (figure 2.6). This
architectural form, previously associated mainly with churches, possessed
"natural" (that is, asymmetrical) floor plans. The symbolic associations of
the architectural style with nature and religion became inextricably linked
with the natural and religious ideals of the cult of domesticity (Sklar 1973:
173; see also Juster 1996; Wall 1991, 1999). The home continued to be an
important locus for socializing children and reproducing social relationships, although the particulars of those relationships had changed (Clark
1988: 536). Residential architecture in the Gothic Revival style increased
in popularity as white, middle-class women became separated from the
mode of production and glorified in their roles as the moral guardians of
children through the ideology of domesticity (Vlach 1995: 142; see also
Rotman 2006, 2009a).

Figure 2.7. Rear view of the Reverend John Farewell Moors family home (ca. 1848). Photograph courtesy of Broughton Anderson.

Architecturally, the house of Reverend Moors was originally constructed in two sections. The first was a newly constructed front portion of one-and-a-half stories in the Gothic Revival style. It contained four rooms on the first floor—two parlors, a dining room, and a bedroom—while the second floor contained only bedrooms and had an open garret above. The second section consisted of a one-story, two-room ell at the rear of the house, constructed by reusing a pre-existing structure, likely an old carriage house (figure 2.7) (Hautaniemi and Paynter 1999: 31).

The archaeological excavation of a buried land surface at the Moors site yielded a variety of refined earthenwares (Hautaniemi 1994; Hautaniemi and Paynter 1996, 1999). It is not surprising that Gothic-paneled ironstone, a known emblem of the cult of domesticity (Wall 1991, 1999; Wetherbee 1985, 1986), was associated with the Moors's occupation of the site (figure 2.8). The presence of this decorative motif correlated perfectly with the Gothic Revival architecture of the home. As such, this particular ceramic pattern served as another icon of domesticity and expression of the gender relations within this middle-class Protestant household (Rotman 2009a: 195).

The Moors site reflected strong evidence for adherence to the cult of domesticity and attendant separation of gender roles, at least as an ideal. The archaeological and architectural data from the site also illustrated the importance of developmental cycle, particularly with regard to gender ideology. Several aspects of the data suggest tensions between idealized vi-

Figure 2.8. Gothic-paneled ironstone plate recovered from the Moors family home during excavations in Deerfield, Massachusetts. Photograph by the author.

sions for social relations within the household and the lived reality of the reverend and his family. Reverend and Esther Moors were ideologically middle class as defined by John's occupation as a minister. Domesticity was largely an ideal of the middle class and, given its association with religion and Christian values, an appropriate guiding principle for a minister and his young family.

By constructing their new home in the Gothic Revival style, John and Esther built a house that embodied the ideals of domesticity in a highly visible form. Yet, realizing their dream home appeared to have required an element of creativity. Although socially middle class, the couple's status as newlyweds created very real financial barriers to acquiring all the associated material trappings. The newlywed Moors may have been able to afford the construction of the cottage by reducing expenses through recycling a pre-existing structure for the back section of the house (Rotman 2001, 2009a, 2009b).

The refined earthenwares from the site revealed another tension between ideology and the ability to enlist its associated material symbols (Rotman

2006). Only two teaware vessels were recovered from the site. This paucity of teawares seemed to indicate that the Moors were not reproducing their social position through the ritual of afternoon tea (Rotman 2001, 2009a). The Moors may have chosen to expend their limited financial resources on hired help rather than elaborate teawares, since domestic servants working in and around the house were a symbol of the family's middle-class status that would have been visible to a larger segment of the community than the tea set in their parlor would have been.

An examination of the data through the additional lens of developmental cycle, however, revealed that material patterning at the Moors site was more than a matter of their middle-class socioeconomic position (Rotman 2006, 2009). The proportionately small number of Gothic-paneled ironstone vessels in the assemblage suggested that their status as newlyweds may have limited their ability to acquire this iconographic tableware. In addition, Esther died about two years after the Moors moved into their new home. Although she was not the primary wage earner, as the matron of the house she would have played a key role in selecting housewares such as ceramic tableware and hosting afternoon tea in the family's parlor, important elements of her gender role as defined under the most idealized model of the cult of domesticity.

The material record of the Moors house reflected both the iconographic *ideals* of gender roles as well as *real* lived experience of the Moors as newlyweds (Rotman 2006, 2009). The ideals of domesticity intersected with other social prisms and, thus, were negotiated along with socioeconomic class, ethnicity, religion, and life cycle.

Beyond Domesticity

Households were the arenas within which children were socialized to domestic ideals. Importantly, however, "children are not simply raised into adults; they become adults with a specific gender identity" (Kamp 2001: 14). Through toys, children learn about their socially prescribed roles in society, normative sexual relations, gender-appropriate work, and other values (Leinaweaver 2013; Rotman 2009a; Voss 2008c). According to Baxter (2008: 163), "this consideration of identity in general and the overlapping constructions of age and gender specifically have been central in attempts to expand understandings of what childhood meant in different times and places."

For nineteenth-century middle-class Victorian America, "ideologies of race and class were inseparable" (Barton and Somerville 2012; Roediger 1991). Racialized mechanical banks, for example, were given to children as toys, but they served to cultivate xenophobia about African-Americans, Chinese, Irish, and Native Americans in particular and reproduced perceptions of white dominance (Barton and Somerville 2012: 63). Thus, socioeconomic class was not the only basis of difference in nineteenth-century America. Increased ethnic diversity due to Emancipation and immigration created additional social categories through which gendered beings enacted daily life and the dominant classes defined deviance and otherness.

The domestic and work lives of free African-Americans at the W.E.B. DuBois site in Great Barrington, Massachusetts, for instance, were very different from those of the Anglo-European families in nearby Deerfield (Battle-Baptiste 2011; Muller 1994). The ideal of a "woman's place in the home" was problematic, since the legacy of enslavement had largely limited women's labor to domestic and institutional service or arduous manual labor outside of the home (Battle-Baptiste 2011). In addition, "the inability of captive African men to actively pursue their patriarchal destiny was controlled in very dehumanizing ways by plantation owners and overseers" (Battle-Baptiste 2011: 40–41). Therefore, cultural constructions of Black womanhood and motherhood were not simply in opposition to European American models of domesticity, but rather occurred at the multifaceted intersection of domestic ideals, post-Emancipation oppression, emerging class distinctions within African-American communities, and other social, political, economic, and ideological forces of the time (Battle-Baptiste 2011; Brandon 2004; Davidson 2004; Muller 1994).

The African-American writer and civil rights activist W.E.B. DuBois spent his boyhood in Great Barrington embedded in the significant maternal kinship of the Burghardts (figure 2.9). Through property ownership and other economic transactions, the Burghardt women—his mother, maternal grandmother, and other maternal kin—wielded uncommon power for the time and created a *homeplace* as the sphere of their interactions with family and community, the labor they undertook to support themselves, and the goods they purchased for consumption (Battle-Baptiste 2011: 158;

Figure 2.9. Mary Burghardt DuBois and W.E.B. DuBois as an infant (ca. 1868). Photograph courtesy of the Department of Special Collections and University Archives, W.E.B. DuBois Library, University of Massachusetts, Amherst.

Muller 1994: 87). Although the archaeological record yielded fragments of dishes, clothing, agricultural implements, and other vestiges of daily life, it was the land and house—"sturdy, small, and old fashioned" (Battle-Baptiste 2011: 139) that were the most significant artifacts from this site. Landownership refuted the myth of the inferiority of the African-American family (Muller 1994). While the men "were out-migrating, selling their labor to more distant markets, the Burghardt women were creating their own unique position in this changing economic field" (Muller 1994: 91). In a myriad of ways, the Burghardt women were at the epicenter of navigating the complex social worlds in which they lived and of forging identities for themselves, their children, and their grandchildren in the post-Emancipation period. Their homeplace elucidated the ways in which domesticity was significantly shaped at the intersection of race, ethnicity, and class.

The domestic residence of another freed African-American family associated with Van Winkle's Mill in northwest Arkansas provides an additional glimpse into the ways in which toys in particular highlighted Victorian ideologies and social relations of class, ethnicity, race, and gender

Figure 2.10. Morris-Butler House, Indianapolis, Indiana (a property of Historic Landmarks Foundation of Indiana). Photograph by the author.

(Brandon 2013). A variety of children's items were recovered, including doll parts and marbles. These artifacts in postbellum contexts may be "seen as a mark of upward mobility and increased humanization through the consumption of increasingly frivolous goods" (Brandon 2013: 44). Parents may have purchased dolls for their daughters, for example, as a way of expressing their aspirations for ascendant social status (Mullins 2001; Wilkie 2000).

The most poignant artifacts from Van Winkle's Mill, however, were the fragments of children's plates with the alphabet encircling the rim. These typical vessels for children in middle-class homes were meant to aid in teaching the ABCs (Kwas 2009). Literacy was discouraged among enslaved Africans and, following Emancipation, education was stressed as a path to equality (Brandon 2013). As at the W.E.B. DuBois site, mainstream white, middle-class Victorian ideals of domesticity were not implemented in the same ways in free African-American households. Alphabet plates were used in Victorian America to signal particular class and gender ideals. For freed slaves Aaron Anderson and Jane Van Winkle, these children's plates

Figure 2.11. The rear section of the Morris-Butler House, facing southwest, showing (*left to right*) the main house, the kitchen ell, the roofed passageway, the summer kitchen, and the attached privy. Photograph by the author.

were used to "imagine new social possibilities, mediate lived contradictions, and envision new personal pleasures, posing new relationships between consumers and society and portraying who we *wish* to be" (Mullins 1999b: 28; see also Brandon 2013).

Socioeconomic status, ethnicity, and gender also converged in complex ways at the Morris-Butler House in Indianapolis (Rotman 2007). The house was a classic example of a middle- to upper-class urban residence of the mid-nineteenth century (figure 2.10). The main floor consisted of an entry hall with a formal parlor on one side and a library/family parlor and a formal dining room on the other. The kitchen was situated beyond the dining room at the back of the first floor. A summer kitchen was attached to the main kitchen by a roofed passage and had an adjoining privy (figure 2.11). A comparative study of the midden around the house revealed a paucity of materials from the public side yard (26.5 percent of the assemblage recovered) compared to intensive use of the rear private yard (73.5 percent of the assemblage), illustrating a classic separation of public and private spaces under domesticity, both ideologically and spatially (Rotman 2007: 104).

A close interrogation of the archaeological, documentary, and oral history data revealed however that understandings of public and private did not correlate neatly with male and female activity areas, respectively (Rotman 2007). Rather, public spaces such as the side yard were used largely by the family for leisure pursuits and entertaining guests, whereas the private rear yard was occupied by African-American domestic servants completing daily household chores. The kitchen of the residence was the only private space within the house that was used exclusively by women (the family's cook, Martha, as well as Mrs. Butler and her daughters). Therefore, at the Morris-Butler House "gender was given primacy in shaping social relations in private interior contexts only, whereas uses of public space and private exterior landscapes were influenced by class and ethnicity" (Rotman 2007: 110).

With the rise of industrial capitalism, additional vectors of social inequality emerged (Orser 2010: 129). Gendered social relations were profoundly influenced by an increase in socioeconomic and racial differentiation.

Domestic Spaces and Evolving Gender Relations

As dynamic social spaces, households corresponded to a nexus of social reproduction and production. The exterior appearance of a residence, the organization of interior spaces, the rituals and artifacts used within it, and their evolution over time linked gender ideologies to class, ethnicity, life cycle, and other social relations. Investigations of households illustrate how colonialism, capitalism, and patriarchy impacted gendered experience through time and across space.

Furthermore, the archaeological records of households illustrate the ways in which individuals, families, and economic units engaged in complex negotiations with the larger social world as choices and adaptations were made (Greenwood and Slawson 2008: 77) and cultural norms were rejected or subverted (Joseph 2004: 19). Dialectical analyses furthermore revealed that artifacts and domestic spaces were significantly shaped by the differential positioning of their users and consumers (interpenetration of opposites) as well as being used in competing or conflicting ways (contradiction). The resulting material world often produced similar artifacts with very different meanings as well as a range of archaeological patterns within similar social and economic contexts.

The gender ideologies that structured social roles and relations within households were not confined only to that arena of cultural engagement. Community-level social interaction also both shaped and was shaped by gender ideologies as they were practiced within domestic units. The dynamic relationship between these two spheres of human experience—household and community—is explored in the next chapter.

3

-ccccccc-

Beyond the Household

Gender in the Community

Gendered social relations were codified and reproduced outside the domestic sphere at the level of the community. In this chapter, I engage in
abstraction of generality, moving from the analytical level of specific households to the communities in which they are situated. Domestic units do
not exist in isolation, but in *relation* to one another within their larger social, political, and economic contexts and elucidate the ways in which they
were connected to wider cultural processes (M. Wood 2004: 210).

Community-level analyses also facilitate the investigation of cultural
groups that are not visible at the scale of an individual household, such as
nineteenth-century Irish immigrants living in tenements in the Five Points
neighborhood of New York City (Brighton 2001; Yamin 2001). Furthermore, a household-level view often belies the integrated and interdependent nature of households within communities, such as in utopian societies
(Nickolai 2003; Savulis 2003).

The ideologies that operated within families and households—and
which were visible in the material records of those domestic spaces—significantly shaped notions of "proper" gender roles, relations, behavior, dress,
and other aspects of social conduct beyond the domestic arena. The foun-
dational gendered ideals of corporate families, republican motherhood,
and the cult of domesticity, for example, permeated all levels of interaction
and often reproduced patriarchal authority and inequality in both domestic units and their larger communities. Thus, the social relations enacted
within homes were replicated outside of it, just as the ideals that structured

social relations within communities were enacted within individual families, households, and economic units. These spheres of interaction were mutually reinforcing, transcending the physical boundaries of individual homelots.

Occasionally, however, community-level social engagement was used to *challenge*, rather than reproduce, gender roles and relations within the home. Domestic reform and equal rights feminism were two such powerful counter-narratives in historic America, particularly during the late nineteenth and early twentieth centuries. These alternative ideals sought to redefine relationships between men, women, and others, as well as expand the range of culturally accepted gender roles and behaviors within society (see chapter 2).

This chapter introduces gender at the level of community social interaction and the ways in which various ideologies were codified, reproduced, and challenged in the public sphere. Just as gendered social relations within communities operate at a different scale than households do, the same is true of their archaeological, material, and spatial correlates. Colonialism, capitalism, and patriarchy continued to be powerful forces in shaping social relations through time and across space, as well as in defining differences in gendered performance or identity as deviance.

Gendered Spaces of Colonialism

Corporate families and other colonial households, as well as the gender relations operating within them, were defined to a large degree by ecclesiastical ideologies that naturalized patriarchal control (Rotman 2009a). Social interaction within colonial outposts and the engagement of these military or religious communities with local Indigenous peoples were significantly shaped by these ideals.

Colonial engagement with Indigenous peoples was particularly gendered in the Massachusetts "Praying Town" of the Ponkapoag. Much like the Pequot of Connecticut, Ponkapoag men were largely absent from the community while they hunted, fished, and participated in trading and war (Clements 2013; O'Brien 1997). As a result of these gendered labor practices, adult populations experienced skewed gender roles. Furthermore, the colonists' plundering of woods and wetlands impacted the ability of Native women to raise crops, produce traditional utensils, and harvest wetland herbs and medicines (O'Brien 1997). Consequently, Ponkapoag women were forced to sell their labor or the products of their labor to their colonial neighbors. Thus, under patriarchy and capitalism, in the colonial praying towns of New England, "traditional gendered and reciprocal divisions of labor were transformed into the exchange of labor for money and the commoditization of community support, including traditional women who assisted each other during labor and childbirth" (Clements 2005, 2013: 121).

Changing gender roles and relations in Ponkapoag villages were not expressed only in the altered demography of Indigenous communities. The negotiation of colonial ideals and conditions was also visible in Native American burials (Clements 2005, 2013; Mandell 2005). More women than men were interred in local cemeteries, reflecting the proportion of females and males living and working in the praying town. Interments also included individuals buried in traditional flexed positions in round pits as well as prone in wooden coffins following the Christian tradition. Grave goods too consisted of both Native American (e.g., red ochre) and colonial artifacts (e.g., earthenware mugs and clay pipes). Placing Indigenous items in the graves of loved ones was an act of defiance to colonial authority (Cipolla 2013). These burials have been interpreted as revealing "women's agency in resisting Puritan patriarchy through ideology as well as the careful manipulation of discourse through material culture" (Clements 2013: 125). As among the Narragansett (Nassaney 2004) and the Pequot (Silliman 2009; Silliman and Witt 2010), Ponkapoag Indigenous women played a critical role in negotiating the evolving social order under colonial rule.

Gender also had distinctive spatial dimensions within Oneota longhouse communities in the Upper Mississippi Valley, where community was defined by gender and clan membership in strongly matrilineal and matrilocal terms (O'Gorman 2010). Men and women experienced longhouse communities differently and in ways that were created, codified, and reproduced through daily mundane practices with meaningful spatial components (Bourdieu 1973; O'Gorman 2010; Sutlive 1978).

A man, for example, experienced his obligations and kinship ties "within a network of places defined by location of his natal longhouse, his marital longhouse, and other clan connections. Men were not divorced from their obligations to their natal community when they moved to their wife's long-house" (O'Gorman 2010: 576–577). Women remained in their natal long-houses, however, and their daily activities were much more localized than men's. Consequently, the spheres of interaction for men and women were fundamentally different, with men experiencing loci of shelter and belonging across a larger landscape than women did. The material correlates of connected village communities were observed in the commonalities of storage and processing facilities for agricultural products, frequencies of the type and size of ceramic vessels, and types of projectile points (O'Gorman 1996; 2010: 587). Oneota communities, therefore, were not constrained by the physical margins of individual longhouses, but rather were distributed broadly across regional landscapes.

Archaeological analyses of longhouses illustrated that, in some Indigenous matrilineal and matrilocal societies, kinship-based obligations produced different communities for men and women in their natal and marital longhouses (O'Gorman 2010: 592). Spatial dimensions of gender roles and relations in agricultural production had relevance for European American settlements in later centuries as well. ˎ

Changing Agricultural Economy and Evolving Social Relations

During the second and third quarters of the eighteenth century, the River Gods of Deerfield experienced increased affluence through intensified agricultural production (Melvoin 1989: 249; Paynter et al. 1987: 6). As individual accumulations of surpluses increased, economic and social differentiation also increased. Simultaneously, however, the power of corporate families and collective enterprises was weakened. This transformation of social relations was most evident in the planned layouts of new towns established in the Connecticut River valley during this period (particularly after the mid-eighteenth century). Surveyors divided up land, effectively scattering families over the entire geographic area of the settlement from its inception (Garrison 1991; Rotman 2001, 2009a). Households were no longer arranged along a central street with long narrow fields stretching out behind them. Farmsteads were now situated upon 100–150-acre blocky parcels with houses more widely dispersed along multiple streets. A town

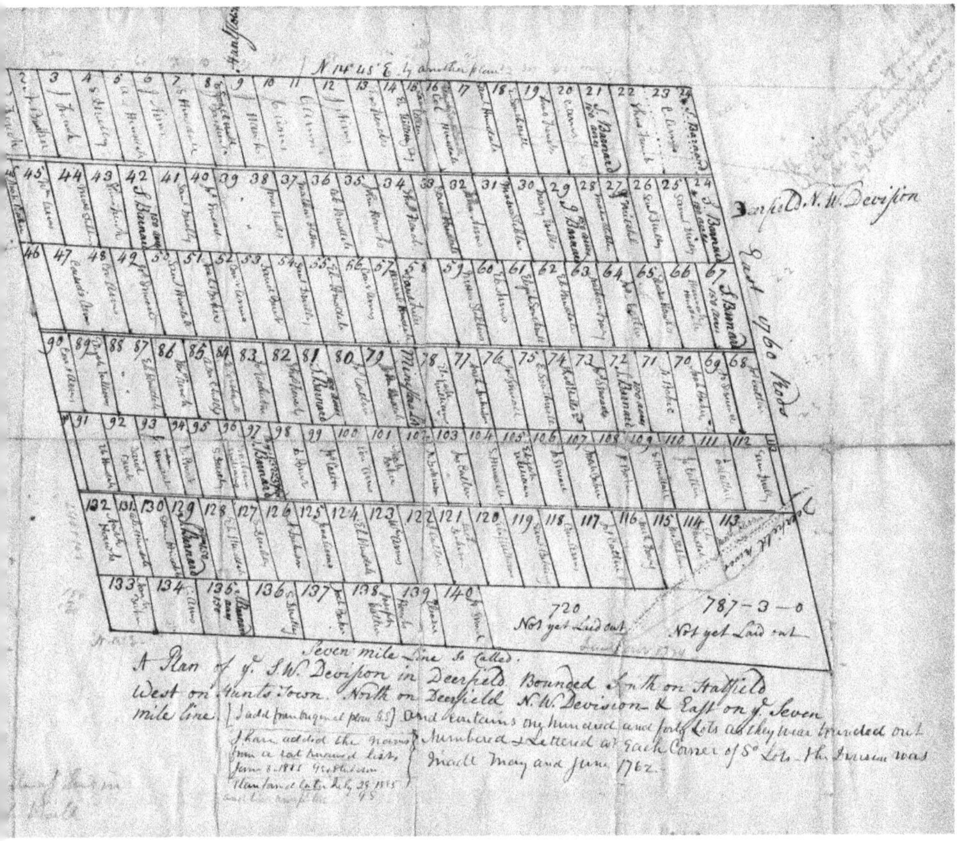

Figure 3.1. Historical map of Conway, Massachusetts (ca. 1762). Courtesy of the Pocumtuck Valley Memorial Association Library, Deerfield, Massachusetts.

center was established for the meetinghouse and perhaps a tavern and a small business or two (Garrison 1991: 21–23).

The village of Conway in the Connecticut River valley was one of the rural agricultural communities settled according to this new scheme (figure 3.1). Interestingly, many of its original proprietors were familiar with or were actually part of the town system of Deerfield. The model of corporate community and mutual responsibility of the 1670s, however, was no longer important by the 1760s. Rather, the village was centered on more rationalized economic principles, such as the efficient undertaking of daily agricultural tasks facilitated by the consolidation of the farmstead and its associated important resources (Garrison 1991: 23). The changed spatial arrangements of newly established towns like Conway "symbolized a shift in values toward a more individualistic type of community in which the needs and goals of the family were elevated in importance over the group" (Garrison 1991: 23). This shift in values had implications for social relations of gender.

Up until the nineteenth century, farms were the most common centers of production, with all members working together to maintain the household. As a result, women made important contributions to the domestic economy and therefore their status was relatively high vis-à-vis men (Hautaniemi and Rotman 2003; McMurry 1988; Rotman 2001, 2009a; Spencer-Wood 1995). Limited market forces were operating, so individual households provided for the majority of their own needs, and an exchange of some labor or goods among neighbors supplied any missing necessities (Stewart-Abernathy 1986; Worrell 1985). A climate of close interdependence among all members of the farm household (men, women, family, hired laborers) and a high degree of self-sufficiency existed (Coontz 1988; Rotman and Nassaney 1997). The nature of farming communities fundamentally changed, however, once neighbors were no longer in close physical proximity and their dependence upon one another began to wane.

By the mid-nineteenth century, earlier rural social arrangements were supplanted by "one based on competition, market orientation, capital accumulation, and profits" (McMurry 1988: 57). New agricultural technologies such as reapers and mowers reduced labor requirements dramatically while increasing crop yields. Fewer individuals could now manage a larger number of acres. Successful farmers added to their landholdings and farm sizes grew. Farming also became more specialized, for it was more cost-effective and profitable for farmers to focus on one or two primary crops, rather than continue to tend to a broad spectrum of livestock and agricultural pursuits for self-subsistence (Coontz 1988; McMurry 1988: 6). Unfortunately, not all farm families were able to meet the increased capital requirements and, coupled with the overall decline in the importance of agriculture in later years, these changes often meant that laborers moved away from rural areas to seek jobs in the surrounding towns and cities (Paynter 1990: 6). This trend has continued to the present, as highly industrialized agribusinesses have spent large amounts of capital to completely mechanize agriculture,

Figure 3.2. Woman with cows. Undated postcard in possession of the author.

driving smaller family farmers and laborers out of farming (Groover 2008). The inward orientation of individual farms continued to intensify as the interdependence of farming communities continued to decline (Rotman 2009a, 2013b). These changes were most visible materially and spatially in the growing size of farm acreage and the virtual disappearance of family subsistence farms from some rural landscapes.

Social and gender relations in rural settings were also changed as agricultural practices underwent transformation (figure 3.2). As farm production became progressively more specialized and influenced by industrial capitalism, tasks formerly completed by women became more significant to farm revenues and were appropriated by men (e.g., production of butter, cheese, and eggs) (McMurry 1988: 61; Rotman 2013b; Yentsch 1991). In central New York state, cheese production became increasingly widespread after 1850 (Gibb et al. 2009). Many farmwives reported to reformers, however, that they were happy to be relieved of the arduous labor involved in household cheese production (McMurray 1987; Spencer-Wood 1995: 124). For most of the nineteenth century, women's earnings from household production belonged to their husbands, so that women's domestic production essentially amounted to domestic servitude (Hautaniemi and Rotman 2003; Kessler-Harris 1982; Rotman 2013b; Spencer-Wood 2006: 154). During the latter half of the nineteenth century, individual farms became increasingly independent with the shift from subsistence farming to agribusiness. Rural gender relations consequently bore greater resemblance to their urban middle-class counterparts, wherein the cult of domesticity dominated and gender separation in both ideology and practice became the norm (McMurry 1988: 6; Wall 1994).

Challenging Gender Norms

The women of Deerfield were not merely passive adherents of the cultural milieu in which they lived, but actively engaged it to empower themselves and shape their worlds (Rotman 2009a, 2013b). As members of a rural village, they were well acquainted with the fluidity of agricultural labor and the interrelation of associated spaces; that is, with performing whatever tasks needed to be done rather than maintaining rigid separations between male and female labors (Rotman 2005, 2009a, 2013b; Stewart-Abernathy 1986). They were also accustomed to contributing to the domestic economy of the household by selling surplus butter and eggs as well as through other productive activities, rather than laboring only for family consumption (McMurry 1988). It was not surprising, then, that Deerfield women, particularly those who lived along the Street, became actively involved in the Arts and Crafts movement during the late nineteenth and early twentieth centuries (Harlow 2001, 2005; Rotman 2005, 2009a, 2013b).

Miller and Lanning (1994: 447) tabulated women's scale of involvement in community craftwork. In 1901, the Society of Blue and White Needlework paid 34 women for contracted work. At least 23 of these women lived on the Street or shared the last name of a Street property owner. In the same year, the Society of Deerfield Industries listed 33 members, 31 of whom either lived on the Street or shared the last name of a Street property owner. By 1914, 13 of the 57 residences, slightly less than one-quarter, contained spaces specifically converted to commercial uses for displaying and selling community crafts (Rotman 2013b: 54).

For village women, participation in craftwork was a logical extension of familiar patterns of social and economic interaction, the deep history of which was emphasized in the re-creation of the colonial past through the "preserving, restoring, producing, and promoting remnants of Deerfield's preindustrial era" (Miller and Lanning 1994: 438). For domestic reformers, the Arts and Crafts movement was part of a nostalgia for the greater gender equality characteristic of farms, where women and men alike produced goods both for consumption *and* for public markets (Spencer-Wood 1991: 237; Rotman 2013b). Further, with the relative absence of men through outmigration and death in the Civil War, the village became predominantly female. Women had considerable latitude in shaping new gendered social relations in the community, particularly with regard to challenging a rigid separation of public and private spaces (Hautaniemi and Rotman 2003; Rotman 2005, 2009a).

Some village women—particularly those who were not native to Deerfield—may have subverted gender ideals like the cult of domesticity by buying property along the Street and reuniting public and private spheres through their involvement in craftwork (Rotman 2009a, 2013b). Gillian Naylor (1971: 15) asserts that "the Arts and Crafts Movement was built upon and expressed, especially in its earlier years, an ideology of radical social reform [that challenged growing inequalities at the turn of the twentieth century], so that the movement was concerned . . . with the ethics as much as with the aesthetics of design." Madeline Yale Wynne and Annie Putnam were two Deerfield women who were particularly influential in bringing both the artistic aspects and political ideals of Arts and Crafts to the village. Wynne, for example, arranged touring exhibitions of Deerfield craftwork and brought in speakers on art or politics, including women's suffrage (Harlow 2001, 2005). These activities illustrate that the ideas of equal rights feminism were present concurrently with the ideals of domesticity, shaping social roles and gender relations within the village (Rotman 2006, 2009a), particularly for affluent women.

In addition, the crafts were not produced exclusively in public spaces; rather, work was undertaken individually in women's homes as well as collectively in centralized locations (Harlow 2005). Some women worked on embroidery or quilts in their parlors or converted a bedroom for part-time craft production. Others, like Wynne and Putnam, worked in studios to pursue their craftwork in private (Harlow 2001: 11). Yet, simultaneously, these women made their porch available to the Pocumtuck Basket Makers for communal production of their wares (figure 3.3). In this way, Wynne and Putnam empowered other women in the village toward economic self-sufficiency and autonomy, while simultaneously ensuring efficient production of wares for sale. Their ability to do so was no doubt facilitated by their

Figure 3.3. Pocumtuck basket makers on the porch of Madeline Yale Wynne and Annie Putnam, Deerfield, Massachusetts, 1901. Photograph courtesy of the Pocumtuck Valley Memorial Association, Memorial Hall Museum, Deerfield, Massachusetts.

status as wealthy women (Rotman 2006, 2007). The individual or communal production of wares may also have been grounded less in ideology than in the technicalities of the craft. Metalsmithing was an individualized pursuit, whereas basket making was more conducive to collective involvement. Thus, in Deerfield, production of goods under the rubric of the Arts and Crafts movement blurred the boundaries between public and private spheres, economic and domestic activities, and male and female gender roles within the home and community.

The participation of Deerfield women in craftwork was a natural extension of their previously experienced social and economic interactions. As members of a farming village, they were accustomed to contributing to a variety of agricultural tasks regardless of social prescriptions for gendered divisions of labor. In the relative absence of men in the village, women were able to construct gendered social relations that met their unique economic, social, and other needs rather than conforming to the dominant gender ideologies of their day.

In 1911, Deerfield women were also particularly effective in the public arena by influencing the installation of a municipal water system (Hautaniemi and Rotman 2003). Logistical and organizational support for municipal water was orchestrated by the Deerfield Improvement Society, a group of women and men committed to civic projects, such as locating benches and trash receptacles in the village and dealing with diseased elm trees. This organization raised funds for its various endeavors through a series of historical pageants in 1910, 1913, and 1916 (Suzanne Flynt, pers. comm. 1999). The "Deerfield water works" was one of the society's beneficiaries (quotation from a privately held diary; Suzanne Flynt, pers. comm. 1999), and pageant proceeds helped ensure that the planned water system became a reality (Hautaniemi and Rotman 2003: 151). In this way, the pageants went beyond an expression of the ideals of domestic reform to play a relatively active role in their implementation (Glassberg 1995).

Many of the women involved with village craftwork also participated in the pageants, thereby taking an active role in securing water to their own homes (Hautaniemi and Rotman 2003; Rotman 2001, 2005, 2009a, 2013b). Their involvement in the municipal water project and associated pageants illustrated that domestic reform and equal rights feminism were part of their ideological landscape along with the ideals of domesticity. Despite having no official political power and supposedly being relegated to the private sphere, many women property owners were instrumental in shaping the very public political, social, and economic townscape of this Massachusetts village. Activities of village women were not confined simply to those of economic necessity. Their civic-oriented work in the Deerfield Temperance Society and other organizations had both public *and* private relevance. These activities were also spatially distinct, being carried out in public arenas like churches and schools. Women and men further blurred the boundaries between the public and private spheres through their active collaboration on the municipal water project and fund-raising through historical pageants (Hautaniemi and Rotman 2003; Rotman 2001, 2009a).

Interestingly, in 1901, the Gothic Revival house built by Reverend Moors and his family passed to Arthur Ware Ball, a farmer who was active in local social and civic activities. The Deerfield Hook and Ladder Company, the local firefighting department, was one community organization in which Ball was very involved (Hautaniemi and Rotman 2003). A concern for an

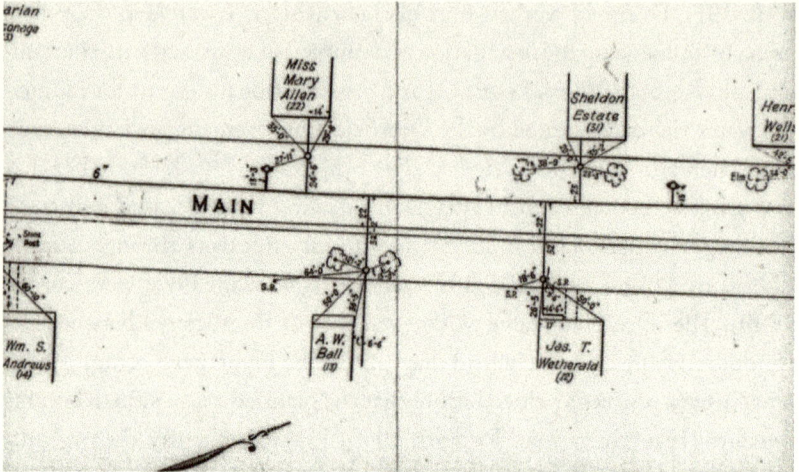

Figure 3.4. Deerfield Fire District plans showing pipes and connections, 1911. Courtesy of the Pocumtuck Valley Memorial Association Library, Deerfield, Massachusetts.

adequate water supply to fight fires may have been a significant motivator for piping water throughout the village and nearby farmland. In fact, the plans for the water system include hydrants evenly spaced along the streets and roads (figure 3.4). Some of these pipes went directly to houses, while others bypassed the residence entirely, presumably continuing to outbuildings located at the backs of lots (not shown on the plans for the water system, but shown on other period maps). The Moors-Ball property was one where the water pipe extended past the house to the barn. Arthur Ware Ball may have used his political position as water commissioner to "exercise his gender privilege to site the water on his homelot nearer to his work needs than those of the women in his household" (Hautaniemi and Rotman 2003: 148). Municipal water was a contested issue with implications for gendered social relations in this household.

Many residents of Deerfield village challenged the dichotomous ideals that dominated late nineteenth- and early twentieth-century gender ideologies. Arts and Crafts work in the community involved a significant segment of the village population and spanned the socioeconomic spectrum (Miller and Lanning 1994; Rotman 2009b, 2013b). The domestic production of craftwork for public markets transformed gendered social relations and challenged the cultural norms of separation between public and private spheres (Rotman 2005, 2009a, 2013b). Their community-level social organization illustrated the complex ways in which Deerfield women in particular negotiated the dominant gender ideal of their time (specifically the cult of domesticity) while incorporating new ideas for gender roles and relations (such as domestic reform and equal rights feminism), all within the unique cultural context of a rural Massachusetts village adapting to the transformations of agricultural production under industrial capitalism.

Other Responses to Changing Social Relations

The women and men of Deerfield were not unique in the ways they confronted the social changes that accompanied economic shifts in the late nineteenth and early twentieth centuries. Other communities in other places, such as Boston and New York, responded in similar ways (e.g., Praetzellis 2013). Similar to republican motherhood, the cult of domesticity emphasized the rearing of children and the importance of enculturating future democratic leaders (Spencer-Wood 2003; see chapter 2).

Domestic reformers, however, extended women's domestic roles into community spaces—such as parks, playgrounds, children's gardens, and other urban green spaces—that were designed to "improve urban morality by bringing people into contact with the purifying influence of God's nature" (Spencer-Wood 2003: 32). Significantly, these forms of community organization and the material outcomes (parks, playgrounds) illustrate that women were active social agents in their communities and not solely relegated to the domestic sphere (Rotman 2005, 2013b; Spencer-Wood 1994, 1999b, 2003). Much like the involvement of Deerfield women in pageants and municipal water projects, normative gender roles and relations in domestic reform movements incorporated both households *and* the communities in which they were situated. As such, the gender ideals within these two realms of social interaction were mutually reinforced while simultaneously challenging and expanding gender roles and relations within individual households.

One of the issues of interest to domestic reformers was dress reform (Nickolai 2013). More than simply functional, the clothes one wears are symbols of both identity and ideology, the basis of differentiation of both economic and cultural power (Bourdieu 1985). Thus, as material culture, clothing is "used to negotiate both personal identity and place in the greater social space" (Nickolai 2013: 215). Clothing was used to distinguish between not only genders but also socioeconomic classes (Gilchrist 1991; Nickolai 2013; White 2005). For example, elite women might wear several different outfits—morning gowns, tea gowns, evening gowns—depending on the time of day and the context of their social interaction (e.g., family only versus entertaining guests) (Nickolai 2013: 219). Thus, knowledge of the cultural codes accompanying different types of dress was a commodity and a highly effective mechanism for social differentiation.

Clothing was also highly symbolic (Giele 1995; Loren 1996; Nassaney 2008). Adherents to domestic ideals advocated restrictive clothing that also effectively conveyed modesty, such as corsets, multiple undergarments, and weighty overdresses. Such restrictive women's clothing was seen to parallel their restricted public roles (Giele 1995). Therefore, "as more middle-class women moved into the public sphere seeking, with some success, economic and political power and independence, they also became interested in reforming women's dress to make it more convenient and, in many cases, healthful" (Nickolai 2013: 220; see also Crane 2001). Equal rights feminists of the 1850s promoted an alternative ideal of "dressing sensibly" in clothing that eschewed restriction and weight (Giele 1995: 53). There were attempts, for instance, to discontinue the binding corsets to which a variety of physical and mental ailments were attributed (Cunningham 2003). Shorter skirts, pantaloons, and other forms of dress were attempted in various contexts, sometimes successfully but very often not (Fischer 2001).

Amelia Bloomer, for instance, designed a short dress that was much more comfortable and practical to wear (Giele 1995). "Bloomers" were perceived as scandalous and women who wore them were ridiculed. Even the spouses of these women were subjected to taunts. Elizabeth Cady Stanton was a very public figure who collaborated with Susan B. Anthony on the important issue of women's suffrage. Stanton's political foes indicted her husband by chanting "Heigh! Ho! The carrion crow, Mrs. Stanton's all the go; Twenty tailors take the stitches, *Mrs.* Stanton wears the britches" (Ward and Burns 1999: 71). Finally, both Stanton and Anthony conceded that wearing bloomers was detracting from their message of women's rights and abandoned the practice. Mrs. Stanton lamented, "Ah! Such is the tyranny of tradition!" (Exhibit, Women's Rights National Historic Park, Seneca Falls, 2000).

Many utopian communities also experimented with distinctive dress that conveyed group identity and great spirituality (Nickolai 2013: 221). Indeed, many intentional communities emerged as alternatives to mainstream American society during the late nineteenth and early twentieth centuries in response to the significant social changes occurring under industrial capitalism.

The Shakers were one such utopian society who settled in several places in the eastern United States and whose membership was derived through recruitment and conversion. Known as the United Society of Believers in Christ's Second Appearing, the group was founded by Ann Lee, a member of a dissenting Quaker sect (Savulis 2003). The group believed in a dual-gender god, which was mediated by celibacy (Crosthwaite 1989). As such, the Shakers' way of life deliberately eschewed heteronormative gender relations, such as the cult of domesticity, that emphasized marriage, reproduction, and patriarchal authority as key features, providing a counter-narrative to the gender roles associated with the capitalist ideology that dominated nineteenth-century social discourse.

Gender and spiritual hierarchies within Shaker communities were reinforced through behavioral regulations, architecture, and landscape design (T. Johnson 1976; Savulis 2003; Starbuck 1994). Those spaces that were "utilized simultaneously by men and women incorporated architectural elements that reinforced gender separation such as separate doorways, hallways, stairs, and bedrooms" (Savulis 2003: 165). Specifically, the structure of the material world was organized to promote celibacy, which was the path to salvation. The highly differentiated spaces of Shaker buildings may have significantly resembled the sexually segregated places of mainstream American architecture, which was designed to isolate women in kitchen ells at the back of the home and constrain their movements to the domestic sphere as much as possible. A dialectical understanding of Shaker spaces, however, reveals that these similarities in structural forms served very different ideological purposes in practice.

Religious ideology—beliefs and behaviors—was part of a dialogue with other secular and religious objects and ideas (Nickolai 2003), particularly during the Second Great Awakening that swept through the eastern

United States in the first half of the nineteenth century. The houselot occupied by Ellen White, a main prophet of the Seventh-day Adventists, for example, illustrated the interesting ways in which households did (or did not) engage with the communities in which they were situated. Although the small rural village of Battle Creek where she resided in the mid-nineteenth century was well connected to global markets, the archaeological record of her home expressed the ideological separation that belied her physical proximity to her neighbors. Thus, gender ideologies, roles, and relations must be assessed at the levels of both individual households and the local communities in which they are located, in order to fully understand the ways in which cultural norms are negotiated, accepted, or rejected.

White and her family embraced healthful eating as a spiritual act, eschewing alcohol, coffee, tea, and tobacco and embracing vegetarianism. Consequently, the faunal remains and artifacts associated with food preparation and storage included "few or no [meat] remains or oyster shells or cans from tinned fish and meats" (Nickolai 2003: 155), an archaeological signature very different from those of her farming neighbors. Neither an idiosyncrasy nor a sampling error, the distinctive material record of one household relative to its community may illustrate the varied responses of different families within a single context. Therefore, it is critical to be mindful of religion as a potentially "important aspect of the social positions and relationships of past people, and an important component in the formation of some aspects of the archaeological record" (Nickolai 2003: 157).

Significantly, the study conducted by Nickolai (2003) highlights that the location of a household in a rural, urban, or other setting is only one factor that may shape uses of the material world. The relative physical isolation or integration of a site is not necessarily an indicator of the degree to which site residents were connected to the community context. Often, families in rather remote locations—such as the Burghardt family of Great Barrington—are intimately connected to the outside world in important social and economic ways, whereas other households—such as the home of Ellen White—are proximal to their physical neighbors but ideologically very much separate. This is not to suggest that "ruralness" or "urbanness" or "suburbanness" plays no role in the formation of the archaeological records of households and communities; but rather, that it is imperative that the local context of each site be carefully examined and understood in order to fully elucidate nuances in social relations.

Gendered Spaces and Industrialization

Urban contexts provide additional interesting loci for examining households and communities as well as the dynamic interactions between these two spheres of human interaction. Immigrants and emancipated slaves flooded into America's industrializing cities during the late nineteenth century. Differences in class, race, and ethnicity often resulted in significant tensions between established economic or political structures and ideologies and those of in-migrating individuals and families.

During the antebellum period, most domestic reformers were "white middle-class or elite men who pushed poor whites, immigrants, and African-Americans to cleanse themselves of behavior that affirmed aspects of their identity, but which the reformers deemed disrespectable and undesirable" (Kruczek-Aaron 2013: 311). Maintaining existing social relations was crucial. Therefore, enforcing norms such as orderliness and cleanliness was of particular interest to American reformers. Newly arrived city dwellers, however, often brought with them beliefs, practices, and traditions that were foreign, both literally and figuratively.

Acculturation for immigrants—both historically and today—is a process (Kivisto 2004: 155). Rather than a straightforward progression of one group becoming like another, however, acculturation is a series of complex negotiations in which some traditions may continue, individual choices and adaptations may be made (Greenwood and Slawson 2008: 77), and cultural norms may be rejected or subverted (Joseph 2004: 19). Murray (2006: 6) describes this process as that of *becoming* or *devenir*.

Protestant missionaries in places such as New York City strongly encouraged newly arrived Irish immigrants to assimilate into American culture and emulate the behaviors of Victoriana, including gender roles and relations as defined by the cult of domesticity (Brighton 2011; Fitts 1999, 2001). In the late nineteenth century, however, gentility and respectability were not the only criteria for membership in the Victorian middle class. Occupation, religion, ethnicity, and race were also very important

(Mullins 2011; Phillips 2013). For at this time "the white-collar middle class was dominated by native-born white Protestants who strongly associated gentility with Protestant Christianity" (Fitts 1999: 41).

Poor, urban, working-class households did not necessarily conform to the separate spheres ideology and patriarchal authority; consequently, nineteenth-century reformers frequently viewed them as depraved and dangerous (Fitts 1999: 117). The material assemblages associated with these families and the tenements in which they lived, however, often contained matched sets and the iconographic Gothic-paneled ironstone strongly associated with domestic ideals (Wall 1985, 1999, 2000). Thus, the use of these fancy ceramics did indeed create an outward appearance of gentility, but these objects and associated social practices were not assigned the same symbolic meanings or values that middle-class families gave them. Rather, Irish immigrants, for example, "adopted elements of Victorianism and fused them with their own concepts of morality" (Brighton 2001: 28). Some of the ceramics were clearly designed for children and would have been important instruments in training boys and girls for their culturally prescribed gendered and other roles in society (Barton and Somerville 2012; Brighton 2008, 2011; Mullins 2011).

Similarly, for Irish Catholic immigrants, ethnic identity trumped class identity (Brighton 2001, 2004). Working-class households of nuclear and extended families in the Five Points neighborhood of New York used ceramic teawares and tablewares to "communicate Irish cultural traditions and middle-class Victorian values" (Brighton 2001: 21). Irish families also transformed the meanings of the cultural rituals of which ceramic teawares and tablewares were a part (Brighton 2001; Rotman 2010, 2012; Shakour et al. 2010). Outwardly, tea drinking was a very Victorian middle-class activity, yet inwardly it served to reinforce the cultural tradition of the céili—a nighttime gathering of neighbors for the sharing of food and stories. Immigrant families used distinctly American material culture and behaviors to engage in authentically Irish practices (Brighton 2004, 2008), just as the Pequot (and likely many other Indigenous groups) used European American ceramics in particularly Native American ways.

As with the Irish tenements in New York, archaeological features on Overseas Chinese sites in the San Francisco Bay region often cannot be associated with specific households. In Chinese communities, "residential arrangements were shaped by institutionalized discrimination, racial violence, labor practices, economic relations, and culturally specific strategies" that resulted in domestic configurations very different from those of their non-Chinese neighbors (Voss 2008e: 42). Indeed, the "household" as an archaeological unit of analysis is not particularly applicable to these communities in which social collectivity was so important to survival. A wide range of social units were relevant to the Overseas Chinese, including the individual, family, kin network, district association, temple membership, occupational groups, and the community at large (Voss 2008d). Like Irish immigration, movement of Chinese peoples is a global phenomenon that cannot be understood in strictly local terms. Many Chinatowns were linked not only to each other, but to European American communities through business relationships, labor practices, district associations, political organizing, and kinship ties (Praetzellis and Praetzellis 1998). Since most Overseas Chinese in the nineteenth century were men, the material culture from sites dating to this period reflect their behaviors, dispositions, activities, and identities (B. Williams 2008).

Excavation of wood-lined rectangular pits at the Market Street Chinatown site in San Francisco illustrated that "good sanitation was a prominent concern in this densely populated community, both for the residents' own health and comfort [and also] to counter racial stereotypes that portrayed the Chinese people as filthy and unclean" (Voss 2008d: 45). Western discourse also emasculated Asian men (Wong and Santa Ana 1999). Traditional Chinese garments along with the customary long braid (or queue), for example, "confounded Western ideals of gender and appropriate dress" (Fosha 2004: 64) and was used to perpetuate a feminized image of Chinese men (B. Williams 2008). The chinoiserie teacups and tea bowls documented in great numbers in the archaeological record of the Market Street Chinatown site were perceived by Westerns as "dainty cups" and the Chinese men who used them were emasculated in particularly racialized ways (B. Williams 2008: 60). As such, the material record reflects the complex intersection of class, racism, and ethnicity with gender in these community contexts.

In other places, however, ethnicity served to unite rather than divide people, intersecting with gender ideals and socioeconomic status in unique ways. Lawrenceburg was a dynamic community in southern Indiana during the nineteenth century. This planned urban center was poised to take advantage of emerging financial opportunities related to commercial activities (Rotman and Clay 2008). The failure of the canal system and its replacement by the railroad, however, altered the character of the city. It also changed the landscape through the addition and deletion of associated transportation features. The shift in transportation patterns affected the local economy and fostered the development of the multiethnic working-class community of Germantown, a walking suburb adjacent to the small factories and other forms of industrialization that came to characterize the community in the latter part of the nineteenth century (Rotman and Clay 2008). Through expansion, urbanization, and industrialization, this neatly platted neighborhood in Lawrenceburg became an economically marginal ethnic enclave within the city. The material records of three houselots were investigated to understand changing social relations within this evolving community: the affluent Macy house (12D502), the owner-occupied working-class Bieger-Gould-Disque site (12D520), and the speculative rental housing of the Tousey-Hofenbeader-Mohr site (12D508).

The most notable difference among the ceramics from the three homelots was the relative percentages of Gothic and other paneled ironstones, which were very strongly associated with an ideological and physical separation of gender roles as part of the cult of domesticity. This pattern dominated the assemblage from the relatively affluent middle-class Macy house, was present in smaller proportions at the working-class Bieger-Gould-Disque site, and was completely absent from the lower-class Tousey-Hofenbeader-Mohr site (Rotman and Clay 2008: 63). At first glance, this distribution is not surprising. Gothic-paneled vessels have been attributed as a nearly exclusive material symbol of the middle class (Fitts 1999; Wall 1994) and the latter households were working and lower class.

Closer examination of the artifacts from these sites, however, revealed that *other* symbols of middle-class Victorian ideals, such as flowerpots, miniature ceramic tea sets, and specialized dining vessels for children were present in the homelots' assemblages (Fitts 1999). These forms of material culture (e.g., flowerpots) were part of establishing the home as a natural haven and refuge from the crass commercializing and industrializing outside world, as well as for socializing children into their prescribed gender roles as adults (through the miniature tea sets and specialized dining vessels). Common clay flowerpot fragments were recovered from all three sites, as were pieces of toy dishes. A dish from a child's place setting was recovered in the assemblage from the working-class Bieger-Gould-Disque duplexes. Although Gothic-paneled wares were absent from the lower-class Tousey-Hofenbeader-Mohr rental property, many other Victorian middle-class symbols were recovered from that site, including flowerpots, toy dishes, and a children's dish. Consequently, it appears that Victorian middle-class ideals may have been operating in each of the households but not necessarily with identical material patterns (Rotman and Clay 2008: 64), illustrating the interpenetration of opposites or that a range of material expressions may be present within a single social context.

The Victorian ideals in Lawrenceburg represent a complex entanglement of gender and class. In addition, the archaeological records of these households once again illustrate the key role that women played in choosing the social rituals of which the household would be a part, purchasing the attendant material culture for the home, and enculturating children into these social worlds.

Historical and archaeological analyses have revealed ways in which Victorian dining rituals were used to emphasize class and nativity statuses within the community (Walker 2008). All of the assemblages from Lawrenceburg consisted primarily of undecorated and minimally decorated teawares and tablewares, even though their location on the Ohio River, a major distribution corridor for manufactured products throughout the eastern United States, would in theory have given them access to a wide range of consumer goods. Fitts (1999: 56) asserted that the penchant for selecting these kinds of white dishes was a uniquely middle-class phenomenon. Yet, *all* families in the Lawrenceburg neighborhood under study, regardless of their financial status, appeared to have used these types of dishes in their homes.

Fitts (1999: 58) further observed that these types of table settings conveyed the ideals of thrift and modesty. Crass et al. (1999: 17–18) noted that Germans, in particular, were known to be conservative materially and would be expected to display different artifacts of gentility than their non-German neighbors would. The residents of the homelots in this study may have felt that predominantly white tea and table settings conveyed the Victorian ideals of purity and the morality of domesticity, even if they were not specifically in the Gothic-paneled pattern.

It is unlikely that the middle-class symbols observed at these sites, particularly those objects with the most recent *termini post quem*, were simply the result of Victorian ideals taking greater hold in the public consciousness toward the end of the nineteenth century. Wall (1991, 1994, 1999, 2000) observed that, despite the codification of the ideals of domesticity in households of different socioeconomic status, the expressions of these ideals did vary according to class.

Indeed, the residents of the homelots in Lawrenceburg appeared to be collectively "behind the times" in terms of what constituted fashionable material displays (Rotman and Clay 2008: 64). It would be expected that the decorations on ceramic vessels would parallel the elaborate ornamentation seen in other aspects of the material world, such as grave markers (McGuire 1988; Sears 1989) and architectural styles (Howard 1989), in the decades surrounding the turn of the twentieth century. The majority of the vessels in the assemblages from the Lawrenceburg sites remained undecorated or minimally decorated. If the middle-class symbols recovered were simply the result of Victorian ideals taking a greater hold in the public consciousness, it would be expected that those material forms would strongly parallel larger social material trends.

Instead, remaining outside the mainstream of Victorian fashion appears to have been evidence of the insular strategy of this German community in southern Indiana around the turn of the twentieth century and not strictly an expression of class ideals. Furthermore, using predominantly white dishes—as their neighbors did—may have been a matter of group uniformity (Wall 1999: 113) and conformity (Fitts 1999: 56). The need for community cohesion may have become increasingly important as the neighborhood underwent dramatic social and economic changes as a result of urban expansion, industrialization, and difficult financial times, both locally and nationally (Rotman and Clay 2008).

Porcelain tea sets, also associated with Victorian middle-class domesticity (Fitts 1999; Wall 1994), were absent from the assemblages. Only a few child's toy dishes and individual vessels were recovered. Although porcelain tea sets were not necessarily expected for the working-class and lower-class families in the study, it was anticipated that some would be recovered from the Macy site, particularly from the earliest occupation by its most affluent residents. Yet, only a single paneled teacup was recovered from the wood-lined privy (Feature 6). Given how expensive porcelain was relative to other refined earthenwares, the absence of porcelain tea sets may have been another deliberate attempt to de-emphasize material symbols that would signal class differences (Rotman and Clay 2008: 64). Ethnic identity would have been important to community cohesion, a priority that was greater than the socioeconomic aspirations of individual families.

In addition, beginning in the decades after the mid-nineteenth century, consumers could purchase dinner sets that contained teacups and tea saucers, so the purchase of a separate tea set was not necessary (although a teapot was not included in the dinner set) (Israel 1968). Such sets were advertised in the 1880 Montgomery Ward catalogue but may have been available even earlier. At the houselots in Lawrenceburg, matching tea sets were recovered from the working-class households in the study (N = 3), but more than twice as many matching table and matching/complementary tea and table sets were identified (N = 7).

The availability of teawares as part of tableware sets in the late nineteenth century raises another interesting question that has particular implications for gendered social relations in Lawrenceburg. The tea ritual in working-class households has been interpreted as serving a function different from that in middle-class residences (Wall 1991, 1994, 1999, 2000). That is, the ritual did not assert familial status within the community; rather, tea drinking affirmed the intimacy and cohesion of the family's close, kin-like social circle.

The similarities of working-class teawares and tablewares (as opposed to the distinct differences between sets used for ritual tea drinking versus familial dining), particularly after 1880 and perhaps earlier, could simply be a matter of what was available for purchase. Teawares and tablewares came together in a set and were identical. Consequently, the matched wares recovered from working-class and lower-class households of this period may be an expression of marketing strategy rather than differential meaning for the social ritual of afternoon tea (Rotman and Clay 2008: 65). These consumer patterns—and the relative absence of social distinctions between families—also suggest that complementary rather than hierarchical gender relations were likely also operating in both households and the community.

Furthermore, purchasing an additional, separate set of teawares might not have been economically feasible in a time when neighborhood residents were becoming increasingly marginalized. An overt material display of a separate tea set may have been viewed as wasteful or decadent in this conservative community, particularly during the financially difficult decades of the late nineteenth century (Rotman and Staicer 2002). Wall (1991, 1999: 113) noted that for some poorer middle-class women in New York, "dazzling their friends with sumptuous ceramics was not necessarily a productive strategy in an environment where they might need the help of their peers to maintain their precarious position at the lower end of the middle class." Thus, ceramic vessels may have been used to highlight group similarities rather than to emphasize differences. This certainly appeared to be true for the economically marginal households in Lawrenceburg as well (Rotman and Clay 2008).

The material assemblages from the three sites were strikingly homogenous, with the notable exception of the uneven distribution of Gothic-paneled vessels. It appears that identity within this Lawrenceburg neighborhood was constructed less on class differences than on ethnic (German) similarities (Rotman and Clay 2008: 65). These commonalities were expressed through the predominantly undecorated or minimally decorated (molded, no color) ceramic vessels recovered from these different households. During the last half of the nineteenth century, as the transportation infrastructure was transformed and the area became increasingly marginalized by urbanization and industrialization, residents appeared to respond to these difficult changes by stressing ethnic identity and community cohesion through their uses of the material world (Rotman and Clay 2008).

The archaeological sites examined here for Irish Catholic immigrants in New York City, Overseas Chinese in California, and German immigrants in southern Indiana all illustrate the simultaneous interplay of gender, class, and ethnicity at the level of the community. Importantly, immigrant groups selectively mediated these various identities through material culture and the built environment, often with reference to both the world they currently inhabited and the world they left behind upon emigrating. It was only through community-level analyses of their material worlds that these interesting nuances of gender, class, and ethnicity became fully visible.

Archaeological excavation in the San Francisco Bay Area also yielded interesting data on class consciousness among nineteenth-century railroad workers. Aspects of diet and dining at a number of households in this working-class community revealed divisions among the railroad workers along the lines of craft or skill and nativity (Walker 2008: 108). "American" identity was based upon ideas of appropriate standards of living and forms of behavior, including gender roles and relations as defined by domesticity (Arnesen 1994; Barrett 1992; Walker 2008). Dining etiquette, for example, was a common public exercise in social competence and class boundary maintenance in nineteenth-century America (Carson 1990; Fitts 1999; Kruczek-Aaron 2002; Wall 1991).

Food consumption was an activity strongly correlated with the domestic sphere, and women were entrusted with the etiquette and knowledge of its rituals. As such, dining was a highly gendered activity. Recovered faunal remains from the railroad sites in California indicated that unskilled immigrant workers tended to prefer more expensive cuts of meat than their skilled U.S.-born counterparts did. Although this may be attributed to cultural, ideological, and economic factors associated with the unskilled workers, it is more likely a reflection of the Victorian ideologies of frugality and respectability to which the native-born skilled workers conformed. Not surprisingly then, skilled workers tended to invest in the material trappings of formal dining to a much greater extent than immigrant workers did. The exclusivity of Victorian dining and "mastery of its rituals signaled that one belonged to a civilized society or, possibly more to the point, *a* civilized society. One that was not immigrant" (Walker 2008: 128). As purchasers and preparers of food, women were especially important cultural agents in this process.

Victorian ideology was also an important element of frontier mining camps in the American West, where notions of manifest destiny and rugged individualism abounded (Parker and Rodseth 2005). Too often, however, these mining camps are incorrectly understood to be bastions of bachelor life with women only present as prostitutes. This characterization belies the reality that many men were married to local Native American or

Hawaiian women and that families were an integral part of these complex communities (Rose 2013).

In the mid-nineteenth-century multiethnic mining camp of Kanaka Flat, Oregon, the narrative of "lonely men and loose women" was utterly false. Instead of "revealing the expected cluster of brothels and saloons, research has shown Kanaka Flat to be a settlement of couples of mixed ethnicity, who married in religious ceremonies when legally able to do so" (Rose 2013: 31). As such, the domestic debris from cabin sites in the settlement must be interpreted as remnants not of bachelor living but of nuclear or possibly extended families. Understanding the demographic composition of the community, therefore, contextualizes the archaeological deposits under study, dispels preconceived myths of site histories, and reveals the intersection of gender with other social prisms, which for mining camps was significant ethnic diversity.

Gendered Social Interaction at the Level of Community

Community-level analysis—the abstraction of generality—is particularly effective for understanding the ways in which gender intersects with other social forces to shape human experience. Spade and Valentine (2004: 1) use the metaphor of a kaleidoscope to help "grasp the complex and ever-changing meaning and practice of gender as it interacts with other social prisms—such as race, age, sexuality, and social class—to create complex patterns of identities and relationships." The kaleidoscope characterizes the dynamic and ever-changing meaning and practice of gendered social relations—including but not limited to competing gender ideologies, socioeconomic class, political agendas, and developmental cycle of individuals and families—to create multifaceted patterns of identities and relationships.

As we look at contexts of human engagement, it is also clear that different gender ideologies are simultaneously separate from and integral parts of one another as well as being combined in a myriad of ways. Very often, women, men, and other gendered beings were aware of the dominant ideals, but created and codified gender roles and relations in ways that made sense within their particular circumstances, belief systems, and family requirements. Although gender ideologies existed in idealized forms, they were rarely adopted wholesale; rather, they were interpreted or combined according to unique labor needs, financial abilities, social positions, and political ideals, among many other cultural forces and processes (Rotman 2001, 2009a).

Furthermore, critical analyses and a dialectical lens for interrogating the material world provide us with nuanced understandings of the social relations operating within households and communities as well as how these spheres of interaction are (typically but not always) mutually reinforcing. The interpenetration of opposites is the understanding that how things function—that is, objects and how people perceive them—is to a large degree due to their surroundings (Ollman 1993:14). The interpenetration of opposites reveals that processes are not monolithic, as the case studies presented in this chapter also illustrate. Individual households within a community—whether the Five Points neighborhood in New York or the Lawrenceburg community in southern Indiana or a railroad camp in California—are all uniquely situated within the social, cultural, economic, and political contexts of their time and, thus, negotiate, contest, or respond to dominant cultural norms from those unique structured positions.

Additionally, the dialectical relation of contradiction recognizes that elements within the same relation "do not only intersect in mutually supportive ways, but are constantly blocking, undermining, otherwise interfering with and in due course transforming one another" (Ollman 1993: 16). Community-level analyses help us to understand households not in isolation, but in *relation* to and engagement *with* one another.

Examining gender roles and ideologies within communities also requires a cognizance of materiality and spatiality beyond the scale of individual houselots. Given the dialectical relationship between households and the communities in which they are situated, however, it is critical to move between these two levels of analysis and back again for the richest view of gendered human experience.

Community organizations also elucidate and reinforce cultural norms and the ways in which individuals and families negotiate and contest dominant ideals. Schools, factories, and other institutions are explored in the next chapter.

4

~~<<<<<<<<~~

Institutions and Social Relations of Gender

Institutions often function as mechanisms for social reproduction and social control. Particularly in the late eighteenth and early nineteenth centuries, "the Western world redefined the social and economic order, morality, sexuality, crime, and punishment" (DeCunzo 1995; Foucault 1978, 1979). As a result, a variety of entities emerged as part of domestic reform activities. These institutions both reflected and imposed community attitudes and identities as well as structured human life in a myriad of ways (Gibb 2009).

As with the mutual interaction between households and communities, institutions were also a dynamic multiscalar dimension of social engagement. The Presidio of San Francisco, for example, consisted of individual domestic residences—that is, a community of colonial residents and Native Californians—*and* was a governmental institution as a military outpost on the frontier. Similarly, utopian societies, particularly those with religious foci as their structuring principles, were both communities and representations of ecclesiastical institutions. Arguably, marriage and family are both critical social institutions in American life through time and across space. Therefore, as with households and communities, it is imperative to consider institutions within the context of the communities of which they are a part and the ways in which they amplify ideologies operating within households.

An archaeological and historical examination of institutions facilitates another abstraction of generality: changing the degree of magnification from households to communities to institutions and back again. Institutions also give particular insights into the dialectical relation of the interpenetration of opposites as the perspectives of the operating institutions may be very different from the views of those whose behavior is being controlled by or within them (Baugher 2009). Indeed, the control of others is a key tenet of colonialism, capitalism, and patriarchy, as the case studies to follow illustrate.

In many ways, the institutional examples explored in this chapter could have been included in the earlier chapters on households and communities. The fluidity and permeability of the spheres of human interaction explored in this volume are reflective of how incredibly dynamic social relations are. The codification, reproduction, and regulation of gender roles and relations are of particular interest. A variety of contexts are explored, but institutions of the military, reform, factories, and education (such as institutions with religious foci and schools) are emphasized.

Military Institutions

Gender homogeneity is sometimes assumed for institutional contexts, particularly in presumed all-male contexts like prisons or institutions of religious instruction such as monasteries. As the Kanaka Flat mining camp in Oregon illustrated, however, incomplete and incorrect interpretations of the materiality of such places occur when gender relations are assumed and the specific context under study is poorly understood. Military encampments are another area where particular biases may distort the nuanced realities of gendered social interactions.

The Presidio of San Francisco was not yet officially part of the United States when it was founded by Spain during the colonization of the California coast in the late eighteenth century. The identities of occupants of the San Francisco Presidio were quickly transformed from military settlers to Californios, however, through several interrelated phenomena (Voss 2008b). The emergence of a ranchero culture and the system of land grants facilitated the accumulation of enormous landholdings in the form of cattle ranches, which concentrated wealth, property, and power among relatively few military families. This, in turn, facilitated the exploitation of Native Californians as labor for managing large herds and converting cattle into marketable hides and tallow. Attendant with the ranchero culture was the emergence of a seigniorial society that emphasized relationships over individualism and created a complex web of obligations and authority extending across the entire social order. A white or European racial identity also became increasingly important as a means of claiming social power, wealth, and privilege in nineteenth-century California. In these complex ways, Californios simultaneously forged new identities while also naturalizing their dominance over Native Californians (Voss 2008a, 2008b).

This *ethnogenesis* (formation of new cultural identities) was observable through changes in the landscape, architecture, ceramics, and clothing, among other artifact classes. Several interrelated trends were observable in the material record. A collective colonial identity emerged and the once-diverse society of the San Francisco Presidio became more homogeneous, particularly in terms of internal representation (Voss 2008a, 2008b). In addition, there was an increasing distinction between the homogeneity of colonial society and Native Californians. This "othering" was accompanied by colonial settlers' rejection of their own indigenous and African ancestries. Adobe became the preferred building material and form as residents of the Presidio of San Francisco articulated a shared colonial identity in the decades surrounding the turn of the eighteenth century (figure 4.1). This architectural style created a very clear distinction between the military settlement and the local indigenous peoples.

Gendered social relations were at the center of daily life at this military colonial outpost (Voss 2008a, 2008b). In addition, "although sexuality is sometimes treated as a trivial or private aspect of social life, the archaeology and ethnohistory of Spanish-colonial San Francisco demonstrates that sexual politics were central, rather than incidental, to the imperial project" (Voss 2008b: 200). The Quadrangle of the San Francisco Presidio was one particularly important gendered space (Voss 2008a). In the 1810s, the Quadrangle was "redesigned, eliminating private yards. Instead, the central plaza was expanded and protected by a narrow gate. The plaza became a visually protected interior space where household activities could be undertaken by the community as a whole, rather than by each family in a private yard" (Voss 2008a: 199–200). These changes to community architecture correlated with intensifying regulation of women's sexuality during a period of increased contact between Europeans and Indigenous peoples as well as rising concerns about ethnic propriety and respectability.

The landscape surrounding the colonial outpost was also gendered and

Figure 4.1. Artist's conception of the Presidio of San Francisco as it may have appeared in 1792. Photograph courtesy of Golden Gate National Recreation Area, National Park Service.

sexualized. Colonial women rarely traveled outside the securely colonized area of the presidio. Therefore, in their absence, "the eastern inland areas were masculinized through colonial men's military expeditions and sexualized through interethnic sexual violence perpetrated by some colonial men on Native Californians" (Voss 2008a: 289). Identities, including gendered identities, at the San Francisco Presidio were shaped and negotiated at the intersection of class, ethnicity, race, and sexuality, among other social relations. Ethnogenesis at the presidio can be traced through changes to "material and spatial practices that occurred during the shift from a pluralistic, multiracial, colonial population to one defined by its common status as colonizers and by a regional and ethnic Californio identity" (Voss 2008a: 115). In particular, gendered social relations at the Presidio of San Francisco elucidated the complexities of negotiating gender identities, roles, and relations under colonialism.

Camp Nelson in Kentucky is another military context where gender was a dynamic dimension of lived experiences. The camp was one of the largest recruitment and training centers for African-American soldiers during the Civil War (S. McBride 2013). Excavations of tent sites, mess houses, and barracks revealed material culture and foodways similar to those of European American soldiers at other camps, suggesting some degree of standardization across military contexts (McBride et al. 2006; McBride and McBride 2006). Soldiers' diets, for example, consisted of primarily beef and beans (S. McBride 2013: 75; see also MacPherson 1998).

The archaeology of Camp Nelson also reveals that soldiers cohabited with their wives and children, even though this was against army regulations (S. McBride 2010). Fragments of dolls, glass beads, a hair barrette, and women's clothing buttons from the allegedly all-male barrack sites clearly illustrate family living arrangements. Camp leaders provided rations only to the soldiers, but food remains illustrate that the women were quite resourceful in provisioning themselves and their children in the absence of military support. Animal bones from pigs, chicken, and wild game demonstrate a diverse diet acquired through trade or purchase (S. McBride 2010). The archaeological record of Camp Nelson "showed the independence, ingenuity, and entrepreneurial skill of the women and certainly contradicts stereotypes of slaves' intelligence and individual initiative" (S. McBride 2013: 77). The archaeological record of Camp Nelson also demonstrates that the army was not successful in controlling either the behaviors of its soldiers or those of the families that accompanied them.

The Johnson's Island prison in Lake Erie, Ohio, was another gendered military context from the Civil War (Bush 2009). The island was a Union-designed prisoner-of-war camp for Confederate officers and, thus, housed men only. The facility was overcrowded, and rations, clothing, and communications were limited. Imprisonment challenged these Southern gentlemen in a variety of ways. Many of the captured officers "had never cooked their own food, mended their own clothes or cleaned their own room, having always lived with servants, mothers, sisters, and/or wives. Even in the military, others often addressed their personal care" (Bush 2009: 164).

The privilege these European American men had enjoyed as officers (a consequence of both their ethnicity *and* gender) was denied them as prisoners of war. Prisoners had to cook, set the table, wash the dishes and the laundry, sew, and do other daily chores as features of life in this institutional context (Bush 2009). These tasks were significantly incompatible with Southern folk culture that emphasized "a hierarchical social structure, ascribed status, patterns of deference, and masculine codes of honor" (MacPherson 1998: 24). Thus, the material record of the Johnson's Island military prison—refined earthenwares, buttons, and needles—represented the prisoners' negotiation of gender roles within this single-gendered environment.

Military encampments and prisons are constructed according to specific governmental standards of social interaction. The actual utilization of those spaces by human agents, however, often goes beyond what the institution envisioned. Reform organizations are similarly dynamic, particularly when reform ideas are contested by those they are meant to "help."

Reform Institutions

By the mid-nineteenth century, America "had reformulated both the methods of and responses to social and moral benevolence, reform, and control" (DeCunzo 1995: 3). The work of domestic reformers in the immigrant tenements of New York City is but one example of the ways in which communities policed residents' compliance with dominant class and gender ideals as well as penalized those who did not conform to societal expectations.

The Magdalen Society of Philadelphia (1800–1850) "reflected not only contemporary concerns about social order, it also expressed fears about environmental decay, disease, war, natural disasters, and economic fluctuations in the gendered language of religious belief" (DeCunzo 1995: 4). The female body, sexuality, and physical and moral pollution were the specific foci of the society and its asylum. Sexual activity outside of marriage was deemed immoral for women, yet many of these "fallen" women were supporting themselves financially through prostitution. Therefore, Magdalens residing at the asylum "received training in spinning yarn, sewing, laundry, and other domestic skills," all of which were consistent with the gendered occupational ideals of the time and were deemed essential for becoming wives to Christian men and mothers to their children (DeCunzo 1995: 126).

The setting of the asylum, its architecture, and its landscape were all designed to enclose the women in a morally pure, gardenlike environment that would protect them from the evils of the city beyond its walls. Plain, functional furnishings and dress curbed the women's social and economic aspirations, and the refined ceramics were decorated with patterns that conveyed moral purity and nature (such as floral hand-painted or transfer-printed decorations) (DeCunzo 1995: 62–63, 87–89).

Most of the "fallen" women who utilized the asylum did so for their own purposes. They did not see themselves as immoral or polluted but sought the services of the institution because "it offered a respite from cold, hunger, life in the streets, and abusive family members and associates" (DeCunzo 1995: 127). Indeed, the women who came to the asylum often stayed for only a short time and returned to their previous lives upon leaving.

The Magdalen Society Asylum illustrates the ways in which institutions were sometimes utilized as a mechanism of social control in an effort to get community members to conform to particular ecclesiastical and patriarchal ideals of gender. Regardless of the actual success of such institutions, these community entities were critical components of the cultural landscape of historic America and central to societal negotiation of the changing economic and social order of the times.

Mental institutions also emerged in the late eighteenth and nineteenth centuries as a societal mechanism for managing "deviant" behavior (Fox 1978). With the emergence of psychiatry as a profession, new models for "othering" emerged. Mental illness was widely thought to be the result of heredity or of immoral living (Psota 2011). Thus, mental illness was defined less as a medical condition than as a social one in which individuals exhibited some kind of inappropriate behavior. Those considered "insane," for example, were "that group of unproductive, bothersome defectives who, though they had committed no crime, required an indefinite and involuntary program of 'treatment and confinement,' whereas the 'mentally ill' were those moderately disturbed whose *productive potential* had yet to be determined" (Fox 1978: 17; emphasis added).

Conformity to social standards was expected, uniting the ideals of domesticity and the Protestant work ethic. Women were frequently targeted for compliance with social ideals in many ways that men were not. Under domesticity, women were responsible for their children's care and education, while fathers were the primary financial support for the family (Brockley 2004). By the 1890s, however, physicians began telling mothers that their special-needs children required specific professional, institutional care, and mothers were often blamed for their children's conditions. Specifically, mothers' overprotecting and spoiling of their children was deemed to cause many mental illnesses, such as autism (Psota 2011: 23), creating even more pressure on Victorian mothers to produce "perfect" children.

Institutions for the treatment of mental illness were constructed in the second half of the nineteenth century. Many families sought to care for ill loved ones at home as long as possible, and decision making about institutionalization was motivated by complex variables, such as the significant social stigma of mental illness and the overcrowded conditions of many mental health facilities. Otillia "Tillie" Sengstacken, born in 1877, is a case example. Though she experienced episodes of psychosis, her mother, Mary, and aunt, Margaritha, cared for her for many years in their home in San Jose, California (Psota 2011). The archaeological assemblage from their residence contained a disproportionately high percentage of grooming and health-product bottles relative to other domestic objects (Psota 2011: 20). Medicines included those for constipation, sedation, and pain relief and clearly illustrate the efforts Tillie's family made to care for her at home.

As her mother and aunt got older, however, effectively managing intense episodes of psychosis may have become more difficult, and in 1920, at 43 years of age, Tillie was admitted to Agnews State Hospital near San Francisco, which had been founded in 1886. Unfortunately, abuse at the institution was commonplace, and, shortly after her admission, Tillie developed abscesses on her wrists, hips, and ankles, consistent with restraints (Psota 2011: 32). She developed septicemia and died a few weeks later.

What is significant about Tillie's story is the impact that mental health institutions had on the behavior of families within households, particularly women. The conflation of mental illness with social deviance and the blaming of mothers for their children's illnesses created very dynamic and particularly gendered approaches to managing afflicted persons. The social ideals of communities created institutions (mental hospitals) that defined all deviant behaviors as illness (particularly when one was not able to fulfill one's expected role as a productive member of society) (Psota 2011). Those institutional ideals in turn shaped behaviors at all levels of society, including the choices families—especially mothers—made regarding the care of their children and loved ones.

With the emergence of industrial capitalism, an individual's productive value to society became a prominent feature of social life in America. The ideology of modern discipline encouraged individuality and time discipline, affecting interactions within households, communities, and institutions.

Institutions of Capitalism: Modern Discipline

Rural farming villages and urban industrial communities each had unique economic and productive needs during the economic transition from agricultural to industrial production. The social forces of the time intersected in ways that at once homogenized and fractured class and gender relations throughout the developing social and spatial order of the United States. The late eighteenth through the early twentieth centuries in particular represented a period of major class change, which was accompanied by the growth of the ideology of modern discipline and an emphasis on definition and control of the individual (Shackel 1993). Ideals of order and productivity were also applied to factories, classrooms, hospitals, libraries, schools, and even prisons (Leone 1999: 203).

The penetration of modern discipline is particularly relevant to understanding gender ideologies. Women, as wives and mothers, were instrumental in socializing children into the ideals of time discipline and individuality as well as ensuring that all members of the household conducted themselves properly in terms of the behaviors associated with personal discipline (Rotman 2001, 2009a; Shackel 1993). Both modern discipline and gender had material manifestations in the increasing segmentation and elaboration in dining.

Ceramic dishes clearly changed over time—whiter wares became preferred over cream-colored wares, and matched sets of ceramics gained favor during the nineteenth century (Yentsch 1991; Wall 1994). These changes have been explained in different ways. Deetz (1996) attributed this transformation to a cognitive shift, a change in the way people saw reality. Specifically, the emergence of the Georgian worldview centered society on the individual. George Miller (1991) argues, however, that falling prices for English ceramics increased consumption of these wares and thereby influenced the process of social emulation by lower classes (Leone 1999).

Changes to ceramic teawares and tablewares corresponded to the emergence of the ideology of modern discipline (Leone 1999; Leone et al. 1987; Shackel 1993). Leone (1999: 200) states:

There should be differential participation in, and subjugation to, a wage-labor system as people shift into classes and are either impoverished or become owners. There should be fluctuations in the use of matched ceramics from household to household as people rent or buy, become debtors or lenders, are workers or owners, or are in or out of the market, since cooking, eating, and associated acts of cleanliness mark the disciplines needed to produce wage earners and rent payers.

Hence, differential participation in the ideology of discipline should be expressed through refined earthenwares. Furthermore, the ideologies that shaped gender roles and relations can also be observed.

In their various publications, Leone, Potter, and Shackel examine the proportion of ceramic types (decorative motifs) to forms (functional categories) and sizes (particularly of plates for specialized functions; that is, salad, dinner, or dessert plates) over time. According to Shackel's (1993: 32) model, if few types and sizes are present in an assemblage, this lack of variation and segmentation indicates the owner's non-participation in the new discipline. Conversely, the presence of few types but many sizes indicates a high degree of acceptance and participation in the new social pattern (i.e., one plate per person, vessels with highly specialized functions, and all of them, at least theoretically, being part of the same matched pattern/set). Therefore, a variety of types and sizes indicates some segmentation and partial participation (Shackel 1993: 32).

The Hyde/Thompson house in Annapolis, Maryland, for example, was consistently owned and occupied by upper-middle-class families, whereas the nearby Carroll house was occupied by working-class renters (Leone 1999: 205–208). The indices of tableware diversity for the former house began high and continued to rise relative to the latter, which began low and remained so over time. The indices generated should not be considered determinations of wealth. Rather, they indicate the degree to which households, through their actions and beliefs, were engaged in the culture of modern discipline that accompanied the growth of capitalism (Leone 1999: 208). Therefore, variations in and among ceramic assemblages were determined by the economic history of individual households and families, as well as their relation to the larger economic milieu.

Men were active participants in the dissemination of and engagement with this new ideology of modern discipline (Rotman 2001, 2009a). Men were indoctrinated into these new ideals as their workplaces became reorganized according to new structures of time, routines, and work disciplines during the Industrial Revolution (Leone 1999: 200; see also Thompson 1967, 1974). Factories became important institutional loci wherein modern discipline operated. Importantly, however, these ideals permeated throughout home, community, and institution and shaped human experiences at all levels of social engagement.

The Russell Cutlery Factory in Turners Falls, Massachusetts, implemented the American scheme of mass production that utilized interchangeable parts and labor organization. Processes were highly segmented, and individual workers were responsible for only a small aspect of the overall manufacturing process—in effect, deskilling workers and making them as interchangeable as the parts they were making on the factory line (Nassaney and Abel 1993, 2000). The production floor was design to control workers and maximize efficiency. The archaeological record of the factory reveals a number of wasters—parts that were not made to standard, either intentionally or unintentionally—which strongly suggest that the workers resisted at least some of their bosses' efforts to control their behavior.

Importantly, production at the Russell Cutlery Factory demonstrates that the ideals of modern discipline that structured the manufacturing process did not operate in isolation. Rather, emphasis on the individual and increasing segmentation permeated all spheres of human interaction (Nassaney and Abel 1993, 2000). The ideals of the workplace were also operationalized at home, where children were socialized into their roles as future workers under industrial capitalism (Nassaney and Abel 2000). Thus, the ideology of modern discipline transcended the boundaries of home, community, and institution and became comingled with the gender ideals of the cult of domesticity.

The Schroeder Saddletree Factory and Residence in Madison, Indiana, was a very different kind of factory setting (Rotman and Staicer 2002). It offered an intriguing opportunity to explore specialty production and associated social interactions, the effects of national economic crises in the formation of the archaeological record, and the intersection of these in displays of gender, class, ethnicity, and status.

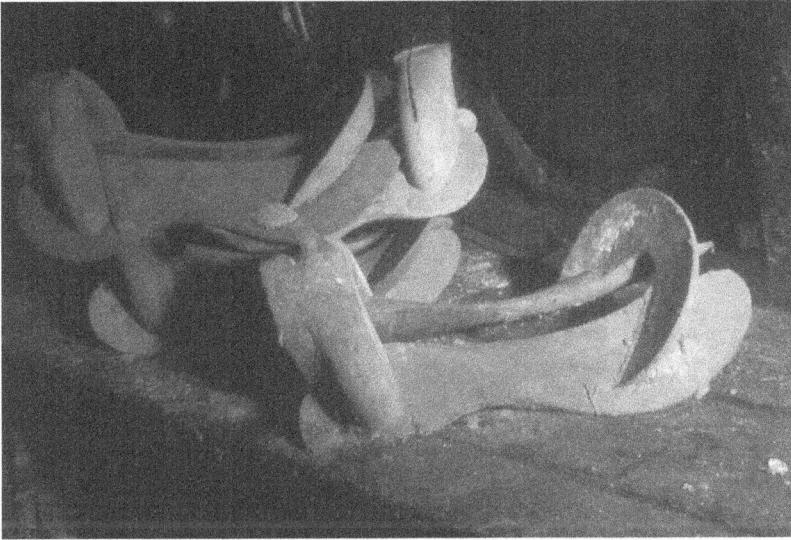

Figure 4.2. Schroeder saddletrees in the woodworking shop. Courtesy of the Schroeder Collection, Madison, Indiana.

The specialty production of saddletrees (the wooden skeletons upon which saddles are assembled) began in the village as early as 1850 (U.S. Bureau of the Census 1850) (figure 4.2). More than 156,000 saddletrees per annum were produced in Madison shops and sold to saddle makers throughout the United States as well as in South America and Cuba (*Madison Weekly Courier* 1879a, 1879b). John Benedict "Ben" Schroeder spent five years as an apprentice in the trade before opening his own shop in 1878 (*Madison Weekly Courier* 1878) (figure 4.3). Ben operated the saddletree factory as a sole proprietorship until his death in 1909. Leo, his eldest son, became the factory manager at age 21. The children continued to operate the business after the death of their mother in 1919, serving as the board of directors, stockholders, and officers of the corporation (figure 4.4).

The relations of specialty production, such as those at the Schroeder Saddletree Factory, must be conceptualized differently from large industrial complexes (Scranton 1997). Corporate paternalism, a form of social control similar to a father-child relationships, was operationalized in both these manufacturing settings to ensure the company's prosperity (Mrozowski 1991; Scranton 1997). In specialty firms, however, paternalistic management sought to strengthen relationships between workers and

Figure 4.3. The Ben Schroeder Saddletree Factory, looking south. Woodworking shop is at right. Blacksmith and assembly shops are at the left, and the brick residence is at the rear. Photo by J. Boucher; courtesy of Historic American Engineering Record, IN-26.

Figure 4.4. The Schroeder family, ca. 1946. *From left*, Leo, Charles, Joseph, and Gertrude. Courtesy of the Schroeder Collection, Madison, Indiana.

employers rather than emphasize divisions (Beaudry 1989; Gutman 1977; Leone et al. 1987; Shackel 1993; Wurst 1991). Consequently, evidence of worker resistance observed at mass-production sites—such as production failures at the Russell Cutlery Factory or illicit alcohol consumption observed in other contexts—was not observed at the Schroeder factory (Rotman and Staicer 2002).

In addition, a kin-ordered mode of production appears to have operated within the capitalist mode of production at this site. All members of the family participated in the business in some way—with the exception of Mrs. Schroeder, who was busy raising eight children and running the household, and Theresa, who died as a young girl. An uncle, Peter Backus, also worked for the firm, as did multiple generations of the same families, many of whom were, like the Schroeders, German immigrants. The Schroeders appeared to have been extremely loyal to their workers—employing them for extended periods (albeit occasionally intermittently), diversifying their product lines to keep craftsmen on the payroll, and occasionally paying employees before drawing salaries for themselves. Clearly, the Schroeders' management style was indeed paternalistic, even familial, rather than bureaucratic (Rotman and Staicer 2002; Staicer 1994).

For the Schroeders, family and business were very closely associated. Understanding this intimate relationship was critical to interpreting the past at the site. Industrial spaces were interspersed with domestic activity areas. The family's vegetable garden was reportedly situated between the lumber piles and the blacksmith shop (Bruce Hackney, pers. comm. 1997). Wrapped saddletrees were hung in the first floor of the north addition to the house, while the dried and finished products were warehoused in the residence until sold (Staicer 1994: 32). The intermixing of industrial and domestic spaces was a function of more than the limited area available on the narrow parcel of land on which the house and factory were located. It illustrated that no clear separation existed between the home and factory.

The role of women in production at this site was also particularly interesting. In addition to his sons, Ben's daughters—Pauline, Rose, and Gertrude—also assisted with business operations by writing out documents for their father, keeping the books, and canvassing trees (binding the wooden components together with canvas covering) (Brady 1994: 20). Another woman, Elizabeth "Lizzie" Koehler, began working for the

Schroeders as a "coverer" in 1917 at the age of 47. She continued to work intermittently for the family until 1947 (when she was 77 years old) and "was one of the last workers on the payroll when business declined in the late 1940s" (Staicer 1994). The integral involvement of women at the site was in stark contrast to the gender segregation that dominated the larger cultural milieu. Much like at Lawrenceburg, just a short distance away along the Ohio River, building community within this German immigrant enclave superseded the class distinctions and gender separation observed elsewhere. Furthermore, much like farm women, who labored alongside their husbands and hired hands, oral history indicated that the women associated with the Schroeder Saddletree Factory had relatively high status vis-à-vis the men at the site as a result of their productive contributions to factory operations (Staicer 1994). Despite the factory's location in a semi-urban setting (the small village of Madison, Indiana) the gender roles and relations of its workers closely paralleled those of rural contexts.

The family was highly regarded for the relationships they fostered with their workers. Yet the only material display of their high social status was the fancy woodwork on the gables of their modest brick residence (Rotman and Staicer 2002). The Schroeders owned the means of production, were active members of the community, and had a reputation for being kindhearted people. Their status was explicit and, therefore, they had no need to assert it materially. The three major economic crises the Schroeders experienced during their occupation of the site may also have influenced material displays of class and status. The high rate of curation and reuse of objects observed archaeologically and throughout the structures at the site appeared to have been more than a mere penchant for saving things (Rotman et al. 1998). Rather, these conservative uses of the material world may have been necessitated by lean economic times and, in turn, were status displays in themselves.

The Schroeder Saddletree Factory and Residence is a complex and fascinating place with an amazingly rich material and documentary record (Rotman and Staicer 2002). It provides intriguing glimpses into handicraft production during the late nineteenth and early twentieth centuries, the social relations that guided human interactions, displays of class and status, and the potential effect of national-scale economic crises upon uses of the material world. Importantly, too, evidence from the Saddletree Factory illustrated that loci of production can have unique class, ethnic, and gendered social relations and, thus, must be considered within the specific context under investigation.

Loci of production are highly visible community institutions that have the power to reproduce social relations of inequality, including those of class and gender, yet can also unite communities, according to various factors such as ethnicity. Educational institutions have similar capabilities and are especially powerful in enculturating members of the community into proscribed social roles.

Institutions of Instruction

Educational institutions are particularly important loci for examining the codification and reproduction of gendered social relations, as schools are explicitly intended to train their members to function within their particular cultural setting. Whether in a highly circumscribed social arena, such as a religious community, or in a more broadly defined context, like a public school, institutions of instruction are particularly gendered arenas of human interaction.

Since 1852, for instance, the Redemptorists, a congregation of ordained priests and lay brothers, have operated on the site of St. Mary's, a historic district in Annapolis, Maryland (Kryder-Reid 1994). During the second half of the nineteenth century, the site was used primarily for training the novitiate for ordination and as a base from which priests led missions to rural areas. Like the Johnson's Island military prison, the Redemptorist site was all-male, but the status of individuals within the community was linked to gender-associated meanings.

The Redemptorist ideology was codified in members' vows of obedience, poverty, celibacy, and perseverance. These tenets had striking parallels to the virtues of women celebrated as part of the cult of domesticity; specifically piety, purity, submissiveness, and domesticity. The lay brothers' "association with female qualities was one means of maintaining their docile acceptance of menial tasks and their position on the lowest rung of the congregation's hierarchy" (Kryder-Reid 1994: 102).

The faunal remains recovered from a nineteenth-century deposit show minimal processing at the site, suggesting that in their domestic chores, the lay brothers were isolated from the outside world in ways that paralleled the isolation of women in kitchen ells under domesticity (Walker n.d.; Kryder-Reid 1994: 109). A later deposit, from 1911, yielded cow bones with signs of significant professional butchering. This period correlated with the congregation's transition to a parochial school and greater participation in the market economy of Annapolis (Kryder-Reid 1994).

Importantly, just as the cultural roles of women are defined in opposition to men, so too are men defined in opposition to women. Moreover, the religious training site of the Redemptorists clearly illustrates that "differentiation in gender roles within a single-sex site is possible" (Kryder-Reid 1994: 111). In this ecclesiastical context, the pervasive ideals of patriarchy required distinctions to be made in gender roles. The priests were defined as masculine, in opposition to the lay brothers who were assigned relatively feminine attributes of subservience and docility. Close interrogation of the historical and archaeological record is critical for understanding the subtle nuances in human experiences and the ways in which individuals are trained into their roles as gendered beings.

Public schools offer different views of the enculturation of individuals. The Wea View School first appeared in the 1866 Titus atlas of Tippecanoe County, Indiana (near West Lafayette) (Rotman et al. 2005) (figure 4.5). In 1852, the state legislature had made school attendance compulsory. Wea View was situated within an agricultural community and student attendance reflected its agricultural cycle. Enrollment was highest during the winter, when children were not required to complete farm labor, and was much less robust during times of planting and harvest. By the turn of the twentieth century, the number of one-room, or common, schools in Indiana declined as consolidation of district schools began. Wea View School was among the first of the schools to open in Tippecanoe County and among the last to close (Rotman 2009b).

Archaeological investigation of the Wea View School yielded an assortment of objects associated with schools and children—fragments of slates (n = 140) and pencils (19 slate, 19 graphite, and 1 wax), chalk and an eraser, a stoneware ink bottle (n = 1), marbles and jacks, and buttons and buckles (Rotman et al. 2005). One of the most surprising finds was a small section of a book page. This likely belonged to a primer or other textbook, but was too fragmentary to read and too fragile to clean. No other educational

Figure 4.5. Wea View Schoolhouse, Tippecanoe County, Indiana,
as it appeared in Hooker (1917).

materials, such as chemistry sets (e.g., microscopes, beakers, test tubes, or
their component parts) or mathematical instruments (such as protractors
and compasses) were recovered during the excavation.

The County Examiner's notes and other historic documentation indicated that education at Wea View focused upon basic skills, such as reading, writing, arithmetic, and spelling. Penmanship, grammar, algebra, phys-
iology, and U.S. history were also taught (Hooker 1917: 76). The dearth
of artifacts recovered from the site was actually entirely consistent with
the school's curriculum. All of the aforementioned subjects were book-
oriented and could have been taught strictly through the use of primers
and other texts, objects likely to be curated and, therefore, not recoverable
archaeologically.

The schoolhouse also served as a community center. A pressed-glass
punch cup, fancy serving spoons, a cake knife, and tobacco pipe bowls provide clear evidence that activities other than teaching and learning occurred
at the site (Rotman 2009b). The community functions that might have
been held at the schoolhouse may have included religious services, political
gatherings, Christmas parties, or spelling bees.

One class of artifacts was unexpectedly informative of community activity at the schoolhouse site—munitions (Musselman 2005). Twenty-two
munitions artifacts, representing five different calibers of guns—were recovered during excavation and were stratigraphically correlated to the use
of the school. Many of these munitions were clustered near a large oak tree

in the southwest corner of the site. This tree may have been used to hold a target for skill-shooting games during a community festivity such as a spring fair. The distribution of other munitions across the site may be indicative of subsistence hunting activities by neighbors after school hours— or perhaps may account for some of the broken window glass from the site!

Another class of artifacts was particularly interesting in that they could conceivably represent education or community activities or both (Rotman et al. 2005). Several straight pins, a needle, and a safety pin were found concentrated in association with buttons in the northeast corner of the schoolhouse foundation. These artifacts may have represented a community event, such as local women meeting at the schoolhouse for a sewing circle. Or perhaps the curriculum during the late nineteenth century (ca. 1873–1891) specifically included domestic training for girls, with instruction in sewing and mending garments. The school board had issued a directive to instruct female students in domestic science, a directive which remained in effect until circa 1910 (Burrell 2005). Sewing, needlework, and embroidery have historically been important activities in the formation of gender identities and social roles (Beaudry 2005; Galle 2004). If these sewing items do indeed represent educational activity, they would provide evidence of compliance with the local school board (Rotman 2009b).

Notes made by the County Examiner illustrated that the community valued character attributes such as order and industriousness (Rotman 2009b). The archaeological evidence also indicated that gender was an important structuring principle in the community and, furthermore, that the people believed in the appropriateness of gender separation. Three privies were identified along the rear fence line of the schoolhouse parcel and excavated. The material culture revealed a distinctive gendered use of these facilities; one was used by females (1870–1910) and two by males (1870–1880 and 1880–1900) (Erickson 2005). If we envision the differential mechanics for women/girls and men/boys using privy facilities—lifting skirts versus dropping drawers—the potential for losing things from one's pockets is reduced for the former and increased for the latter. The gendered use of privies, however, was based in part on the proportions of objects intentionally disposed of versus (at least probably) inadvertently lost.

The women's privy contained predominantly domestic objects, including container glass, ceramic sherds, metal food containers, a cake knife, and a serving spoon (Rotman et al. 2005). The women, who were charged with domestic duties at home under the prevailing ideology of domesticity, were likely the ones who attended to the cleanup and disposal of items accidentally broken during social events. Furthermore, these women were likely to have dumped this refuse in the privy designated for them, even if the men's facility was unoccupied at the time, as much out of habit as propriety (Erickson 2005; Rotman et al. 2005). The men's privies, by contrast, contained only one-tenth as many domestic artifacts but held objects such as hex nuts, pocketknives, rubber balls, marbles, and a bicycle license plate—all of which would have fit easily in trouser pockets and none of which were also recovered from the women's privy. The features were also spatially distinct. The women's privy was located in the southwestern corner of the schoolyard, while the men's privies were adjacent to one another in the opposite, southeastern corner of the site.

The community was revealed through the archaeological record of the schoolhouse in another way as well. A total of 298 ceramic sherds were recovered during field investigations; 249 of these were refined earthenwares (180 whiteware, 60 ironstone, two porcelain, and seven semi-porcelain), representing a minimum of 72 different vessels. It was expected that the ceramics from the site would include a variety of fine platters, plates, and bowls—due to "putting one's best foot forward" during community gatherings and celebrations. Only 25 of the 72 refined earthenware vessels (34.7 percent), however, were decorated with transfer prints (green, maroon, and brown), flow blue, annular (green and maroon), solid blue glaze, molded decoration, or decalcomania. The remaining vessels (65.3 percent) were undecorated. The variety of refined earthenwares may hint at the multivocality of the community and the range of families who participated in events at the site over its more than five decades of use.

The predominance of undecorated ceramics might be interpreted as an indication of relative poverty. The results of ceramic cost indexing, for example, would certainly suggest that the families who used the Wea View School were not wealthy. Although it is possible that more expensive vessels were also handled more carefully (resulting in less breakage), material culture at the site appears to have been used to emphasize group identity rather than differences (Rotman 2009b). When families gathered at the schoolhouse for worship or the spring spelling bee or the Christmas hoedown, they gathered as friends, neighbors, and family (through both blood relationships and family-like bonds). These events may have been opportunities for socializing and building group solidarity rather than venues for asserting social position (Rotman et al. 2005; Wall 1991). As such, uses of the material world at this site closely parallel those observed in the German immigrant enclave of Lawrenceburg as well as at the Schroeder Saddletree Factory in Madison (Rotman and Clay 2008; Rotman and Staicer 2002)—places where belonging was emphasized over status displays.

Archaeological and historical investigations revealed that the building served as more than a locus of education. It was also a community center and gathering place for friends, neighbors, and family (Rotman et al. 2005). The punch cup, serving spoons, cake knife, and munitions are all evidence of non-educational activities at the site. The use of space—notably the separation of the privies—illustrates that gender was a powerful force shaping social relations in the community, which was reflected in the spatial organization of the schoolyard. Historical documents also reveal an emphasis on gender difference through a curriculum that likely consisted of manual training for boys and domestic skills for girls (Rotman 2009b).

Children acquire "their identities through formal and informal education and usually have to reconcile input from their families, neighbors, and religious and social leaders" (Lindauer 2009: 86). While the mission of all schools is to enculturate children into socially prescribed roles, some of these institutions were more pernicious than others.

Native American children who were students at the Phoenix Indian School (1891–1990) were forcibly removed from reservations and subjected to involuntary assimilation (Lindauer 2009). The curriculum of the boarding school sought to teach boys trades, such as carpentry, blacksmithing, wagon making, and tin working; meanwhile girls were instructed in housekeeping skills, sewing, cooking, and laundry. The goals of such schools were for Indians to "assimilate, acculturate, and become Anglicized; they were to speak only English, learn a trade, dress as other Americans, and practice Christianity" (D. Adams 1995; Lindauer 2009: 94). The curriculum strongly reflected the highly segregated gender roles of domesticity that dominated the larger American cultural milieu, particularly during the late nineteenth and early twentieth centuries.

Pupils were stripped of all outward signs of their Indigenous identity. They were also forbidden to speak their Native language, practice their religion, or wear Indigenous clothing (Lindauer 2009). A school identity was imposed upon them through practices such as cutting their hair short and requiring a school uniform. A steam whistle was used to divide the day into different activities, teaching Native children the unfamiliar rigors of time discipline. Dishes and eating utensils, as well as regimented meals three times a day, instilled ideas of individuality, order, courtesy, and health awareness. Finally, the playthings not only reinforced gender roles, but also lessons of self-sufficiency and responsibility (Lindauer 2009: 95). Artifacts associated with these cultural practices illustrated the ideals with which students were indoctrinated.

The Phoenix Indian School and similar institutions, furthermore, taught self-reliance and individualism; concepts that were very challenging for Indigenous children who had been raised in a society where communal ownership and interdependence were stressed (Lindauer 2009: 96). Items such as toothbrushes and combs were used to teach cleanliness, germ transmission, and personal property. Few of these objects were inscribed or marked with the owner's name, suggesting that the ideas of individualism were not widely internalized in the student population.

Practicing of Indigenous religion was explicitly forbidden at the school and thus a form of resistance. Oral history and documentary evidence confirm that children would sneak off campus to perform Native ceremonies, dances, and prayers. Two clay figures were found—a miniature bird and a four-legged animal—which may have "provided a sense of security and connection to the customs and traditions of home as effigy representations or clan symbols" (Lindauer 2009: 99). These objects would have been perceived as contraband and thus confiscated by school staff.

The archaeological record of the Phoenix Indian School exemplifies the dialectical relation of contradiction; that is, that the social relations operating at the site were not always mutually supportive. The children's resistance to acculturation, furthermore, attests to the ways in which they fought to maintain traditional identities through their engagement with the material world. The dialectical relation of the interpenetration of opposites is also illustrated through the differential positioning of the administrators and students at the school, who assigned very different meanings to the objects used; for example, perceiving an effigy figure as either contraband (administrators) or a powerful symbol of home and community (children).

Schools are especially powerful loci of institutional and community power that seek to train children and others for their socially prescribed roles within their particular cultural contexts. Similar training was also reinforced through other cultural entities, such as the military, factories, and reform institutions. In this way, the ideals of societal institutions provided multiple avenues through which expectations for conformity were conveyed and enforced (Wilkie 2010).

Institutions as Lenses of Home and Community

The institutions of society express dominant cultural ideals, including those of gender. They are also instruments of power because they have the capacity to enforce hegemonic views and penalize those who fail to conform.

On the surface, the military, reform institutions, prisons, and schools may appear to have very different missions; however, a deep interrogation of their policies and practices reveals many common goals. Patriarchal authority and differential gender roles, for example, are codified and reproduced in all of these contexts. In addition, those ideals permeate all levels of social engagement within the communities in which institutions were situated, transcending the boundaries between household and community. Abstractions of generality move the level of investigation between these different scales of human activity. The abstraction of vantage point allows us to examine different sides of the same social relations (e.g., officer versus enlisted man at Camp Nelson; priest versus lay brother at the Redemptorists monastery; and administrator versus pupil at the Phoenix Indian School).

Examining the archaeological and historical records of these various arenas through a multiplicity of lenses reveals the complexity of human experience as well as the ways in which individual agents reconcile the ideals being communicated. Dominant ideologies do indeed structure cultural discourse, and institutions are the most visible mechanism for their conveyance. Ideologies are rarely adopted wholesale, however, as individuals negotiate the cultural landscapes of which they are a part. That is, human beings engage aspects of class, gender, and other ideologies that are meaningful to them, reject or subvert other dimensions, and otherwise create amalgamations of those ideals and identities.

5

-⟨⟨⟨⟨⟨⟨⟨⟨⟨-

Summary

The Archaeology of Gender in Historic America

Gendered social relations are fundamental to the human experience. Gender is codified and reproduced at multiple scales—from the household to the community to broader regional and national institutions. Individuals and families in historic America both negotiated and mediated gender ideologies through the material world. Using a feminist perspective, this volume examined gendered social relations as they intersected with other social prisms.

Colonialism, patriarchy, and the capitalist mode of production, as well as other ideological, economic, and political forces, have shaped gender through time and across space. Specifically, the power relations embedded within them structure social relations in significant ways (Paynter and McGuire 1991; Voss 2006: 111). An individual's gender affects her or his interactions and connections to other people (including kinship and marriage) as well as access to economic resources and social power, among many other things (Paynter 2000; Rotman 2009a; Voss 2008a, 2008b). Therefore, gender is inextricably linked to class, ethnicity, race, sexuality, identity, and life cycle, among other social dimensions.

Several gender ideologies—corporate families, republican motherhood, the cult of domesticity, domestic reform, and equal rights feminism—represented the dominant cultural discourses of their respective times and locations. These ideals were defined largely by white, middle-class Protestants in heteronormative sexual relations. Adherence to prevailing gender norms was expected and those who did not conform, whether by choice or by circumstance, were often perceived as a threat to the social order (Rotman 2009a). These dominant ideals thus became the standard by which deviance and "otherness" were defined, and acted as powerful forms of social power and control.

How individuals and families understood, interpreted, and operationalized gender ideologies was significantly influenced by the rural, urban, or suburban context in which they lived. Household settings, whether rural or urban or suburban, actively shaped the creation and codification of gender roles. Yet while the cultural differences that defined these varied contexts were important, it is also essential to recognize the continuum of experience that was represented by rural, suburban, and urban settings as well as the social, political, and economic interconnectedness of these loci (Rotman 2009a).

In addition, the changes and transformations that were part of the natural life course from a child to an adult to a young parent to an elderly individual also shaped gender roles and relations, particularly within families and households. Therefore, the adoption and implementation of gender ideologies varied according to the developmental cycles of families, their financial and social circumstances, and the abilities and desires of human agents (Rotman 2005). Very often, there were disconnects between the "ideal" and the realities of one's life that required "concessions" to be made (Demos 1970).

The social and historical *context* for interpreting gendered social relations is also critical. Historical archaeologies of gender must move beyond "women's objects" and "men's objects" to understand how the creation, codification, and negotiation of gendered roles and relations are represented in space and the material world (Rotman 2009a; Singleton and Bograd 2000). Dialectics is an ideal tool for such analyses as it explores the *web* of social relations of which gender was a part. The interpenetration of opposites elucidates that objects, how any thing functions, and how people perceive them are largely due to their surroundings. Similarly, the abstraction of vantage point facilitates the examination of different sides of the same relation, while the dialectical relation of contradiction highlights interactions and negotiations within relations. Collectively, these tools allow for dynamic and nuanced examinations of social relations as they shaped human experiences.

Households and domestic spaces are particularly important loci of gendered social relations. The activities within households "serve to 'produce' material things (such as food, clothing, and shelter), but they do so in a way that both reifies and transforms social structure—along with such things as gender constructions and power relations" (Barile and Brandon 2004: 8; Bourdieu 1977; H. Moore 1988, 1994, 1996). Therefore, domestic residences as dynamic social entities are both the medium and outcome of social practices (Barber 1994; Giddens 1984; Pearson and Richards 1994). A variety of ideologies have structured gendered social relations within families and household through time and across space.

The corporate family was the economic, social, and political unit that tied each household to the larger community in a web of interdependence during the colonial period in New England, while patriarchal authority structured that order within both households and villages. There was a gendered division of labor, but not distinct and separate spheres. The materiality and spatiality of Deerfield, as one example, with its organic forms of architecture and orientation of households along the Street, expressed the corporate nature of community life, including hierarchical but complementary gendered social relations.

Native American male and female roles were often highly interdependent and more flexible than the gender systems of their Anglo-European neighbors, particularly in colonial New England. For instance, Narragansett women had greater autonomy vis-à-vis men than European women, in part because they controlled the production of maize (Nassaney 2004: 334). In the colonial economic system, however, tobacco was distributed beyond traditional male ceremonial uses, resulting in increased use by Native women and children. As a result, an activity that had once served to reproduce gender relations and ideologies was undermined and social tensions between Indigenous men and women became marked (Nassaney 2004: 356).

Women *and* men in both Indigenous and European American families contributed to the domestic economy of the household and were integrated into complex webs of social and economic interaction in the colonial world of the northeastern United States. A dialectical analysis reveals, however, that structural similarities belie significant differences in social power and access to resources, especially for women.

The Pequot of Connecticut also became inextricably bound to colonial settlers through wage labor, exchange, and indebtedness. As a result, European and locally manufactured ceramics, such as redware, replaced traditional Native-produced vessels, since consumer choices within this context of racism, disenfranchisement, and marginalization were significantly limited (Silliman 2009). Rather than constituting evidence of acculturation, however, these items become Eastern Pequot objects when used in Native American reservations and households. Choosing to buy consumer goods that were both available and affordable "did not translate directly into the dilution of native cultural practices, attachment to indigenous communities or connections to reservation land. These choices represented strategies of survival" (Silliman and Witt 2010: 62).

Consumer items were also important for enslaved Africans. Objects of personal adornment and ceramic dishes were excellent material expressions that varied considerably according to gender, age, ethnicity, and life cycle of the members of the complex domestic households of which they were a part (Scott 1991a, 1992b; Thomas and Thomas 2004; White 2008). Importantly, "an individual's desire and ability to participate in the market economy changed as children were born, as people aged, as spouses or children died, were sold, or ran away" (Galle 2010: 38; see also Danforth 2004). Thus, daily life for enslaved Africans was structured at the intersection of gender, socioeconomic class, and life cycle, including age and marital status, factors that were expressed through material practices.

During the later colonial period, republican motherhood represented an increased ideological separation of gender roles within families and households. Architecturally, kitchen ells emphasized differential perceptions of public and private spaces and relocated female activities to the back of the house. This change in domestic spaces was the beginning of a process by which women became increasingly isolated from the community and their labor became differentially valued as public and private spheres diverged (M. Johnson 1993: 137; Rosaldo 1974: 68; Wall 1994:19; Yentsch 1991: 201).

The gendered uses of space—as well as lived experiences—were more complex than simple dichotomies of production/reproduction, public/private, agricultural/domestic, male/female, elite/non-elite would suggest (Beaudry 2004; Conkey and Gero 1991; Wurst 2003; Wylie 1991). While these distinctions were real, they did not always produce mutually exclusive spaces (Borish 1995: 88; Hautaniemi and Rotman 2003; Rotman 2005, 2013b). The divergence of gendered roles, tasks, and spaces paralleled other ideological changes during the late eighteenth and early nineteenth centuries in historic North America.

Modern discipline also emerged as an important ideology that intersected with both class and gender. Human agents, particularly those belonging to the middle and lower classes, learned to think and conduct themselves according to social ideals that encouraged individuality and time discipline. This ideology found expression in the increased variation (e.g., salad plates, dinner plates, dessert plates) and segmentation of ceramic vessels (e.g., individual place settings).

At about the same time, the cult of domesticity emerged as the dominant gender ideal, emphasizing piety, purity, domesticity, and submissiveness, while also further elaborating an ideological and physical separation of public and private spheres (Beetham 1996; Rotman 2006; Ryan 1985). In particular, white, middle-class women became separated from economic production and their roles as the moral guardians of children were glorified (Vlach 1995: 142; see also Rotman 2006, 2009a). The symbolic associations of nature and religion through architecture and material culture (e.g., Gothic Revival architecture and Gothic-paneled ironstone) became inextricably linked with the natural and religious ideals of domesticity (Sklar 1973: 173; see also Juster 1996; Wall 1991, 1999).

Other domestic ideals were pervasive in the wider cultural milieu of early nineteenth-century America. For emancipated Blacks, for example, the notion and practice of a "woman's place in the home" was problematic. The legacy of enslavement had largely limited women's labor to domestic and institutional service or arduous manual labor outside of their homes (Battle-Baptiste 2011). In addition, "the inability of captive African men to actively pursue their patriarchal destiny was controlled in very dehumanizing ways by plantation owners and overseers" (Battle-Baptiste 2011: 40–41). Consequently, cultural constructions of Black womanhood and motherhood were not simply in opposition to European American models of domesticity, but rather occurred at the multifaceted intersection of domestic ideals, post-Emancipation oppression, emerging class distinctions within African-American communities, and other social, political, economic, and ideological forces of the time (Battle-Baptiste 2011; Brandon 2004; Davidson 2004; Muller 1994). Property ownership through a "homeplace" symbolized the ways in which for Black families domesticity was significantly shaped at the juncture of race and class.

Although domestic units are critical units of analysis in historical archaeology, they do not exist in isolation. Rather, households are situated in *relation* to one another within their larger social, political, and economic contexts. Examinations of communities, therefore, elucidate the ways in which households were connected to wider cultural processes (M. Wood 2004: 210). Since gendered social relations operate at a different scale within communities than in households, the same is true of their archaeological, material, and spatial correlates. Communities and farming villages, for example, were reconfigured to accommodate the changing social order and shift in societal emphasis from communal interaction to individual achievement.

These social changes were often the focus of domestic reform efforts as reformers sought to reconcile their internal contradictions and often directly to resist them. The ideals of the Arts and Crafts movement, for example, appealed to the residents of Deerfield. Madeline Yale Wynne arranged touring exhibitions of village craftwork and brought in speakers on art and politics, including women's suffrage (Harlow 2001, 2005). These activities illustrate that the ideas of equal rights feminism were present simultaneously with the ideals of domesticity, shaping social roles and gender relations within the village (Rotman 2006, 2009a).

Through their reform activities, Deerfield women also influenced the installation of the municipal water system and staged historical pageants to raise money for the undertaking (Hautaniemi and Rotman 2003). The pageants went beyond an expression of the *ideals* of domestic reform to contribute actively to their implementation (Glassberg 1995). Women and men also blurred the boundaries between the public and private spheres through their active collaboration on the municipal water project and fundraising through the pageants (Hautaniemi and Rotman 2003; Rotman 2001, 2009a).

Domestic reformers in other locations throughout historic America extended their ideals into community spaces—such as parks, playgrounds, children's gardens, and other urban green spaces (Spencer-Wood 2003:

32). Significantly, these forms of community organization and their material outcomes illustrate that women were active social agents in their communities and not solely relegated to the domestic sphere (Rotman 2005; Spencer-Wood 1999b, 2003). Much like the involvement of Deerfield women in pageants and the municipal water project, domestic reform incorporated both households *and* the communities in which they were situated. As such, the gender ideals within these two realms of social interaction were mutually reinforcing while simultaneously challenging gender roles and relations within individual households.

Within the framework of domestic reform during the late nineteenth and early twentieth centuries, many intentional communities emerged as alternatives to mainstream American society in response to the significant social changes occurring under industrial capitalism (Savulis 2003). The Shakers' way of life was in stark contrast to the heteronormative gender relations (e.g., domesticity) that emphasized marriage, reproduction, and patriarchal authority as key features. The Shakers' material world was organized to promote celibacy, which was viewed as the path to salvation (T. Johnson 1976; Savulis 2003; Starbuck 1994).

The highly gendered spaces of Shaker buildings may have significantly resembled the sexually segregated places in mainstream architecture, which was designed to isolate women in kitchen ells at the back of the home and constrain their movements to the domestic sphere as much as possible. A dialectical understanding of Shaker spaces, however, reveals that although the structural forms were similar, they served very different ideological purposes in practice.

Reform ideals were also the focus of nineteenth-century Protestant missionaries in places such as New York City. Newly arrived Irish immigrants were strongly encouraged to assimilate into American culture and emulate the behaviors of Victoriana, including gender roles and relations as defined by domesticity (Brighton 2011; Fitts 1999, 2001). Poor, urban, working-class households did not conform to the separate spheres ideology or to patriarchal authority; consequently, they were frequently viewed as depraved and dangerous (Fitts 1999: 117).

Victorian dining rituals often emphasized class and nativity statuses within communities (Walker 2008). Food consumption was strongly correlated with the domestic sphere and women were entrusted with the etiquette and knowledge of its rituals. As such, dining was a highly gendered activity (Rotman 2009a; Wall 1999, 2000). Victorian dining was used to divide communities, such as with San Francisco railroad workers, as well as unite them, as with the German immigrant enclave in Lawrenceburg, Indiana. Importantly, dining rituals clearly illustrate the articulation of gender ideals with social relations of class and ethnicity (Rotman 2009a; Rotman and Clay 2008; Rotman and Staicer 2002).

Reformers also frequently used formal community institutions as mechanisms for social reproduction and social control (Foucault 1978, 1979; DeCunzo 1995). A variety of entities that emerged during the late nineteenth and early twentieth centuries were rooted in domestic reform ideals. These institutions reflected and imposed community attitudes as well as structured human life in a myriad of ways (Gibb 2009), albeit with varied degrees of success.

The Magdalen Society of Philadelphia sought to control women's sexual activity outside of marriage. Although many "fallen" women had resorted to prostitution as a way of financially supporting themselves, reformers viewed this activity as immoral (DeCunzo 1995). Consequently, residents of the Magdalen Society Asylum received domestic training that was consistent with the gendered occupational ideals of the time and deemed essential for becoming wives of Christian men and mothers to their children (DeCunzo 1995: 126). The reform work of the Magdalen Society was an example of how communities, through their institutions, sought to enforce conformity to particular ecclesiastical and patriarchal ideals for gender roles and relations. The efficacy of the Magdalen Society is doubtful, however, as many women returned to their previous lives upon leaving the asylum. Regardless of the actual success of such institutions, these community entities were critical components of the cultural landscape of historic America and were central to societal negotiation of the changing economic and social orders of their times.

Industrial production also sought to control human actions. The Russell Cutlery Factory in Turners Falls, Massachusetts, implemented the American scheme of mass production that utilized interchangeable parts and highly segmented labor organization (Nassaney and Abel 2000). Thus the modern discipline that mothers were inculcating in their children also operated outside households. Individual workers within the factory were responsible for only a small aspect of the overall manufacturing process. In effect, workers were deskilled and became as interchangeable as the parts they were making (Nassaney and Abel 1993; Shackel 1993, 1996). The production floor was designed to control workers and maximize efficiency. The archaeological record of the factory, however, reveals a number of wasters—parts that were not fashioned to standard, either intentionally or unintentionally—strongly suggesting that the workers resisted at least some of their bosses' efforts at controlling their behavior.

The ideologies that operated in households and institutions were also reproduced through educational institutions. The explicit role of schools is training individuals, particularly children, to function within their particular cultural setting and conform to societal norms and ideals. Children acquire "their identities through formal and informal education and usually have to reconcile input from their families, neighbors, and religious and social leaders" (Lindauer 2009: 86). The curriculum of the Phoenix Indian School taught boys and girls trades and skills that were deemed gender appropriate. Through these boarding schools, Native American children were forced to "assimilate, acculturate, and become Anglicized; they were to speak only English, learn a trade, dress as other Americans, and practice Christianity" (Lindauer 2009: 94; see also D. Adams 1995). The curriculum provided to Indigenous children strongly reflected the highly segregated gender roles of domesticity that dominated the larger European American cultural milieu, particularly during the late nineteenth and early twentieth centuries.

The case studies presented in this volume illustrate a broad spectrum of gendered social relations through time and across space in historic America. They have highlighted the multiscalar nature of gender as it has operated in households, communities, and institutions, as well as some of the material and spatial correlates of gendered engagement. The metaphor of a kaleidoscope captures the complex and ever-changing meaning and practice of gendered social relations—including but not limited to competing ideologies, socioeconomic class, political agendas, race and ethnicity, sexuality, and developmental cycles—to create complex patterns of identities and relationships.

REFERENCES CITED

Abel, Marjorie
1987   Women, Labor Force Participation, and Economic Development: The Issues of Occupational Segregation. Unpublished PhD dissertation, Department of Anthropology. University of Massachusetts, Amherst.

Adams, David Wallace
1995   *Education for Extinction: American Indians and the Boarding School Experience, 1875–1928*. University of Kansas Press, Lawrence.

Adams, William H.
1990   Landscape Archaeology, Landscape History, and the American Farmstead. *Historical Archaeology* 24(4): 92–101.

Agnew, Agnes B.
1995   Women and Property in Early 19th-Century Portsmouth, New Hampshire. *Historical Archaeology* 29(1): 62–74.

Alcott, W. A.
1838   *The Young Wife, or Duties of Women in the Marriage Relation*. 6th ed. George W. Light, Boston.

1849   *The Young Wife's Guide to Excellence*. 13th ed. Strong and Broadhead, Boston.

1851   *The Young Mother, or Management of Children in Regards to Health*. 20th ed. Charles D. Strong, Boston.

Arkush, Brooke S.
2011   Native Responses to European Intrusion: Cultural Persistence and Agency among Mission Neophytes in Spanish Colonial Northern California. *Historical Archaeology* 45(4): 62–90.

Arnesen, Eric
1994   "Like Banquo's Ghost, It Will Not Down": The Race Question and the American Railroad Brotherhoods, 1880–1920. *American Historical Review* 99(5): 1601–1633.

Baker, Paula
1984   The Domestication of Politics: Women and American Political Society, 1780–1920. *American Historical Review* 89(3): 620–647.

1991   *The Moral Frameworks for Public Life: Gender, Politics, and the State in Rural New York, 1870–1930*. Oxford University Press, New York.

Barber, J. Russell.
1994   *Doing Historical Archaeology: Exercises Using Documentary, Oral, and Material Evidence*. Prentice Hall, Englewood Cliffs, New Jersey.

Barile, Kerri S.
2004   Hegemony within the Household: The Perspective from a South Carolina Plantation. In *Household Chores and Household Choices: Theorizing the Domestic Sphere in Historical Archaeology*, edited by K. S. Barile and J. C. Brandon, pp. 121–137. University of Alabama Press, Tuscaloosa.

Barile, Kerri S., and Jamie C. Brandon (editors)
2004   *Household Chores and Household Choices: Theorizing the Domestic Sphere in Historical Archaeology*. University of Alabama Press, Tuscaloosa.

Barrett, James R.
1992   Americanization from the Bottom Up: Immigration and the Remaking of the Working Class in the United States, 1880–1930. *Journal of American History* 79(3): 996–1020.

Barron, Hal S.
1986   Rediscovering the Majority: The New Rural History of the Nineteenth-Century North. *Historical Method* 19(4): 141–152.

Barth, Frederick
1969   *Ethnic Groups and Boundaries: The Social Differentiation of Culture Difference*. Little, Brown, Boston, Massachusetts.

Barton, Christopher P., and Kyle Somerville
2012   Play Things: Children's Racialized Mechanical Banks and Toys, 1880–1930. *International Journal of Historical Archaeology* 16: 47–85.

Battle-Baptiste, Whitney
2011   *Black Feminist Archaeology*. Left Coast Press, Walnut Creek, California.

Baugher, Sherene
2009   Historical Overview of the Archaeology of Institutional Life. In *The Archaeology of Institutional Life*, edited by A. Beisaw and J. Gibb, pp. 5–16. University of Alabama Press, Tuscaloosa.

Baxter, Jane E.
2005a   *Children in Action: Perspectives on the Archaeology of Childhood*. Archaeological Papers of the American Anthropological Association, No. 15. Arlington, Virginia.

2005b   *The Archaeology of Childhood: Children, Gender, and Material Culture*. AltaMira Press, Walnut Creek, California.

2008   The Archaeology of Childhood. *Annual Review of Anthropology* 37: 159–175.

Beaudry, Mary
1989   The Lowell Boot Mills Complex and Its Housing: Material Expressions of Corporate Ideology. *Historical Archaeology* 23(1): 19–32.

2004   Doing the Housework: New Approaches to the Archaeology of Households. In *Household Chores and Household Choices: Theorizing the Domestic Sphere in Historical Archaeology*, edited by K. S. Barile and J. C. Brandon, pp. 255–262. University of Alabama Press, Tuscaloosa.

2005   Stitching Women's Lives: Interpreting the Artifacts of Sewing and Needlework. Paper presented at the annual meeting of the Society for Historical and Underwater Archaeology, York, England.

Beaudry, Mary, and Stephen Mrozowski

1987a   *Interdisciplinary Investigations of the Boot Mills, Lowell, Massachusetts*. Vol. I: *Life at the Boarding Houses*. Cultural Resource Management Study No. 18, Division of Cultural Resources, North Atlantic Region, National Park Service, Boston.

1987b   *Interdisciplinary Investigations of the Boot Mills, Lowell, Massachusetts*. Vol. II: *The Kirk Street Agent's House*. Cultural Resource Management Study No. 18, Division of Cultural Resources, North Atlantic Region, National Park Service, Boston.

Beecher, Catherine

1841   *The Treatise on Domestic Economy for the Use of Young Ladies at Home and at School*. T. H. Webb, Boston.

Beers, F. W.

1871   Historic Map of "The Street" in Deerfield, Massachusetts. F. W. Beers & Company Atlases, New York.

Beetham, Margaret

1996   *A Magazine of Her Own?: Domesticity and Desire in the Woman's Magazine, 1800–1914*. Routledge, London and New York.

Beisaw, April, and James Gibb (editors)

2009   *The Archaeology of Institutional Life*. University of Alabama Press, Tuscaloosa.

Bell, Alison

2005   White Ethnogenesis and Gradual Capitalism: Perspectives from Colonial Archaeological Sites in the Chesapeake. *American Anthropologist* 107(3): 446–460.

Berg, Barbara J.

1978   *The Remembered Gate: Origins of American Feminism; The Woman and the City, 1800–1860*. Oxford University Press, New York.

Blackwood, Evelyn

1997   Native American Genders and Sexualities: Beyond Anthropological Models and Misrepresentations. In *Two-Spirit People: Native American Gender Identity, Sexuality, and Spirituality*, edited by S. E. Jacobs, W. Thomas, and S. Lang, pp. 284–296. University of Illinois Press, Urbana and Chicago.

Blades, Brooke S.

1976   Cultural Behavior and Material Culture in Eighteenth-Century Deerfield, Massachusetts: Excavations of the Dr. Thomas Williams House. Manuscript on file, Henry Flynt Library, Historic Deerfield, Inc., Deerfield, Massachusetts.

1977   Doctor Williams' Privy: Cultural Behavior as Reflected in Artifact Deposition at the Dr. Thomas Williams House, Deerfield, Massachusetts. In *Dublin Seminar for New England Folklife: Annual Proceedings*, edited by P. Benes, pp. 56–63. Boston University Press, Boston.

Bleier, Ruth

1984   *Science and Gender: A Critique of Biology and Its Theories on Women*. Pergamon Press, New York.

Boag, Peter

2011a   The Trouble with Cross-Dressers: Researching and Writing the History of Sexual and Gender Transgressiveness in the Nineteenth-Century American West. *Oregon Historical Quarterly* 112(3): 322–339.

2011b   *Re-Dressing America's Frontier Past*. University of California Press, Berkeley.

Bograd, Mark

1989   Whose Life Is It Anyway?: Ceramics, Context, and the Study of Status. Unpublished MA thesis, Department of Anthropology, University of Massachusetts, Amherst.

Bonine, Mindy

2004   Analysis of Household and Family at a Spanish Colonial *Rancho* along the Rio Grande. In *Household Chores and Household Choices: Theorizing the Domestic Sphere in Historical Archaeology*, edited by K. S. Barile and J. C. Brandon, pp. 15–32. University of Alabama Press, Tuscaloosa.

Borish, Linda

1995   "Another Domestic Beast of Burden": New England Farm Women's Work and Well-Being in the Nineteenth Century. *Journal of American Culture* 18(3): 83–100.

Boserup, Esther

1970   *Women's Roles in Economic Development*. George Allen and Unwin, London.

Bourdieu, Pierre

1973   The Berber House. In *Rules and Meanings*, edited by M. Douglas, pp. 98–110. Penguin, Harmondsworth and New York.

1977   *Outline of a Theory in Practice*. Translated by R. Nice. Cambridge University Press, Cambridge.

1984   *Distinction: A Social Critique of the Judgment of Taste*. Harvard University Press, Cambridge, Massachusetts.

1985   The Social Space and the Genesis of Groups. *Social Science Information: Theory and Methods* 24(2): 195–220.

1993   *The Field of Cultural Production: Essays on Art and Literature*, edited by R. Johnson. Columbia University Press, New York.

Brady, Carolyn

1994   Schroeder Saddletree Factory Workers. Manuscript on file, Schroeder Saddletree Factory, Historic Madison, Inc./Historic Madison Foundation, Inc., Madison, Indiana.

Bragdon, Kathleen J.

1996   Gender as a Social Category in Native Southern New England *Ethnohistory* 43(4): 573–592.

Brandon, Jamie C.

2004   Reconstructing Domesticity and Segregating Households: The Intersection of Gender and Race in the Postbellum South. In *Household Chores and Household Choices: Theorizing the Domestic Sphere in Historical Archaeology*, edited by K. S. Barile and J. C. Brandon, pp. 197–209. University of Alabama Press, Tuscaloosa.

2013   Reversing the Narrative of Hillbilly History: A Case Study Using Archaeology at Van Winkle's Mill in the Arkansas Ozarks. *Historical Archaeology* 47(3): 36–51.

Brandon, Jamie C., and Kerrie S. Barile

2004   Introduction: Household Chores; or, the Chore of Defining the Household. In *Household Chores and Household Choices: Theorizing the Domestic Sphere in Historical Archaeology*, edited by K. S. Barile and J. C. Brandon, pp. 1–14. University of Alabama Press, Tuscaloosa.

Brashler, Janet

1991   When Daddy Was a Shanty Boy: The Role of Gender in the Organization of the Logging Industry in Highland West Virginia. *Historical Archaeology* 25(4): 54–68.

Brighton, Stephen A.

2001   Prices That Suit the Times: Shopping for Ceramics at the Five Points. *Historical Archaeology* 35(3): 16–30.

2004   Symbols, Mythmaking, and Identity: The Red Hand of Ulster in Late Nineteenth-Century Paterson, New Jersey. *International Journal of Historical Archaeology* 8(2): 149–162.

2008   Degrees of Alienation: The Material Evidence of the Irish and Irish American Experience. *Historical Archaeology* 42(4): 132–153.

2009   *Historical Archaeology of the Irish Diaspora: A Transnational Approach*. University of Tennessee Press, Knoxville.

2011   Middle-Class Ideologies and American Respectability: Archaeology and the Irish Immigrant Experience. *International Journal of Historical Archaeology* 15(1): 30–50.

Brockley, Janice

2004   Rearing the Child Who Never Grew Up. In *Mental Retardation in America: A Historical Reader*, edited by S. Noll and J. W. Trent, Jr., pp. 130–164. New York University Press, New York.

Brodkin-Sacks, Karen

1989   Toward a Unified Theory of Class, Race, and Gender. *American Ethnologist* 16(3): 534–550.

Brooks, Alison S., Fatimah Collier Jackson, and Roy Richard Grinker

1993   Race and Ethnicity in America. *Anthro Notes* 15(3): 1–3, 11–15.

Brown, Elsa Barkley

1992   "What Has Happened Here": The Politics of Difference in Women's History and Feminist Politics. *Feminist Studies* 18(2): 295–312.

Brown, Marley

1987   *"Among Weighty Friends": The Archaeology and Social History of the Jacob Mott Family, Portsmouth, Rhode Island, 1640–1800 (Quaker)*. PhD dissertation, Brown University. University Microfilms, University of Michigan, Ann Arbor.

Bruegel, Martin

2002   Work, Gender, and Authority on the Farm: The Hudson Valley Countryside, 1790s–1850s. *Agricultural History* 76(1): 1–27.

Brumfiel, Elizabeth, and Cynthia Robin

2008   Gender, Households, and Society: An Introduction. In *Gender, Households, and Society: Unraveling the Threads of the Past and the Present*, edited by E. Brumfiel and C. Robin, pp. 1–16. Archaeological Papers No. 18. American Anthropological Association, Arlington, Virginia.

Brydon, Lynne, and Sylvia Chant

1989   *Women in the Third World: Gender Issues in Rural and Urban Areas*. Rutgers University Press, New Brunswick, New Jersey.

Burrell, Japhia

2005   Architectural Change and Use of Space. Paper presented at the Annual Symposium on Ohio Valley Urban and Historical Archaeology, Carter Caves State Resort Park, Kentucky.

Bush, David R.

2009   Maintaining or Mixing Southern Culture in a Northern Prison: Johnson's Island Military Prison. In *The Archaeology of Institutional Life*, edited by A. Beisaw and J. Gibb, pp. 153–171. University of Alabama Press, Tuscaloosa.

Butler, Judith

1990   *Gender Trouble: Feminism and the Subversion of Identity.* Routledge, New York.

1993   *Bodies That Matter: On the Discursive Limits of "Sex."* Routledge, New York.

Carson, Barbara G.

1990   *Ambitious Appetites: Dining, Behavior, and Patterns of Consumption in Federal Washington.* American Institute of Architects Press, Washington, D.C.

Casella, Eleanor C.

2009   On the Enigma of Incarceration: Philosophical Approaches to Confinement in the Modern Era. In *The Archaeology of Institutional Life*, edited by A. M. Beisaw and J. G. Gibb, pp. 17–32. University of Alabama Press, Tuscaloosa.

Chambers-Schiller, Lee Virginia

1984   *Liberty a Better Husband: Single Women in America, The Generations of 1780–1840.* Yale University Press, New Haven, Connecticut.

Cheek, Charles, and Amy Frielander

1990   Pottery and Pigs' Feet: Space, Ethnicity, and Neighborhood in Washington, D.C., 1880–1940. *Historical Archaeology* 24(1): 34–60.

Child, Mrs.

1831   *The Mother's Book.* Carter, Hendee, and Babcock, Boston.

1833   *The American Housewife.* 12th ed. Carter, Hendee, Boston.

Cipolla, Craig N.

2013   Native American Historical Archaeology and the Trope of Authenticity. *Historical Archaeology* 47(3): 12–22.

Clark, Clifford E., Jr.

1982   Household, Market, and Capital: The Process of Economic Change in the Connecticut Valley of Massachusetts, 1800–1860. Unpublished PhD dissertation, Harvard University, Cambridge, Massachusetts.

1988   Domestic Architecture as an Index to Social History: The Romantic Revival and the Cult of Domesticity in America, 1840–1870. In *Material Life in America, 1600–1860*, edited by R. B. St. George, pp. 535–549. Northeastern University Press, Boston.

Clements, Joyce M.

2005   A Winding Sheet for Deborah George: Searching for the Women of Ponkapoag. Unpublished PhD dissertation, York University, Toronto.

2013   Intimate Matters in Public Encounters: Massachusetts Praying Indian Communities and Colonialism in the Seventeenth and Eighteenth Centuries. In *Historical and Archaeological Perspectives on Gender Transformations: From Private to Public*, edited by S. M. Spencer-Wood, pp. 105–128. Contributions to a Global Historical Archaeology, series ed. C. E. Orser, Jr. Springer Academic, New York and London.

Clinton, Catherine
1984   *The Other Civil War: American Women in the Nineteenth Century*. Hill and Wang, New York.

Collier, Jane, Michelle Z. Rosaldo, and Sylvia Yanagisako
1992   Is There a Family? New Anthropological Views. In *Rethinking the Family: Some Feminist Questions*, edited by B. Thorne and M. Yalom. Rev. ed. Northeastern University Press, Boston.

Conkey, Margaret W., and Joan Gero
1991   Tensions, Pluralities, and Engendering Archaeology: An Introduction to Women and Prehistory. In *Engendering Archaeology: Women in Prehistory*, edited by J. M. Gero and M. W. Conkey, pp. 3–30. Basil Blackwell, Oxford.

Coontz, Stephanie
1988   *The Social Origins of Private Life: A History of American Families, 1600–1900*. Verso, London.

1992   *The Way We Never Were: American Families and the Nostalgia Trap*. Basic Books, New York.

Corber, Robert J., and Stephen Valocchi
2003   *Queer Studies: An Interdisciplinary Reader*. Blackwell, Malden, Massachusetts.

Cott, Nancy F.
1977   *The Bonds of Womanhood: "Woman's Sphere" in New England. 1780–1835*. Yale University Press, New Haven, Connecticut.

Cowan, Ruth
1982   The "Industrial Revolution" in the Home: Household Technology and Social Change in the Twentieth Century. In *Material Culture Studies in America*, edited by T. J. Schlereth, pp. 222–236. American Association for State and Local History, Nashville, Tennessee.

Crane, Diana
2001   *Fashion and Its Social Agendas: Class, Gender, and Identity in Clothing*. University of Chicago Press, Chicago.

Crass, David, Bruce Penner, and Tammy Forehand
1999   Gentility and Material Culture on the Carolina Frontier. *Historical Archaeology* 33(3): 14–31.

Crosthwaite, Jane F.
1989   "A White and Seamless Robe": Celibacy and Equality in Shaker Art and Theology. *Colby Library Quarterly* 25(3):188–198.

Cunningham, Patricia
2003   *Reforming Women's Fashion, 1850–1920: Politics, Health, and Art*. Kent State University Press, Kent, Ohio.

Danforth, Marie Elaine
2004   African American Men, Women, and Children in Nineteenth-Century Nat-

chez, Mississippi: An Analysis of the City Cemetery Sexton's Records. In *Engendering African American Archaeology: A Southern Perspective*, edited by J. E. Galle and A. L. Young, pp. 237–262. University of Tennessee Press, Knoxville.

Davidson, James M.

2004   "Living Symbols of Their Lifelong Struggles": In Search of the Home and Household in the Heart of Freedman's Town, Dallas, Texas. In *Household Chores and Household Choices: Theorizing the Domestic Sphere in Historical Archaeology*, edited by K. S. Barile and J. C. Brandon, pp. 75–108. University of Alabama Press, Tuscaloosa.

Davies, Sharyn Graham

2007   *Challenging Gender Norms: Five Genders among the Bugis in Indonesia*. Case Studies in Anthropology. Thomson Wadsworth, Belmont, California.

Day, Grant

1996   Finding Ethnicity in the Material Record. Paper presented at the Annual Meeting of the Society for Historical Archaeology, Cincinnati, Ohio.

Day, Grant, and Deborah L. Rotman

2001   Archaeological Data Recovery Plan for the Armstrong Farmstead (15Fa185), Fayette County, Kentucky. With contributions by Berle Clay and James T. Kirkwood. Manuscript on file, Cultural Resource Analysts, Inc., Lexington, Kentucky.

DeCunzo, LuAnn

1995   Reform, Respite, Ritual: An Archaeology of Institutions; The Magdalen Society of Philadelphia, 1800–1850. *Historical Archaeology* 29(30).

Deetz, James

1977   *In Small Things Forgotten*. Anchor Press, New York.

1982   Households: A Structural Key to Archaeological Explanation. In *Archaeology of the Household: Building a Prehistory of Domestic Life*, edited by R. Wilk and W. Rathje. *American Behavioral Scientist* 25(6): 717–724.

1988   Material Culture and Worldview in Colonial Anglo-America. In *The Recovery of Meaning*, edited by M. P. Leone and P. Potter, Jr., pp. 219–233. Smithsonian Institution Press, Washington, D.C.

1996   *In Small Things Forgotten*. Expanded and revised edition. Anchor Books, Doubleday, New York.

Delle, James

1998   *An Archaeology of Social Space: Analyzing Coffee Plantations in Jamaica's Blue Mountains*. Plenum Press, New York.

2000   Gender, Power, and Space: Negotiating Social Relations Under Slavery on Coffee Plantations in Jamaica, 1790–1834. In *Lines That Divide: Historical*

Archaeologies of Race, Class, and Gender, edited by J. A. Delle, S. A. Mrozowski, and R. Paynter, pp. 168–204. University of Tennessee Press, Knoxville.

Demos, John
1970   *A Little Commonwealth: Family Life in Plymouth Colony*. New York: Oxford University Press.

Deslandes, Paul R.
2007   The Boundaries of Manhood in Eighteenth- and Nineteenth-Century Britain. *Gender and History* 19(2): 376–379.

Dierkes-Thrun, Petra
2014   Transgender Studies Today: An Interview with Susan Stryker. *Boundary 2: An International Journal of Literature and Culture*, August 20. Blog accessed online at http://boundary2.org/2014/08/20/transgender-studies-today-an-interview-with-susan-stryker/.

Dixon, Kelly J.
2006   Sidling Up to the Archaeology of Western Saloons: Historical Archaeology Takes on the Wild of the West. *World Archaeology* 38(4): 576–585.

Downing, Andrew Jackson
1841   *Treatise on the Theory and Practice of Landscape Gardening . . . With Remarks on Rural Architecture*. Wiley and Putnam, New York and London.
1842   *Cottage Residences; or A Series of Designs for Rural Cottages and Cottage Villas*. Wiley and Putnam, New York and London.

Driskill, Qwo-Li, Chris Finley, Brian Joseph Gilley, and Scott Lauria Morenson
2011   *Queer Indigenous Studies: Critical Interventions in Theory, Politics, and Literature*. University of Arizona Press, Tucson.

Driskill, Qwo-Li, Daniel Heath Justice, Deborah Miranda, and Lisa Tatonetti
2011   *Sovereign Erotics: A Collection of Two-Spirit Literature*. The University of Arizona Press, Tucson.

DuBois, Ellen C.
1978   *Feminism and Suffrage: The Emergence of an Independent Women's Movement, 1848–1869*. Cornell University Press, Ithaca, New York.

Ember, Carol
1983   The Relative Decline in Women's Contributions to Agriculture with Intensification. *American Anthropologist* 85: 285–305.

Ember, Carol R., Melvin Ember, and Peter N. Peregrine
2012   *Human Evolution and Culture: Highlights of Anthropology*. 7th ed. Pearson Higher Education, Boston.

Erickson, Kristie
2005   Gendered Social Relations and Privies. Paper presented at the Annual Symposium on Ohio Valley Urban and Historical Archaeology, Carter Caves State Resort Park, Kentucky.

Evans, Sara M.

1989 *Born for Liberty: A History of Women in America.* Free Press, New York.

Fausto-Sterling, Anne

2000 *Sexing the Body: Gender Politics and the Construction of Sexuality.* Basic Books, New York.

Fennell, Christopher C.

2011 Early African America: Archaeological Studies of Significance and Diversity. *Journal of Archaeological Research* 19: 1–49.

Ferguson, Ann

1989 *Blood at the Root: Motherhood, Sexuality, and Male Dominance.* Pandora, London.

Ferguson, Leland

1992 *Uncommon Ground: Archaeology and Early African America, 1650–1800.* Smithsonian Institution Press, Washington, D.C.

Fesler, Garrett R.

2004 Living Arrangements among Enslaved Women and Men at an Early Eighteenth-Century Virginia Quartering Site. In *Engendering African American Archaeology: A Southern Perspective*, edited by J. E. Galle and A. L. Young, pp. 177–236. University of Tennessee Press, Knoxville.

Fischer, Gayle V.

2001 *Pantaloons and Power: A Nineteenth-Century Dress Reform in the United States.* Kent State University Press, Kent, Ohio.

Fitts, Robert K.

1999 The Archaeology of Middle-Class Domesticity and Gentility in Victorian Brooklyn. *Historical Archaeology* 33(1): 39–62.

2001 The Rhetoric of Reform: The Five Points Missions and the Cult of Domesticity. *Historical Archaeology* 35(3): 115–132.

Flexner, E.

1968 *Century of Struggle.* Atheneum Books, New York.

Folbre, Nancy R.

1985 The Wealth of Patriarchs: Deerfield, Massachusetts, 1760–1840. *Journal of Interdisciplinary History* 16(2): 199–220.

Fosha, Rose

2004 The Archaeology of Deadwood's Chinatown: A Prologue. In *Ethnic Oasis: The Chinese in the Black Hills*, edited by L. Zhu and R. Fosha, pp. 44–68. South Dakota Historical Society Press, Pierre.

Foucault, Michel

1978 *The History of Sexuality.* Translated by R. Hurley. Pantheon Books, New York.

1979 *Discipline and Punish: The Birth of the Prison.* Translated by A. Sheridan. Vintage Books, New York.

Fowler, Bridget
1997   *Pierre Bourdieu and Cultural Theory: Critical Investigations.* Sage Publications, London.
Fox, Richard W.
1978   *So Far Disordered in Mind: Insanity in California, 1870–1930.* University of California Press, Berkeley.
Franklin, Maria
2001   The Archaeological Dimensions of Soul Food: Interpreting Race, Culture, and Afro-Virginian Identity. In *Race and the Archaeology of Identity*, edited by C. E. Orser, Jr., pp. 88–107. University of Utah Press, Salt Lake City.
Friedan, Betty
1963   *The Feminine Mystique.* W. W. Norton, New York.
Galindo, Mary Jo
2004   The Ethnohistory and Archaeology of Nuevo Santander *Rancho* Households. In *Household Chores and Household Choices: Theorizing the Domestic Sphere in Historical Archaeology*, edited by K. S. Barile and J. C. Brandon, pp. 179–196. University of Alabama Press, Tuscaloosa.
Galle, Jillian E.
2004   Designing Women: Measuring Acquisition and Access at the Hermitage Plantation. In *Engendering African American Archaeology: A Southern Perspective*, edited by J. E. Galle and A. L. Young, pp. 39–72. University of Tennessee Press, Knoxville.
2010   Costly Signaling and Gendered Social Strategies among Slaves in the Eighteenth-Century Chesapeake: An Archaeological Perspective. *American Antiquity* 75(1): 19–43.
Galle, Jillian E., and Amy Young (editors)
2004   *Engendering African American Archaeology: A Southern Perspective.* University of Tennessee Press, Knoxville.
Garfinkel, Harold
2006   Passing and the Managed Achievement of Sex Status in an "Intersexed" Person. In *The Transgender Studies Reader*, edited by S. Stryker and S. Whittle, pp. 58–93. Routledge, New York and London.
Garrison, J. Ritchie
1991   *Landscape and Material Life in Franklin County, Massachusetts, 1770–1860.* University of Tennessee Press, Knoxville.
Geller, Pamela
2009   Identity and Difference: Complicating Gender in Archaeology. *Annual Review of Anthropology* 38: 65–81.
Gero, Joan M., and Margaret W. Conkey
1991   *Engendering Archaeology: Women and Prehistory.* Basil Blackwell, Oxford.

Gibb, James

2009   Introduction. In *The Archaeology of Institutional Life*, edited by A. Beisaw and J. Gibb, pp. 1–4. University of Alabama Press, Tuscaloosa.

Gibb, James, and April Beisaw

2001   Learning Cast Up from the Mire: Archaeological Investigations of School-houses in the Northeastern United States. *Northeast Historical Archaeology* 29: 107–129.

Gibb, James G., David J. Bernstein, and Stephen Zipp

2009   Farm and Factory: Agricultural Production Strategies and the Cheese and Butter Industry. *Historical Archaeology* 43(2): 83–107.

Gibb, James G., and Julia A. King

1991   Gender, Activity Areas, and Homelots in the 17th Century Chesapeake Region. *Historical Archaeology* 25(4): 109–131.

Giddens, Anthony

1979   *Central Problems in Social Theory: Action, Structure, and Contradiction in Social Analysis*. University of California Press, Berkeley.

1984   *The Constitution of Society: Outline of the Theory of Structuration*. Polity, London.

Giele, Janet

1995   *Two Paths to Equality: Temperance, Suffrage, and the Origins of Modern Feminism (Social Movements Past and Present)*. Twayne, New York.

Gilchrist, Roberta

1991   Women's Archaeology?: Political Feminism, Gender Theory, and Historical Revision. *Antiquity* 65: 495–501.

2005   Introduction: Scales and Voices in World Historical Archaeology. *World Archaeology* 37(3): 329–336.

Gilje, Paul A.

1996   The Rise of Capitalism in the Early Republic. *Journal of the Early Republic* 16(2): 159–181.

Glassberg, David

1995   Historical Pageants: Public Epic in the Midwest. In *Invisible America: Unearthing Our Hidden History*, edited by M. P. Leone and N. A. Silberman, pp. 210–211. Henry Holt Reference Book, New York.

Glassie, Henry

1975   *Folk Housing in Middle Virginia: A Structured Analysis of Historic Artifacts*. University of Tennessee Press, Knoxville.

Glazier, David C.

1987   From the Commons to Private Property: Institutional Change in Deerfield, Massachusetts. Unpublished PhD dissertation, Department of Anthropology, University of Massachusetts, Amherst.

Goody, Jack

1971 [1958]   *The Developmental Cycle in Domestic Groups*. Cambridge Papers in Social Anthropology No. 1. Cambridge University Press, Cambridge, New York.

1972   The Evolution of the Family. In *Household and Family in Past Time*, edited by P. Laslett and R. Wall, pp. 103–124. Cambridge University Press, Cambridge, New York.

Green, Harvey

1983   *The Light of the Home: An Intimate View of the Lives of Victorian Women in America*. Pantheon, New York.

Greenwood, Roberta S., and Dana N. Slawson

2008   Gathering Insights on Isolation. *Historical Archaeology* 42(3): 68–79.

Greven, P. J.

1970   *Four Generations: Population, Land, and Family in Colonial Andover, Massachusetts*. Cornell University Press, Ithaca, New York.

Groover, Mark

2003   *An Archaeological Study of Rural Capitalism and Material Life: The Gibbs Farmstead in Southern Appalachia, 1790–1920*. Kluwer Academic/Plenum, New York.

2008   *The Archaeology of North American Farmsteads*. The American Experience in Archaeological Perspective, edited by M. S. Nassaney. University Press of Florida, Gainesville.

Gurko, M.

1974   *The Ladies of Seneca Falls: The Birth of the Women's Rights Movement*. Macmillan, New York.

Gutman, Herbert G.

1977   *Work, Culture, and Society in Industrializing America*. Vintage Books, New York.

Hahn, Stephen, and Jonathon Prude

1985   *The Countryside in the Age of Capitalist Transformation: Essays in the Social History of Rural America*. University of North Carolina Press, Chapel Hill.

Halttunen, Karen

1982   *Confidence Men and Painted Women: A Study of Middle-Class Culture in America, 1830–1870*. Yale University Press, New Haven, Connecticut.

Harlow, Elizabeth A.

2001   Madeline Yale Wynne, the Arts and Crafts Movement, and Deerfield. Manuscript on file, Department of Anthropology, University of Massachusetts, Amherst.

2005   Madeline Yale Wynne and the Arts and Crafts Movement: An Archaeological Assemblage from Deerfield, Massachusetts. Unpublished MA thesis, Department of Anthropology, University of Massachusetts, Amherst.

Harvey, David

1996   *Justice, Nature, and the Geography of Difference*. Blackwell, Malden, Massachusetts.

Hautaniemi, Susan I.

1994   Archaeological Site Survey at the Moors Homelot, Deerfield, Massachusetts. Manuscript on file, Historic Deerfield, Inc., Deerfield, Massachusetts.

1999   A Living Ell: Servant and Farm Labor Architecture in 19th Century New England. Paper prepared for the Annual Meeting of the Society for American Archaeology, Chicago, Illinois.

2001   Demography and Death in Emergent Industrial Cities of New England. Unpublished PhD dissertation, Department of Anthropology, University of Massachusetts, Amherst.

Hautaniemi, Susan I., and Robert Paynter

1996   Preliminary Report and Request for Permit Extension. Manuscript on file, Massachusetts Historical Commission, Boston.

1999   *Archaeological Investigations Final Report, Permit 1265: Moors Homelot, Deerfield, Massachusetts*. Submitted to the Massachusetts Historical Commission, Boston. Copies available from the Department of Anthropology, University of Massachusetts, Amherst.

Hautaniemi, Susan I., and Deborah L. Rotman

2003   To the Hogs? Or to the Homestead?: Municipal Water and Gender Relations at the Moors Site in Deerfield, Massachusetts. In *Shared Spaces and Divided Places: Exploring the Material and Spatial Dimensions of Gender Relations and American Historical Landscapes*, edited by D. L. Rotman and E. R. Savulis, pp. 135–159. University of Tennessee Press, Knoxville.

Hayden, Dolores

1980   What Would a Non-Sexist City Look Like?: Speculations on Housing, Urban Design, and Human Work. *Signs: Journal of Women, Culture, and Society* 5(3, Supplement): S170–S187.

1995   *The Grand Domestic Revolution*. MIT Press, Cambridge, Massachusetts.

Heath, Barbara J.

2004   Engendering Choice: Slavery and Consumerism in Central Virginia. In *Engendering African American Archaeology: A Southern Perspective*, edited by J. E. Galle and A. L. Young, pp. 19–38. University of Tennessee Press, Knoxville.

Hendon, Julia A.

1996   Archaeological Approaches to the Organization of Domestic Labor: Household Practice and Domestic Relations. *Annual Review of Anthropology* 25: 45–61.

Herbert, Christopher
2011   "Life's Prizes Are by Labor Got": Risk, Reward, and White Manliness in the California Gold Rush. *Pacific Historical Review* 80(3): 339–368.

Holly, Henry Hudson
1878   *Modern Dwellings in Town and Country: Adapted to American Wants and Climate with a Treatise on Furniture and Decoration.* Harper and Brothers, New York.

Hood, J. Edward
1996   Social Relations and the Cultural Landscape. In *Landscape Archaeology: Reading and Interpreting the American Historical Landscape,* edited by R. Yamin and K. B. Metheny, pp. 121–146. University of Tennessee Press, Knoxville.

Hooker, Brainard
1917   *The First Century of Public Schools of Tippecanoe County, Indiana.* Haywood, Lafayette, Indiana.

Howard, Hugh
1989   *How Old Is This House?: A Skeleton Key to Dating and Identifying Three Centuries of American Homes.* Noonday Press; Farrar, Straus, and Giroux, New York.

Hunt, W. J., Jr.
1993   Ethnicity and Firearms in the Upper Missouri Bison-Robe Trade: An Examination of Weapon Preference and Utilization at Fort Union Trading Post, N.H.S., North Dakota. *Historical Archaeology* 27(3): 74–101.

Israel, Fred
1968   *1897 Sears, Roebuck Catalogue.* Introduction by S. J. Perelman. Chelsea House, New York.

Jacobs, Margaret
2011   Western History: What's Gender Got to Do with It? *Western Historical Quarterly* 42(3): 297–304.

Jacobs, Sue-Ellen, and Christine Roberts
1989   Sex, Sexuality, Gender, and Gender Variance. In *Gender and Anthropology,* edited by S. Morgen, pp. 438–462. American Anthropological Association, Washington, D.C.

Johnson, Matthew
1993   *Housing Culture: Traditional Architecture in an English Landscape.* Smithsonian Institution Press, Washington, D.C.

Johnson, Theodore E. (editor)
1976   The "Millennial Laws" of 1821. *Shaker Quarterly* 7(2): 35–58.

Joseph, Joseph W.
2004   Resistance and Compliance: CRM and the Archaeology of the African Diaspora. *Historical Archaeology* 38(1): 18–31.

Joyce, Rosemary A.

2008   Ancient Bodies, Ancient Lives: Sex, Gender, and Archaeology. Thames and Hudson, New York.

Juster, N.

1996   A Woman's Place: Yesterday's Women in Rural America. Fulcrum, Golden, Colorado.

Kaestle, Carl F.

1983   Pillars of the Republic: Common Schools and American Society, 1780–1860. Hill and Wang, New York.

Kamp, Kathryn A.

2001   Where Have All the Children Gone?: The Archaeology of Childhood. Journal of Archaeological Method and Theory 8(1): 1–34.

Kasper, Kimberly

2012   Seeds for the Future: The Materialities of Traditional Ecological Knowledge. Archaeologies: Journal of the World Archaeological Congress 8(3): 269–292.

Kehoe, Alice B.

1997   On the Commensurality of Gender Categories. In Two-Spirited People: Native American Gender Identity, Sexuality, and Spirituality, edited by S. E. Jacobs, W. Thomas, and S. Lang, pp. 265–271. University of Illinois Press, Urbana and Chicago.

Kerber, Linda

1976   The Republican Mother: Women and the Enlightenment, An American Perspective. American Quarterly 28(2): 187–205.

Kerber, Linda, Nancy F. Cott, Robert Gross, Lynn Hunt, Carroll Smith-Rosenberg, and Christine M. Stansell

1989   Beyond Roles, Beyond Spheres: Thinking about Gender in the Early Republic. William and Mary Quarterly 46(3): 565–585.

Kessler-Harris, Alice

1982   Out to Work: A History of Wage-Earning Women in the United States. Oxford University Press, New York.

Kimmel, R. H.

1993   Notes on the Cultural Origins and Functions of Sub-floor Pits. Historical Archaeology 27(3): 102–113.

King, Julia

2006   Household Archaeology, Identities, and Biographies. In The Cambridge Companion to Historical Archaeology, edited by Dan Hicks and Mary Beaudry, pp. 87–103. Cambridge University Press, Cambridge.

Kivisto, Peter

2004   What Is the Canonical Theory of Assimilation? Journal of the History of Behavioral Sciences 40(2): 149–63.

Kockelman, Paul
2007   Agency: The Relation between Meaning, Power, and Knowledge. *Current Anthropology* 48(3): 375–402.

Kruczek-Aaron, Hadley
2002   Choice Flowers and Well-Ordered Tables: Struggling over Gender in a Nineteenth-Century Household. *International Journal of Historical Archaeology* 6(3): 173–185.
2013   Making Men and Women Blush: Masculinity, Femininity, and Reform in Nineteenth-Century Central New York. In *Historical and Archaeological Perspectives on Gender Transformations: From Private to Public*, edited by S. M. Spencer-Wood, pp. 307–336. Contributions to a Global Historical Archaeology, edited by C. E. Orser, Jr. Springer Academic, New York.

Kryder-Reid, Elizabeth
1994   "With Manly Courage": Reading the Construction of Gender in a Nineteenth-Century Religious Community. In *Those of Little Note*, edited by E. M. Scott, pp. 97–114. University of Arizona Press, Tucson.

Kulikoff, Allan
1992   *The Agrarian Origins of American Capitalism*. University Press of Virginia, Charlottesville.

Kwas, Mary
2009   *Digging for History at Old Washington*. University of Arkansas, Fayetteville.

Lamb Richmond, Trudie, and Amy E. Den Ouden
2003   Recovering Gendered Political Histories: Local Struggles and Native Women's Resistance in Colonial Southern New England. In *Reinterpreting New England Indians and the Colonial Experience*, edited by C. G. Calloway and N. Salisbury, pp. 174–213. Colonial Society of Massachusetts, Boston.

Lamphere, Louise
2001   The Domestic Sphere of Woman and the Public World of Men: The Strengths and Limitations of an Anthropological Dichotomy. In *Gender in Cross-Cultural Perspective*, edited by C. B. Brettell and C. F. Sargent, pp. 100–109. Prentice Hall, Upper Saddle River, New Jersey.

Lang, Sabine
1998   *Men as Women, Women as Men: Changing Gender in Native American Cultures*. University of Texas Press, Austin.

Lasch, C.
1997   *Women and the Common Life: Love, Marriage, and Feminism*. W. W. Norton, New York and London.

Leinaweaver, Jessaca B.
2013   Practice Mothers. *Signs* 38(2): 405–430.

Leone, Mark P.

1984   Interpreting Ideology in Historical Archaeology: Using the Rules of Perspective in William Paca Garden in Annapolis, Maryland. In *Ideology, Power, and Prehistory*, edited by D. Miller and C. Tilley, pp. 25–35. Cambridge University Press, Cambridge.

1999   Ceramics from Annapolis, Maryland: A Measure of Time Routines and Work Discipline. In *Historical Archaeologies of Capitalism*, edited by M. Leone and P. Potter, Jr., pp. 195–216. Kluwer Academic/Plenum, New York.

Leone, Mark, Parker Potter, Jr., and Paul Shackel

1987   Toward a Critical Archaeology. *Current Anthropology* 28(3): 283–302.

Leone, Mark P., and Neil A. Silberman (editors)

1995   *Invisible America: Unearthing Our Hidden History*. Henry Holt, New York.

Lindauer, Owen

2009   Individual Struggles and Institutional Goals: Small Voices from the Phoenix Indian School Track Site. In *The Archaeology of Institutional Life*, edited by A. Beisaw and J. Gibb, pp. 86–104. University of Alabama Press, Tuscaloosa.

Little, Barbara

2007   *Historical Archaeology: Why the Past Matters*. Left Coast Press, Walnut Creek, California.

Löfgren, Orvar

2003   The Sweetness of Home: Class, Culture, and Family Life in Sweden. In *The Anthropology of Space and Place: Locating Culture*, edited by S. M. Low and D. Lawrence-Zúñiga, pp. 142–159. Blackwell, Malden, Massachusetts.

Loren, Diana DiPaolo

1996   Colonial Dress and Identity at the Spanish Presidio of Los Adaes. *Southern Studies* 7: 45–64.

2000   The Intersections of Colonial Policy and Colonial Practice: Creolization on the Eighteenth-Century Louisiana/Texas Frontier. *Historical Archaeology* 34(3): 85–98.

Ludlow Collective

2001   Archaeology of the Colorado Coal Field War, 1913–1914. In *Archaeologies of the Contemporary Past*, edited by V. Buchli and G. Lucas, pp. 94–107. Routledge, London.

MacPherson, James M.

1998   The Differences between the Antebellum North and South. In *Major Problems in the Civil War and Reconstruction*, edited by M. Perman, pp. 21–30. Houghton Mifflin, Boston.

Madison Weekly Courier [Madison, Indiana]

1878   "City News" column, 26 June: 5.

1879a   "City News" column, 28 February: 5.

1879b   Untitled article, 5 March: 4.

Mandell, Daniel R.

2005   "The Times Are Exceedingly Altered": The Revolution and Southern New England Indians. In *Eighteenth Century Native Communities of Southern New England in the Colonial Context*, edited by J. Campisi, pp. 160–190. Occasional Paper No. 1, Mashantucket Pequot Museum and Research Center, Ledyard, Connecticut.

Margolis, M. L.

1984   *Mothers and Such: Views of American Women and Why They Changed*. University of California, Berkeley.

Marilley, S. M.

1996   *Woman Suffrage and the Origins of Liberal Feminism in the United States, 1820–1920*. Harvard University Press, Cambridge, Massachusetts.

Marks, Jonathon

1994   Black, White, Other: Racial Categories Are Cultural Constructs Masquerading as Biology. *Natural History* (December): 32–35.

Marx, Karl, and Frederick Engels

1972   *Ireland and the Irish Question*. International, New York.

Matthews, G.

1989   *"Just a Housewife": The Rise and Fall of Domesticity in America*. Oxford University Press, New York and Oxford.

McBride, Kevin

2007   Transformation by Degree: Eighteenth-Century Native American Land Use. In *Eighteenth-Century Native Communities of Southern New England in the Colonial Context*, edited by Jack Campisi, pp. 35–54. Occasional Paper No. 1, Mashantucket Pequot Museum and Research Center, Ledyard, Connecticut.

McBride, W. Stephen

2010   African-American Women, Power, and Freedom in the Contested Landscape of Camp Nelson, Kentucky. In *Archaeology and Preservation of Gendered Landscapes*, edited by S. Spencer-Wood and S. Baugher, pp. 95–112. Springer Academic, New York.

2013   Camp Nelson and Kentucky's Civil War Memory. *Historical Archaeology* 47(3): 69–80.

McBride, W. Stephen, Susan C. Andrews, J. Howard Beverley, and Tracey Sandefur

2006   *From Supply Depot to Emancipation Center, the Archaeology of Camp Nelson, Kentucky*. Wilber Smith Associates, Lexington, Kentucky.

McBride, W. Stephen, and Kim A. McBride

2006   Civil War Housing Insights from Camp Nelson, Kentucky. In *Huts and History: The Historical Archaeology of Military Encampment during the American*

Civil War, edited by C. R. Geier, D. G. Orr, and M. B. Reeves, pp. 136–171. University Press of Florida, Gainesville.

McGowan, Susan, and Amelia F. Miller

1996   *Family & Landscape: Deerfield Homelots from 1671.* Pocumtuck Valley Memorial Association, Deerfield, Massachusetts.

McGuire, Randall H.

1988   Dialogues with the Dead: Ideology and the Cemetery. In *The Recovery of Meaning: Historical Archaeology in the Eastern United States*, edited by M. P. Leone and P. B. Potter, Jr., pp. 435–480. Smithsonian Institution Press, Washington, D.C.

1991   Building Power in the Cultural Landscapes of Broome County, New York, 1880 to 1940. In *The Archaeology of Inequality*, edited by R. H. McGuire and R. Paynter, pp. 102–124. Blackwell, Oxford and Cambridge, Massachusetts.

2006   Marxism and Capitalism in Historical Archaeology. In *The Cambridge Companion to Historical Archaeology*, edited by D. Hicks and M. Beaudry, pp. 123–142. Cambridge University Press, Cambridge.

McMurry, Sally

1987   Women and the Expansion of Dairying: The Cheesemaking Industry in Oneida County, New York, 1830–1860. Paper presented at the annual Berkshire History Conference, Wellesley College, Wellesley, Massachusetts.

1988   *Families and Farmhouses in Nineteenth-Century America: Vernacular Design and Social Change.* Oxford University Press, Oxford and New York.

Melvoin, R.

1989   Secular Trends in Mortality in the Connecticut Valley, 1700–1850. *Human Biology* 49(3): 389–414.

Middleton, Angela

2007   Silent Voice, Hidden Lives: Archaeology, Class, and Gender in the CMS Missions, Bay of Islands, New Zealand, 1814–1845. *International Journal of Historical Archaeology* 11(1): 1–31.

Miller, Daniel

1987   *Material Culture and Mass Consumption.* Basil Blackwell, New York.

Miller, George

1991   A Revised Set of CC Index Values for Classification and Economic Scaling of English Ceramics from 1787 to 1880. In *Approaches to Material Culture Research for Historical Archaeologists*, edited by D. R. Brauner, pp. 86–110. Second edition. Society for Historical Archaeology, California, Pennsylvania.

Miller, Marla R., and Anne Digan Lanning

1994   "Common Parlors": Women and Recreation of Community Identity in Deerfield, Massachusetts, 1870–1920. *Gender and History* 6(3): 435–455.

Mintz, Sidney W.
1987   *Sweetness and Power: The Place of Sugar in Modern History.* Penguin Books, New York.

Moore, Henrietta L.
1988   *Feminism and Anthropology.* University of Minnesota Press, Minneapolis.
1994   *A Passion for Difference.* Indiana University Press, Bloomington.
1996   *Space, Text, and Gender: An Anthropological Study of the Marakwet of Kenya.* Guilford Press, New York and London.

Moore, Lisa
1992   "Something More Tender Still Than Friendship": Romantic Friendships in Early-Nineteenth-Century England. *Feminist Studies* 18(3): 499–520.

Moore, Rose G., and Deborah L. Rotman
2003   Rural, but Not Isolated: Connectedness at the Armstrong Farmstead (15Fa185) in the Central Bluegrass Region of Kentucky. Paper presented in the Revisiting Rural Contexts: Dispelling Agrarian Myths symposium, co-organized by D. L. Rotman and L. Wurst for the Annual Meeting of the Society for Historical Archaeology, Providence, Rhode Island, January 14–19.

Morgenson, Scott Laria
2011   *Spaces Between Us: Queer Settler Colonialism and Indigenous Decolonization.* University of Minnesota Press, Minneapolis.

Mrozowski, Stephen
1984   Prospects and Perspectives on an Archaeology of the Household. *Man in the Northeast* 27: 31–49.
1991   Landscapes of Inequality. In *The Archaeology of Inequality*, edited by R. H. McGuire and R. Paynter, pp. 79–101. Basil Blackwell, Oxford.

Mrozowski, Stephen A., Maria Franklin, and L. Hunt
2008   Archaeobotanical Analysis and Interpretations of Enslaved Virginian Plant Use at Rich Neck Plantation. *American Antiquity* 73: 699–728.

Muller, Nancy Ladd
1994   The House of the Black Burghardts: An Investigation of Race, Gender, and Class at the W.E.B. DuBois Boyhood Homesite. In *Those of Little Note: Gender, Race, and Class in Historical Archaeology*, edited by E. M. Scott, pp. 81–96. University of Arizona Press, Tucson.

Mullins, Paul
1999a   Race and the Genteel Consumer: Class and African-American Consumption. *Historical Archaeology* 33(1): 22–38.
1999b   *Race and Affluence: An Archaeology of African American and Consumer Culture.* Klewer Academic Press, New York.
2001   Racializing the Parlor: Race and Victorian Bric-a-Brac Consumption. In *Race*

and the *Archaeology of Identity*, edited by C. E. Orser, Jr., pp. 158–176. University of Utah Press, Salt Lake City.

2004   Ideology, Power, and Capitalism: The Historical Archaeology of Consumption. In *A Companion to Social Archaeology*, edited by L. Meskell and R. W. Preucel, pp. 195–211. Blackwell, Malden, Massachusetts.

2011   *The Archaeology of Consumer Culture. The American Experience in Archaeological Perspective*, edited by M. S. Nassaney. University of Florida Press, Tallahassee.

Munroe, Robert L., and Ruth Munroe

1987   *Samoan Time Allocation*. HRAF Press, New Haven, Connecticut.

Murray, Edmundo

2006   *Becoming Irlandés: Private Narratives of the Irish Emigration to Argentina (1844–1912)*. Buenos Aires: Literature of Latin America.

Musselman, Matthew

2005   Munitions from the Schoolhouse. Paper presented at the Annual Symposium on Ohio Valley Urban and Historical Archaeology, Carter Caves State Resort Park, Kentucky.

Nanda, Serena

1986   The Hijras of India: Cultural and Individual Dimensions of an Institutionalized Third Gender Role. In *The Many Faces of Homosexuality: Anthropological Approaches to Homosexual Behavior*, edited by E. Blackwood, pp. 35–54. Harrington Park Press, New York.

2000   Introduction. Gender Diversity: Crosscultural Variations. Waveland Press, Long Grove, Illinois.

Narotzky, Susana

2007   The Project in the Model: Reciprocity, Social Capital, and the Politics of Ethnographic Realism. *Current Anthropology* 48(3): 403–424.

Nash, Margaret A.

1997   Rethinking Republican Motherhood: Benjamin Rush and the Young Ladies' Academy of Philadelphia. *Journal of the Early Republic* 17(2): 171–191.

Nassaney, Michael

2004   Native American Gender Politics and Material Culture in Seventeenth-Century Southeastern New England. *Journal of Social Archaeology* 4(3): 334–367.

2008   Identity Formation at a French Colonial Outpost in the North American Interior. *International Journal of Historical Archaeology* 12(4): 297–318.

Nassaney, Michael S., and Marjorie R. Abel

1993   The Political and Social Contexts of Cutlery Production in the Connecticut Valley. *Dialectical Archaeology* 18(3–4): 247–289.

2000   Urban Spaces, Labor Organization, and Social Control: Lessons from New England's Nineteenth-Century Cutlery Industry. In *Lines That Divide: His-*

torical Archaeologies of Race, Class, and Gender, edited by James A. Delle, Stephen A. Mrozowski, and Robert Paynter, pp. 239–275. University of Tennessee Press, Knoxville.

Nassaney, Michael S., José António Brandão, William M. Cremin, and Brock A. Giordano

2007 Archaeological Evidence of Economic Activities at an Eighteenth-Century Frontier Outpost in the Western Great Lakes. *Historical Archaeology* 41(4): 3–19.

Naylor, Gillian

1971 *The Arts and Crafts Movement: A Study of Its Sources, Ideals, and Influences on Design Theory.* MIT Press, Cambridge, Massachusetts.

Newcomb, H.

1855 *How to Be a Lady: A Book for Girls Containing Useful Hints on the Formation of Character.* 15th ed. Gould and Lincoln, Boston.

Newton, Michael

2010 "Did You Hear about the Gaelic-Speaking African?": Scottish Gaelic Folklore about Identity in North America. *Comparative American Studies* 8(2): 88–106.

Nickolai, Carol

2003 The Relevance of Nineteenth-Century Religion to the Archaeological Record: An Example from the Home of Ellen White, Prophetess of Seventh-day Adventism. *International Journal of Historical Archaeology* 7(2): 145–159.

2013 Decently Dressed: Women's Fashion and Dress Reform in the Nineteenth-Century United States. In *Historical and Archaeological Perspectives on Gender Transformations: From Private to Public*, edited by S. M. Spencer-Wood, pp. 215–230. Contributions to a Global Historical Archaeology, edited by C. E. Orser, Jr. Springer Academic, New York.

Nuttall, Sarah

2009 *Entanglement: Literary and Cultural Reflections on Post-apartheid.* Wits University Press, Johannesburg, South Africa.

Nylander, Jane

1994 *Our Own Snug Fireside: Images of the New England Home, 1760–1860.* Yale University Press, New Haven, Connecticut.

O'Brien, J. M.

1997 *Dispossession by Degrees: Indian Land and Identity in Natick, Massachusetts, 1650–1790.* Cambridge University Press, Cambridge.

O'Gorman, Jodie

1996 Domestic Economies and Mortuary Practices: A Gendered View of Oneota Social Organization. Unpublished PhD dissertation, University of Wisconsin, Madison.

2010   Exploring the Longhouse and Community in Tribal Society. *American Antiquity* 75(3): 571–597.

Ollman, Bertell

1993   *Dialectical Investigations*. Routledge, London.

2003   *Dance of the Dialectic: Steps in Marx's Method*. University of Illinois Press, Champaign-Urbana.

Orser, Charles E., Jr.

1996   *A Historical Archaeology of the Modern World*. Contributions to Global Historical Archaeology. Plenum Press, New York.

2007   *The Archaeology of Race and Racialization in Historic America*. The American Experience in Archaeological Perspective, edited by M. S. Nassaney. University Press of Florida, Gainesville.

2010   Twenty-First-Century Historical Archaeology. *Journal of Archaeological Research* 18: 111–150.

Orser, Charles E., Jr. (editor)

2001   *Race and the Archaeology of Identity*. University of Utah Press, Salt Lake City.

Osterud, Nancy G.

1991   *Bonds of Community: The Lives of Farm Women in Nineteenth-Century New York*. Cornell University Press, Ithaca, New York.

Pappas, Efstathios I.

2004   Fictive Kin in the Mountains: The Paternalistic Metaphor and Households in a California Logging Camp. In *Household Chores and Household Choices: Theorizing the Domestic Sphere in Historical Archaeology*, edited by K. S. Barile and J. C. Brandon, pp. 159–178. University of Alabama Press, Tuscaloosa.

Parker, Bradley J., and Lars Rodseth (editors)

2005   *Untaming the Frontier in Anthropology, Archaeology, and History*. University of Arizona Press, Tucson.

Paynter, Robert

1990   The Transformation of the W.E.B. DuBois Boyhood Homesite: A Consideration of Race, Class, Gender, and Space. Paper presented for the Archaeology of Cultural Landscape symposium, co-organized by E. Hood and J. Garman for the Annual Meeting of the Society for American Archaeology, Las Vegas, Nevada.

1998   Steps to an Archaeology of Capitalism: Material Change and Class Analysis. In *The Recovery of Meaning: Historical Archaeology in the Eastern United States*, edited by M. P. Leone and P. B. Potter, Jr., pp. 407–434. Smithsonian Institution Press, Washington and London.

1999   Epilogue: Class Analysis in Historical Archaeology. *Historical Archaeology* 33(1): 184–195.

2000   Historical Archaeology and the Post-Columbian World of North America. *Journal of Archaeological Research* 8(3): 169–217.

2002   Time in the Valley: Narratives about Rural New England. *Current Anthropology* 43(S4): S85–S101.

Paynter, Robert, and Randall H. McGuire

1991   *The Archaeology of Inequality: Material Culture, Domination, and Resistance.* In *The Archaeology of Inequality*, edited by R. McGuire and R. Paynter, pp. 1–27. Basil Blackwell, Oxford and Cambridge.

Paynter, Robert, Rita Reinke, J. Ritchie Garrison, J. Edward Hood, Amelia Miller, and Susan McGowan

1987   Vernacular Landscapes in Western Massachusetts. In *Annual Meeting of the Society for Historical Archaeology. The Archaeological Use of Landscape Treatment in Social, Economic, and Ideological Analysis*, F. Harrington, general editor, Savannah, Georgia.

Pearson, Michael Parker, and Colin Richards

1994   Ordering the World: Perceptions of Architecture, Space, and Time. In *Architecture and Order: Approaches to Social Space*, edited by M. P. Pearson and C. Richards, pp. 1–37. Routledge, New York.

Phillips, Danielle Taylor

2013   Moving with the Women: Tracing Racialization, Migration, and Domestic Workers in the Archive. *Signs* 38(2): 379–404.

Pluckhahn, Thomas J.

2010   Household Archaeology in the Southeastern United States: History, Trends, and Challenges. *Journal of Archaeological Research* 18: 331–385.

Porter, Susan L.

1996   Introduction. In *Women of the Commonwealth: Work, Family, and Social Change in Nineteenth-Century Massachusetts*, edited by S. L. Porter, pp. 1–16. University of Massachusetts Press, Amherst.

Praetzellis, Adrian, and Mary Praetzellis

1998   A Connecticut Merchant in Chinadom: A Play in One Act. *Historical Archaeology* 32(1): 86–93.

Praetzellis, Mary

2013   Sisters across the Bay: Archaeology and the Influence of Two Late Nineteenth-Century Kindergartens in Northern California. In *Historical and Archaeological Perspectives on Gender Transformations: From Private to Public*, edited by S. Spencer-Wood, pp. 337–362. Springer Academic, New York.

Psota, Sunshine

2011   The Archaeology of Mental Illness from the Afflicted and Caretaker Perspective: A Northern California Family's Odyssey. *Historical Archaeology* 45(4): 20–38.

Purser, Margaret
1991 "Several Paradise Ladies Are Visiting in Town": Gender Strategies in the Early Industrial West. *Historical Archaeology* 25(4): 6–16.

Reiner, Jacqueline S.
1982 Rearing the Republican Child: Attitudes and Practices in Post-Revolutionary Philadelphia. *William and Mary Quarterly* 39: 150–163.

Reis, Elizabeth
2009 *Bodies in Doubt: An American History of Intersex.* Johns Hopkins University Press, Baltimore, Maryland.

Rifkin, Mark
2011 *When Did Indians Become Straight?: Kinship, the History of Sexuality, and Native Sovereignty.* Oxford University Press, Oxford and New York.

Roediger, David R.
1991 *The Wages of Whiteness: Race and the Making of the American Working Class.* Verso Press, London.

2007 *The Wages of Whiteness: Race and the Making of the American Working Class.* New ed. Verso Press, London.

Romero, L.
1997 *Home Fronts: Domesticity and Its Critics in the Antebellum United States.* Duke University Press, Durham, North Carolina.

Rosaldo, M.
1974 Woman, Culture, and Society: A Theoretical Overview. In *Woman, Culture, and Society,* edited by M. Z. Rosaldo and L. Lamphere, pp. 17–42. Stanford University Press, Stanford, California.

Rose, Chelsea
2013 Lonely Men, Loose Women: Rethinking the Demographics of a Multiethnic Mining Camp, Kanaka Flat, Oregon. *Historical Archaeology* 47(3): 23–35.

Rothschild, Nan A.
2006 Colonialism, Material Culture, and Identity in the Rio Grande and Hudson River Valleys. *International Journal of Historical Archaeology* 10(1): 73–108.

Rotman, Deborah L.
1995 Class and Gender in Southwestern Michigan: Interpreting Historical Landscapes. Unpublished MA thesis, Department of Anthropology, Western Michigan University, Kalamazoo.

2001 *Beyond the Cult of Domesticity: Exploring the Material and Spatial Expressions of Multiple Gender Ideologies in Deerfield, Massachusetts, ca. 1750–ca. 1911.* PhD dissertation, Department of Anthropology, University of Massachusetts, Amherst.

2003 Introduction: Exploring Shared Spaces and Divided Places on the American Historical Landscape. In *Shared Spaces and Divided Places: Exploring the Ma-*

terial and Spatial Dimensions of Gender Relations and the American Historical Landscape, edited by D. L. Rotman and E. R. Savulis, pp. 1–23. University of Tennessee Press, Knoxville.

2005   Newlyweds, Young Families, and Spinsters: A Consideration of Life Cycle in the Historical Archaeologies of Gender. International Journal of Historical Archaeology 9(1): 1–36.

2006   Separate Spheres?: Beyond the Dichotomies of Domesticity. Current Anthropology 47(4): 666–674.

2007   Public Displays and Private Tasks: Historical Archaeology of Landscape Utilization and Gender Relations in Indianapolis. Midcontinental Journal of Archaeology 32(1): 89–116.

2009a   Historical Archaeology of Gendered Lives. Contributions to a Global Historical Archaeology, edited by C. E. Orser, Jr. Springer Academic, New York.

2009b   Rural Education and Community Social Relations: Historical Archaeology of the Wea View Schoolhouse No. 8, Wabash Township, Tippecanoe County, Indiana. In The Archaeology of Institutional Life, edited by A. Beisaw and J. Gibb, pp. 69–85. University of Alabama Press, Tuscaloosa.

2010   "The Fighting Irish": Historical Archaeology of 19th-Century Catholic Immigrant Experiences in South Bend, Indiana. Historical Archaeology 44(2): 113–31.

2012   Irish-Catholic Immigrant Life in South Bend, Indiana: Refined Earthenwares and the 19th-Century Social Worlds of the Midwest. Midcontinental Journal of Archaeology 37(1): 25–44.

2013a   Engendering Historical Archaeology. Encyclopedia of Global Archaeology, edited by Claire Smith. Springer Academic, New York. DOI 10.1007/978-1-4419-0465-2.

2013b   Domestic Production for Public Markets: The Arts and Crafts Movement in Deerfield, Massachusetts (1850–1911). In Historical and Archaeological Perspectives on Gender Transformations: From Private to Public, edited by S. Spencer-Wood, pp. 45–62. Springer Academic, New York.

Rotman, Deborah L., Japhia Burrell, Kristie Erickson, and Matt Musselman

2005   Wea View School No. 8: Historical Archaeologies of Education and Social Relations in Wabash Township, Tippecanoe County, Indiana. Ohio Valley Historical Archaeology 20: 88–98.

Rotman, Deborah L., and R. Berle Clay

2008   Urban Archaeology at the Site of the Argosy Casino: The Materiality of Social Change in the Canal Town of Lawrenceburg, Indiana. In Urban Archaeology: Updates on Method and Theory, edited by P. Mullins and M. Wagner. Historical Archaeology 42(1): 46–69.

Rotman, Deborah L., Rachel Mancini, and Mark Boatwright

1998   Archaeology and Preservation at the Ben Schroeder Saddletree Factory and Residence: Deciphering Nearly a Century of Domestic and Industrial Activity. Archaeological Resources Management Service, Ball State University, Report of Investigations No. 49. Muncie, Indiana.

Rotman, Deborah L., and Michael S. Nassaney

1997   Class, Gender, and the Built Environment: Deriving Social Relations from Cultural Landscapes in Southwest Michigan. *Historical Archaeology* 31(2): 42–62.

Rotman, Deborah L., and Ellen-Rose Savulis (editors)

2003   *Shared Spaces and Divided Places: Exploring the Material and Spatial Dimensions of Gender Relations and American Historical Landscapes.* University of Tennessee Press, Knoxville.

Rotman, Deborah L., and John Staicer

2002   Curiosities and Conundrums: Deciphering Social Relations and the Material World at the Ben Schroeder Saddletree Factory and Residence, Madison, Indiana. *Historical Archaeology* 36(2): 92–110.

Rubertone, Patricia E.

2000   The Historical Archaeology of Native Americans. *Annual Review of Anthropology* 29: 425–446.

Russell, W. C.

1981   Women's Political Rights in Connecticut, 1830–1980. Manuscript on file, Yale–New Haven Teachers Institute, New Haven, Connecticut.

Ryan, M.

1985   *The Empire of the Mother: American Writing about Domesticity, 1830–1860.* Harrington Park Press, New York and London.

Salmon, Marylynn

2000   The Limits of Independence, 1760–1800. In *No Small Courage: A History of Women in the United States*, edited by Nancy Cott, pp. 109–178. Oxford University Press, Oxford.

Samford, Patricia

2004   Engendering Enslaved Communities on Virginia's and North Carolina's Eighteenth- and Nineteenth-Century Plantations. In *Engendering African American Archaeology: A Southern Perspective*, edited by J. E. Galle and A. L. Young, pp. 151–176. University of Tennessee Press, Knoxville.

Savulis, Ellen-Rose

2003   Zion's Zeal: Negotiating Identity in Shaker Communities. In *Shared Spaces and Divided Places: Material Dimensions of Gender Relations and the American Historical Landscape*, edited by D. L. Rotman and E. R. Savulis, pp. 160–189. University of Tennessee Press, Knoxville.

Schneider, Jane C., and Peter T. Schneider
1996   *Festival of the Poor: Fertility Decline and the Ideology of Class in Sicily, 1860–1980.* University of Arizona Press, Tucson.

Scott, Elizabeth M.
1991a   A Feminist Approach to Historical Archaeology: Eighteenth-Century Fur Trade Society at Michilimackinac. *Historical Archaeology* 25(4): 42–53.
1991b   Gender in Complex Colonial Society: The Material Goods of Everyday Life in a Late Eighteenth-Century Fur Trading Community. In *The Archaeology of Gender: Proceedings of the 22nd Annual Chacmool Conference*, edited by D. Walde and N. D. Willows, pp. 490–495. Archaeological Association of the University of Calgary, Calgary, Alberta.
1994   *Those of Little Note: Gender, Race, and Class in Historical Archaeology.* University of Arizona Press, Tucson.
2001   "An Indolent Slothfull Set of Vagabonds": Ethnicity and Race in a Colonial Fur-Trading Community. In *Race and the Archaeology of Identity*, edited by C. E. Orser, Jr., pp. 14–33. University of Utah Press, Salt Lake City.
2004   Introduction: Gender Research in African American Archaeology. In *Engendering African American Archaeology: A Southern Perspective*, edited by J. E. Galle and A. L. Young, pp. 1–18. University of Tennessee Press, Knoxville.

Scranton, Philip
1997   *Endless Novelty: Specialty Production and American Industrialization, 1865–1925.* Princeton University Press, Princeton, New Jersey.

Sears, John
1989   *Sacred Places: American Tourist Attractions in the Nineteenth Century.* Oxford University Press, Oxford and New York.

Seifert, Donna J. (editor)
1991   Gender in Historical Archaeology. *Historical Archaeology* 25(4).
1994   Mrs. Starr's Profession. In *Those of Little Note: Gender, Race, and Class in Historical Archaeology*, edited by E. M. Scott, pp. 149–173. University of Arizona Press, Tucson.

Shackel, Paul
1993   *Personal Discipline and Material Culture: An Archaeology of Annapolis, Maryland, 1695–1870.* University of Tennessee Press, Knoxville.
1996   *Culture Change and the New Technology: An Archaeology of an Early American Industrial Era.* Contributions to a Global Historical Archaeology. Plenum Press, New York and London.

Shakour, Katherine, Casey McNeill, and Deborah L. Rotman
2010   Social Customs of Irish Immigrants: An Analysis of Tablewares and Teawares from an Irish American Family at the Turn of the 20th Century in South Bend, Indiana. *Ohio Valley Historical Archaeology* 29: 9–23.

Sheldon, George

1972 A History of Deerfield, Massachusetts: The Times When and the People by Whom It Was Settled, Unsettled and Resettled: With a Special Study of the Indian Wars in the Connecticut Valley. 2 vols. New Hampshire, Somersworth, New Hampshire.

1983 A History of Deerfield, Massachusetts, 1895–1896. Reprint. Pocumtuck Valley Memorial Association, Deerfield, Massachusetts.

Silliman, Stephen

2005 Culture Contact or Colonialism?: Challenges in the Archaeology of Native North America. American Antiquity 70(1): 55–74.

2009 Change and Continuity, Practice and Memory: Native American Persistence in Colonial New England. American Antiquity 74(2): 211–230.

Silliman, Stephen, and Thomas A. Witt

2010 The Complexities of Consumption: Eastern Pequot Cultural Economies in Eighteenth-Century New England. Historical Archaeology 44(4): 46–68.

Singleton, Teresa, and Mark Bograd

2000 Breaking Typological Barriers: Looking for the Colono in Colonoware. In Lines That Divide: Historical Archaeology of Race, Class, and Gender, edited by J. A. Delle, S. A. Mrozowski, and R. Paynter, pp. 3–21. University of Tennessee Press, Knoxville.

Skibo, James M., William H. Walker, and Axel E. Nielsen

1995 Expanding Archaeology. In Archaeological Theory, edited by J. M. Skibo, W. H. Walker, and A. E. Nielsen. University of Utah, Salt Lake City.

Sklar, K. K.

1973 Catharine Beecher: A Study in American Domesticity. W. W. Norton, New York and London.

Smith, Monica L.

2007 Inconspicuous Consumption: Non-Display Goods and Identity Formation. Journal of Archaeological Method and Theory 14(4): 412–438.

Snyder, Terri L.

2012 Refiguring Women in Early American History. William and Mary Quarterly 69(3): 421–450.

Spade, Joan Z., and Catherine Valentine

2004 The Kaleidoscope of Gender: Prisms, Patterns, and Possibilities. Thomson Wadsworth, Belmont, California.

Spain, Daphne

1992 Gendered Spaces. University of North Carolina Press, Chapel Hill and London.

2001 How Women Saved the City. University of Minnesota Press, Minneapolis.

Spencer, L.

1987   Victorian Domesticity in Deerfield: A Case Study of Agnes Gordon Higginson Fuller (1838–1924). Summer Fellows Program. Manuscript on file, Historic Deerfield, Inc., Deerfield, Massachusetts.

Spencer-Wood, Suzanne M.

1991   Toward an Historical Archaeology of Materialistic Domestic Reform. In *The Archaeology of Inequality*, edited by R. H. McGuire and R. Paynter, pp. 231–286. Basil Blackwell, Cambridge, Massachusetts.

1994   Diversity in Nineteenth-Century Domestic Reform: Relationships among Classes and Ethnic Groups. In *Those of Little Note: Gender, Race, and Class in Historical Archaeology*, edited by E. Scott, pp. 175–208. University of Arizona Press, Tucson.

1995   Toward Further Development of Feminist Archaeology. *1993 World Archaeological Bulletin* 7: 118–136.

1996   Feminist Historical Archaeology and the Transformation of American Culture by Domestic Reform Movements, 1840–1925. In *Historical Archaeology and the Study of American Culture*, edited by L. DeCunzo and B. L. Herman, pp. 397–446. Winterthur Museum and University of Tennessee Press, Knoxville.

1999a   The World Their Household: Changing Meanings of the Domestic Sphere in the Nineteenth Century. In *The Archaeology of Household Activities*, edited by P. M. Allison, pp. 162–189. Routledge, London.

1999b   Gendering Power. In *Manifesting Power: Gender and the Interpretation of Power in Archaeology*, edited by T. L. Sweely, pp. 284–307. Routledge, London.

2003   Gendering the Creation of Green Urban Landscapes in America at the Turn of the Century. In *Shared Spaces and Divided Places: Material Dimensions of Gender Relations and the American Historical Landscape*, edited by D. L. Rotman and E. R. Savulis, pp. 24–61. University of Tennessee Press, Knoxville.

2004   What Difference Does Feminist Theory Make in Researching Households?: A Commentary. In *Household Chores, Household Choices: Theorizing the Domestic Sphere in Historical Archaeology*, edited by K. Barile and J. C. Brandon, pp. 235–254. University of Alabama Press, Tuscaloosa.

2006   A Feminist Theoretical Approach to the Historical Archaeology of Utopian Communities. *Historical Archaeology* 40(1): 152–185.

2007   Feminist Theory and Gender Research in Historical Archaeology. In *Women in Antiquity: Theoretical Approaches to Gender and Archaeology*, edited by S. M. Nelson, pp. 29–74. Altamira Press, Lanham, Maryland.

2009   Feminist Theory and the Historical Archaeology of Institutions. In *The Archaeology of Institutions*, edited by A. Beisaw and J. Gibb, pp. 3–48. University of Alabama Press, Tuscaloosa.

2012   Commentary: How Feminist Theory Increases Our Understanding of the Archaeology of Poverty. *Historical Archaeology* 45(3): 183–193.

2013   Commentary: How Feminist Theories Increase Our Understanding of Processes of Gender Transformation. In *Historical and Archaeological Perspectives on Gender Transformations: From Private to Public*, edited by S. M. Spencer-Wood, pp. 391–424. Contributions to a Global Historical Archaeology, edited by C. E. Orser, Jr. Springer Academic, New York.

Spencer-Wood, Suzanne M., and Sherene Baugher

2001   Introduction and Historical Context for the Archaeology of Institutions of Reform. Part I: Asylums. *International Journal of Historical Archaeology* 5(1): 3–17.

Spencer-Wood, Suzanne M., and Stacey L. Camp

2013   Introduction. In *Historical and Archaeological Perspectives on Gender Transformations: From Private to Public*, edited by S. M. Spencer-Wood, pp. 1–22. Contributions to a Global Historical Archaeology, edited by C. E. Orser, Jr. Springer Academic, New York.

Spencer-Wood, Suzanne M., and Christopher N. Matthews

2011   Impoverishment, Criminalization, and the Culture of Poverty. *Historical Archaeology* 45(3): 1–10.

Spicer, Edmund H.

1975   *Indian Identity versus Assimilation.* Occasional Paper of the Weatherhead Foundation. Weatherhead Foundation, New York.

St. George, Robert B.

1988   Artifacts of Regional Consciousness in the Connecticut River Valley, 1700–1780. In *Material Life in America, 1600–1860*, edited by R. B. St. George, pp. 335–356. Northeastern University Press, Boston.

Staicer, John

1994   A History of the Ben Schroeder Saddle Tree Company, Madison, Indiana, 1878–1972. Graduate research paper for the Cooperstown Graduate Program in History Museum Studies, State University of New York, College at Oneota, Oneota.

Starbuck, David

1994   The Identification of Gender at Northern Military Sites of the Late Eighteenth Century. In *Those of Little Note: Gender, Race, and Class in Historical Archaeology*, edited by E. M Scott, pp. 115–128. University of Arizona Press, Tucson.

Stewart-Abernathy, Leslie C.

1986   Urban Farmsteads: Household Responsibilities in the City. *Historical Archaeology* 20(2): 5–15.

1992   Industrial Goods in the Service of Tradition: Consumption and Cognition on an Ozark Farmstead before the Great War. In *The Art and Mystery of Historical Archaeology*, edited by A. E. Yentsch and M. C. Beaudry, pp. 101–126. CRC Press, Boca Raton, Florida.

2004   Separate Kitchens and Intimate Archaeology: Constructing Urban Slavery on the Antebellum Cotton Frontier in Washington, Arkansas. In *Household Chores and Household Choices: Theorizing the Domestic Sphere in Historical Archaeology*, edited by K. Barile and J. C. Brandon, pp. 51–74. University of Alabama Press, Tuscaloosa.

Stewart-Abernathy, Leslie C., and Barbara L. Ruff

1989   A Good Man in Israel: Zooarchaeology and Assimilation in Antebellum Washington, Arkansas. *Historical Archaeology* 23(2): 96–112.

Stillinger, E.

1992   *Historic Deerfield: A Portrait of Early America*. Dutton Studio Books, New York.

Stine, Linda F.

1990   Social Inequality and Turn-of-the-Century Farmsteads: Issues of Class, Status, Ethnicity, and Race. *Historical Archaeology* 24: 34–79.

1991   Early Twentieth-Century Gender Roles: Perceptions from the Farm. In *The Archaeology of Gender: Proceedings of the 22nd Annual Conference of the Archaeological Association of the University of Calgary*, edited by D. Walde and N. D. Willows, pp. 496–501. Archaeological Association of the University of Calgary, Calgary, Alberta.

Strasser, S.

1982   *Never Done: A History of American Housework*. Pantheon Books, New York.

Stryker, Susan

2006   (De)Subjugated Knowledges: An Introduction to Transgender Studies. In *The Transgender Studies Reader*, edited by S. Stryker and S. Whittle, pp. 1–17. Routledge, New York and London.

Stryker, Susan, and Aren Z. Aizura

2013   Transgender Studies 2.0. In *The Transgender Studies Reader 2*, edited by Susan Stryker and Aren Z. Aizura, pp. 1–12. Routledge, New York and London.

Sutlive, Vinson H., Jr.

1978   *The Iban of Sarawak: Chronicle of a Vanishing World*. Waveland Press, Prospect Heights, Illinois.

Sweeney, Kevin

1984   Mansion People: Kinship, Class, and Architecture in Western Massachusetts in the Mid-Eighteenth Century. *Winterthur Portfolio* 19: 231–256.

1986   River Gods and Related Minor Deities: The Williams Family and the Connecticut River Valley, 1637–1790. Unpublished PhD dissertation, Department of History, Yale University, New Haven, Connecticut.

Swierenga, Robert
1982   Theoretical Perspectives on the New Rural History: From Environmentalism to Modernization. *Agricultural History* 56: 495–502.
Sweitz, Sam R.
2012   Consumer Strategy and Household Consumption in the Cripple Creek Mining District, Colorado, USA. *International Journal of Historical Archaeology* 16: 227–266.
Takaki, R.
1993   *A Different Mirror: A History of Multicultural America.* Little, Brown, Boston, Massachusetts.
Temkin-Greener, H.
1979   Fertility Transitions and Patterns of Family Formation: Connecticut River Valley Communities During the Eighteenth and Nineteenth Century. Unpublished PhD dissertation, Department of Anthropology, University of Massachusetts, Amherst.
Thomas, Brian W., and Larissa Thomas
2004   Gender and the Presentation of Self: An Example from the Hermitage. In *Engendering African American Archaeology: A Southern Perspective*, edited by J. E. Galle and A. L. Young, pp. 101–132. University of Tennessee Press, Knoxville.
Thompson, E. P.
1967   Time, Work-Discipline, and Industrial Capitalism. *Past and Present* 38: 56–96.
1974   Patrician Society. *Journal of Social History* 7: 382–405.
Tomášková, Silvia
2007   Mapping a Future: Archaeology, Feminism, and Scientific Process. *Journal of Archaeological Method and Theory* 14(3): 264–284.
Towle, Evan B., and Lynn M. Morgan
2002   Romancing the Transgender Native: Rethinking the Use of the "Third Gender" Concept. In *The Transgender Studies Reader*, edited by S. Stryker and S. Whittle, pp. 666–684. Routledge, New York and London.
Tringham, Ruth
1988   Households, Housefuls, and Archaeological House Remains: Social Archaeology at a Microscale. Paper presented at the Chacmool Conference, Calgary, Alberta.
Van Bueren, Thad
2004   *Contemplating Household Transitions: Investigations at the Carnduff Dump (CA-SMA-368/H) in San Mateo County, California.* Submitted to the California Department of Transportation, Oakland.

Van Buren, Mary

2010   The Archaeological Study of Spanish Colonialism in the Americas. *Journal of Archaeological Research* 18: 151–201.

Vlach, J. M.

1995   Greek Revival Architecture. In *Invisible America: Unearthing Our Hidden History*, edited by M. P. Leone and N. A. Silberman, pp. 144–145. Henry Holt Reference Book, New York.

Voss, Barbara L.

2006   Engendering Archaeology: Men, Women, and Others. In *Historical Archaeology*, edited by M. Hall and S. W. Silliman, pp. 107–127. Blackwell Studies in Global Archaeology. Blackwell, Malden, Massachusetts, and Oxford.

2008a   *The Archaeology of Ethnogenesis: Race and Sexuality in Colonial San Francisco.* University of California Press, Berkeley.

2008b   Domesticating Imperialism: Sexual Politics and the Archaeology of Empire. *American Anthropologist* 110(2): 191–203.

2008c   Sexuality Studies in Archaeology. *Annual Review of Anthropology* 37: 317–336.

2008d   Gender, Race, and Labor in the Archaeology of Spanish Colonial America. *Current Anthropology* 49(5): 861–893.

2008e   Between the Household and World System: Social Collectivity and Community Agency in Overseas Chinese Archaeology. *Historical Archaeology* 42(3): 57–52.

Walker, Mark

n.d.   Faunal Remains from Feature 82. In Preliminary Report of the St. Mary's Site (18AP45), 1987–1990 Seasons, edited by E. Kryder-Reid. Manuscript on file, Archaeology Lab, University of Maryland, College Park, Maryland.

2008   Aristocracies of Labor: Craft Unionism, Immigration, and Working-Class Households in West Oakland, California. *Historical Archaeology* 42(1): 108–132.

Wall, Diana diZerega

1985   The Beginnings of the Family Consumer Economy: Toward the Archaeological Analysis of Social Change. *American Archaeology* 5(3): 190–194.

1991   Sacred Dinners and Secular Teas: Constructing Domesticity in Mid-nineteenth-Century New York. *Historical Archaeology* 25(4): 69–81.

1994   *The Archaeology of Gender: Separating the Spheres in Urban America.* Plenum Press, New York and London.

1999   Examining Gender, Class, and Ethnicity in Nineteenth-Century New York City. *Historical Archaeology* 33(1): 102–117.

2000   Family Meals and Evening Parties: Constructing Domesticity in Nineteenth-Century Middle-Class New York. In *Lines That Divide: Historical Archaeolo-*

gies of Race, Class, and Gender, edited by J. A. Delle, S. A. Mrozowski, and R. Paynter, pp. 109–141. University of Tennessee Press, Knoxville.

Ward, Geoffrey C., and Kenneth Burns

1999 *Not for Ourselves Alone: The Story of Elizabeth Cady Stanton and Susan B. Anthony*. Alfred A. Knopf, New York.

Weber, Max

1976 *The Protestant Work Ethic and the Spirit of Capitalism*. George Allen and Unwin, New York.

Wegars, Patricia

1991 Who's Been Working on the Railroad?: An Examination of the Construction, Distribution, and Ethnic Origins of Domed Rock Ovens on Railroad-Related Sites. *Historical Archaeology* 25(1): 37–65.

Weismantel, Mary

2013 Towards a Transgender Archaeology: A Queer Rampage through Prehistory. In *The Transgender Reader 2*, edited by S. Stryker and A. Z. Aizura, pp. 319–334. Routledge, New York and London.

Wetherbee, Jean

1985 *A Second Look at White Ironstone*. Wallace-Homestead, Lombard, Illinois.

1986 *White Ironstone: A Collector's Guide*. Antique Trader Books, Dubuque, Iowa.

White, Carolyn

2005 *American Artifacts of Personal Adornment, 1680–1820: A Guide to Identification and Interpretation*. Altamira Press, Lanham, Maryland.

2008 Personal Adornment and Interlaced Identities at the Sherburne Site, Portsmouth, New Hampshire. *Historical Archaeology* 42(2): 17–37.

Wilkie, Laurie

2000 *Creating Freedom: Material Culture and African Identity at Oakley Plantation, 1840–1950*. Louisiana State University, Baton Rouge.

2003 *The Archaeology of Mothering: An African-American Midwife's Tale*. Routledge, New York and London.

2004 Granny Midwives: Gender and Generational Mediators of the African American Community. In *Engendering African American Archaeology: A Southern Perspective*, edited by J. E. Galle and A. L. Young, pp. 73–100. University of Tennessee Press, Knoxville.

2010 *The Lost Boys of Zeta Psi: A Historical Archaeology of Masculinity at a University Fraternity*. University of California Press, Berkeley.

Wilkie, Laurie A., and Kevin M. Bartoy

2000 A Critical Archaeology Revisited. *Current Anthropology* 41(5): 747–777.

Williams, Bryn

2008 Chinese Masculinities and Material Culture. *Historical Archaeology* 42(3): 53–67.

Williams, Raymond
1973   *The Country and the City.* Oxford University Press, New York.
Wolf, Eric
1997   *Europe and the People without History.* University of California Press, Berkeley.
Wong, Sau-Ling, and Jeffrey Santa Ana
1999   Gender and Sexuality in Asian American Literature. *Signs* 25(1): 171–226.
Wood, Gordon
1969   *The Creation of the American Republic, 1776–1787.* University of North Carolina Press, Chapel Hill.
Wood, Margaret C.
2004   Working-Class Households as Sites of Social Change. In *Household Chores and Household Choices: Theorizing the Domestic Sphere in Historical Archaeology*, edited by K. S. Barile and J. C. Brandon, pp. 210–234. University of Alabama Press, Tuscaloosa.
Worrell, J.
1985   Ceramic Production and Exchange Network of an Agricultural Neighborhood. In *Domestic Pottery of the Northeastern United States 1625–1850*, edited by S. P. Turnbaugh, pp. 153–170. Academic Press, New York.
Wright, Gwendolyn
1981   *Building the Dream: A Social History of Housing in America.* MIT Press, Cambridge, Massachusetts, and London.
Wurst, LouAnn
1991   "Employees Must Be of Moral and Temperate Habits": Rural and Urban Elite Ideologies. In *The Archaeology of Inequality*, edited by R. McGuire and R. Paynter, pp. 125–149. Basil Blackwell, Oxford.
1994   America's Rural Myths and Historical Archaeology: An Introduction. Paper presented for the Revisiting Rural Contexts symposium, organized by L. Wurst for the Annual Meeting of the Society for Historical Archaeology, Cincinnati, Ohio.
1999   Internalizing Class in Historical Archaeology. *Historical Archaeology* 33(1): 7–21.
2003   The Legacy of Separate Spheres. In *Shared Spaces and Divided Places: Material Dimensions of Gender Relations and the American Historical Landscape*, edited by D. L. Rotman and E. R. Savulis, pp. 225–237. University of Tennessee Press, Knoxville.
2006   A Class All Its Own: Explorations of Class Formation and Conflict. In *Historical Archaeology*, edited by M. Hall and S. W. Silliman, pp. 190–208. Blackwell Studies in Global Archaeology. Blackwell, Malden, Massachusetts, and Oxford.

Wurst, LouAnn, and Robert Fitts (editors)

1999   Confronting Class. *Historical Archeology* 33(1).

Wylie, Alison

1991   Gender Theory and the Archaeological Record: Why Is There No Archaeology of Gender? In *Engendering Archaeology: Women and Prehistory*, edited by J. M. Gero and M. W. Conkey, pp. 31–54. Basil Blackwell, Oxford.

Yamin, Rebecca (editor)

2001   Becoming New York: The Five Points Neighborhood. *Historical Archaeology* 35(3).

Yanagisako, S. J.

1987   Toward a Unified Analysis of Gender and Kinship. In *Gender and Kinship: Essays Toward a Unified Analysis*, edited by J. F. Collier and S. J. Yanagisako, pp. 107–132. Stanford University Press, Stanford, California.

Yentsch, Anne

1991   The Symbolic Divisions of Pottery: Sex-Related Attributes of English and Anglo-American Household Pots. In *The Archaeology of Inequality*, edited by R. H. McGuire and R. Paynter, pp. 192–230. Basil Blackwell, Oxford and Cambridge, Massachusetts.

Young, Amy

1997   Risk Management Strategies among African-American Slaves at Locust Grove Plantation. *International Journal of Historical Archaeology* 1(1): 5–37.

2003   Gender and Landscape: A View from the Plantation Slave Community. In *Shared Spaces and Divided Places: Material Dimensions of Gender Relations and the American Historical Landscape*, edited by D. L. Rotman and E. R. Savulis, pp. 104–134. University of Tennessee Press, Knoxville.

2004   Risk and Women's Roles in the Slave Family: Data from Oxmoor and Locust Grove Plantations in Kentucky. In *Engendering African American Archaeology: A Southern Perspective*, edited by J. E. Galle and A. L. Young, pp. 133–150. University of Tennessee Press, Knoxville.

Zagarri, Rosemarie

1992   Morals, Manners, and the Republican Mother. *American Quarterly* 44(2): 192–215

INDEX

Page numbers in *italics* refer to illustrations.

Abstraction of extension, 36
Abstraction of level of generality, 36, 37, 71, 98, 120
Abstraction of vantage point, 36, 37, 120
Acculturation, 87
African-Americans, 30, 87, 126; Burghardts and Dubois, 66–67, 126; Camp Nelson (Kentucky) and, 101–2; Van Winkles, 67–69
Africans, enslaved, 22, 48–50, 66, 125
Age, 16. *See also* Children
Agnews State Hospital (San Francisco), 105
Algonquian, 45; effigy pestles and, 46
Anthony, Susan B., 22, 84
Architecture: Georgian, 51–52, *52, 57, 57*; Gothic Revival, 62–63, *62–63*; Greek Revival, 61–62, *61*; Shakers and, 85
Arts and Crafts movement, 78–83, 127; community involvement and, 82; transformation of gendered social relations and, 82–83
Assimilation, 118

Backus, Peter, 111
Banks, childrens', xenophobia and, 65–66
Barnard, David, 56; color coding of ceramics and, 58
Barnard, Eliza, 56; color coding of ceramics and, 58
Beecher, Catharine, 19
Black womanhood, 66, 126
Bloomer, Amelia, 84

Boston marriages, 4
Bugis (Indonesia), 4, 5
Burghardts (Massachusetts), 66–67, 86, 126; Mary Burghardt DuBois, 67
Burghardts (New York), 29
Burials, Ponkapoag, 73
Buttons: Camp Nelson (Kentucky) and, 102; enslaved Africans and, 49; Johnson's Island prison and, 103; Wea View Schoolhouse (Indiana), 116

Camp Nelson (Kentucky), 101–2
Capitalism, 19; Arts and Crafts movement, 78–83; clothing reform and, 85; productive capacity of individuals and, 104, 105; social control and, 99
Catholic, 88
Ceramics: childrens' dishes, 68, 90–91; Chinese immigrants and, 89; color coding of, 57–58; enslaved Africans and, 49; flowerpots, 90–91; German immigrants and, 90–94; Gothic-paneled ironstone, 63, *64*, 88, 90; Johnson's Island prison (Ohio), 103; modern discipline, 106–8, 126; Pequot usage of, 47, 125; reform institutions and, 104; teawares, 65, 88, 92–94; time discipline and, 53; Wea View Schoolhouse (Indiana), 117–18
Children, 6, 16; childrearing, 21, 53, 59, 83; toys and enculturation, 65–66, 68–69; Wea View Schoolhouse (Indiana) and, 114–18
Chinese, 66, 88–89; masculinity and, 89; racism and, 89
Civil War, 102–3

Class: business class and, 59; clothing, 84; defined, 29; different scales of, 29; fluidity of, 30; middle class, 20, 59, 60, 87, 91; modern discipline, 106–7; performance of, 30; social relations of, 28–30; working class and, 59, 60

Clothing: Chinese immigrants and, 89; dress reform, 83–84; Phoenix Indian School (Arizona), 119; utopian societies and, 85

Colonialism: corporate families and, 17; gendered spaces of, 72–74; Indigenous groups and, 45–47, 72–73; republican motherhood and, 18; social control and, 99

Communities: households in relations to, 71; Oneota longhouses, 73–74; Ponkapoag Praying Town, 72–73; Wea View Schoolhouse (Indiana), 114–18

Consumption, 16; African-Americans in the post-Emancipation period and, 66; enslaved Africans and, 48–50, 125; farms and, 34; middle class and, 20, 60; racial privilege and, 60, 61; teawares and, 92–94

Context, importance of, 8, 14, 27, 123

Contradiction, 37, 38, 50, 70, 97, 119, 123

Conway (Massachusetts), 75–76, 75

Cooperatives, 23, 24

Corporate families, 16–17, 124

Corporate paternalism, 109

Cross-dressers, 4

Cultural feminists. See Domestic reform

Deerfield (Massachusetts), 11, 12, 43, 56–58, 74; Arts and Crafts movement and, 78–83, 127; changes to agricultural production and, 58; corporate families in, 42, 124; historical pageants and, 81–83, 127; municipal water in, 81–83, 82, 128; republican motherhood in, 51–54

Deerfield Hook and Ladder Company, 81

Deerfield Improvement Society, 81

Deerfield Temperance Society, 81

Developmental (life) cycle, 63, 123, 125; Rev. Moors and family, 64–65

Dialectics: abstraction, 36; of class, 29; defined, 36; Shakers and, 85; social relations, 36, 97, 123, 124. See also Abstraction of extension; Abstraction of level of generality; Abstraction of vantage point; Contradiction; Interpenetration of opposites

Dining etiquette, 30, 91; Phoenix Indian School (Arizona), 119; railroad workers and, 95, 128–29

Domesticity: African-Americans and, 66, 68; childrearing, 21; cult of, 15, 19–23; Deerfield and, 64–65, 79, 127; gentility and, 87; Gothic-paneled ironstone, 63, 64, 88, 90, 126; Gothic Revival architecture and, 62–63; middle class and, 19; Phoenix Indian School (Arizona), 118; power and, 21; Redemptorists and, 113

Domestic reform, 23–25, 127; Arts and Crafts movement and, 78–79; community spaces (parks, playgrounds) and, 83, 127–28; dress reform and, 83–84; immigrant tenements and, 103; municipal water in Deerfield and, 81

DuBois, W.E.B., 66–67, 67

Economic roles/units, 17, 78–79. See also Production

Educational institutions, 113–20; Phoenix Indian School (Arizona), 118–20, 130; Redemptorists (Maryland), 113–14; Wea View School, 114–18, 115

Effigy pestles, 45–46, 46; Algonquian and, 46

Emancipation (post-Emancipation): identity formation and, 67; oppression and, 66

Enlightenment, 18

Equal Rights feminism, 22–23, 127; cloth-

ing and, 84; Deerfield and, 79; World
Anti-Slavery Conference and, 22
Ethnicity, 30–33; archaeological record
and, 32; defined, 30–31; Morris-Butler
House and, 69–70; race and, 30
Ethnogenesis, 101; defined, 100

Fa'afafines (Samoa), 4
Family size: class status and, 20; fertility,
21; respectability and, 20
Farmsteads: mechanization of, 55–56,
76; urban, 34
Female invalidism, cult of, 25–26
Five Points Neighborhood (New York
City), 71, 88
Foodways: Camp Nelson (Kentucky)
and, 102; railroad workers and, 95,
128–29; Redemptorists, 113–14; Rich
Neck Plantation, 49; Saragossa Planta-
tion, 49–50; Seventh-day Adventists
(Ellen White), 86
French and Indian War, 54

Gender: binary systems of, 3, 7, 8, 16,
25; biological basis of, 3; body and,
5; capitalism and, 19; challenges to
norms and, 72; class and, 19; cultural
production of, 5–6; defined, 2–8;
differentially experienced, 38; enslaved
Africans and, 48–50; history of analyses, 13–14; ideology, 14; Indigenous
peoples and, 45–48; multiplicity of
ideals, 15–16, 24, 25; negotiated, 5, 70,
101; plurality of dimensions and, 5;
systems of, 8
Georgian architecture, 51–52, 52, 57, 57;
implications for gender, 52; worldview,
106
German immigrants, 90–94, 129; Schroeder Saddletree Factory (Indiana),
108–12, 109–10
Gothic-paneled ironstone, 63–64, 64,
88, 90

Gothic Revival architecture, 62–63, 62–63
Greek Revival architecture, 61–62, 61;
masculinity and, 61
Grimké sisters, 23

Habitus, defined, 40
Hierarchy, 17, 18, 51; on farms, 55; Shakers
and, 85
Hijras (India), 4
Historical archaeology, 6, 8–9
Home religion, cult of, 26
Hooker, Isabella Beecher, 22
Households, 17, 124; Chinese immigrants
and, 89; enslaved Africans and, 48–50;
Indigenous peoples and, 45–48; Irish
immigrants and, 88; loci of enculturation, 42, 62, 65; production and, 40;
property-ordered, 18; social reproduction and, 40, 70
Houses: African-American homeplaces
and, 66, 126; authority in, 44; corporate
families and, 44; housing reformers,
23–24; social configurations of space
and, 41; social practice in, 41
Hunting, constructions of masculinity
and, 50
Huron, 45

Identity, 7, 9, 18, 42; class, 28–30; ethnic,
30–33; Presidio of San Francisco and,
100; Wea View Schoolhouse (Indiana),
114–18
Ideology: defined, 31; modern discipline
and, 106–8; social discourse and, 120
Immigrants: Chinese, 66, 88–89; German,
90–94, 108–12, 129; Irish, 66, 71, 88,
128; laborers, 29
Industrialization: agricultural production
and, 58; cities and, 87; domesticity
and, 20; ethnicity and, 32–33; modern
discipline and, 106–8; republican
motherhood and, 19; Victorian ideals
and, 90

Inequality, 14; communities and, 71; loci of production, 106–13; republican motherhood and, 17, 18–19, 51

Intentional communities. *See* Utopian societies

Interdependence, 17, 48, 124; corporate families and, 45; farms and, 76; households and communities, 71

Interpenetration of opposites, 37, 48, 70, 91, 97, 98–99, 119, 123

Irish, 66, 71, 88, 89, 128

Johnson's Island prison (Ohio), 102–3

Kaleidoscope, 16, 30, 96, 130

Kinsey, Alfred, 6

Kitchens: domestic reform and, 23; ells, 52, 56, 114, 125, 128; habitus and, 40; Morris-Butler House and, 69–70; Redemptorists and, 114

Koehler, Elizabeth "Lizzie," 111–12

Labor: Chinese immigrants and, 89; divisions of, 20, 44; on farms, 55; wage labor, 59

Landscapes: factors in change, 35; modifications to, 35

Longhouses, Oneota, 73–74

Magdalen Society (Philadelphia), 103–4, 129

Marriage: Boston, 4; heteronormative, 4, 26, 128

Masculinity, 6, 16; Chinese immigrants and, 89; enslaved Africans and, 66, 126; Greek Revival architecture and, 61; hunting and, 50; Johnson's Island prison (Ohio) and, 103

Medicine bottles, 105

Mental institutions, 104–6

Military institutions, 99–103; Camp Nelson, 101–2; Presidio of San Francisco, 98, 99–101, *101*

Mining camps, 95–96

Modern discipline, 106–8, 126; Phoenix Indian School (Arizona), 119; Russell Cutlery Factory (Massachusetts), 108, 129. *See also* Time discipline

Moors, Reverend John and families, 56, 62–64, 81; color coding of ceramics and, 58; developmental cycle and, 64–65; Gothic-paneled ironstone, 64, *64*; Gothic Revival architecture, 62–6362–63; middle class, 64

Morality, 18; institutions as enforcement of, 98; moral authority, 59

Morris-Butler House (Indianapolis), 68, 69–70, *69*

Mothering: domesticity and, 21; intensive, 26; mental illness caused by, 104–5; modern discipline and, 106; scientific, 26

Mott, Lucretia, 22

Narragansett, 45, 124

Native Americans, 4, 66, 95, 124; Algonquian, 45; Huron, 45; Narragansett, 45, 124; Native Californians, 98; Oneota, 73–74; Pequot, 46–48, 125; Phoenix Indian School (Arizona), 118–20, 130; Ponkapoag, 72–73

Native Hawaiians, 96

Nuclear family, 18, 51

Oneota, 73–74

Parochial spaces, domestic reform and, 24–25

Passing, 4

Patriarchy, 26, 58, 128; communities and, 71; corporate families and, 42, 124; domesticity and, 21; domestic reform, 24; enslaved Africans and, 66, 126; equal rights feminism, 22; republican motherhood and, 18; Shakers and, 85; social control and, 99, 129

Patriotism, 18

Peirce, Melusina Fay, 24

Pequot, 46–48, 125; traditional ecological knowledge and, 48; wage labor under colonialism, 46

Personhood, 9

Phoenix Indian School (Arizona), 118–20

Pocumtuck Basket Makers, 79, *80*

Political: roles/units, 17, 18; equal rights feminism, 22; power, 18

Ponkapoag, 72–73

Power: changing agricultural production and, 58; domesticity and, 20, 21; domestic reform and, 24; ethnicity and, 31; institutions as loci of, 120; republican motherhood and, 18; social relations and, 122; social spaces and, 55

Praying Town (Massachusetts), Ponkapoag, 72–73

Presidio of San Francisco, 99–101, *101*

Private sphere, 16; domesticity, 19; domestic reform and, 23; equal rights feminism and, 22

Production, 13, 16, 17, 21, 26; Arts and Crafts movement in Deerfield and, 78–83; corporate families and, 54; farms and, 34, 55–56, 58, 76; gendered spaces of, 55; households and, 40; Russell Cutlery Factory (Massachusetts), 108; Schroeder Saddletree Factory (Indiana), 108–12, *109–10*; social control and, 129

Protestant, 16, 63, 122; gentility and, 88; mental institutions and, 104; missionaries in New York City, 87, 128

Public sphere, 16; communities and, 72; domesticity, 19; domestic reform and, 23; equal rights feminism, 22

Putnam, Annie, 79–80

Quakers, 85

Race: defined, 30; ethnicity and, 30, 87; racism and, 31, 66; social category of, 31

Railroad workers, 95

Redemptorists (Maryland), 113–14

Reform institutions, 103–6

Religion: domesticity and, 126; Phoenix Indian School (Arizona), 119; Redemptorists (Maryland), 113–14; Second-day Adventists, 86; Second Great Awakening, 85; Shakers and, 85; Victorian middle class, 87

Reproduction: agriculture and, 58; biological, 13, 16; corporate families and, 54; gendered spaces of, 55; home and, 26, 40; social, 17, 65, 98

Republican motherhood, 15, 17–19, 83, 125

Revolutionary War, 17–18

Rich Neck Plantation (Virginia), 49

Rose, Ernestine, 23

Rural settings/spaces, 33, 123; characteristics of, 33; contrast with urban, 34, 86

Russell Cutlery Factory (Massachusetts), 108, 111, 129

Saragossa Plantation (Mississippi), 49

Schools. *See* Educational institutions

Schroeder Family, 108–12; Charles, *110*; Gertrude, *110*, 111; John Benedict "Ben," 109; Joseph, *110*; Leo, 109, *110*; Mrs. Schroeder, 111; Pauline, 111; Rose, 111; Teresa, 111

Schroeder Saddletree Factory (Indiana), 108–12, *109–10*

Second Great Awakening, 85

Sengstacken, Otillia "Tillie," 105

Separation of spheres, 15, 20, 127; agricultural production and, 58, 77–78; domesticity and, 59; industrialization and, 20; reform institutions and, 103; religious ideology and, 85–86; republican motherhood and, 51; Wea View Schoolhouse (Indiana) and, 116

Seventh-day Adventists, 86

Sexuality, 6; Magdalen Society (Philadelphia), 103; Presidio of San Francisco and, 100

Shakers (United Society of Believers in Christ's Second Appearing), 85, 128

Single blessedness, cult of, 15, 26
Social control, 98; corporate paternalism, 109; Presidio of San Francisco and, 101; reform institutions and, 103–6
Social Darwinism, 60
Social personae, 5
Society of Blue and White Needlework, 78
Society of Deerfield Industries, 78
Space: false dichotomies of, 55, 80, 81, 83, 127; gendered uses of, 55, 125–26; Morris-Butler House and, 68, 69–70, 69; Oneota longhouses and, 73–74; Quadrangle at the Presidio of San Francisco and, 100; Shakers and, 85; village layouts and, 42–44, 75–76
Stanton, Elizabeth Cady, 22, 84–85
Status: agricultural production, 58, 76, 77–78; corporate families and, 17, 45; domesticity and, 20–21; domestic reform and, 24; equal rights feminism and, 24; republican motherhood and, 19, 54
Stone, Lucy, 23

Time discipline, 108; defined, 52–53. See also Modern discipline
Toys, childrens': banks, 65–66; Camp Nelson (Kentucky) and, 102; dolls, 68; marbles, 68; Wea View Schoolhouse (Indiana), 114–18
Traditional ecological knowledge, 47–48; Pequot and, 48

Urban farmsteads, 34
Urban settings/spaces, 19, 33, 122; contrast with rural, 34, 86
Utopian societies, 24, 71, 128; clothing and, 85; Shakers and, 85

Van Winkle, Aaron, 68–69
Van Winkle, Jane, 68–69
Variation as deviance, 7, 15, 16, 66, 104, 105, 122–23
Vocabulary, limitations of, 7

Ware, Arthur Ball, 81
Ware, Edwin, and family, 61, 61
Wea View School (Indiana), 114–18, 115
White, Ellen, 86–87
Whiteness, defined, 31
Williams, Anna, 56–58, 57
Williams, Ebenezer Hinsdale, 56–58, 57
Williams, Esther, 52, 52–54
Williams, Lydia, 56
Williams, Thomas, 52, 52–54
Women's suffrage, 22, 84
Wright, Fanny, 23
Wynne, Madeline Yale, 79–80, 127

Yards: enslaved Africans and, 48–49; Morris-Butler House and, 69–70

Deborah L. Rotman is a Fulbright U.S. Scholar (Ireland, 2015–2016) and an Associate Professional Specialist in the Department of Anthropology at the University of Notre Dame. She is the author of *Historical Archaeology of Gendered Lives* and coeditor of *Shared Spaces and Divided Places: Material Dimensions of Gender Relations and the American Historical Landscape.*

The American Experience in Archaeological Perspective
Edited by Michael S. Nassaney

The Archaeology of Collective Action, by Dean J. Saitta (2007)

The Archaeology of Institutional Confinement, by Eleanor Conlin Casella (2007)

The Archaeology of Race and Racialization in Historic America, by Charles E. Orser Jr. (2007)

The Archaeology of North American Farmsteads, by Mark D. Groover (2008)

The Archaeology of Alcohol and Drinking, by Frederick H. Smith (2008)

The Archaeology of American Labor and Working-Class Life, by Paul A. Shackel (2009; first paperback edition, 2011)

The Archaeology of Clothing and Bodily Adornment in Colonial America, by Diana DiPaolo Loren (2010; first paperback edition, 2011)

The Archaeology of American Capitalism, by Christopher N. Matthews (2010; first paperback edition, 2012)

The Archaeology of Forts and Battlefields, by David R. Starbuck (2011; first paperback edition, 2012)

The Archaeology of Consumer Culture, by Paul R. Mullins (2011; first paperback edition, 2012)

The Archaeology of Antislavery Resistance, by Terrance M. Weik (2012; first paperback edition, 2013)

The Archaeology of Citizenship, by Stacey Lynn Camp (2013)

The Archaeology of American Cities, by Nan A. Rothschild and Diana diZerega Wall (2014; first paperback edition, 2015)

The Archaeology of American Cemeteries and Gravemarkers, by Sherene Baugher and Richard F. Veit (2014; first paperback edition, 2015)

The Archaeology of Smoking and Tobacco, by Georgia L. Fox (2015; first paperback edition, 2016)

The Archaeology of Gender in Historic America, by Deborah L. Rotman (2015; first paperback edition, 2018)

The Archaeology of the North American Fur Trade, by Michael S. Nassaney (2015; first paperback edition, 2017)

The Archaeology of the Cold War, by Todd A. Hanson (2016)

The Archaeology of American Mining, by Paul J. White (2017)

The Archaeology of Utopian and Intentional Communities, by Stacy C. Kozakavich (2017)

www.ingramcontent.com/pod-product-compliance
Lightning Source LLC
Chambersburg PA
CBHW032351280326
41935CB00008B/528